9342

MARY

THE VIRGIN MARY IN THE LIFE AND WRITINGS OF JOHN HENRY NEWMAN

The editor wishes to express his gratitude to Sr Christiana Fritsch, FSO, for assistance with typing, indexing and proofreading; to Gerard Tracey for help with a few Oratorian references and to Fr Reginald Foster OCD, a friend of many years, for references to some classical authors.

JOHN HENRY NEWMAN

MARY

THE VIRGIN MARY IN THE LIFE
AND WRITINGS OF
JOHN HENRY NEWMAN

EDITED WITH
INTRODUCTION AND NOTES

BY PHILIP BOYCE

GRACEWING PUBLISHING
LEOMINSTER, HEREFORDSHIRE

WILLIAM B. EERDMANS PUBLISHING COMPANY
GRAND RAPIDS, MICHIGAN

This selection of texts was first published in Italian as *Maria: Pagine scelte*
by Paoline Editoriale Libri, Milan, 1999
© Figlie di San Paolo
via Francesco Albani, 21–20149 Milan

This edition published jointly in 2001

in England by

Gracewing
2 Southern Avenue
Leominster
Herefordshire HR6 0QF

and in the United States of America by

Wm. B. Eerdmans Publishing Company
255 Jefferson Avenue S.E.
Grand Rapids, Michigan 49503
www.eerdmans.com

GRACEWING ISBN   0 85244 529 6
EERDMANS ISBN   0-8028-3929-0

05 04 03 02 01   5 4 3 2 1

Typesetting by
Action Publishing Technology Ltd, Gloucester, GL1 5SR
Printed in England by MPG Books Ltd, Bodmin, PL31 1EG

CONTENTS

INTRODUCTION

TEXTS

*footnotes in square brackets [ ] are by Newman himself.

INTRODUCTION

JOHN HENRY NEWMAN: A BIOGRAPHICAL SKETCH

One of the great names of ninetenth-century England was that of John Henry Newman. He was a man of genius and of noble ideals, who became famous as a preacher and as a writer, especially on religious and educational matters. He was a man willing to suffer for his convictions, that is, for what he firmly believed to be the truth, especially when it was a matter of revealed truth. Hence during his lifetime he was intensely loved and admired by some people, and equally as intensely hated and persecuted by others. As with most great personalities, few people remained indifferent to him.

This man – John Henry Newman – about whom so much is still spoken and written today, was born in London on 21 February 1801. He died in Birmingham on 11 August 1890 – his span of years covering most of the nineteenth century. The Anglican family into which he was born, as the eldest of six children, was a God-fearing one, whose religion consisted mainly in the frequent reading of the Bible. This early knowledge of Scripture impressed high moral standards on the receptive mind of the young boy, together with a deep sense of divine Providence and of the sufferings of Christ. However, the maturing intellectual powers needed something more precise and binding. We soon find the fifteen-year-old Newman tempted to unbelief and self-sufficiency: he wanted to be virtuous and proper like any gentleman, but not religious and devotional. He even read through some books that put God's existence in doubt and thought to himself: 'How dreadful but how plausible'.[1]

This line of thought was abruptly changed by an illness the young Newman suffered during the summer of 1816. He came under the influence of a pious clergyman who lent him some theological books. This became the occasion of a profound 'change of thought' which has ever since been called Newman's 'first conversion'. He himself always regarded it as one of the most important graces of his life. It consisted of a keen awareness of God's presence which made him distrust material phenomena and pay much more attention to the invisible world. Following on this 'conversion', he wholeheartedly accepted the doctrine of the revealed religion of Christianity. He began to see the importance of great dogmas such as the Incarnation of the Son of God, the work of redemption by Christ, the gift of the Holy Spirit in the souls of the baptized and the Catholic belief in the unending warfare between the powers of good and evil in the world. This was the first great turning-point in his life: his young mind was captured

---

[1] *Apologia pro vita sua. Being a History of his Religious Opinions.* London, Longmans, Green & Co., 1908, p. 3.

by the truths of Christian revelation; his heart was touched with the scriptural ideal of holiness.[2] He saw that Christian perfection was not a merely intellectual theory. It would involve daily practice. His quest for truth and holiness would entail constant growth and development.

From his youth, then, we can say that one of his guiding mottoes was 'Holiness rather than peace'.[3] As the years went by, he found that fidelity to this principle caused him much suffering. Many a time he could have chosen the road of compromise and made life more peaceful for himself. He never did that, for he was a man of principle. The ideal of holiness which he contemplated in his youth continued to guide him to the end of his days.

The second principle that directed the course of his life was that of development. As he said himself: 'Growth the only evidence of life'.[4] He understood clearly that all living things must grow and develop: where this process stops, life itself begins to stagnate and to die. So also with great ideas and truths: they evolve as men live them and put them into practice, yet they remain what they always were. What is true today cannot be false tomorrow. This principle would later enable Newman to understand the truth of the position of the Roman Catholic Church.

To return to the story of his life: Newman entered

---

[2] Cf. Charles Stephen Dessain, 'Newman's First Conversion. "A great change of thought" August 1st till December 21st 1816', in *Newman Studien*. Herausgegeben von Heinrich Fries und Werner Becker. Nürnberg, Glock und Lutz, 1957, Vol. 3, pp. 37–53.

[3] *Apologia,* p. 5.

[4] *Ibid.*

Trinity College, Oxford, at the age of sixteen. There he met and mingled with men of learning and culture. He soon began to be known and respected for his outstanding intellectual talent. At the age of twenty-one he was elected a Fellow of Oriel College. It was a mark of the greatest distinction at such a young age and raised him from obscurity to reputation. Newman then decided on a clerical and celibate life. In 1825 he was ordained a priest of the Church of England. He always gave the utmost importance to his spiritual and pastoral duty as a priest: it meant for him to have the care of souls upon him until the end of his days. When he was only twenty-seven years of age, he was appointed Vicar of St Mary the Virgin, which was the University Church of Oxford. From the pulpit of this church, at the heart of Oxford and of the Church of England, he wielded untold influence for a period of fifteen years. As a preacher he tried to awaken his listeners to a deeper awareness of their Christian dignity, to a more consistent and practical faith and to all the demands of the Gospel. To many he was a living example of what he preached. His fame and prestige grew steadily: 'A mysterious veneration had by degrees gathered round him, till it was almost as though some Ambrose or Augustine of older ages had reappeared.'[5]

In fact, Newman had begun a systematic reading of the works of the Fathers of the Church. These old heroes and doctors of the faith, who lived in the early centuries of Christianity, began to make him dissatisfied with the spiritual state of the Church of England.

---

[5] Cf. Wilfrid Ward, *The Life of John Henry Cardinal Newman based on his private Journals and Correspondence*. London, Longmans, Green & Co., 1912, Vol. 1, pp. 63–4.

While pondering this fact he went with friends on a Mediterranean voyage, where he was struck down with a high fever as he journeyed through Sicily. While in bed struggling for life, he had a strange confidence that he would not die, and kept repeating the famous words: 'I have not sinned against light'. He recovered and returned to England, humbled and purified by the trial, and confident that God had 'a work for him to do'.[6] This work turned out to be what is now known as the Oxford Movement. It was a return to primitive Christianity, 'to that ancient religion which had well nigh faded out of the land, and which must be restored'.[7]

After five years of the Oxford Movement, the theory developed by Newman about the Anglican Church being a *via media* between the errors of Protestantism on the one hand and the exaggerations and corruption of Rome on the other, began to crumble. The reading of the Fathers of the Church, and especially of St Augustine, convinced him that the Church of Rome was the legitimate successor of the Church of the Apostles and of early Christianity. He resigned his Anglican offices and withdrew to Littlemore, a hamlet near Oxford, for three years of prayer and study. There he sorted out his final difficulty, namely, how to justify the presence of certain doctrines in the Roman Catholic Church of his day,

[6] Cf. *Autobiographical Writings*. Edited with Introduction by Henry Tristram of the Oratory. London and New York, Sheed & Ward, 1956, pp. 122–7, 136; *Apologia*, pp. 34–5.

[7] Cf. Philip Boyce, OCD, 'Illness and Conversion in Newman's Life', in *Luce nella solitudine. Viaggio e crisi di Newman in Sicilia 1833*. A cura di Rosario La Delfa e Alessandro Magno. Palermo, Ila Palma, 1989, pp. 51–72.

doctrines which seemed to him not to have been held in primitive Christianity. The principle of genuine development which he elucidated enabled him to see in the teachings of the Church of Rome in the last century the legitimate and vital growth of the doctrines that had been taught by the Apostles and believed in the first centuries. Even though accidentals were different, the substance of doctrine had ever remained the same: later dogmas were authentic developments of the original Revelation. This for Newman was an 'ineffably cogent argument' which he illustrated in his masterpiece of theological writing: *An Essay on the Development of Christian Doctrine.*

The Church of Rome was after all the Church of the Fathers, the true Church of Christ. Hence he felt himself gravely bound in conscience to join it. We can scarcely comprehend what a sacrifice this step meant for Newman – the abandonment of people he loved, the disappointment and scandal he caused to Anglican friends who had been guided by him, and the rejection of the Church of his birth which he had deeply loved. On 9 October 1845, he was received into the Catholic Church by Blessed Dominic Barberi, an Italian Passionist Father who was working as a missionary in England.

It was like 'coming into port after a rough sea'.[8] Dr Wiseman urged him to study for the Catholic priesthood and sent him to the College of Propaganda Fide in Rome. In the chapel of this College he was ordained a Catholic priest on Trinity Sunday, 30 May 1847, by Cardinal Fransoni.

[8] *Apologia*, p. 238.

He had decided after much thought and investigation that the Oratory of St Philip Neri would be the religious Institute most suited to himself and to Englishmen like him. Consequently he entered their Novitiate at Santa Croce in Rome, and there he made a deep study of the Oratorian Rule, considering how it could be adapted to England.

He returned to Birmingham in December 1847, where he founded the first English Oratory of St Philip Neri on the vigil of the Feast of the Presentation, 2 February 1848. In this city he worked among the poor for two years until he was appointed by the Pope and the Bishops of Ireland as the first Rector of the new Catholic University in Dublin. He remained in Ireland for five years, trying amid many difficulties to put into practice his comprehensive ideas of Catholic education – subservient to the cause of religion, but with its own purpose of enlarging the mind and forming Christian gentlemen, as well as preparing an educated laity, 'men of the world for the world' but guided by an enlightened faith, which they could defend when called upon to do so.[9]

Newman's ideas were often ahead of his times and as a result he went through some dark years of suspicion and persecution. Some of his theories (especially about the position of the laity in the Church) were even brought to Rome as suspect. There were also the customary difficulties faced by the fledgling Community of Oratorians in Birmingham; the Catholic bishops of the time failed to understand him

[9] Cf. Louis McRedmond, *Thrown among Strangers. John Henry Newman in Ireland*. Dublin, Veritas, 1990; Fergal McGrath, SJ, *Newman's University. Idea and Reality*. Dublin, Browne & Nolan, Ltd., 1951.

fully; the rumour went out among Anglicans that he had regretted the step he took in converting to Rome. Then unexpectedly, in 1864, he was publicly challenged to defend the integrity of his motives and of the Catholic clergy in general. He responded with the famous *Apologia pro vita sua*, a classic of religious biography, which won him fame and respect once again, and helped to remove many psychological barriers between Protestants and Catholics in Britain.

In 1870, Newman published *A Grammar of Assent*. It too is a classic. In it the author analyses philosophically the act of assent by the human mind to revealed truths. Throughout his life, Newman had always defended the right of the ordinary uneducated man to certitude in those religious beliefs, which, if questioned about, he could not scientifically demonstrate. In this treatise, he shows how the mind arrives at certitude in general and specifically in matters of religious belief.

Newman spent the remainder of his years living a quiet and simple life as an Oratorian in Birmingham. It is difficult to condense such a long and active life in a few pages without giving an inadequate picture: a man with a literary output of over 80 volumes and 20,000 letters; an intellectual genius, a religious leader, a renowned convert, a gifted preacher, a master of the English language, a heroic lover of truth and 'spiritual father and guide' of many souls 'in the paths of holiness'.[10] Honours came to him late in life: in December 1877, he was made the first honorary Fellow of

---

[10] *Addresses to Cardinal Newman with His Replies etc. 1879–81*. Edited by the Rev. W. P. Neville (Cong. Orat.). Longmans, Green & Co., 1905, p. 72.

Trinity College, Oxford,[11] and in 1879 the newly elected Pope Leo XIII conferred on him the honour of the Cardinalate.[12] It was the highest recognition he could receive for the long labours of a lifetime. Shortly afterwards he confided to a friend: 'I have ever tried to leave my cause in the Hands of God and to be patient – and He has not forgotten me'.[13]

God called him to himself on 11 August 1890, to receive the unspeakable reward reserved for those who sacrifice all for the sake of truth and the love of Christ.

[11] Newman considered this honour as one of the greatest compliments he had ever received. He always had fond memories of Trinity College. There he had many friends and in the *Apologia* he declared that Trinity 'had never been unkind' to him (p. 237).

[12] If the honour bestowed on him by Trinity College was one of the greatest Newman received from Oxford, the Cardinalate was what corresponded to it from the part of Rome. It put an end to all the stories that were abroad about his being under a cloud of suspicion in the highest ecclesiastical circles.

[13] *The Letters and Diaries of John Henry Newman*. Edited at the Birmingham Oratory. Vols. XI–XXII (London, Nelson, 1961–72); Vols. XXIII–XXXI; I–VIII (Oxford, Clarendon Press, 1973–99), Vol. XXIX (1976), p. 72. Henceforth abbreviated: *The Letters and Diaries*.

II

NEWMAN'S ANGLICAN ATTITUDE TO THE BLESSED VIRGIN

1. The unlikeliness of Marian devotion in a staunch Anglican

One would not expect, *a priori*, to find the Blessed Virgin Mary venerated in the life of any young Anglican minister during the first half of the nine-teenth century in England. Newman, moreover, found himself at the heart of all that was noblest and best in the university milieu of Oxford. As a pastor and preacher of the Anglican Church, he kept faithful to its teachings and traditions, and showed an instinc-tive dread and distrust of what he considered to be the corrupt and idolatrous practices of Roman Catholics.

At the impressionable age of fifteen, at the time of that first deep conversion in his life, he read extracts from the Church Fathers which enchanted him, but at the same time he studied a book by Thomas Newton which convinced him that the Pope was the Antichrist.[1] The anti-Catholic milieu in which he

[1] Cf. *Essays Critical and Historical*. London, Longmans, Green & Co., 1910, Vol. II, pp. 112–85, on 'The Protestant Idea of Antichrist', where Newman in 1840 writes critically about how prophecies from Daniel and St Paul are too easily applied exclusively to the Roman Catholic branch of the Church.

grew up, and this work by Newton, would seem to make devotion to our Lady an unthinkable practice in his Anglican days.

2. What Newman feared in honours attributed to Mary

In fact, extreme devotional manifestations in the honour paid by Catholics to our Lady had been, as Newman himself confesses in the *Apologia* his 'great *crux* as regards Catholicism'.[2] They were the spontaneous expression of popular feelings towards the Blessed Virgin, and were produced by a particular cultural and historical context. Newman thought that they had received the wholehearted approval of the highest ecclesiastical authorities in Rome and were meant to be imposed universally. They formed part of what Anglicans considered to be the 'Mariolatry' of the Roman Church. Even during the period of the Oxford Movement, at least up until 1839, he considered the honours paid by Catholics to the Saints, and in particular to Saint Mary, to be the very 'essence' of Rome's corruption and theological error.

In 1836, Newman wrote a whole Tract[3] which was to be a manual for use in Anglican controversy with Roman Catholics. He pointed out what he then considered to be the weak points and some errors in certain Catholic beliefs. The honour paid to our Lady was one point particularly condemned. He quoted from some

[2] *Apologia,* p.195.
[3] No. 71. The Tracts were at first short pamphlets and later theological and historical studies on various points of doctrine and religious practices. They were the literary weapons used by the members of the Oxford Movement between 1833 and 1841. Newman himself was the author of approximately twenty-seven of the Tracts.

Catholic authors who ascribe a certain 'omnipotence' to the Blessed Virgin. On account of her office as Mother of God, she is said to be able 'to command' her divine Son with a mother's authority. Moreover, certain Catholic writers claimed that Mary's Son never refuses her any request, so that she could be said to have the same power as Christ himself, 'she being by her omnipotent Son made herself omnipotent'.[4]

Some expressions taken literally are certainly misleading and indeed imprudent. No wonder that it was popular opinion among Anglicans that Catholics (especially in Latin countries) 'worship the Virgin as a goddess'.[5] In fact, the place held by our Lady in Catholic beliefs and devotions was not simply Newman's *crux* with Catholicism: it lay at the heart of many an Anglican's suspicion and fear. It was also a stumbling-block for Pusey, as he states in his *Eirenicon:* 'that vast system as to the Blessed Virgin, which to all of us has been the special 'crux' of the Roman system ... her intercession is held to be coextensive with His'.[6]

---

[4] Cf. *Tracts for the Times.* By Members of the University of Oxford. London, Rivington & Parker, 1834–41, Vol. 3, pp. 19, 24–25; also published in *The Via Media of the Anglican Church.* In two volumes. London, Longmans, Green & Co., 1908, 1911, Vol. II, pp. 122, 129–30.

[5] *Loss and Gain.* The Story of a Convert. London, Longmans, Green & Co., 1911, p. 176.

[6] E. B. Pusey, *The Church of England a portion of Christ's one holy Catholic Church, and a means of restoring visible unity. An Eirenicon, in a Letter to the Author of 'The Christian Year'.* London, Oxford and Cambridge, John Henry and James Parker, and Rivingtons, 1865, p. 101. Edward Bouverie Pusey (1800–82) was also a member of the Oxford Movement and a close friend of Newman. He was elected Fellow of Oriel College in 1823. For some years he studied in Germany and on his return was appointed (in 1828) Regius Professor of Hebrew. He was a canon of Christ Church. He defended the Anglican Church, basing himself on the Fathers of the Church as interpreted by English divines. When Newman retired from the Oxford Movement, Pusey became its leader.

In short, for Anglicans, the Roman practice seemed to eclipse the honour due to our Lord and to interfere with his role as the unique Mediator.[7] Newman was convinced all his life that the divine glory was essentially incommunicable. Consequently, Christ's feelings of devotion towards his Mother, just as his special love for St John, the beloved disciple, are not disclosed in detail in the New Testament. It would be dangerous and could not be done 'without a risk lest the honour which those Saints received through grace should eclipse in our minds the honour of Him who honoured them'.[8]

Apart from the charge of putting honour and devotion to Christ in the shade, Newman as an Anglican, at least up to the writing of the *Via Media,* held that some Marian doctrines and many devotional practices in the Church of Rome were not to be found in the early Church. An 'undue veneration' had sprung up towards our Lady and the Saints. It was a typical example of that 'intolerable offence of having added to the Faith',[9] which made Anglicans so sure of their disapproval of Catholic practices. To them it seemed like a form of idolatry and was often referred to as 'Mariolatry'. Those who judged Catholic forms of

---

[7] Writing to his bishop in 1841 Newman expresses this thought succinctly: 'Every feeling which interferes with God's sovereignty in our hearts, is of an idolatrous nature; and, as men are tempted to idolize their rank and substance, or their talent, or their children, or themselves, so may they easily be led to substitute the thought of Saints and Angels for the one supreme idea of their Creator and Redeemer, which should fill them' (*The Via Media of the Anglican Church,* Vol. II, pp. 410–11).

[8] *Parochial and Plain Sermons.* In eight volumes. London, Longmans, Green & Co., 1907–11, Vol. II, p. 133.

[9] *Apologia*, p.107. Cf. p. 53.

worship from what appeared to a public onlooker, without understanding the real meaning of these mysteries of faith, simply thought, as Newman himself said in 1841, that the Roman system 'goes very far indeed to substitute another Gospel for the true one. Instead of setting before the soul the Holy Trinity, and heaven and hell; it does seem to me, as a popular system, to preach the Blessed Virgin and the Saints, and Purgatory.'[10]

The authorities in Rome justified it, Newman claimed in his Anglican years, by arguing unfairly from the writings of the Fathers of the Church. On the one hand, they professed to recognize and follow their authority; on the other hand, they seemed to him to be eclectic in their attitude, accepting the teaching of the Church Fathers only on those points that did not contravene modern Roman beliefs and practices. The points of doctrine and practice commonly held in the nineteenth century and which the Fathers would censure were quietly explained away as if the Fathers who would disagree were not in harmony with the mind of the Church of their day. On this line of argument, Newman thought he was on sure ground, in 'an impregnable position'. He seemed to have caught Roman theology in a fatal trap.[11]

At that time Newman did not understand how Catholic theology uses Patristic writings as a witness to divine and revealed truth. In fact, as he himself would also claim,[12] it is not the assertion of an indi-

---

[10] *A Letter addressed to the Rev. R. W. Jelf, DD,* published in *The Via Media of the Anglican Church,* Vol. II, pp. 367–93. Cf. p. 369.

[11] Cf. *The Via Media,* Vol. I, pp. 68, 78–9.

[12] Cf. *ibid.* p. 52.

vidual Father that carries weight, but their common testimony, by which they witness to an apostolic tradition, handed down from the time of the Apostles in the living body of the Church.[13] Moreover, the Patristic writings do not contain revelation as does Sacred Scripture: they simply give a doctrinal interpretation and exposition of revealed truth as handed down in a living ecclesial tradition. The Church itself interprets that same body of revealed truth, but does so with the authority received from Christ, at certain times even with an infallible proclamation.[14]

3. *Newman's surprising devotion while still an Anglican to the Virgin Mary*

Notwithstanding the foregoing premises, our Lady did play a significant role in Newman's life, even as an Anglican. He always had a special personal devotion to Mary, the Mother of the Saviour. There is no doubt about this fact. He himself testifies to it: 'In spite of my ingrained fears of Rome, and the decision of my reason and conscience against her usages, in

[13] The role of the Church Fathers is excellently portrayed in the document of the Congregation for Catholic Education: *Instruction on the Study of the Fathers of the Church in the Formation of Priests*. Rome 1989.

[14] Thus for Catholics, as distinct from Anglicans, the first and proximate rule of faith is the Magisterium of the Church in its authoritative declarations, which of course are guided by the words of Scripture and of a living Tradition, of which the Fathers are privileged witnesses. In this sense, St Thomas Aquinas affirms: 'The very doctrine of Catholic Doctors has its authority from the Church. Hence, we have to be guided by the authority of the Church more than by the authority of Augustine or Jerome or any other Doctor' (*Summa Theologiae*, II-II, q.10, a.12). Cf. 'the greatest doctors have sometimes failed' (*The Letters and Diaries,* XII, 98).

spite of my affection for Oxford and Oriel,[15] yet I had a secret longing love of Rome the Mother of English Christianity, and I had a true devotion to the Blessed Virgin, in whose College I lived, whose Altar I served, and whose Immaculate Purity I had in one of my earliest printed Sermons made much of'.[16] This devotion and reverence for Mary increased as the years went by, especially after 1833, when he admits that his devotion did continue to grow.[17]

This Anglican devotion of his was based on what he knew from Scripture on the mystery of the Incarnation and of our Lady's nearness to Christ. When he began to study the Church Fathers, new possibilities of development of the seminal facts of the sacred text began to open up before his mind. However, in what he said and wrote he normally observed a tone of reserve and moderation, in order not to upset his Anglican friends and also for fear of being caught up in Roman beliefs and usages which he still considered to be erroneous.

The sermon which has just been referred to above, namely, 'The Reverence due to the Virgin Mary', is most noteworthy, and gives us one of the best

[15] Oriel was the College in Oxford, renowned at the time for its high academic standards, where Newman in 1822 was elected Fellow (a resident member who had the obligation of pursuing some specific branch of studies and who received a salary from College revenues) and in 1826 was appointed a tutor (a Fellow with responsibility for undergraduates).

[16] *Apologia.*, p. 165. The Sermon referred to is 'The Reverence due to the Virgin Mary', which was preached on 25 March, 1832, and published in *Parochial and Plain Sermons,* Vol. II, pp. 127–38. It contained a passage which to many Anglicans seemed to go perilously near the Roman doctrine of the Immaculate Conception.

[17] Cf. *Apologia*, p. 53.

summaries we have of Newman's thought as an Anglican on our Lady. It was preached for the Feast of the Annunciation, 1832. He makes much of the words of the Archangel Gabriel to Mary. These same words form the scriptural foundation of the Church's teaching on the Divine Motherhood, the perpetual Virginity and Immaculate Conception of Mary.

While summing up the reasons why the Virgin Mary is called blessed in Scripture, Newman touches on most of his Anglican thought about her. The first reason for this blessedness arises from Mary's parallel role to Eve in the history of salvation, a point which would become a distinctive feature of Newman's Mariology. First of all, in Mary, 'the curse pronounced on Eve was changed to a blessing'.[18] God did not decide to destroy his sinful children who transgressed his original purpose, but he proposed to forgive and save them. Hence he sent his only Son, born of a woman (cf. Gal. 4: 4), to redeem them and initiate a new creation from what had become old and corrupt.

Moreover, woman's subjection to man, subsequent on Eve's initial disobedience and most evident in the pagan world, was rectified through Mary's obedience. Christ vindicated the rights and honour of his Mother and through her of all women according to God's eternal plan for creation. The original dignity of marriage was restored, its spiritual value and symbolism were reinstated. If Newman were alive today he would surely enlarge on this passage of the inspired

---

[18] *Parochial and Plain Sermons*, Vol. II, p. 129. Cf. Paul Schneider, OSB, 'Das Marienbild des anglikanischen Newman', in *Newman Studien* II (1954) pp. 103–19.

text in order to shed light on the contemporary
discussion on women's rights which is being brought
to extremes by certain feminist groups.

Another ground for Mary's blessedness is connected
with her holiness, which sprang from her nearness to
Christ, the incarnate Son of God. Indeed this relation
of hers to Christ and to the mystery of the Incarnation
lies at the heart of Newman's teaching on Mary. From
this basic dogma of the Incarnation all the theology of
the redemption takes its meaning. Christ was 'truly
God and truly Man, One Person, – as we are soul and
body, yet one man, so truly God and man are not two,
but One Christ'.[19] The nature of the Church, the
power of the sacraments, the dignity of man rests on
the reality of the Incarnation. In Christmas sermons
and in those dealing with the Passion, Newman
frequently returns to this doctrine in order to illustrate
the deepest significance of the birth and sufferings of
Christ.[20]

From the truth of the Incarnation as revealed in

[19] *Parochial and Plain Sermons,* Vol. II, p. 32.

[20] The historian, James A. Froude recalls how, many years after he had
heard Newman preach a sermon on 'The Incarnate Son, a Sufferer
and Sacrifice' (cf. *Parochial and Plain Sermons*, Vol. VI, pp. 69–82), he
still remembered it because of the preacher's emphasis on the *reality*
of the Incarnation of the Son of God. Froude tells us that after a biblical description of the way of the Cross and the Crucifixion, there
followed a moment of complete silence. After the pause, the silence
was rent by the low clear voice of the preacher: 'Now I bid you
recollect that He to whom these things were done was Almighty
God.' It was as if those listening received an electric stroke and understood for the first time the deep meaning of the doctrine of the
Incarnation (Cf. James A. Froude, *Short Studies in Great Subjects*,
London 1907, Vol. V, pp. 206–7). Cf. John Henry Newman, *Gesù*.
Pagine scelte. Introduzione, traduzione e note di Giovanni Velocci.
Milano, Edizioni Paoline, 1992.

Scripture it follows that Mary is the Mother of Jesus. The eternal Son of God became a true man, with a human nature like ours, but without sin. He derived 'His manhood from the substance of the Virgin Mary; as it is expressed in the articles of the Creed, "conceived by the Holy Ghost, born of the Virgin Mary".'[21] Thus he was truly God and truly man. In this Anglican sermon, from which we quote, Newman calls Mary the Mother of Christ.

Newman the Anglican has no doubt then about calling Mary the Mother of Jesus. However, in this very same sermon he seems to hesitate to call her the Mother of God. In fact, a few lines after he had referred to her as 'His (Christ's) Mother', he says: 'Thus He came into this world, not in the clouds of heaven, but born into it, born of a woman; He, the Son of Mary, and she (if it may be said), the mother of God'.[22]

The hesitancy, culled from the parenthesis, would seem to arise from Newman's desire in his Anglican milieu not to go beyond the plain words of Scripture in their reference to Mary. Since the inspired word consistently calls her the Mother of Jesus, he refrained from making an unqualified use of the title 'Mother of God' which could be falsely understood by his hearers. But there does not seem to be any doubt in Newman's mind: there are in fact other instances previous to and following on this date (December 1834) where he explicitly calls Mary the Mother of God.

For example, in a sermon for Christmas Day, nine

---

[21] *Parochial and Plain Sermons,* Vol. II, p. 31.
[22] *Ibid.* p. 32.

years before that date, namely in 1825, he had written: 'A daughter of man became the Mother of God – to her, indeed, an unspeakable gift of grace; but in Him, what condescension!'[23] Later, in 1838, he would claim that the Blessed Virgin was holy in soul and body on account of her nearness to God, and in this context, he declares that 'all but heretics have ever called (her) the Mother of God'.[24]

It is clear then that Newman while still an Anglican had the highest regard for Mary, whose holiness he admired and considered to come from her proximity in body and spirit to the Incarnate Word of the eternal Father. One could ask, however: did his estimation of Mary's holiness go as far as to include freedom from sin even at the moment of her conception? We must remember that the Immaculate Conception was not yet defined as a dogma by the Catholic Church. Still, we should not be unduly surprised to find traces of that doctrine in Newman's Anglican preaching, since he relied so heavily on the teaching of the Fathers of the Church.[25] And indeed we know that he was accused on one occasion of secretly holding this doctrine. It was after the sermon to which we already referred, preached on the Feast of the Annunciation, 1832. The passage that gave offence was the following, in particular the concluding lines: 'Who can estimate the holiness and perfection of her, who was chosen to be the Mother of Christ? If to him that

---

[23] *Parochial and Plain Sermons*, Vol. VIII, p. 252.

[24] *Discussions and Arguments on various Subjects*. London, Longmans, Green & Co., 1911, p. 223.

[25] Cf. Charles Stephen Dessain, *Cardinal Newman's Teaching about the Blessed Virgin Mary*. Birmingham, Friends of Cardinal Newman, no date. 2nd edition, pp. 7–8.

hath, more is given, and holiness and Divine favour go together (and this we are expressly told), what must have been the transcendent purity of her, whom the Creator Spirit condescended to overshadow with His miraculous presence? . . . This contemplation runs to a higher subject, did we dare follow it; for what, think you, was the sanctified state of that human nature, of which God formed His sinless Son; knowing as we do, "that which is born of the flesh is flesh," and that "none can bring a clean thing out of an unclean?"[26] He seemed to his listeners to imply that Mary's human nature had always been in a sanctified state of grace, hence always without sin.

Scholars discuss and disagree about what Newman really held as an Anglican concerning the doctrine of the Immaculate Conception. Some hold that until he became a Catholic he did not fully understand or believe this doctrine. Others claim that he did arrive personally at this belief but refrained from saying it explicitly in order not to give offence to his co-religionists.

There may have been some initial hesitation but one can certainly say that all the premises were there for such a belief. As an Anglican he had the highest regard for Mary as the Mother of the Incarnate Son of God. He saw how fitting it was that a person so near to God's Son should be completely without sin. From his Patristic readings he learned to make much of the parallel between Eve and Mary: if Eve was sinless on the day she was created it seemed appropriate that Mary should be equally free from sin at the dawn of a

[26] *Parochial and Plain Sermons*, Vol. II, pp. 131–2.

new creation. The balance in the argument then would seem to favour his personal acceptance of this doctrine. In fact, his response to his Anglican accusers in 1835 when the sermon was published, was simply that 'there was nothing against the doctrine in the Thirty-Nine Articles' of the Anglican faith.[27]

Another point on which Newman dwells in his Anglican writings is the reserve with which Sacred Scripture refers to the Mother of Jesus. It comes as a surprise: one would expect to be told more details. However, Newman regards this relative silence as containing an important message for believers. It was a point that coloured his own Marian devotion and which confirmed him in his reluctance to accept as an Anglican some of the Roman teaching on our Lady and most expressions of popular devotion to her. Revelation, he stated, was written down by the inspired authors to give glory to God, not to honour individual saints. If the sacred text were to amplify on what God had bestowed on his friends the saints, it could be dangerous for us. We would be tempted to love and think more of them – creatures after all – than of the Creator himself. And on account of the sublime privileges bestowed on the Blessed Virgin, from whom Christ took his manhood, it would be particularly dangerous: 'We cannot combine, in our thought of her, all we should ascribe with all we should withhold. Hence, following the example of Scripture, we had better only think of her with and for her Son, never separating her from Him . . .'[28]

---

[27] Cf. Letter of 30 May 1860 in *The Letters and Diaries,* XIX, 346–7. The Thirty-Nine Articles (often referred to as the Articles), dated from 1576 and were the set of clauses and formulas that defined the principle tenets of the Anglican faith.

[28] *Parochial and Plain Sermons,* Vol. II, p. 135.

Looking at the whole arc of Newman's Anglican days, we can easily perceive a constant development in his Mariology. He himself, as already mentioned, refers to the growth of his devotion to the Saints and our Lady during the years he led the Oxford Movement.[29] At the very beginning of the *Apologia*, he tells us that, in one of his boyhood copybooks, he drew what seemed to him to be a rosary beads with a little cross attached.[30] From that moment until the last months of his life when, as an old and feeble Cardinal, he could no longer celebrate Mass or read his breviary but could merely use his rosary beads, the Blessed Virgin Mary was a constant presence in his life.

Shortly after his return from Rome as a Catholic priest, he writes to a friend (Henry Wilberforce) telling him how he and his companions 'went round by Loreto' on their journey from the eternal City, in order 'to get the Blessed Virgin's blessing'. This gives him the cue to sum up briefly our Lady's presence in his life: 'I have ever been under her shadow, if I may say it. My College was St Mary's, and my Church; and when I went to Littlemore, there, by my own previous disposition, our Blessed Lady was waiting for me. Nor did she do nothing for me in that low habitation, of which I always think with pleasure'.[31]

Some acquaintances exerted an importance influence on Newman's approach to Rome and on his developing respect for our Lady. Notable among

[29] Cf. *Apologia*, p. 53

[30] *Ibid.* p. 13.

[31] *The Letters and Diaries,* XII, 153–4. The College he refers to was Oriel (the House of St Mary) and the Church was St Mary the Virgin's. Newman was elected Fellow of Oriel in 1822 and made Tutor in 1826.

Anglicans was R. Hurrell Froude who 'fixed deep' in his mind 'the idea of devotion to the Blessed Virgin' and led him 'gradually to believe in the Real Presence'.[32] They had first met in 1826 and Froude became a very close friend of Newman, especially from 1829 until his death in 1836. It was Froude who introduced him to Keble in 1828 and the latter also influenced his veneration for the Blessed Virgin and his esteem for the Church of Rome.[33]

After 1841 it was a Catholic correspondent who became most helpful in explaining certain beliefs to Newman, namely, Dr Charles Russell, who presented himself as 'an humble Irish Catholic priest'. Newman

---

[32] Cf. *Apologia,* p. 25. Richard Hurrell Froude was born in 1803, the son of an archdeacon from Devon. He was brilliantly gifted intellectually and also had a deeply religious mind. His youngest brother was James Anthony Froude, the historian. He was elected Fellow of Oriel College in 1826 and made Tutor the following year. In 1829 he received Anglican Orders. He was particularly devoted to the Blessed Virgin Mary and closely collaborated with Newman at the beginning of the Oxford Movement. He died of consumption on 28 February 1836. His *Remains,* consisting of extracts from his poetry and private diary, were published posthumously by Newman (in 1838 and 1839) with the help of Keble. In the *Apologia,* Newman acknowledges his debt to him (cf. pp. 24–5).

[33] John Keble was born in 1792 and was an ardent defender of the High Church. He was elected, while still very young, Fellow of Oriel in 1811. He was ordained a priest in 1816 and made a Tutor the following year. He was deeply concerned about the liberal trends in the Church of England. His famous Assize Sermon in St. Mary the Virgin on 14 July 1833 was regarded by Newman as the beginning of the Oxford Movement, of which Keble was a leading member. He wrote some of the *Tracts for the Times.* After Newman's secession to Rome, he worked with Pusey in the defence of the High Church elements in the Church of England. In 1836 he was appointed Vicar of Hursley, where he remained as a faithful parish priest until his death in 1866. For his influence on Newman, cf. *Letters and Diaries,* XI, p. 172; *Essays Critical and Historical,* Vol. II, pp. 436–40.

avows that he had more to do with his conversion than any one else. With regard to difficulties concerning our Lady, he was instrumental in helping Newman to understand that all popular and traditional devotions were not universally approved and imposed. In October 1842, he sent him a volume of sermons by St Alphonsus Liguori and helped to explain what was doctrinally accurate and what was the expression of a local exuberant devotion. Some such devotional manifestations had been the most puzzling point of the problem for Newman. Dr Russell was able to assure Newman that the translator had published the entire collection of sermons by St Alphonsus and not a selected number, but that at least some few passages of the original were not to be found in the English translation. Although they may be defended, the omission of such passages, Newman concluded, 'in the case of a book intended for Catholics, at least showed that such passages as are found in the works of Italian Authors were not acceptable to every part of the Catholic world'.[34] Although unknown to himself perhaps, Russell was a significant help to Newman on his conversion journey and in clarifying some points of Marian teaching.

Scholars normally trace the Anglican development

[34] *Apologia,* p. 195. cf. pp. 389–90. Charles William Russell (1812–80) entered St Patrick's College, Maynooth, the principal National Seminary of Ireland, where he was ordained in 1835. He was made professor of Church History in 1845, and from 1857 he was the President of the College. After reading *Tract 90* he began correspondence with Newman in 1841. His humble and unobtrusive manner greatly influenced Newman's conversion journey. Cf. Henry Tristram, 'Dr Russell and Newman's Conversion' in *The Irish Ecclesiastical Record* 66 (1945) pp. 195–6.

of Newman's belief in our Lady, and corresponding devotion, into four easily-defined periods.[35] The first period stretches up to 1834. It is dominated by Newman's strong belief in the mystery of the Incarnation of God's Son. From Scripture he understood that the Son of God, coming into this world, took a human mother who was a virgin. He even considered the possibility of her Immaculate Conception, as a consequence of the role she played in the Incarnation. Thus 'Newman's first statements concerning Mary contain and give expression to the core ideas of his future Mariology. From his faith in the Incarnation, he was led to faith in Mary ... As his faith in Christ was the central belief of his life, so also his faith in Mary led him to have a genuine veneration for her, one which he practised first of all as an Anglican in the Anglican Church'.[36]

A second period covers the initial four years of the Oxford Movement, up until 1837. It is characterized by Newman's discovery of the difference between intercession and invocation. The doctrine of the Communion of Saints made it clear to him that the members of the Body of Christ can pray and intercede for each other. Therefore, St Mary and the Saints do intercede for us, but that does not warrant us to invoke them. Strangely enough, this distinction between intercession and invocation, although tacitly

---

[35] Cf. Lutgart Govaert, *Kardinal Newmans Mariologie und sein persönlicher Werdegang*. Salzburg und München, Universitätsverlag Anton Pustet, 1975, pp. 23–80; Paul Schneider, OSB, 'Das Marienbild des anglikanischen Newman', in *Newman Studien* II (1954) pp. 103–19; Francis J. Friedel, SM, *The Mariology of Cardinal Newman*. New York, Benziger Brothers, 1928, pp. 1–87.

[36] Lutgart Govaert, *Kardinal Newmans Mariologie, op. cit.* p. 38

recognized by two of the Thirty-Nine Articles, was not approved by the Anglican authorities in general, who firmly rejected the belief in the intercession of our Lady and the Saints, since invocation of the Saints was clearly condemned by these Articles.

Nor did Newman, until the very end of his Anglican days, accept the practice of invoking the Saints. In a sermon dating from 1837 on 'The Communion of Saints', he states that the blessed in heaven may be active promoters of the Church's welfare by their prayer, but that we do not know how they do that. And he adds, lamenting the Roman practice: 'While we thus think of the invisible Church, we are restrained by many reasons from such invocations of her separate members as are unhappily so common in other Christian countries.'[37]

Newman thought that invocation of the saints was not a practice in the early Church and that it could easily become a prayer to the saint, which he regarded as idolatrous. Invocation of our Lady or of any saint seemed to him to obscure the unique mediation role of Christ. Although he came to realize that the Anglican Church tacitly approved certain invocations, in the sense that the *ora pro nobis* of litanies was not directly condemned, he nevertheless refrained from invoking the Blessed Virgin Mary, in obedience to the directives of his Anglican allegiance, until the day he was received into the Roman Catholic Church. Even while reciting the Roman Breviary in Littlemore in the years leading up to his conversion, he and his companions still omitted the direct invocations it

---

[37] *Parochial and Plain Sermons*, Vol. IV, p. 183.

contained, claiming that they were not an essential part of the Divine Office. Instead of *ora pro nobis* (pray for us), they would say *oret pro nobis* (may she pray for us) and they omitted the *Salve Regina* altogether.[38]

A third period, covering the next few years (1837–39), saw Newman basing himself on arguments from renowned writers such as St Vincent of Lerins[39] and Bishop Bull[40] to prove that Marian devotion as practised in the Roman Church was not known in the early centuries. The only Church tradition he accepted at the time was one to be found in Scripture and handed on by the Apostles. The development in such a tradition would only be one of words or formulation. Consequently he condemned, as unscriptural and contrary to the practice of the Church Fathers, modern Catholic veneration and especially invocation of our Lady. It was, he said, a corruption of the original teaching of primitive times

[38] Cf. Henry Tristram, *Dr. Russell and Newman's Conversion, ibid.* p. 198; Lutgart Govaert, *Kardinal Newmans Mariologie, op. cit.* pp. 42–48.

[39] The only authentic work known of this Saint and ecclesiastical writer of the fifth century is the *Commonitorium adversus profanas omnium haereticorum novitates*. He was a monk in the monastery of Lérins, an island off the south coast of France. He died in 434 or shortly afterwards. He is remembered especially for his famous passage concerning true development of doctrine and for one in which he treats of the 'notes' that distinguish true doctrine from heresy, namely: *quod ubique, quod semper, quod ab omnibus creditum est:* 'what has been believed in all places, at all times and by everybody' must be regarded as orthodox (*Commonitorium,* c. II, 3).

[40] George Bull (1634–1710), an Anglican bishop, is known for a renowned work of Anglican theology in which he studied the historical development of the doctrine of the Trinity before the Council of Nicea in 325. Newman as an Anglican quoted Bull in an effort to prove that the Church of Rome tried at times to explain away certain doctrines of the Church Fathers in order to safeguard its own innovations (cf. *The Via Media,* Vol. I, pp. 61–63).

and of the way Scripture urges us to venerate the Virgin Mary. By going to excess in such devotional practices in honour of the Mother of God, he thought that her divine Son's position and his redemptive role was put in the shade and misunderstood.

Nevertheless, in this period Newman's own veneration for the Blessed Virgin continued to grow. It was firmly rooted in Scripture, and it would seem that he even came to believe privately in the Immaculate Conception, but he still saw no possibility of accepting the practice of invocation.[41]

The fourth and final period covers the six years preceding his conversion to Roman Catholicism (1839–45), during which Newman deepened his understanding of true doctrinal development, no longer restricting it to a mere verbal kind. In his *Apologia* he even hints at an interaction between his Marian devotion and his discovery of the principle of doctrinal development. The growth in his understanding of Catholic teaching was still considerable in these years. In 1841, he states quite clearly that in conscience he could not change his allegience: 'I could not go to Rome, while she suffered honours to be paid to the Blessed Virgin and the Saints which I thought in my conscience to be incompatible with the Supreme, Incommunicable Glory of the One Infinite and Eternal'.[42]

While writing the *Essay on the Development of Christian Doctrine*, he came to an understanding of Mary as the first among created beings. In this fact he

---

[41] Cf. Lutgart Govaert, *Kardinal Newmans Mariologie, op. cit.* pp. 48, 49; 58–9.

[42] *Apologia*, p. 148.

also found the reason why Catholic devotion to Mary remains clearly distinct from the worship of Christ and is not detrimental to it. He discovered that in Catholic devotional writings all the glory that a creature can receive is given to the Blessed Virgin. Consequently, a distinct cult is assigned to Mary by reason of her unique dignity as the Mother of God and, even more so, on account of the transcendent dignity of her Son. Despite the fervent devotion and exalted position of Mary, he found 'evidence of its not interfering with that incommunicable and awful relation which exists between the creature and the Creator.'[43] Newman now saw that the way was clear for him to accept the various expressions of genuine Catholic devotion but, obedient as he was to the Church to which he still belonged, he refrained from invoking her until the day he became a Roman Catholic.

---

[43] *Development of Christian Doctrine*, p. 434. Cf. below, Text XVII, p. 300.

III

THE BLESSED VIRGIN MARY IN NEWMAN'S CATHOLIC DAYS

1. Solidly based on Scripture.

Newman contemplates Mary's place and dignity in the ensemble of Catholic doctrine as consequent on the doctrine of the Incarnation. So closely was she united to her divine Son that it seemed to him most fitting that she be adorned with all the graces and privileges which the Catholic Church had recognized as belonging to her. All her glories are for her Son's sake. She is entirely relative to him and all she has redounds to his praise.

Moreover, the entire corpus of Catholic beliefs is so harmonious and interconnected that one doctrine often implies and postulates another, or several others. An example given by our author is that seemingly improbable title 'Mother of the Creator'. Yet, if we deny that it can be rightly attributed to our Lady, we then find ourselves in difficulty with the title 'Son of God'. Human reason may at first find it absurd, 'and yet on further consideration we shall see that we cannot refuse the title to Mary without denying the Divine Incarnation – that is, the great and fundamental truth of revelation, that God became man'.[1]

In this sense, Newman regards the doctrine of the divine Motherhood of Mary as a safeguard to the doctrine of the Incarnation, protecting it from false interpretations. In an early Catholic sermon he writes:

> If you would bring out distinctly and beyond mistake and evasion, the simple idea of the Catholic Church that God is man, could you do it better than by laying down in St. John's words that 'God became man'? ... And the confession that Mary is *Deipara*, or the Mother of God, is that safeguard wherewith we seal up and secure that doctrine of the Apostle from all evasion ... It declares that He is God; it implies that He is man; it suggests to us that He is God still, though He has become man, and that He is true man though He is God.[2]

Throughout his Catholic days we can easily perceive Newman's ecumenical sensitivity in dealing with Marian themes. He himself had personal experience of the ingrained suspicion in the mind of non-Catholics towards what they saw as an undue veneration and exaltation of a creature at the expense of the Creator. Consequently, he is keen to make the important distinction between doctrine that is untouchable and devotion which can have many and varying expressions: 'I fully grant that *devotion* towards the blessed Virgin has increased among Catholics with

[1] *Meditations and Devotions of the late Cardinal Newman*, London, Longmans, Green & Co., 1911, p. 39.

[2] *Discourses addressed to Mixed Congregations*, London, Longmans, Green & Co., 1909, pp. 346–8.

the progress of centuries; I do not allow that the *doctrine* concerning her has undergone a growth, for I believe that it has been in substance one and the same from the beginning'.[3]

For this same ecumenical reason, he was careful to base his teaching on Sacred Scripture and on Patristic teaching. Here he was on common ground with his Anglican friends. Even his own private *Meditations and Devotions*, in particular his reflections on the Litany of Loreto for the month of May, are thoroughly biblical in their tone and spirit. And in his main treatise on Mary, the *Letter to Pusey*,[4] he calls repeatedly on the witness of the early Church as enshrined in the writings of the Church Fathers: 'As regards our teaching concerning the Blessed Virgin, with the Fathers I am content ... the Fathers are enough for me. I do not wish to say more than they suggest to me, and will not say less'.[5]

On certain particular points Newman tries to rectify popular misunderstanding. He is at pains to point out that Mary has been redeemed by her Son's passion just as any other child of Adam. Indeed for her, Christ did more than for anyone else. Newman also stresses the truth, so difficult for Anglicans to understand, that devotion to our Lady does not in any way come between the believer and his creator. The following

[3] *Certain Difficulties felt by Anglicans in Catholic Teaching.* Two volumes. London, Longmans, Green & Co., 1908, 1910, Vol. II, p. 26.

[4] *A Letter addressed to the Rev. E. B. Pusey, D.D., on occasion of his Eirenicon of 1864* offers us Newman's thought as a Catholic on our Lady. It is published with Notes in *Certain Difficulties felt by Anglicans in Catholic Teaching*, Vol. II, pp. 1–170. We shall presently discuss it at greater length.

[5] *Ibid.* Vol. II, pp. 24–5.

celebrated words resound from the pages of the *Apologia*: 'Only this I know full well now, and did not know then, that the Catholic Church allows no image of any sort, material or immaterial, no dogmatic symbol, no rite, no sacrament, no Saint, not even the Blessed Virgin herself, to come between the soul and its Creator. It is face to face, "solus cum solo," in all matters between man and his God. He alone creates; He alone has redeemed; before His awful eyes we go in death; in the vision of Him is our eternal beatitude'.[6]

Newman always avoided untheological exaggerations in Marian devotion. His preference was for those expressions of devotion more in keeping with the English character and culture. That does not mean that he himself did not have an intense prayer life, rich in fervent devotion. He took Mary as his Confirmation name.[7] He maintained that the ethos of his group of Tractarian converts possessed 'a special devotion to Mary' and had domestic qualities of mind, such as being 'easy, familiar and not rigid' of which our Lady was the 'special patroness'.[8] In his correspondence, he did not hesitate to suggest a lively devotion to the Blessed Virgin. When Rector of the Catholic University in Dublin, he chose *Sedes Sapientiae* as its title and patroness.

In his private meditations he himself asks to be set free from languor and inability, and to be filled with energy

[6] *Apologia*, p. 195.

[7] Note where he uses it when writing to Pius IX on 20 June 1847: *The Letters and Diaries*, XII, 87.

[8] *Ibid.* Vol. XI, p. 305. Cf. *Sermon Notes of John Henry Newman 1849–1878*. Edited by Fathers of the Birmingham Oratory, London, Longmans, Green & Co., 1914, pp. 102–3.

and fervour of soul.[9] He did not hesitate to incorporate many Roman customs into the Oratorian community in Birmingham. It is sufficient to glance at the litanies, the novenas and prayers that are to be found in his *Meditations and Devotions*. So while Newman wisely advocated forms of piety and, in particular, of Marian devotions among English Catholics that were more congenial to their nature, 'at the same time', as Wilfrid Ward writes, 'there were Italian prayer-books like the *Raccolta,* to which he was always devoted. Indeed, his own personal taste in devotion was always far more in sympathy with the Continental forms than was that of the old Catholics.[10] What he deprecated was untheological exaggerations.'[11]

It was however the publication of Pusey's *Eirenicon* that offered the context and the call to draw up the most systematic elaboration of his Mariology that we possess. What the *Apologia* means for our knowledge of his religious opinions and of his spiritual journey from Oxford to Rome, his *Letter to Pusey* represents for what we know of his Catholic theological thinking on our Lady.

2. The context of the Eirenicon and of Newman's Letter to Pusey

The context that prompted this Mariological work by Newman was the following. The Definition of

---

[9] Cf. *Meditations and Devotions*, pp. 430–1.

[10] The 'old Catholics' were those English Catholics, a relatively small number, who had remained faithful to the Roman Catholic faith since the time of the Reformation.

[11] *The Life of John Henry Newman, op. cit.* Vol. I, p. 204, footnote 2.

the dogma of the Immaculate Conception by Pope Pius IX in 1854 raised many fears and criticisms of Rome from outside the Church. Some of them stemmed from ignorance or misconceptions of what the doctrine exactly meant.[12] Others came from prejudice against the See of Rome and against any solemn declaration made by the Pope. Although Papal Infallibility had not yet been defined, there was a clear reference to it in the Papal pronouncement of 1854. This dogma was not proclaimed by an Ecumenical Council but by the Pope alone, ('by virtue of the authority of the holy Apostles Peter and Paul and of Our own authority,') using the full weight of his apostolic authority to bind the consciences of all the faithful on a particular point of doctrine. Some Anglicans were upset. Their displeasure and doubts arose not simply from the doctrine itself but from the implications of this papal pronouncement that raised a Marian truth, already commonly held by Roman Catholics, to the status of a dogma. Some others had intellectual difficulties with this doctrine, not seeing how it could be reconciled with the universality of original sin, a point that had also caused perplexity among Catholics for many centuries.

Pusey had the merit of formulating in his *Eirenicon* the fears and objections of sincere Anglicans in a learned and exhaustive fashion, and thus evoking a singularly well-balanced, documented and ecumenical response from Newman. Although Newman considered that his friend discharged his olive-branch

---

[12] *Sermon Notes,* p. 106.

of peace (*Eirenicon*) 'as from a catapult',[13] Pusey's aim was not as polemical as his text would at times suggest.

In a letter dated 2 November 1865, he manifested his objectives and the spirit that inspired him in the composition of his *Eirenicon*. He stated that his intention was not polemical and that he took issue only with matters which he considered to be important. He concentrated on the practical difficulties experienced by Anglicans in the Roman system of doctrine and, above all, of devotion. He declared that he relied on popular and widely circulated books by St Alphonsus Liguori and W. Faber, while limiting himself to questions which he considered to be theological opinions and not issues which were *de fide*. In an effort to keep the two Churches from drifting further apart on doctrinal matters, he wished to forestall certain theological opinions from being declared points of dogmatic faith, as happened in 1854 with the Immaculate Conception:

I thought that none of the system of the B.V. had been *de fide*, and this is what I wished to be said by your authorities indirectly ... But, after the doctrine of the Immaculate Conception had been so long a pious opinion, it has been declared to be *de fide*, and many bishops said that it was so held among their people ... In view of the Synod of next year,[14] I was

---

[13] *Difficulties felt by Anglicans,* Vol. II, p. 7.

[14] There was much political unrest in Italy at the time and the Council would not begin until 1869. In 1867, with hundreds of bishops present in Rome for the eighteenth centenary of the deaths of St Peter and St Paul, Pope Pius IX announced that an ecumenical Council would take place in Rome. It was solemnly opened on 8 December 1869.

not sorry, since I wrote at all, to say what are our difficulties, lest any of them should be made matters of faith too. But then too I wished to show that our difficulties lay outside the Council of Trent, and, as I thought, outside what is *de fide* (the Immaculate Conception is a perplexity), and so I thought it no attack, since I was mostly speaking of things not *de fide*, as I believed, but which, as things stand, individuals of us, if we joined the Roman Church, must receive.[15]

There was a latent dread in the minds of many Englishmen that a multitude of devotions, pious opinions and popular beliefs could well be imposed by papal authority (especially if it were to be proclaimed to be infallible) upon anyone who would wish to be received into the Catholic Church. They considered the Church of the sixteenth-century Reformation to have been purified of such devotional and erroneous excesses. Most things feared by them were not dogmatic issues but expressions of popular religiosity. Even Pusey admitted that Anglican difficulties lay outside the Council of Trent, in that collection of popular beliefs and practices, which no Roman Catholic would ever claim to be matters of dogmatic faith, but which to the Anglicans smacked of superstition and error.

And yet, take not ourselves only, but the general body of Englishmen, whether instructed or not instructed, it will be of this ... undefined body of

---

[15] Henry Parry Liddon, *Life of Edward Bouverie Pusey*. In 4 volumes. London, Longmans, Green & Co., 1893–7, Vol. IV, p. 122. Cf. p. 121.

practical belief that they will be thinking when they speak of our 'reformed' Church, or against becoming Roman Catholics. If they speak against Papal authority, it is not in itself (which would be a matter of indifference), but as an authority, which, if they submitted to it, would enforce upon them that practical system.[16]

Therefore, in the *Eirenicon*,[17] Pusey spoke of many religious subjects, underlining the amount of Catholic doctrine preserved by the Anglican body and thus making it similar to fundamental tenets of Rome, while also showing the points of divergence. He touched on the doctrine of the Sacraments, the Eucharistic Presence, the meaning of Transubstantiation, Papal Infallibility, the authority of the Church and of the Pope, Scripture and Tradition, Church unity, the Invocation of Saints, Purgatory, Indulgences and, of course, the doctrine concerning the Blessed Virgin Mary.

A substantial part of Pusey's treatise dealt with our Lady, either directly, or indirectly when expounding on topics such as intercession, the invocation of Saints and the question of Purgatory. The subject of the Immaculate Conception became the crux of the problem, simply because it was a topical theme in those decades and illustrated very clearly what Englishmen feared in the Roman Catholic system,

---

[16] E. B. Pusey, *An Eirenicon, In a Letter to the Author of 'The Christian Year'*. Oxford 1865, p. 99.

[17] The *Eirenicon* was in fact a reply to a letter by Dr Manning, published as a pamphlet in 1864: *The Workings of the Holy Spirit in the Church of England, a Letter to the Rev. E. B. Pusey*.

since it was also closely connected with the infallible authority of the Pope.

Newman wrote his *Letter to Pusey* during nine days of intensive work[18] preceding the Feast of the Immaculate Conception, 1865. It may seem a short period of time in which to compose a book that was universally recognized as a most noteworthy contribution to Marian studies. However, it was not put together on the spur of the moment: Newman had been long familiar with the arguments treated. He simply put into systematic form what he had studied, pondered upon and lived in his personal life for over twenty years. As Francis J. Friedel, in his fine exposition of Newman's Mariology, says:

> If Newman was able to produce so finished a composition within the space of a few weeks, it was because he had the material ready for service a long time since. In fact, this masterpiece of Marian literature is but the systematization, the crystallization of what Newman had taught and preached since the day when he set himself to write the *Essay on Development*.[19]

Despite Pusey's proposed eirenical intention, Newman considered that even his friend's method was unfair; that he had made much of, instead of smoothing down, points of divergence between Anglicanism and Roman Catholicism; and that some of the authors he quoted from were extreme in their

---

[18] Ian Ker, *John Henry Newman. A Biography*. Oxford, Oxford University Press, 1988, p. 580.

[19] Francis J. Friedel, *The Mariology of Cardinal Newman., op. cit.* p. 107.

views and not representative of genuine Catholic teaching in the points on which they were cited as authorities. With regard to veneration for the Mother of God, Newman found that Pusey's *Eirenicon* was likely to produce further prejudice and distrust among Anglicans towards Catholics: 'Have you even hinted that our love for her is anything else than an abuse? Have you thrown her one kind word yourself all through your book?'[20] He thought that Pusey's treatment was 'one-sided' in its presentation of Catholic belief on the subject of the Blessed Virgin Mary, and that the content and tone were 'calculated to wound those who love you well, but love truth more'.[21]

In undertaking the composition of his *Letter to Pusey*, Newman was guided by what we would nowadays call an ecumenical intention. He felt called on to clear up the confused and at times false notions which many non-Catholics entertained about Marian belief and practice in the Catholic Church: 'There just now seems a call on me, under my circumstances, to avow plainly what I do and what I do not hold about the Blessed Virgin, that others may know, did they come to stand where I stand, what they would, and what they would not, be bound to hold concerning her.'[22]

Whatever Newman's desires and whatever the general hopes of Catholics were for reunion with the Anglican Church, they would never accept it at the price of compromise on even one of the Marian doctrines handed down by a long tradition and taught by the Church: 'In truth, the honour of our

[20] *Difficulties felt by Anglicans,* Vol. II, p. 116.

[21] *Ibid.* p. 6.

[22] *Ibid.* p. 25.

Lady is dearer to them than the conversion of England.'[23] Nor would he himself allow ecumenical considerations to make him compromise on doctrinal issues. Unity he knew could be built only on dogmatic truth.

Our author gives a solid exposition of Catholic theology on the subject of the Blessed Virgin Mary. In order to have a sound foundation he showed that Marian devotion, as it was then customary among Roman Catholics, was simply a consequence of what Scripture said about her and of what the Fathers of the Church had taught. By claiming to follow the inspired text and the Patristic writings, he was on common ground with his Anglican friend. Both were aware that it would be the dear wish of those venerable Fathers to see Anglicans and Catholics reunited, without either of them doing violence to their own conscience. Newman admits that he would be the last person in the world to deny conscience its rights and duties. Indeed, he could well understand the position of Anglicans since he had suffered for many years in the same situation. Sincerity and fidelity to conscience, however, would eventually lead to the fullness of the light of truth. In proof of this, he could point to his own experience: 'A faulty conscience, faithfully observed, through God's mercy, had in the long-run brought me right.'[24]

Having answered some incidental statements in the *Eirenicon* that referred mainly to his position before his reception into the Catholic Church, Newman

[23] *Ibid.* p. 116.
[24] *Ibid.* p. 6.

declares what his method will be. He intends to base his argumentation on the teaching of the Fathers of the Church. It was they who led him into the Catholic Church and he professes that 'as regards our teaching concerning the Blessed Virgin, with the Fathers I am content ... [They] are enough for me. I do not wish to say more than they suggest to me, and I will not say less.'[25]

In an age when there was an inflation of popular and devotional writing on our Lady and when many Mariological treatises did not show a thorough knowledge of or respect for Patristic literature, Newman's *Letter to Pusey* appeared as a breath of fresh air. It dissipated many prejudices and was widely acclaimed. It became a best seller, and within months a second edition (with a few corrections) had to be published. German and French translations appeared already in 1866. Friedel justly remarks:

> Newman, too, wished to give a new impulse to Catholic studies so as to enable the Catholic to meet the Protestant on the common footing of Antiquity. His small work, priceless for its profundity, solidity, and conformity to all the canons of historical criticism, was the forerunner of considerable subsequent research on similar lines and in other domains of theology.[26]

Even those Catholics who had a different outlook from Newman, such as Cardinal Manning and W. G.

[25] *Ibid.* pp. 24–5.
[26] Francis J. Friedel, *The Mariology of Cardinal Newman, op. cit.* p. 140.

Ward and F. W. Faber, could not but acknowledge the theological depth and patristic knowledge displayed by the author. There were parts of it they criticized, especially those sections where Newman endeavoured to show that Catholic veneration of our Lady, if rightly understood, coincided with Patristic teaching and was consequently quite acceptable to Anglicans.[27] They thought that Newman's treatment of the subject might diminish at least the fervour of Catholic devotion to the Blessed Virgin Mary and the Saints. In particular they did not relish the language used by Newman when he explained that Mary needed a Redeemer as much as any other human person, because 'in Adam, she died, as others . . . that she incurred his debt . . .; but that, for the sake of her Son who was to redeem her and us upon the Cross, to her the debt was remitted by anticipation'.[28] To one such Catholic, a barrister and one of Manning's converts, Newman explained his position:

> What I have said in my Letter was but a matter of fact, viz. that the Decree of 1854 did not deny that our Lady was under the debitum – that no Catholic was called to deny it – that I did not deny it – that Suárez,[29] the greatest theological authority of these latter times, affirmed it.

[27] *Ibid.*

[28] *Difficulties felt by Anglicans,* Vol. II, p. 48.

[29] Francisco Suárez (1548–1617) was an eminent Jesuit theologian and Scholastic philosopher from Spain. He was known for the depth of his thought and displayed a wide knowledge of the writings of the Church Fathers. In Scholasticism, he gave rise to a school of his own known as 'Suarism.' He wrote extensively and was very highly regarded in his day. Many editions and compendiums of his theological and philosophical thought were published up until the nineteenth century.

I did not say that every Catholic was obliged to affirm – or that there was not a certain particular sense of the word in which divines, such as Viva[30] and your own Jesuit author, considered that they were at liberty to deny it.

For myself, such subtleties, touch neither my heart nor my reason. They don't seem to me to add one atom of honour to our Lady – they do but deprive her Son of subjects. I do but associate them with the loss of souls. It would not lead me to say with a clearer conscience '*Per te, Virgo, sim defensus, in die judicii*' to have the misgiving within me, that by my officious zeal for her honour, I had prevented my brethren from submitting to the Catholic Church, and enjoying the blessings of Catholic communion.[31]

In fact, after reading it, many said: 'If this is the meaning of the Doctrine, there is no reason why all Christians should not hold it'.[32] Newman's tone was much more acceptable to Anglicans. They felt in it a sympathy and broad-mindedness which they found lacking in the writings of other less sensitive writers, such as Ward. Whereas Newman advocated a certain tolerance in points not strictly dogmatic, his Catholic critics wished at times to display as unchangeable and essential to the faith certain opinions and popular

---

[30] Domenico Viva (1648–1726) was an Italian Jesuit who worked and taught mainly in Naples. He wrote various volumes of dogmatic and moral theology. His most famous work is *Trutina theologica damnatarum thesium* (1708) in two volumes.

[31] *The Letters and Diaries*, XXII, 225.

[32] Charles Stephen Dessain, *Cardinal Newman's Teaching about the Blessed Virgin Mary, op. cit.* p. 11.

practices which were not theologically certain. They endeavoured to prove them by the mere fact that they were accepted by Church authority and widely practised by Catholics.

On 31 March 1866, a long and significant review of seven columns appeared in *The Times*.[33] Although unsigned, most people knew immediately that it was the work of R. W. Church.[34] While appreciative of Newman's effort and admitting that Anglican readers 'would much care to know' his reflections on Pusey's *Eirenicon*, the writer claims that the voice of this respected Oxford convert did not reflect the opinions of those who had ruling power in Roman circles and those whom they trusted throughout the Church. In other words, the popular excesses in Marian devotion among some Catholic authors and worshippers were in his opinion countenanced by Catholic authorities, and that remained at a practical level a stumbling-block to reunion and to the conversion of many.[35]

Newman was not unduly annoyed by this article in *The Times*. He thought that indirectly it would do

[33] The significance of such a long review of a book of Catholic theology may be lost on us now. It is helpful to know that 'an article of such length in *The Times* in those days proclaimed, as a rule, a public event of first-rate national importance. That Newman's brief letter to Dr Pusey should call forth a review nearly as long as itself, was an eloquent comment on the position Newman now held in the public mind; and to the initiated who knew that it came from the pen of R. W. Church, afterwards Dean of St Paul's, this fact added to its interest'. (Wilfrid Ward, *The Life of John Henry Cardinal Newman, op. cit.* Vol. II, p. 109).

[34] Published also in R. W. Church, *Occasional Papers.* Selected from the *Guardian*, *The Times*, and the *Saturday Review* 1846–1890. 2 Volumes. London, Macmillan, 1897, Vol. II, pp. 398–440.

[35] Cf. Wilfrid Ward, *The Life of John Henry Newman, op. cit.* Vol. II, pp. 108–12.

good to the Catholic cause, for it meant publicity for his book, and he knew that more Anglicans would be impressed by genuine Catholic teaching on our Lady. He was right, as Dr Ullathorne testifies: 'The exposition of the Mystery of the Immaculate Conception in the letter to Dr. Pusey ... has cleared away the difficulties that obscured the minds of several earnest inquirers with respect to the whole subject of the Blessed Virgin.'[36] To Pusey himself, who sympathized with him for the attacks made upon his *Letter*, Newman responded that he was not irritated by them for they 'are a proof that one is doing a work'.[37]

Therefore, on the whole, Newman's book was well received. Various bishops and theological schools throughout England expressed their approval. Particularly gratifying was the praise given by his own bishop, Dr Ullathorne, in a letter to *The Tablet*, published 4 April 1866. He came out strongly in defence of Newman's orthodoxy; he drew up a long list of facts that illustrated Newman's personal devotion to our Lady and that of his Oratory at Birmingham; and declared that it was the genuine Roman tradition that he and his fellow converts had learned in Rome. Dr Ullathorne deprecated some 'petty cavilling from Catholics without authority' which he claimed to be an ungrateful attitude towards a man who wrote 'a masterly exposition of the subject most difficult for a Protestant to comprehend, and which has made that subject classical in the English tongue'. In particular he singled out for praise the

---

[36] *The Letters and Diaries*, XXII, 343.
[37] *Ibid*. 201.

orthodoxy of Newman's Marian teaching which 'defends every inch of the ground of Catholic principle from ... Pusey, and the earnestness with which he puts forth his whole soul in exalting each glorious privilege of the Immaculate Mother of Our Lord'.[38]

38 *Ibid.* 343. Cf. 341–4.

THEMES OF NEWMAN'S MARIOLOGY

1. Mary, conceived without original sin

In many ways, the truth of the Immaculate Conception was the focal point of Newman's teaching on our Lady: it touched on many points of his Mariology. He contemplated it as a logical consequence of Mary being the Second Eve.[1] It was a fitting preparation for her who was to be the Mother of God Incarnate. From her divine Motherhood flow all her other privileges. Even in his Anglican days, he came to understand how fitting and how logical it was that Mary should be immaculate in every way, so that it did not prove to be a problem for him to accept it personally – 'for why should it not have been difficult to me at that time, if there were a real difficulty in receiving it?'[2] As we already saw, he preached about it in equivalent words, yet dared not use the term, as it was not recognized by the Anglican creed.

The point that seemed to Newman 'to be conclu-

[1] Cf. *The Letters and Diaries,* XXIV, 283.
[2] *Meditations and Devotions,* p. 80.

sive'[3] in proving the Immaculate Conception of Mary
was that it flows as an immediate inference from that
other doctrine (already taught by the Fathers and
universally accepted in the Christian tradition) of Mary
being the Second Eve. This argument has a strong
ecumenical weight as well. All agree that Eve was sinless
and endowed with grace. It is an open question,
whether our first parents were created in a state that
enjoyed nothing more than the qualities of their
untainted human nature or whether, as is more likely,
they were elevated beyond nature to the state of grace
from the very first instant of their existence. The question was not decided by the Council of Trent. Newman
simply states that Adam received the gift of grace before
Eve, 'at the very time (it is commonly held) of his original formation'.[4] What is certain is that they were not
created in a state of sin or enmity with God. Adam and
Eve were sinless at the first instant of their existence.

This suffices for Newman, who regards Mary as the
counterpart of Eve: as the latter collaborated with
Adam in our fall from grace, Mary co-operated with
Christ in restoring our lost privileges. The Virgin
Mary, who had a vital role to play in the work of
redemption as the Mother of the Saviour, conquered
the tempter by obeying in faith, thus undoing the
harm of Eve's transgression and failure. Consequently,
Newman argues, she must have been endowed at least
as highly as Eve was. She too must have been sinless
from the beginning of her existence: otherwise the
parallel with Eve would be definitely faulty. Both of
them were placed by Providence at a critical juncture

[3] *Difficulties felt by Anglicans,* Vol. II, p. 49.
[4] *Ibid.* pp. 44–5.

in human history. Following on Mary's obedience to God's designs, a new and better creation dawned for the human race.

> Is it any violent inference, that she, who was to co-operate in the redemption of the world, at least was not less endowed with power from on high, than she who, given as a help-mate to her husband, did in the event but co-operate with him for its ruin? If Eve was raised above human nature by that indwelling moral gift which we call grace, is it rash to say that Mary had even a greater grace? ... And if Eve had this super-natural inward gift given to her from the first moment of her personal existence, is it possible to deny that Mary too had this gift from the very first moment of her personal existence? I do not know how to resist this inference: – well, this is simply and literally the doctrine of the Immaculate Conception.[5]

Newman of course makes reference here simply to the supernatural gift of grace. He does not mean that Mary was given the so-called 'preternatural' gifts of immortality, knowledge and immunity from suffering that our first parents possessed before the Fall. Like her Son, she advanced in knowledge and age, she suffered even more keenly than others owing to her extreme purity and innocence, and she ended her days on earth passing through the doors of death (as is commonly held) to be glorified however in soul and body: 'Mary came into a fallen world, and resigned herself to its laws; she, as also the Son she bore, was exposed to

[5] *Ibid.* pp. 45, 46.

pain of soul and body, she was subjected to death; but she was not put under the power of sin.'[6]

The Immaculate Conception seems to Newman to be also included in the fact that the Blessed Virgin never committed any venial sin. 'Her personal sanctity' leads Catholics on to 'the doctrine of the Immaculate Conception.'[7] Those who come near God, the All-Holy Creator and source of all sanctity, must also be holy. No one came as near to him as Mary, the Mother of Christ, who was the living tabernacle of his Incarnate Son, carrying him in her womb and accompanying him from his birth to his death on Calvary. 'An instinctive sentiment has led Christians jealously to put the Blessed Mary aside when sin comes into discussion.'[8] To profess in the fullest sense Mary's personal sinlessness is the equivalent of stating that she was conceived immaculately: 'Indeed, it is almost saying what has been said in other words, for if no venial sin, *must* there not be Immaculate Conception?'[9]

---

[6] *Discourses to Mixed Congregations*, p. 354. Cf. Francis J. Friedel, *The Mariology of Cardinal Newman, op. cit.* pp. 304–5.

[7] *The Letters and Diaries*, XII, 334.

[8] *Difficulties felt by Anglicans*, Vol. II, pp. 49–50; cf. p. 136.

[9] *Sermon Notes*, p. 106. The only real objection which Newman knows against the doctrine was the fact that some eminent Fathers of the fourth century, such as Origen, Tertullian, St Basil, St Chrysostom and St Cyril of Alexandria, thought that our Lady did become a victim to some of the infirmities of our nature by committing slight imperfections or venial sins (such as initial doubt) at the moment of the Annunciation and under the Cross. Consequently, Newman added a lengthy examination of these texts in the published volume of his *Letter to Pusey*. He shows that these were mere personal opinions of individual Fathers and not indications of a living and widespread tradition in the Church (cf. *Difficulties felt by Anglicans,* Vol. II, Note III, pp. 128–152). On this question one can get a fuller summary in Domenico Bertetto, *Maria la serva del Signore.* Trattato di Mariologia. Napoli, Dehoniane, 1988, pp. 88–108.

The theological argumentation is exact. In fact, would it be possible for her to commit a venial sin at all? Considering her position and privileges, her freedom from those wounds that original sin leaves on our nature, attracting us strongly to sinful pleasures, darkening our mind and weakening our will, would not any transgression in her case be very serious – just as the personal sin committed by Eve and Adam was extremely grave?

Indeed, the Church also teaches this absolute freedom of our Lady from even the slightest personal sin. The Council of Trent, excluding the case of our Lady from its treatment of original sin, declared that it was the faith of the Church that she was kept free from all venial sin through a special privilege granted by God.[10] Pius IX, in his Bull *Ineffabilis Deus* for the dogmatic definition of the Immaculate Conception, repeated this thought which he had culled from the Fathers of the Church, saying that Mary was 'always free from every stain of sin, all fair and perfect, a virgin undefiled, immaculate, ever blessed, and free from all contagion of sin, from which was formed the new Adam, a reproachless, most sweet paradise of innocence'.[11]

Newman, however, not only bases his conviction

---

[10] In Canon 23 of the Decree on Justification, the Council of Trent states: 'If anyone maintains that a person once he is justified ... can avoid all sin, even venial sin, throughout the whole of life, without a special divine privilege, as the Church believes was the case with the Blessed Virgin, *anathema sit*' (Cf. H. Denziger – A. Schönmetzer, SJ, *Enchiridion Symbolorum Definitionum et Declarationum de Rebus Fidei et Morum*. Freiburg im Breisgau, Herder, 1963, No. 1573).

[11] Cf. *Acta Pii IX*, Vol. I, pp. 608–12 *passim*. Pius XII in his Encyclical *Mystici Corporis* has the same teaching. He declares that Mary was 'free from every stain, both personal and hereditary, and was always most closely united with her Son' (AAS 35 (1943) p. 247).

on theological argumentation but, as always, goes to the sure foundation of Sacred Scripture. He reads the pertinent texts in the light of the interpretation given to them by the Fathers of the Church. Thus he recalls the words of Genesis 3:15 and defends the Vulgate reading: '*She* shall bruise thy head' – the same procedure as was used by Pope Pius IX in the Bull *Ineffabilis Deus*. He adds that the parallel Eve–Mary shows up the full content of the Archangel's words to Mary: 'full of grace'.[12] Newman's exposition is completely in harmony with the mind of the Church and is a fine specimen of theological writing.

Moreover, he draws on another passage from Scripture that speaks of an enduring war between the serpent and the woman. It is the famous vision of St John in the Apocalypse (ch. 20) where the serpent is called Satan, the Evil Spirit. The woman with child is understood by Newman as referring to Mary with Christ. The parallels with the passage in Genesis 3:15 are obvious: the vision of a woman in both texts; she is with a 'seed' in Genesis, and with a 'child' in the Apocalypse; present in both cases is the serpent and

[12] The same interpretation was given by Pope Pius IX when promulgating the dogma of the Immaculate Conception and was echoed by Pope Pius XII in his Encyclical *Fulgens Corona*. Exegetes admit the messianic and eschatological meaning of Genesis 3:15, although they dispute how Christ and his Mother are referred to in the text. Tradition recognizes a Mariological interpretation. Pius XII relying on this tradition affirms: 'If therefore the Blessed Virgin Mary was deprived at any moment of divine grace, as a result of being stained in her conception by the hereditary stain of sin, then at least for that instant even though a very brief one, there would not have existed between her and the serpent that enmity, which is spoken about from the earliest tradition down to the solemn definition of the Immaculate Conception, but on the contrary there would have been a certain subjection.'(Encyclical Letter, *Fulgens Corona*, 8 September 1953).

the enmity between them. Newman cannot help but conclude that 'the woman is Mary in the third [chapter] of Genesis'. The parallel Eve–Mary becomes still clearer. And the implications for the doctrine of the Immaculate Conception are evident: the enmity between them is understandable 'if she had nothing to do with sin – for, so far as any one sins, he has an alliance with the Evil One'.[13]

Our Lady's Immaculate Conception is also closely connected with her divine Maternity. In fact, it is this unique privilege of being the Mother of God, a privilege that is evident from the Gospels, that gives even greater force to the texts already mentioned in support of the Immaculate Conception. The text of the Dogmatic Constitution on the Church, *Lumen Gentium* of Vatican II portrays her as being prepared to be a worthy dwelling place for God's Son.[14]

[13] *Meditations and Devotions*, p. 84. The Mariological interpretation of this text from the Apocalypse (ch. 20) is admittedly not the one commonly used by the Fathers of the Church and theologians of former centuries. Neither is it used by Pius IX in his Bull of promulgation of the dogma of the Immaculate Conception (*Ineffabilis Deus*), nor by Pius XII in his Marian Encyclical *Fulgens Corona*, nor by the Fathers of Vatican II. The usual interpretation is ecclesial. However, Pope Paul VI in his Exhortation *Signum magnum* in 1967 does give it a Mariological interpretation. Moreover, it has come to be recognized by some eminent exegetes and theological scholars of the present time as containing first of all a reference to the Church, but one which also has a Mariological content. The Church and Mary appear from this text of the Apocalypse (12:1–6) as closely conjoined in the struggle against Satan and in the victory over the powers of evil (cf. Domenico Bertetto, *Maria la Serva del Signore, op. cit.* pp. 289–92).

[14] For example, this important document of Vatican II recalls how the holy Fathers of the Church were accustomed to refer to Mary, the Mother of God, as 'all holy and free from every stain of sin, as though fashioned by the Holy Spirit and formed as a new creature'. (*Lumen Gentium*, 56).

God himself is infinitely holy and it was fitting that he should prepare an immaculate Mother for his Incarnate Son. Even in the order of nature, the honour or dishonour of a mother is reflected in her son. Therefore, an intuition of faith enables us to see how 'convenient' or appropriate it was that the Word made flesh should do what his almighty power enabled him to do, namely, preserve his Mother free from all sin. 'The divine Maternity, then, if attentively considered, postulates the privilege of the Immaculate Conception.'[15]

This method of the 'fittingness' of a truth is also used in theology, especially to confirm a point that is known from other sources. Newman himself had recourse to it on occasion[16] but he was particularly pleased with the procedure used by Pius IX in preparing the definition of the Immaculate Conception. In fact, on 2 February 1849, the Pope published the Encyclical Letter *Ubi primum,* in which he requested all the bishops of the Church to express their views on the question of the Immaculate Conception and to consult the faithful in their dioceses so as to find out the opinion of the entire body of believers of the universal Church. He thought it most significant that the Pope should wish to know if the Catholic people called for this proclamation: 'It is very joyous news – strange that in our day what has been a controversy for so many centuries should at length be defined – but it is a wonderful time.'[17]

---

[15] Martino Jugie, *L'immaculée Conception dans l'Écriture sainte et dans la Tradition Orientale.* Roma 1952, p. 51

[16] He has an entire Sermon entitled 'On the Fitness of the Glories of Mary' (*Mixed Congregations,* pp. 360–76)

[17] *The Letters and Diaries,* XIII, 84–5. Cf. 81–2.

Newman strongly advocated the place of the laity in the Church. An article he wrote for the July 1859 issue of *The Rambler,* entitled 'On Consulting the Faithful in Matters of Doctrine', was severely criticized. Some regarded it as meaning that the Pope was almost obliged to take counsel with the laity before important doctrinal statements were issued. Newman explains, however, that he meant the verb 'consult' in the more idiomatic sense of the English language, namely, to ask the opinion of someone in order to ascertain a matter of *fact*. As one may 'consult' the barometer about the weather – 'the barometer only attests the *fact* of the state of the atmosphere'.[18] It is simply a question of finding out the mind of the Church, the implicit faith of the multitude of believers which reflects an apostolic tradition and mirrors the teaching which the faithful have universally received from their bishops through preaching, catechetical instructions, pastoral letters and liturgical worship. Thus by consulting the faithful he means the effort to find out what the faithful believe. 'Doubtless their advice, their opinion, their judgment on the question of definition is not asked; but the matter of fact, viz. their belief, *is* sought for, as a testimony to that apostolic tradition, on which alone any doctrine whatsoever can be defined.'[19] Once again we see the importance of a living tradition in the life of the Church.

This 'source' of divine revelation is naturally very

---

[18] John Henry Newman, *On Consulting the Faithful in Matters of Doctrine.* Edited with an Introduction by John Coulson. London, Collins, 1986, p. 54.

[19] *Ibid.* pp. 54–5.

difficult to use. Nowadays especially, it is not easy to 'consult' the faithful, since public opinion can be so easily manipulated by the media and by pressure groups, even in matters concerning the faith. However, the Second Vatican Council reiterated the importance and trustworthiness of this *sensus fidei* of the holy people of God.[20] And as mentioned, Pius IX made explicit use of it in the preparation and proclamation of the dogma of the Immaculate Conception.[21]

Thus Newman's teaching on the Immaculate Conception is theologically very rich in content and is linked with many other aspects of his Marian doctrine and theological thought. In this light it is understandable that he had a particular devotion to this mystery and to the Immaculate Virgin. He had the principal liturgical celebration of the Oratory changed from the Assumption to the Conception and in 1851 (three years before the definition) dedicated the Birmingham Oratory Church to the Immaculate Conception. He was very pleased that his was one of the Congregations that had got permission to have the word *immaculata* inserted in the Preface of the Mass after the word *conceptione*.[22]

In the last century, Protestants often thought that the doctrine of the Immaculate Conception was the

---

[20] Vatican II, *Lumen Gentium*, 12. Cf. 35.

[21] In the document with which he promulgated the definition, Pope Pius IX wrote that he had asked the bishops of all the Catholic world, in his Encyclical Letter *Ubi Primum*, 'what was the piety and devotion of their flocks towards the Immaculate Conception of the Mother of God, and especially, what the bishops themselves thought about promulgating the definition or what they desired' so that he could pronounce his supreme judgment as solemnly as possible (*Ineffabilis Deus*, of 8 December 1854).

[22] Cf. *The Letters and Diaries*, XIII, 82.

one that offered Catholics greatest difficulty. Newman had no intrinsic difficulty with the dogma as such. He saw it intimately harmonizing with the body of other dogmatic truths recognized by the Church.[23] The faithful had come to accept it long before it was declared a dogma. Led by an instinct of faith and guided by the Holy Spirit, they accepted it with enthusiasm and almost demanded that the highest Church authority declare it to be a certain point of their faith. In no way was it 'a burden' to Catholic believers. In fact, Newman thought that no holy person 'in any age has ever really denied it'.[24] By the last century, theological reflection and pastoral preaching had arrived at explaining it in a way that it seemed obvious to the vast majority of Catholics that it must be true. People were able to see that it formed an integral part of the entire body of dogmatic truths. It did not appear in any way to be a spurious idea that could not be assimilated into the theological doctrines approved by the Church. This is a sign of authenticity: 'It is a great evidence of truth, in the case of revealed teaching, that it is so consistent, that it so hangs together, that one thing springs out of another, that each part requires and is required by the rest'.[25]

Newman thought that those who seemed to have denied it, or at least thought it not necessary, had in mind some other notion. In the Middle Ages, the difficulty of men like St Thomas and St Bernard 'consisted in matters of words, ideas, and argu-

[23] Cf. *Apologia*, pp. 254–5.
[24] *Sermon Notes*, p. 106.
[25] *Mixed Congregations*, pp. 360–1.

ments'.[26] They did not see how it harmonized with other doctrines.

In fact, it is easy to have misconceptions about the precise meaning of this doctrine. Newman went to much trouble in explaining the real notion of the Immaculate Conception since many people were troubled by this doctrine simply because they had a false understanding of its genuine nature. Some people thought that the privilege referred not to Mary but to her mother, St Anne. This of course is not true. The Catholic dogma of the Immaculate Conception refers to Mary as being conceived (passively) without sin, not to her mother who (actively) conceived her.[27]

Others understood it to mean that Mary did not need to be redeemed, that she was an exception to the universal effect of Christ's saving sacrifice. Newman reacted decisively, stating with emphasis that she, first of all, was redeemed by her Son's Passion, but in a more excellent way, a way that prevented her fall rather than repaired the damage inflicted by the fall. Or, as Pope Pius IX would say, repeating former Pontiffs, she was saved from sin by the foreseen merits of Jesus Christ, the Saviour of the human race. To Robert Wilberforce, Newman writes clarifying these false notions:

> We do not say that she did not owe her salvation to the death of her Son. Just the contrary, we say that she, of all mere children of Adam, is in the truest sense the fruit and the purchase of His Passion. He

[26] *Apologia*, p. 255.
[27] Cf. *Meditations and Devotions*, p. 82; *The Letters and Diaries*, XIX, 365–6.

has done for her more than for anyone else. To others He gives grace and regeneration at a point in their earthly existence; to her, from the very beginning. [...] She and we are both simply saved by the grace of Christ.[28]

Another misunderstanding concerning this doctrine arose from the different views of original sin and of grace held by Catholics and by Protestants: to the former, original sin means a negative quality, a deprivation of something that is due though not merited, a missing grace of friendship with God on a supernatural level. Protestants take it to mean a positive infection, 'an active poison corrupting the soul',[29] 'an *infection* of nature, so that man's nature is not what it was before the fall'.[30] Consequently, they regard the doctrine of the Immaculate Conception as postulating for Mary a different nature from ours. To which Newman replies emphatically: 'We do not make her *nature* different from others. [...] Certainly, she *would* have been a frail being, like Eve, *without* the grace of God.'[31]

From these divergent views of original sin, it is clear that 'grace' is regarded differently by Catholics and Protestants. In general, for the latter, it is a purely external approbation given by God to a soul that is still internally corrupt, although its indignity is, as it were, covered over or at least not imputed by God.

[28] *Meditations and Devotions*, pp. 80, 81. Cf. *Difficulties felt by Anglicans*, Vol. II, p. 49.

[29] *Difficulties felt by Anglicans*, Vol. II, p. 48.

[30] *The Letters and Diaries*, XIX, 363.

[31] *Meditations and Devotions*, p. 80. Cf. *Difficulties felt by Anglicans*, Vol. II, p. 48.

Catholics on the other hand regard grace as a thing of transforming and justifying beauty: 'a real inward condition or superadded quality of the soul'.[32] In other words, Mary had that positive quality of supernatural grace which Eve had before her fall – and this is what the doctrine of the Immaculate Conception means for Catholics.

We have given more prominence to this point of Marian doctrine, because of the eminent role it played in Newman's Mariological teaching, and because of its ecumenical importance in his days on account of its difficulty for Protestants and the preparation of its promulgation as a dogma.

However, Newman touched on many other points in his Mariology. The following deserve particular notice.

2. Mary, the Second Eve

Newman's reading of the Fathers and of the history of the early Church led him to begin his theological exposition on our Lady, by recalling what he terms 'the great rudimental teaching of Antiquity from its earliest date'[33] concerning Mary. He quotes ten authors dating from the second to the sixth centuries, representing the Western and Eastern Churches, and how they witness to an apostolic tradition that, from the beginning, regarded Mary as the Second Eve. More than the nature of her motherhood – a fact taken for granted in the Gospels and clarified theologically only when heretics questioned the divinity of

[32] *Difficulties felt by Anglicans*, Vol. II, p. 46.
[33] *Ibid.* p. 31.

Christ, – it was this position of hers in the work of redemption, as the counterpart of Eve, that came in for most attention in the earliest times.

In his argumentation, Newman gives considerable weight to the fact that these authors, especially the first three he mentions, namely, St Justin, Tertullian and St Irenaeus, witness independently of each other and derive their knowledge from a common source – namely, the universal faith of the early Church, which in turn was derived from an apostolic tradition. In fact, as Francis J. Friedel points out, this mutual independence in their knowledge is not all that important for 'even though they were not independent, they could have derived their doctrine from some common source'.[34] Moreover, the parallelism between the first Adam and the second Adam, Christ, which St Paul elaborates in his treatment of original sin (Rom. 5:12–29), would easily have led ecclesiastical writers of the earliest centuries to see the implications for the first and the second Eve.

The parallelism between Eve and Mary enhances our estimation of our Lady's role in our redemption. The Blessed Virgin, representing the whole human race, was placed like Eve in a position of having to choose between obedience and disobedience to God. Obedience demanded of her an act of faith in God's almighty power that could make a reality of what was humanly impossible: to remain a virgin and yet become the mother of the Messiah. Unlike Eve, Mary consented and obeyed, and thus became the Mother of God, the true mother of all the living (cf. Gen.

[34] *The Mariology of Cardinal Newman,* p. 201. cf. pp. 186–203.

3:20). What Eve lost by her incredulity and proud disobedience, Mary restored to us through her humble obedience and strong faith.

Consequently Newman is led, from his reading of the early Fathers on this point, to speak of the Blessed Virgin as meriting her place in the plan of salvation, since she actively and personally corresponded with God's grace. At the moment of her own conception she was passive in God's creative hands, but at the moment of the Annunciation, when she became the Mother of God and of divine mercy, she was not simply a passive and physical instrument, but a living, responsible and intelligent cause of God taking flesh within her. Had she not willingly made the act of obedience and faith, she would not have become the Mother of God.[35] Cardinal Newman makes much of this point. 'As Eve was a cause of ruin to all, Mary was a cause of salvation to all; as Eve made room for Adam's fall, so Mary made room for our Lord's reparation of it; and thus, whereas the free gift was not as the offence, but much greater, it follows that, as Eve co-operated in effecting a great evil, Mary co-operated in effecting a much greater good.'[36] Our author is here in line with a long tradition going from the earliest times down to the present day. In fact, the Second Vatican Council refers to the Patristic doctrine according to which Mary, as the Second Eve, was not merely 'a passive

[35] This is a thought that was echoed not only by the Fathers of the Church but also by some saints and mystics, for example, St Catherine of Siena who prays as follows: 'The eternal deity knocked at your door, Mary, but if you had not opened the gate of your will, God would not have become incarnate in you' (cf. *Le Orazioni*. A cura di G. Cavallini. Roma, Ed. Catheriniane, 1978, p. 128).

[36] *Difficulties felt by Anglicans,* Vol. II, p. 36.

instrument in the hands of God, but co-operated in the work of human salvation through free faith and obedience'.[37]

All this shows us what a mother we have in the spiritual order, and it also gives us a deeper grasp of Newman's respect and love for her.

3. The Mother of God

Steeped as he was in the Scripture and in the writings of the ancient Fathers of the Church, Newman was firmly convinced of the Blessed Virgin's highest prerogative – her divine maternity. That Mary is the Mother of God (*Theotokos* from the Greek or *Deipara* from the Latin) is 'an integral portion of the Faith, fixed by Ecumenical Council'.[38] This is her fundamental dignity.

Newman delves once more into his knowledge of Patristic literature in order to show how the title *Theotokos* was deeply rooted in the apostolic tradition. The doctrine was clear from the beginning; when devotion began to extend and false developments of a heretical kind made their appearance, the Church reacted in solemn Council, and formulated with dogmatic precision what it had always believed. The third Ecumenical Council of the Church in 431 ended controversy, proclaimed that in Christ there

---

[37] Cf. *Lumen Gentium*, 56. cf. also in his private devotions, where Newman writes: 'As regards the Blessed Virgin, it was God's will that she should undertake willingly and with full understanding to be the Mother of our Lord, and not to be a mere passive instrument whose maternity would have no merit and no reward' (*Meditations and Devotions*, p. 37).

[38] *Difficulties felt by Anglicans*, Vol. II, p. 62.

was only one Person – a divine One – and accordingly declared Mary to be the *Theotokos*, the Mother of God and not merely of the humanity of Christ.[39]

It is evident from Newman's writings that he remains in profound admiration of this exaltation of a mere creature. So much so that in his meditations he asks himself in wonderment which mystery is most astounding – that God should become man without ceasing to be God, or that Mary, a mere creature, should become the Mother of God.[40]

It is truly an awe-inspiring title, indicating the origin of her greatness, and making it extremely fitting that she should be adorned with countless other privileges of grace. For this title is no extravagant expression of human admiration for the mother of the promised Messiah: 'it intends to express that God is her Son, as truly as any one of us is the son of his own mother'.[41]

Consequently Newman states that no honour, compatible with the nature of a creature, is too exalted for her, no praise too great. 'Nothing is too high for her to whom God owes his human life; no exuberance of grace, no excess of glory, but is becoming, but is to be expected there, where God has

---

[39] Cf. *Select Treatises of St Athanasius in Controversy with the Arians*. London, Longmans, Green & Co., 1903. Two volumes. Vol. II. pp. 210–15; *Difficulties felt by Anglicans*, Vol. II, pp. 61–7. For further reading on the importance of the Incarnation in Newman's theology, cf. the following studies: Roderick Strange, *Newman and the Gospel of Christ*. Oxford University Press, 1981; Fortunato Morrone, *Cristo il Figlio di Dio fatto uomo*. L'Incarnazione del Verbo nel pensiero cristologico di J. H. Newman. Milano, Jaca Book, 1990.

[40] Cf. *Meditations and Devotions*, p. 40.

[41] *Difficulties felt by Anglicans*, Vol. II, p. 62.

lodged Himself, whence God has issued.'[42]
Accordingly, it is understandable, almost to be
expected, that when this truth of faith finds its expression in devotion, it gives rise to an exalted and
exuberant form of language. The poets and scholars of
the Eastern Churches in particular vied with each
other in their panegyrics, adding metaphor to
metaphor, in their efforts to extol the greatness of a
Virgin Mother, whose only Son was the only-begotten of the Father. Newman defends this development:
'No wonder if their language should become unmeasured, when so great a term as 'Mother of God' had
been formally set down as the safe limit of it.'[43]

Coming back to theological sobriety as distinct
from the exuberant expressions of filial devotion,
Newman makes the penetrating remark that the truth
of the divine motherhood of Mary is a safeguard for
the very doctrine of the Incarnation. This intuition
was part of Newman's faith from his early Anglican
days. He expressed it, as we saw, in a sermon preached
in 1832[44] and it would remain a constant conviction
of faith throughout his entire life. He repeats it in his
Essay on the Development of Christian Doctrine in 1845:
'it protects the doctrine of the Incarnation and
preserves the faith of Catholics from a specious
Humanitarianism'.[45] And in his Catholic days he again
teaches and preaches this same truth: those who

---

[42] *Mixed Congregations,* p. 363. Cf. *Difficulties felt by Anglicans,* Vol. II,
   pp. 62–3.
[43] *Difficulties felt by Anglicans,* Vol. II, pp. 65–6.
[44] Cf. *Parochial and Plain Sermons,* Vol. II, p. 136.
[45] Cf. *An Essay on the Development of Christian Doctrine.* London,
   Longmans, Green & Co., 1909, p. 426.

rejected the Catholic teaching about our Lady and her divine Maternity, ended by losing their clear perception of the real nature of the Incarnation.[46] For there is no more unequivocal way of declaring that God became incarnate than to say that he was born in our flesh and had a Mother. Thus the confession that Mary is the Mother of God safeguards what St John the Evangelist states so clearly: 'The Word was made flesh and dwelt among us'(John 1:14). 'It declares that He [Christ] is God; it implies that He is man; it suggests to us that He is God still, though He has become man, and that He is true man though He is God. By witnessing to the *process* of the union, it secures the reality of the two *subjects* of the union, of the divinity and of the manhood. If Mary is the Mother of God, Christ must be literally Emmanuel, God with us.'[47]

We should not be surprised that Newman made so much of this point, for the doctrine of the Incarnation was central to his entire religious and theological thought.[48]

Finally in Mary's Motherhood, Newman contemplates a truth which our present age has taken to heart, and which the Church has seen as a positive sign of the times, namely the promotion and dignity of women. Part of the punishment of Eve's sin – being 'ruled over' by her husband (cf. Gen. 3:16) – is reversed by the birth of Christ from the Virgin Mary. In the heathen world before the coming of the Redeemer, women were often in a state of unworthy

---

[46] Cf. *Sermon Notes*, p. 23; *Difficulties felt by Anglicans*, Vol. II, pp. 82–6.

[47] *Mixed Congregations*, pp. 347–8. Cf. *Sermon Notes*, p. 23.

[48] Cf. John Henry Newman, *Gesù*. Pagine scelte, *op. cit.* pp. 62–75; Francis J. Friedel, *The Mariology of Cardinal Newman*, *op. cit.* p. 5.

subordination to men. Newman gives two examples, namely, polygamy and divorce, both of them detrimental to the dignity of women. 'But when Christ came as the seed of the woman, He vindicated the rights and honour of His Mother.'[49] In doing so, he vindicated the rights and honour of all women. That was the genuine 'liberation' of women. Their distinctive role is not changed, Newman hastens to add; their place in the order of creation, intimated by St Peter (1 Pet. 3:7) and St Paul (1 Tim. 2:15) is not altered, any more than man's 'inferiority' to Christ, 'but the slavery is done away with.'[50] And to the seemingly harsh words of St Paul: 'woman shall be saved by child-bearing' (1 Tim. 2:15), Newman gives a thought-provoking interpretation: in a spiritual reading of the text, he understands it to refer implicitly to Mary's child-bearing: women 'shall be saved through the Child-bearing, that is, through the birth of Christ from Mary, which was a blessing, as on all mankind, so peculiarly upon the woman'.[51] Accordingly, marriage began to be restored to its original dignity and became a sign of the union between Christ and his Bride, the Church: 'Thus has the Blessed Virgin, in bearing our Lord, taken off or lightened the peculiar disgrace which the woman inherited for seducing Adam'.[52]

On this point, Newman was speaking with a prophetic voice for our contemporary world. In these considerations by him, Catholic feminist movements

---

[49] *Parochial and Plain Sermons,* Vol. II, pp.130–1.
[50] *Ibid.* p. 131.
[51] *Ibid.*
[52] *Ibid.*

would find enlightened insights into the mystery of
woman, in harmony with the divine plan for creation
and supernatural salvation. It would help them to safeguard the rights of women in a manner that would not
jeopardize their dignity.[53]

4. *The Assumption*

In Newman's day, belief in Mary's Assumption into
heaven was generally held by Catholics, but it was not
as yet part of the definitive dogmatic teaching of the
Church. Newman duly refers to it in his Mariological
writings. He contemplates it in the light of her role as
the Second Eve, and sees how it flows harmoniously
from the privileges of the Immaculate Conception and
the divine Maternity. Therefore, it is in a special way
the 'fittingness' of this Marian privilege that impresses
him. He regards this doctrine to be 'most probable', in
so far as it was intimately bound up with other Marian
doctrines which were revealed more explicitly.[54]

Newman does maintain that our Lady died like
other people and like her Son. Death in itself would

---

[53] The thought of Pope John Paul II, who has done much to exalt the
rightful position and personal dignity of women, runs on similar lines:
'The biblical exemplar of the "woman" finds its culmination in the
motherhood of the Mother of God.' (Apostolic Letter *Mulieris
Dignitatem*, On the dignity and vocation of women, on the occasion
of the Marian Year. Vatican City, Libreria Editrice Vaticana, 1988,
No.19, p. 71). Cf. No. 5, pp. 15–17.

[54] Writing to an Anglican who would later be received into the
Catholic Church, influenced in no small manner by Newman
himself, he corrects a statement made by his correspondent, namely,
that the fact of the Assumption being a pious belief did 'not mean to
say that it was not also probable'. Newman continues: 'For myself I
think it *most* probable. I think its probability grows on the mind
contemplating it steadily.' (*The Letters and Diaries*, XXV, 302.)

not be inconsistent with her dignity as Mother of God and Immaculate Virgin. He dedicates a sermon to this subject, precisely on the Feast of the Assumption. In the notes he made for this sermon he gives the reason: 'Because she was under the laws of fallen nature, and inherited its evils, except so far as sin [is concerned]. Thus our Blessed Lord [suffered fatigue, pain and death] ... Hence, since all men die, she died. Our Lord died.'[55] Her Son wished to share our lot. She was like Him also in this respect. She did not enjoy the preternatural gifts of knowledge and freedom from death enjoyed by Eve before her transgression. Hence, Newman believes that although she did not undergo the ravages of disease and infirmities that weaken and deform the body, she did so suffer in her mind and heart as to be the Queen of Martyrs, but her body was exempt from corruption. What took her life in the end was the ardent love that burned in her heart. 'She died from love'.[56] In this she was also like her Son: 'Therefore we believe that, though she died for a short hour, as did our Lord Himself, yet, like Him,

---

[55] *Sermon Notes,* p. 104.

[56] *Ibid.* p. 105. St John of the Cross when describing the death of those who have reached the state of transforming union with God, affirms that love is the cause of their death: 'If the death of other people is caused by sickness or old age, the death of these persons is not so induced, in spite of their being sick or old; their soul is not wrested from them unless by some impetus and encounter of love far more sublime than previous ones; of greater power, and more valiant, since it tears through the veil and carries off the jewel, which is the soul. The death of such persons is very gentle and very sweet, sweeter and more gentle than was their whole spiritual life on earth' (*The Living Flame of Love* B, I, 30: *The Collected Works of St John of the Cross.* Translated by Kieran Kavanaugh, OCD and Otilio Rodriguez, OCD Washington, DC, ICS Publications, 1991, pp. 653–4).

and by his Almighty power, she was raised again from the grave.'[57]

The fact of her death, as distinct from her Assumption, is open to theological discussion. The question was not touched upon in the declaration of the Assumption which merely states that 'the Immaculate Virgin, preserved free from all stain of original sin, when the course of her earthly life was finished, was taken up body and soul into heavenly glory'.[58] Therefore, Newman's position on Mary's death is the commonly accepted one, and indeed the more probable opinion, if we take into consideration the full meaning of the Incarnation as illustrated in the life and death of Christ.

However, when her appointed time on earth had run its course, she enjoyed the unique privilege of being raised body and soul to heaven. This truth appears as altogether appropriate when we take into consideration her close association with Christ. 'What dignity can be too great to attribute to her who is as closely bound up, as intimately one, with the Eternal Word, as a Mother is with a son? ... Is it surprising then that on the one hand she should be immaculate in her Conception? or on the other that she should be honoured with an Assumption, and exalted as a queen with a crown of twelve stars, with the rulers of day and night to do her service?'[59] This is Newman's line of approach when discussing this Marian prerogative. He could have based his argument on a long Church

---

[57] *Meditations and Devotions*, p. 65. Cf. *Mixed Congregations*, pp. 372–3.

[58] Pius XII, Apostolic Constitution, *Munificentissimus Deus*, in Denzinger-Schönmetzer, *op. cit.* No. 3903.

[59] *Difficulties felt by Anglicans*, Vol. II, pp. 62–3.

tradition, on liturgical texts,[60] and on the universal belief of the faithful. However, since there is no explicit mention of this point of faith in Scripture and since the Fathers begin to write about it only in the fifth century, he did not treat it explicitly in his *Letter to Pusey*. Elsewhere, in his sermons and private meditations, he does manifest his devotion to this mystery of Mary's life and 'takes it for granted that Christian sense necessarily accepts the Assumption as a fitting conclusion to the life of the Divine Mother, and thus concerns himself only with exposing the fact itself, its suitableness, and its connection with other prerogatives of Mary'.[61]

In one of his most beautiful sermons on our Lady: 'On the Fitness of the Glories of Mary', addressed to a congregation of Catholics and non-Catholics in the Oratory Church in 1850, Newman makes explicit mention of this method of argumentation from what seems 'fitting' in the context of faith and of other Marian doctrines. Scripture itself warrants the proof of certain truths by the fact that they are *fitting*. They appear to us to fit in and hang together with other revealed truths. They are consistent with the general body of revelation and seem to be required by other truths for a complete and harmonious whole. The bodily Assumption of our Lady is precisely one such truth that imposes itself on the minds of believers on account of its very suitability and its connection with other Marian and Christological doctrines. 'We feel it

[60] The Feast of the Dormition was a most important Marian Feast in the Byzantine Liturgy.

[61] Francis J. Friedel, *The Mariology of Cardinal Newman*, op. cit. p. 314. Cf. Charles Stephen Dessain, *Cardinal Newman's Teaching about the Blessed Virgin Mary*, op. cit. pp. 11–13.

'ought' to be; that it 'becomes' her Lord and Son thus
to provide for one who was so singular and special,
both in herself and her relations to Him. We find that
it is simply in harmony with the substance and main
outlines of the doctrine of the Incarnation, and that
without it Catholic teaching would have a character
of incompleteness, and would disappoint our pious
expectations.' Indeed, Newman goes on to affirm that
'it would be a greater miracle if, her life being what it
was, her death was like that of other men'.[62]

Later on, in a sermon to a Catholic congregation, of
which we have his notes, he would be more specific:
'it *became* our Lord to raise His mother, and her so
sinless' [...] it is 'more difficult not to believe
Assumption than to believe it after the Incarnation'.[63]

In fact, our Lady's Assumption follows on coher-
ently from the doctrine of the Incarnation. The Son of
God took mortal flesh in Mary's womb. Accordingly,
'no exuberance of grace, no excess of glory, but is
becoming, but is to be expected there, where God has
lodged Himself, whence God has issued'.[64] Moreover,
her immaculate holiness and her nearness to God
outstripped that of all the Saints. If some of them rose
from the dead after the Lord's resurrection and
appeared in Jerusalem (Matt. 27. 52–3), why should
his own Mother not be raised from the tomb? 'It was
surely fitting then, it was becoming, that she should be
taken up into heaven and not lie in the grave till
Christ's second coming.'[65]

---

[62] *Mixed Congregations,* pp. 361, 371.
[63] *Sermon Notes,* pp. 13, 15.
[64] *Mixed Congregations,* p. 363.
[65] *Ibid.* pp. 370–1.

Mary's active part in the mystery of the Incarnation adds to her personal greatness and holiness. We have seen how much Newman revered her in her role as the Second Eve. This parallel, which he learned from the Church Fathers, he also applies when arguing in favour of the doctrine of the Assumption. Eve would not have seen the corruption of death and the grave had she not sinned against her Creator. This line of thought gives us a glimpse of how fitting it was that Mary, who never sinned, should not have forfeited this preternatural privilege, lost by Eve. Explaining to a correspondent in 1869 that the Pope or a General Council cannot define any doctrine that is not revealed and contained in the apostolic tradition of the Church, Newman writes: 'If the Assumption of Our Lady were now defined at the Vatican Council, I should say that plainly it, as the Immaculate Conception, is contained in the dogma "Mary the Second Eve" – I have drawn out this argument as regards the latter doctrine in my letter to Dr Pusey – as to the Assumption, if Mary is like Eve but greater, then, as Eve would not have seen death or corruption, so, while Mary underwent death because she was a child of fallen Adam and sinned in Adam, she did not see corruption because she had more than the prerogatives of Eve'.[66]

We cannot but admire Newman's deft theological argumentation. We now possess the presentation of the Assumption given by Pope Pius XII in the Apostolic Constitution, *Munificentissimus Deus,* of 1 November 1950, by which he promulgated the

---

[66] *The Letters and Diaries*, XXIV, 330. Cf. *Meditations and Devotions,* p. 65.

dogma. He affirms that there is no explicit revelation
of it in Scripture or explicit mention in the earliest
apostolic tradition. It is revealed implicitly and has a
necessary connection with other doctrines that belong
to the revealed deposit of faith.

Pope Pius XII links the Assumption first of all with
the dogma of the divine Maternity. Not only is it fitting
that the all-powerful Son should not allow his Mother's
body to decay in the tomb, but there exists a harmonious
consistency between the Assumption and other Marian
privileges and truths, such as her integral virginity, her
association with Christ as the Second Eve, her unparalleled fullness of grace and holiness, the singular privilege
of her Immaculate Conception, all of which make it
inconceivable that she should undergo the chastisement
of sin, namely, corruption in the grave.

5. *Mary, an All-Powerful Intercessor*

A characteristic feature of Newman's teaching on the
Blessed Virgin Mary is his insistence on the intercessory power of her prayer. She truly merits the title
Auxilium Christianorum. Like all of his Marian belief
and devotion, this aspect is also firmly founded on
theological arguments. In this sense he is a model for
the contemporary age, with its ecumenical sensitivity
and its historical and critical mentality. Intercession
made by St Mary and by all the other Saints is theologically explained by the creature's sharing through
grace in the mediation of Christ, the universal
Mediator; it is justified by the doctrinal truth of the
Communion of Saints in the Mystical Body of Christ;
its effective power arises from the intense love of God

and close union with his divine will enjoyed by the elect in heaven.

The type of prayer that came most spontaneously to Newman himself was that of intercession. It seemed to him to be the kind most specifically recommended by Sacred Scripture. He does not take it to mean a selfish petition, simply for personal needs, but a supplication on behalf of others, or as he expresses it 'for ourselves with others, for the Church, and for the world, that it may be brought into the Church'.[67]

John Henry Newman was a man who easily made friends and who united them in a chain of intercessory prayer that remained constant throughout his life. In his private journals we come across lists of prayers and petitions written down and used by him from his teenage days. The Fathers of the Oratory in Birmingham still have three small notebooks, thumb-soiled and worn by constant use, which contain prayers he said, and the intentions and names of people he prayed for. The earliest prayer in this collection dates from 1817 when he was sixteen years old. It was composed for his first Holy Communion in the Anglican Church. The last entry is dated seventy-two years later – the year before his death. Few people preserve their prayers and prayer intentions over a period of seven decades![68] These lists became familiar

---

[67] *Parochial and Plain Sermons*, Vol. III, p. 350.

[68] Cf. *Newman the Oratorian*. His unpublished Oratory Papers edited with an Introductory Study on the Continuity between his Anglican and his Catholic Ministry by Placid Murray, OSB, Dublin, Gill & Macmillan Ltd., pp. 59–69. Cf. also: Thomas R. Ivory, 'When you Pray ... The Way of Newman': *The Way* 17(1977) pp. 145–55; Philip Boyce, OCD, 'At Prayer with Newman': in *In Search of Light. Life Development Prayer. Three Essays on John Henry Newman.* Rome, International Centre of Newman Friends, 1985, pp. 63–85.

to Newman with regular usage. Among those who found a place in his petitions were: Protestants; those kind to me; those cold to me; godchildren; cousins; Catholics; benefactors; Irish friends; converts; the Dead. And from his diaries we have confirmation that he was faithful to these mementoes.[69]

This Christian obligation to pray for others was not simply part of his own life of faith, but also a topic he dealt with in a number of sermons. The most explicit treatment is in a sermon entitled 'Intercession' which was preached on 22 February 1835 and which contains the basic ideas that would be expanded and applied to the intercessory prayer of our Lady in his *Letter to Pusey*.[70] In general we can say that he considered it a privilege and duty of every Christian and of the ordained ministry in particular. Prayer for others is a typical mark of a baptized person and is a sharing in the work of Christ's own mediation: 'Christ died to bestow upon man that privilege which implies or involves all others, and brings him into nearest resemblance to Himself, the privilege of Intercession ... Christ intercedes above, and he intercedes below ... His prayer thenceforth takes a higher range, and contemplates not himself merely, but others also.'[71] When

[69] To give but one example: his friend, the Rev. Walter Mayers, a clergyman who had been instrumental in turning him to God at the age of fifteen, died prematurely in 1828. Newman was never to forget a prayer for him. In fact, we find that 42 years later he still prayed for him at Mass on the anniversary of his death (cf. *The Letters and Diaries*, XXV, 38).

[70] *Parochial and Plain Sermons*, Vol. III, pp. 350–66; *Difficulties felt by Anglicans*, Vol. II, pp. 68–76.

[71] *Parochial and Plain Sermons*, Vol. III, p. 363.

a person is holy and submissive to God's will, his intercession is particularly powerful.

Of course, there does exist an ordered course in nature, determined by the fixed laws that govern the universe.[72] Faith, however, enables us to perceive a higher order of things, ruled by God's providence and subjected to divine laws. The intercession of angels and saints, the persevering prayer of the just on earth, does have a power that goes beyond the laws of nature and can make possible what seems to unbelieving eyes as utterly unachievable. In fact, the mysterious thing in Newman's view is not so much that prayer should be so powerful as the fact that it should have any influence at all. 'Prayer in its effect, though the idea is so familiar to us, is one of the greatest of mysteries and miracles, yet it is the clear doctrine of Scripture.'[73] The force of our Lady's intercession is simply the highest instance we have of this human power to influence the divine will and obtain blessings from God.

Prayerful mutual assistance between souls is certainly not limited to people on earth. The Communion of Saints signifies above all the personal intercommunion of a spiritual nature that exists, in Christ, between the members of his Mystical Body, whether they are saints in heaven, souls in the state of purification in Purgatory or the faithful on their pilgrimage of faith on earth. It is a reality that spans the abyss between this life and the life to come. Only to the Church is it given to be equally at home on

---

[72] Cf. *Sermon Notes,* pp. 42, 117: *Meditations and Devotions,* pp. 70–1.

[73] *Sermon Notes,* p. 42.

both sides of the frontier of death. The members of the Church, whether they are journeying in this world or have crossed the threshold of death, are closely knit together in the Mystical Body of Christ and in the Communion of Saints.

The doctrinal truth of the Communion of Saints in Newman's view gives rise to prayer in common and to mutual intercession. It is a solemn duty of Christians to pray for each other. The fact is evident from Scripture, in particular from the writings of St Paul: 'I urge then, first of all that petitions, prayers, intercessions and thanksgiving should be offered for everyone' (1 Tim. 2:1).[74]

However, such intercession also extends to the Church suffering and triumphant. We have examples of Newman's prayers for the souls in Purgatory.[75] He also taught that, because of the communion that exists between the faithful on earth and the elect in heavenly glory, the saints do intercede for us at God's throne. From the Apocalypse we know that the angels offer the prayers of all the saints upon the altar before the throne of God (Rev. 8:3–4). Newman argues from this text that 'on this occasion, surely the Angel performed the part of a great Intercessor or Mediator above for the children of the Church Militant below'.[76] Moreover, it is not simply angels who enter into this communion of prayer and intercession with the Church on earth: the Letter to the Hebrews speaks of 'the spirits of the just' as partaking of this same

---

[74] Cf. *Parochial and Plain Sermons, Vol.* III, pp. 351–2; *Difficulties felt by Anglicans*, p. 69.

[75] Cf. *Meditations and Devotions*, pp. 205–6.

[76] *Difficulties felt by Anglicans*, Vol. II, p. 70.

communion (cf. Heb. 12: 23–4) This was one of Newman's favourite texts. He quotes it freely in his sermons. He makes use of it also in his *Letter to Pusey* precisely in order to give a biblical and theological foundation to the intercession made for us by the citizens of the heavenly Jerusalem and in a special way by the Virgin Mary:

> 'Ye have come to Mount Zion, to the heavenly Jerusalem, to myriads of angels, to God the Judge of all, to the spirits of the just made perfect, and to Jesus the Mediator of the New Testament.' What can be meant by having 'come to the spirits of the just,' unless in some way or other, they do us good, whether by blessing or by aiding us? that is, in a word, to speak correctly, by praying for us, for it is surely by prayer that the creature above is able to bless and aid the creature below.[77]

From these basic doctrinal considerations on human sharing in the Mediation of Christ and on the Communion of Saints, Newman proceeds to a further reflection on the theology of prayer, namely, its power or effectiveness. The holier and more pleasing to God is the person who intercedes, the more effective will be his prayer. To prove his point, Newman collects various examples from Sacred Scripture where the remarkable results of the intercession of some holy men and women are put in evidence: Elijah who shut up the heavens and later made fire to fall (1 Kings 17:1; 18:36–8); Abraham and Moses who averted the

---

[77] *Ibid.* p. 71.

wrath of God against sinful people (Gen. 18: 22–33; Exod. 32:11–14; 17:10–12); the importunate widow in the Gospel (Luke 18:2–7); even the Holy Spirit who is presented as the supreme Intercessor within the hearts of the faithful (Rom. 8: 26–7). Indeed, it is love alone that obtains from God whatever it desires. This truth is confirmed by the Mystical Doctor, St John of the Cross: 'When God is loved he very readily answers the requests of his lover ... Nothing is obtained from God except by love'.[78]

The Church itself, Newman remarked, is built on prayer. It was founded in an atmosphere of prayer, as is evident from the presence of the Apostles with our Lady in the Cenacle imploring the outpouring of the Holy Spirit at the first Pentecost (cf. Acts 1:12–14; 2: 1–4). During periods of persecution and distress, never absent in the history of the Church, the faithful always had recourse to prayer for those in trial, following the example of the primitive Christian community who prayed for Peter in prison (cf. Acts 12:5). In his Anglican days, Newman inculcated this ecclesial duty that rests on every Christian:

How can we complain of difficulties, national or personal, how can we justly blame and denounce evil-minded and powerful men, if we have but lightly used the intercessions offered up in the Litany, the Psalms, and in the Holy Communion? How can we answer to ourselves for the souls who have been lost and are now waiting for judgment

---

[78] St John of the Cross, *The Spiritual Canticle* B, 1,13 : *The Collected Works, op. cit.* p.483.

... seeing that, for what we know, we were ordained to influence or reverse their present destiny and have not done it?'[79]

The theological precision of Newman on this question of intercession is remarkable. The Council of Trent taught 'that the Saints who reign with Christ, offer to God their prayers for men; that it is a good and profitable thing to invoke them humbly so as to obtain God's favours, through his Son Jesus Christ, our Lord, who is the only Saviour and Redeemer.'[80] A contemporary Dictionary of Spiritual Theology, when treating of the Communion of Saints, declares that this truth of faith underlies the exercise of Christian prayer, which is essentially a prayer of the community of believers.[81] The foundation of the mediation exercised by saints through their intercession for the faithful is precisely the mediation of Christ, the supreme and unique Mediator in an

[79] *Parochial and Plain Sermons,* Vol. III, p. 365.

[80] Cf. Conc. Tridentinum, Sessio 25, b, in Denzinger-Schönmetzer, No. 1821. This is the constant teaching of the Church. It was recently reiterated with authority by the Catechism: 'The witnesses who have preceded us into the Kingdom, especially those whom the Church recognizes as saints, share in the living tradition of prayer by the example of their lives, the transmission of their writings and their prayer today ... Their intercession is their most exalted service to God's plan. We can and should ask them to intercede for us and for the whole world' (*Catechism of the Catholic Church,* No. 2683).

[81] 'This dogma (of the Communion of Saints) is the basis of personal and community prayer ... The prayer of the Christian should be the voice of the community that prays with him and for him; it should form a brotherhood of prayer. Only in this way do we give full meaning to the words we always say to God: "Our Father" and not "My Father"' (*Dizionario Enciclopedico di Spiritualità.* A cura di Ermanno Ancilli e del Pontificio Istituto di Spiritualità del Teresianum. Nuova edizione. Roma, Città Nuova Editrice, 1990, v. I, p. 586).

absolute sense (cf. 1 Tim. 2:5; Heb. 8:6), in whose mediation all intercessors participate.[82] The *Catechism of the Catholic Church* sums it all up succinctly with the phrase: 'In the age of the Church, Christian intercession participates in Christ's, as an expression of the communion of saints'.[83]

Moreover, St Thomas teaches that the efficacy of the prayer of the Saints, who intercede for us in heaven, comes from their love, holiness and nearness to God.[84]

This doctrinal foundation leads Newman to the conclusion that the Blessed Virgin Mary is especially equipped, by reason of her surpassing sanctity and eminent dignity among the saints, to be a uniquely powerful intercessor on behalf of the faithful on earth. She was never sullied by the slightest sin; she is nearer to her divine Son through her fidelity to God's word than through her physical motherhood; and she intercedes according to the divine will, leaving the outcome to Him. A fine paragraph sums up Newman's teaching on the power of Mary's intercession:

> I consider it impossible then, for those who believe the Church to be one vast body in heaven and on earth, in which every holy creature of God has his

[82] Cf. St Thomas Aquinas, *Summa Theologiae*, III, q. 26, a. 1.

[83] No. 2635.

[84] In answer to the question, 'Do the Saints in heaven pray for us?', St Thomas writes: 'Since prayer for others proceeds from charity . . . the more perfect the charity of the Saints in heaven, the more they pray for people on earth, who can be helped by prayer; and the more united they are to God, the more effectual are their prayers' (*Summa Theologiae*, II-II, q. 83, a. 11).

place, and of which prayer is the life, when once they recognize the sanctity and dignity of the Blessed Virgin, not to perceive immediately, that her office above is one of perpetual intercession for the faithful militant, and that our very relation to her must be that of clients to a patron, and that, in the eternal enmity which exists between the woman and the serpent, while the serpent's strength lies in being the Tempter, the weapon of the Second Eve and Mother of God is prayer.[85]

Therefore, she is *par excellence* the Advocate of the Church and, as we greet her in our prayers, *Advocata nostra*. Newman is quick to remark that there is an essential difference between interceding and the redemptive work of atoning for sin. It was Christ alone who redeemed us by his Paschal Mystery. His Mother Mary was also redeemed, although it was in a unique manner – preserved from sin by virtue of the foreseen merits of her Son. Her prayer of petition is indeed of the same kind as our own, 'not different from us except in degree and perfection'.[86]

Her manner of supplicating is a pattern for us. She is the greatest human exemplification of that gift conferred by God on creatures whereby they can beseech Him on behalf of others for his graces and blessings – something that is even more urgent 'in a generation, which emphatically denies the power of prayer *in toto*'.[87]

---

[85] *Difficulties felt by Anglicans*, Vol. II, p. 73.
[86] *Sermon Notes*, p. 118. Cf. *The Letters and Diaries*, XXII, 68. 90.
[87] *Difficulties felt by Anglicans*, Vol. II, p. 76. Cf. *Sermon Notes*, p. 42.

Newman himself did not hesitate to have recourse to our Lady's intercession. As we already saw when dealing with the development of his life, he did not consider the intercession of Saints to be a necessary part of his Anglican faith, and drew a sharp distinction between intercession and invocation. Nevertheless, shortly after the beginning of the Oxford Movement he became more and more willing to admit the intercession of the Saints, and began to regard it as an open question in the Anglican collection of prescribed prayers.

As a Catholic he had no doubts about the matter. In letters of spiritual counsel, he urged his directees to have trustful recourse to the Blessed Virgin, as for example in the case of Miss Holmes, who was disheartened by her imperfections and lack of fervour which she seemed unable to overcome: 'Put yourself ever and utterly into Mary's hands, and she will nurse you and bring you forward. She will watch over you as a mother over a sick child'.[88] And as for himself, he could state at a moment when he was going through the distressing months leading up to the Achilli trial: 'I assuredly have a simple faith in the omnipotence of her intercession – and I know well, (not to say that my Lord expressly tells me) that we cannot ask too much, so that we are but importunate and unwearied in asking.'[89]

Newman had a deep trust in Mary's prayer, consid-

[88] *The Letters and Diaries*, XIV, 29.

[89] *The Letters and Diaries*, XV, 10. Thirteen years later, writing to his friend, John Keble who remained an Anglican, he said: 'I never can deny my belief that the Blessed Virgin prays efficaciously for the Church, and for individual souls in and out of it' (*The Letters and Diaries*, XXII, 68).

ering her to be all-powerful because of the strength of
her intercession. In one of his meditations he writes:
'No one has access to the Almighty as His Mother has;
none has merit such as hers. Her Son will deny her
nothing that she asks; and herein lies her power'.[90] He
pleads for a correct understanding of the statement
that attributes omnipotence to our Lady. It simply
means that she is all-powerful through her prayer, that
she has 'a delegated omnipotence *in her own sphere*, i.e.
of *intercession*'.[91] Admittedly the expression could be
taken to mean an absurd affirmation. However, as
Newman points out, in the linguistic usage of his day,
lawyers spoke of the 'omnipotence' of the British
parliament – a phrase which nobody understood literally as if it attributed superhuman powers to the
national legislative body of the country: 'Parliament is
omnipotent, as having the power to do what it will,
not in France, or in Germany, or in Russia, much less
all over the earth, much less in heaven, but within the
United Kingdom; and in like manner the Blessed
Virgin is called omnipotent as being able to gain from
God what she desires by the medium of prayer'.[92]
When the word is used by Catholics in reference to
the Virgin it is done so in an improper sense, in a sense
of its own, and as such it has to be understood.[93]

Thus in Newman's life and teaching, Mary the
Mother of Christ is acclaimed as the greatest exemplification of the power of prayer. She is seen as a person

[90] *Meditations and Devotions*, p. 71.

[91] *The Letters and Diaries*, XXXI, 15★. Cf. *ibid*. XII, 291.

[92] *Lectures on the Present Position of Catholics in England*. London,
Longmans, Green & Co., 1913, p. 344.

[93] Cf. *ibid*. pp. 406–7; 24–41.

who through her holiness, her union with the divine will and her nearness to God, is the greatest Advocate of the human race before the throne of God, and a luminous witness to the value of intercession in a world that has turned its back on providence and that denies any direct link between this earth and a future heaven.

6. Newman the Mariologist

Given Newman's Anglican background, it could seem strange that he can be admired and read as a Catholic Mariologist of considerable fame. Yet, this is the truth. Two Anglican friends of his in Oxford (Hurrell Froude and John Keble) and a Catholic priest from the Maynooth seminary in Ireland (Charles Russell) influenced his Anglican attitudes to Mary. Both before and after his reception into the Catholic Church he preached with evident courage and eagerness on the privileges of the Mother of Jesus. In his Catholic days, providence gave him the opportunity of replying to the criticisms raised by his friend, E. B. Pusey, against Catholic beliefs and practices, which had always convinced Anglicans that Rome sanctioned a kind of semi-idolatry in its veneration of the Blessed Virgin.

Newman's reply to his friend, his *Letter to Pusey,* did try to be as charitable as possible while it defended Roman Catholic beliefs. It was publicly defended and praised shortly after its publication by Newman's own bishop, Dr W. B. Ullathorne in a letter which he wrote to the *Tablet*. In it he refuted some Catholic critics of Newman who thought his treatment of Mary was too meagre and cold. Bishop Ullathorne gave special praise for Newman's explanation of the mystery of the Immaculate Conception, so difficult for Protestants to understand, and he claimed that it had 'made that subject classical in the English tongue'.[94] A modern scholar has termed it a 'masterpiece of Marian literature'.[95] And more recently, Jean Guitton has claimed that 'Newman is *par excellence* the *Doctor Marianus* of the nineteenth century' in so far as he did not simply repeat what theologians and mystics had said but added a new key of intelligibility to the mysteries of our Lady's life 'by linking the theology of the Virgin Mary and forms of Marian devotion to the development of the idea of Christ and of the Church'.[96] All this is high praise indeed, but well-deserved.

In fact, Newman's Mariology is profound and solid. It is based above all on what Sacred Scripture tells us about our Lady. This is his first source and it keeps him from all exaggerated devotional deviations, which were not uncommon in his time. With fine theological penetration he is able to bring out the full meaning of each text relating to the Mother of the Saviour.[97]

---

[94] *The Letters and Diaries*, XXII, 343.

[95] Francis J. Friedel, *The Mariology of Cardinal Newman, op. cit.* p. 107. Cf. P. Marie-Martin Olive OP, 'Un petit traité de Mariologie selon les Pères des premiers siècles: la "Lettre à Pusey" de Newman (1865), in *De primordiis cultus Mariani. Acta Congressus Mariologici-Mariani in Lusitania anno 1967 celebrati.* Vol. III De Fundamento Cultus B. V. Mariae in operibus Sanctorum Patrum et Scriptorum ecclesiasticorum (post saec. II). Romae, Pontificia Academia Mariana Internationalis, 1970, pp. 303–32. José Morales also states that the *Letter to Pusey*, despite its polemical nature, can be termed a complete Mariological synthesis (cf. his study: *Religión Hombre Historia.* Estudios Newmanianos. Pamplona, Ediciones Universidad de Navarra, SA, 1989, p. 289).

[96] *Newman Studien*, 3 (1957) 84–5 (footnote 7).

[97] Cf. Piero Chiminelli, 'Maria nella vita e nel pensiero di J. H. Newman': *Studium* 35 (1939) pp. 290–2.

Moreover, Newman learned much from his Patristic readings. The Fathers had led him into the Church and were his guides in theology. At the beginning of his *Letter to Pusey,* he declares that the Fathers are enough for him: 'I do not wish to say more than they suggest to me, and will not say less'.[98] From them he came to appreciate the depth of meaning in the title of Second Eve which was the rudimentary teaching of the early centuries on our Lady. This intuition was to have immense consequences for his Marian doctrine. It is a truth of Marian doctrine which has been reiterated in many papal documents during the present century. Most significantly of all, it was used in the dogmatic Constitution on the Church, *Lumen Gentium,* of the Second Vatican Council in its chapter on our Lady.

Given this biblical and Patristic foundation, Newman's teaching on our Lady has a considerable ecumenical value. He himself was well aware of the difficulties faced by non-Catholics, their ingrained suspicion of quasi-idolatrous practices in the Marian devotions and beliefs of the Roman Church. Consequently, he was able to enter into their mentality, give a clear explanation of genuine Catholic doctrine, correct misconceptions, dispel suspicion and put forward a clear and convincing argument. Moreover, very few writers could clothe their theological script in such graceful and elegant English. His intellectual integrity and his spiritual way of life were so well known and respected that people paid attention and listened with care when he wrote or spoke

---

[98] *Difficulties felt by Anglicans,* Vol. II, p. 25.

about any religious subject. In this sense, his work helped to break down much bigotry between Protestants and Catholics in England during the last century. And as we saw, when his study on our Lady was published and read, many Anglicans were enlightened on the real meaning of certain Mariological doctrines, in particular that of the Immaculate Conception, and were known to say that after Newman's explanation many Christians would be able to accept this doctrine.[99]

Of particular value for their understanding of Catholic Marian practices, was what we could term an original contribution by Newman, namely, the manner in which he highlighted and explained the difference between doctrine and devotion. The former is constant and solid, the latter can have many expressions; it changes with time, place and culture; it may wane in some periods, only to run to excess at other times.

Most helpful, too, from an ecumenical viewpoint, was his explanation of how the honour paid to the Blessed Virgin Mary can in no way come between the soul and its Creator. It does not belittle or interfere with the unique mediation of Christ. Newman points out that it is not possible to lower God by exalting a saint, who is his creature. There is an essential difference between the worship given to Christ and the veneration shown to his Mother. Christ alone has entrance into the sanctuary of our souls; he alone gives new birth, divine grace and spiritual pardon. 'Mary is

---

[99] Cf. Charles Stephen Dessain, *Cardinal Newman's Teaching about the Blessed Virgin Mary, op. cit.* p. 11.

only our mother by divine appointment, given us
from the Cross; her presence is above not on earth;
her office is external, not within us. Her name is not
heard in the administration of the Sacraments.'[100]

If we rightly understand her position and her role,
then we can say that nothing is too great for her
within the order of creation. On one point at least she
'surpasses all even possible creations, viz., that she is
Mother of her Creator.'[101] Veneration given to her by
Catholics is not a form of idolatry; they recognize she
is not divine. Newman says very appropriately that she
took the place that the heretic Arius wished to ascribe
to Christ, a place that was very high and exalted but
one not sufficiently high for the Son of Mary, because
his heretical explanation did not make Him divine.
The Arians exalted Christ more than the most devoted
of Catholics exalt our Lady, yet they still left him a
creature. Newman exclaims in words that betray his
personal love and admiration for Mary: 'The votaries
of Mary do not exceed the true faith, unless the blasphemers of her Son came up to it. The Church of
Rome is not idolatrous, unless Arianism is orthodoxy'.[102]

Indeed, Newman rightly claims that Mary's divine
Maternity is a bulwark of our Lord's divinity. It safeguards the truth of the Incarnation. There could be no
more certain way of saying that God became man
with a nature like ours than by declaring that Mary is
his Mother. The enemies of the Church knew this full
well. Mother and Son go together, and when they

---

[100] *Difficulties felt by Anglicans,* Vol. II, p. 84.
[101] *Ibid.* p. 62.
[102] *An Essay on the Development of Christian Doctrine,* p. 144.

wished to attack the Son, they often began with dishonouring the Mother. Church history since the Protestant Reformation confirms this statement by Newman. Countries who maintained an ardent devotion to Mary still worship her Son, whereas those who rejected many points of Marian doctrine and devotion, on the ground of worshipping Christ more purely, have also ceased to pay him the adoration that is his due.[103]

Another remarkable element of Newman's Mariology is the importance, not simply theoretical but practical, which he attributes to the power of our Lady's intercession. It was clear to him from the Apocalypse (8:3) that the angels and saints do intercede for people on earth. Intercession is a vital part of the life of the Church. The power of their heavenly intercession comes from their holiness. So too with Mary, she is powerful by her prayer for us because she is so holy and so near to Christ. In truth, she is our Advocate – *Advocata nostra.* Jesus loves her too much to refuse anything she asks on behalf of her spiritual sons and daughters, of whom she became the Mother in the order of grace, as she stood beneath the Cross, sharing in and consenting to her Son's redemptive sacrifice. Hence, her intercession is called powerful, even all-powerful, 'because she has, more than anyone else, more than all Angels and Saints, this great, prevailing gift of prayer'.[104]

Newman's veneration for Mary was not simply an intellectual theory; it descended into practical living and expressed itself in personal devotion. He changed

[103] *Ibid.* p. 426.
[104] *Meditations and Devotions,* p. 71.

the name of the College buildings, offered to him and his companions by Bishop Wiseman, from Old Oscott to Maryvale, a name that remains to the present day.[105] He chose the title '*Sedes Sapientiae*' for Mary as patroness of the Catholic University in Dublin. He had a special personal veneration for her as a pattern of faith to be lived out in the humble accomplishment of daily duties. For him, Mary, pondering the word of God, excelled in her theological knowledge the greatest of theologians.[106] In her immaculate purity, she is an example for an impure age, in which celibacy and Christian modesty are under attack. He meditated with wonder her beautiful sinless soul, regarding it as more beautiful than anything in the supernatural world. And he preached about that spiritual beauty of hers that emanated from her soul to her pure body: 'the most perfect image after (Christ) Himself of what is beautiful and tender, and gentle and soothing, in human nature'.[107]

Proof of the authenticity of Newman's devotion and of the excellence of his theological and spiritual writings on our Lady is the fact that their salient points are the same as we still find expounded in the most solemn documents of the Church's Magisterium. His Marian writings, like his theological works in general, are timeless, for they are based on the revealed truth contained in Sacred Scripture, handed on by a living tradition in the Church, doctrinally expounded by the ancient Fathers of the Church and proclaimed with

---

[105] Cf. Beth Mulvey, *St Mary in the Valley. A History of Maryvale House.* Birmingham, Maryvale Books, 1994, pp. 33–8.

[106] *Meditations and Devotions,* p. 34.

[107] *Mixed Congregations,* p. 69.

authority by the Magisterium. They provide us with sure guidance for theological inquiry and rich nourishment for the spiritual life.

Chronology of the Principal Events of Newman's Life

1801   21 February, born in London, son of John Newman and Jemima Fourdrinier.
       9 April, baptized in the church of Saint Benet Fink.

1808   1 May, enters school at Ealing.

1816   His father in financial difficulties (March). Newman ill in the summer. Experiences his first conversion (August … December). Inscribed as a commoner in Trinity College (14 December).

1817   8 June, enters Trinity College as an under-graduate.

1822   12 April, elected Fellow of Oriel College.

1824   13 June, ordained Anglican deacon; his father dies on 29 September.

1825   March, Vice-Principal of Alban Hall under Richard Whately.
       29 May, ordained Anglican priest at Christ Church, Oxford.

1826   20 January, appointed tutor of Oriel.

1827   Made acquaintance of Pusey

1828   14 March, appointed Vicar of the University Church, St Mary the Virgin, Oxford. Here he gave his famous Parochial Sermons until 1843.

1832   Completed his first book, *The Arians of the Fourth Century* and leaves with the Froude family for a Mediterranean journey.

1833   May, seriously ill in Sicily
       June, during return journey composes *Lead Kindly Light*

July, arrives back to England. Keble preaches the Assize Sermon on 'National Apostasy'.

September, the first of the *Tracts for the Times* is published and Newman becomes the leading figure in the Oxford Movement until 1841.

1834   March, the first volume of the *Parochial and Plain Sermons* is published.

1837   *Lectures on the Prophetical Office of the Church (Via Media,* I*)* is published.

1838   He publishes the *Lectures on Justification* and (with Keble's help) Froude's *Remains.*

1839   September, Newman reads Wiseman's article on Augustine and the Donatists.

1841   27 February, publishes *Tract 90,* the final and most controversial one. It was soon condemned by the University and the Anglican bishops. Begins correspondence with Dr Russell (April). In September he retires to Littlemore (where he was to stay until February 1846).

1842   A life of prayer and study at Littlemore. Translations of St Athanasius.

1843   Resigns as Vicar of St Mary's (7 September). His last sermon as an Anglican in Littlemore church, 'The Parting of Friends'.

1845   Resigns his Fellowship of Oriel College (3 October). Received into the Roman Catholic Church by Fr Dominic Barberi (9 October). Confirmed by Dr Wiseman at Oscott (1 November). The *Essay on the Development of Christian Doctrine* is published (November).

1846   Leaves Littlemore for Maryvale, near Oscott, in February. Sets sail for Rome in September and begins study at the College of *Propaganda Fide* with his English convert friends in November.

1847 30 May, ordained a priest by Cardinal Fransoni. In June they go to the Oratorian Novitiate at Santa Croce in Rome, under the guidance of Fr Rossi.

1848 Evening of 1 February, the English Oratory is established by Newman, in Maryvale.

1849 2 February, opening of the Oratory in Alcester Street, Birmingham.
      November, *Discourses to Mixed Congregations* published.

1850 22 August, Newman receives the Doctorate of Divinity, conferred by Pope Pius IX.
      29 September, the new Catholic Hierarchy is established in England.

1851 November, the Achilli trial begins; Newman is appointed Rector of the Catholic University of Ireland.

1852 The Oratory is transferred to Edgbaston, Birmingham (10 February). The sermon, 'The Second Spring' (13 July). Newman gives a series of Discourses on the scope and nature of University education, which would be published in *The Idea of a University*.

1858 12 November, resigns as Rector of the Catholic University, in Dublin.

1864 Controversy with Charles Kingsley and the publication of the *Apologia*.

1865 *The Dream of Gerontius* is published.
      December, Newman writes *A Letter to Pusey*.

1866 31 January, *A Letter to Pusey* is published.

1868   4 January, *Verses on Various Occasions* is published.
1870   *An Essay in Aid of a Grammar of Assent* is published.
1875   January, the publication of *A Letter to His Grace the Duke of Norfolk, on the occasion of Mr. Gladstone's recent Expostulation. (Difficulties felt by Anglicans,* II).
1877   14 December, Newman invited to become Honorary Fellow of Trinity College.
1878   26–28 February, he visits Oxford again to receive from Trinity College the Honorary Fellowship, of which he said: 'No compliment could I feel more intimately'.
1879   12–15 May, Newman is elevated to the Cardinalate by Pope Leo XIII.
1881   *Select Treatises of St Athanasius* is published.
1890   11 August, death of Cardinal Newman at the Oratory in Birmingham.
       19 August, burial at Rednal. *Ex umbris et imaginibus in veritatem.*

PART ONE

LITURGICAL AND PASTORAL TEXTS

I

THE ANNUNCIATION. THE HONOUR DUE TO THE BLESSED VIRGIN[1]

'From henceforth all generations shall call me blessed'
(Lk 1:48).

St Mary, the Mother of our Lord, says in her hymn 'From henceforth all generations shall call me blessed'.[a] Accordingly she has ever been styled in the Church the Blessed Virgin. Yet, alas, in these latter times, it cannot be denied, we have in great measure forgotten to fulfil her meek anticipation of her own praise, and though we retain her day and call it Lady Day,[2] how much more do we look upon it as a date in the civil year than account ourselves honoured by

---

[1] This is Newman's first sermon on our Lady. It lay unpublished in the Archives of the Birmingham Oratory, until Fr Stephen Dessain put it at the disposal of Lutgart Govaert. It was published for the first time in her doctoral thesis *Kardinal Newmans Mariologie und sein persönlicher Werdegang* in 1975 (pp. 136–9). Since Newman himself never prepared it for publication, it lacks precise biblical references and has stylistically incomplete sentences. The manuscript has various words and phrases pencilled in by the author.

[2] 'Lady Day' was a term commonly used to designate the Feast of the Annunciation (25 March).

the coming of the Mother of our Lord unto us.[3]

Yet this spirit of reverence and love towards her memory is what Elizabeth filled with the Holy Ghost injoins us by her own example. 'Blessed art thou among women and blessed is the fruit of thy womb. And whence is this to me, that the Mother of my Lord should come unto me?'[b] And further again she seems to exhort us to this benediction and pious remembrance of the Virgin when she further declares that in God's Providence the honour promised her should be paid her. 'Blessed is she that believed, for there shall be a performance of those things which were told her from the Lord.'[c] And the angel Gabriel, first of all, had said with the same purpose: 'Hail thou that art ...'[d] etc.

Why should we not devoutly pay that honour which is promised as the Virgin's reward? Why not honour our Lord (the Son) in our respectful mention of His Mother? Why because some Christians[4] exceed in their devotion, become irreverent? Yet so it is. We do not think of St Mary as we ought.

Yet some men will answer that St Paul's doctrine stands in the way of it, for he declares, he would not

---

[3] It may seem strange that a young Anglican curate in Oxford should lament the lack of religious devotion and honour paid to our Lady by members of the Church of England. It shows how grounded in Scripture he was and how deeply he appreciated the full implications of the Incarnation – God the Son taking on our human nature and being born of a woman (cf. Gal. 4:4). The fact that he had a human mother meant that he was truly one of us. As a result of Mary's association with her divine Son she shared in his honour and blessedness. Scripture itself urges us to venerate the Mother of Jesus.

[4] The 'Christians' to whom he refers were the Roman Catholics. Anglicans regarded Catholic veneration for our Lady as excessive and detrimental to the honour due to Christ.

know Christ after the flesh,[e] which they would interpret (to mean) 'since Christ died for all men, the
apostle did not claim glory in being a Jew and coun-
tryman of our Lord's; that all men now are Christ's
countrymen and friends; that Christ has now no
kindred and that His Mother is now no more to Him
than any one else'. And they think they confirm their
view by our Lord's own words on one occasion to His
disciples: 'Whosoever shall do the will of God, the
same is My brother and My sister and mother'.[f] Thus
they think to keep us from thinking reverently of the
Virgin as our Lord's Mother in contradiction to her
own words:[5] 'All generations shall call me blessed.'

But let us examine this argument. It by no means
follows because the peculiar privileges of Jews are
repealed, or because St Paul did not glory in his
national connection with Christ, that therefore we are
to leave Christ's Mother out of our thoughts. For this
would prove too much. 'If any man is in Christ, he is
a new creature',[g] he is brought into a new state, gifted
with a new parentage and inheritance. He is a son of
God. But does he for that reason forget he is still a
man and wipe away all his attachment to his natural
relations? Far from it. St Paul expressly warns us: 'If
any provides not for his own, and especially for those
of his own house, he hath denied the faith, and is
worse than an infidel.'[h] It seems that, according to the
Apostle's judgment, a man who forgets his natural

---

[5] Notice Newman's power of argumentation. He never fears to present
his adversary's case with clarity and force. In the next paragraphs he
proceeds to give his own viewpoint, using the same source of demonstration, namely, Sacred Scripture. He confirms it with arguments
from his own keen discernment of the laws of human nature.

friends is worse than if he disbelieved the Gospel.[6]
How then can we consider it be pious to forget and
irreligious to remember Christ's kindred in our
thoughts of Him? How can we suppose that He
would separate Himself from His own Mother, when
He bids us remember our relations? Certainly He
thought of her on the cross; at the very hour that He
was dying for all.[i] And if He remembers her, how can
it be right in us to pass her by in silence, especially
with the implied command, already referred to, to
count her blessed to all generations?

Let us see to it, lest we forget that Christ is perfect
man in our desire to be what we consider spiritual.
We are told He will come as He went,[j] with the same
heart and affections, soul and body the same. Our
Article[7] reminds us that Christ on rising from the dead
'took again ... all things, appertaining to the perfection of man's nature; wherewith He ascended into
heaven, and there sitteth until He returns to judge all
men at the last day'. Doubtless, having loved His own
which were in the world, He loved them unto the
end:[k] and should He not (love) His Mother first of all,
whose welfare I say was on His thoughts even when
He was on the cross? Why is it told to us (Why, what
is our very comfort in temptation but) that Christ
having suffered under it, is able to succour them that
are tempted;[l] that he was touched with the feeling of

---

[6] Newman was a man who made friends easily and who was always very
loyal to them. To his two sisters, Mary and Jemima, he was particularly
near. (cf. Henry Tristram, *Newman and his Friends*. London, John Lane
The Bodley Head Ltd., 1933; John Coulson, 'John Henry Newman: his
genius for Friendship': *The Clergy Review* 62 (1977) pp. 18–21.)

[7] One of the Thirty-Nine Articles of the Anglican faith.

our infirmities, and in all points tempted like as we are? And can He remember His own sorrow, and not the sword which pierced His Mother's soul?[m] Can He remember Judas who betrayed Him[n] and Pilate who crucified Him,[o] and not her who bore Him? And when the Holy Ghost has distinctly declared that she is blessed, can it consist with our duty to Him, not to bless her?[8] He is in heaven, but we are to think of Him just as if He were here. He is still what He is described to be—in the Gospel—He has no variableness. Now do we suppose that, were He on earth, He would allow anyone to treat His Mother's name with disrespect or rather, would not be pleased with our affectionate and respectful remembrance of Her? How strange it is to bring the blessing He pronounces on His faithful servants in disparagment of His love towards her? 'Whosoever shall do the will of God ...'[p] What does it show but the excess of His attachment to her, that the highest reward He can give them is their being as dear to Him as His mother and other immediate relatives?[9]

Will it be said that in heaven all difference between saint and saint is lost, that though the Virgin is dear to

---

[8] Newman distinguishes between the blessing which God gives and through which Mary is 'blessed' (*eulogémené*: cf. Lk 1:28 and 42) and that which comes to her from all generations who call her 'blessed' (*makarizo*: cf. Lk 1:48). After 'the Holy Ghost ... declared that she is blessed', Newman adds '*eulogémené*' in his manuscript; and after 'our duty ... to bless her,' he writes '*makarios*' (cf. Lutgart Govaert, *Kardinal Newmans Mariologie, op. cit.* p. 141).

[9] Following the teaching of St Augustine and other Church Fathers, Newman often explains that Mary's blessedness and nearness to Christ rested not simply on her having been chosen to be his mother, but on her obedience to God's will (cf. below, Text V, pp. 169–70, and p. 170, footnote 5.)

Christ, all His saints are equally dear to Him? Observe how far this principle would carry us. Would it not at once follow that we should thereafter be debarred the happiness of especial intercourse with our earthly friends? That we should not know them again when we met them? How contrary is this cold theory to the notices of Scripture in the subject! St Paul speaks of his Thessalonian converts as his 'glory and joy'^{q} 'in the presence of our Lord Jesus'.^{r} Has not God in His life too made His Gospel flow to us through the channel of natural relationship? Did he indeed elect His followers by some unknown inscrutable law, here and there, as He would have it; raising them one by one in isolated places, with no visible bonds of union but only the promise of a future gathering together in heaven, then indeed we should be forced to leave out associations of this world in our anticipations of heaven. But far from so doing, He has bound us into one body, in one intelligible bond now; He has given us common privileges. He has bid us grow together one and all edifying each other; He has made our natural relations the groundwork of our spiritual relations. The Holy Ghost is poured upon us in infancy for our parents' sake, the promise is unto us because it was unto our fathers before us. And thus having bound together nature and grace in our first days of existence, shall the two ever be separated? Shall those who become sons of God by being sons of Christians ever cease to acknowledge the obligation of that benefit which has brought them through God's Providence to heaven? And if these remembrances of earth remain in heaven, how shall we think that our Lord does not still with ineffable feelings regard His

Mother Mary, and how can we be really said to comprehend His character, to enter into the mind of Christ and to be united to Him in spirit, unless we carefully cherish the remembrance of His doings and feelings while we walk after Him, gathering up the fragments that remain, feeding on those crumbs which He has left us, and though we know not much of the blessed Virgin, yet making much of what is told us about her, and knowing her for her Gracious Son's sake?

Surely the very reason the Gospels were given us at all, was in order to see our Lord as man.[10] Why was it not enough for St Paul to tell us that Christ had died for us and risen again?[s] Why should four Evangelists go over the same ground, reviewing in different thoughts our Lord's same actions, and dwelling upon His words, but in order to give us an example and a consolation in all we do and suffer? Christ was not an angel. He was a man like us, in all points but sin.[t] Have we natural affections? He had them too. Where are we to see them exemplified? He had no brother, sister, wife or father. It is His mother who concentrates them all. Why should we disjoin Him from human nature, as if He were an angel such as came to

---

[10] In these paragraphs, Newman's understanding of the full meaning and implications of the Incarnation are evident. The divine Son of the Father assumed everything in our human nature, sin alone excepted. If he had not shared our feelings, our natural affections, our special love for family and 'friends', our joys, our sorrow, and our fatigue, then these human realities would not have been purified and redeemed. Newman had a deep understanding of human nature and an equally good knowledge of Scripture and theology. Grace, he knew, built on nature without destroying it. Consequently, his argumentation is very sound and convincing (cf. the following sermon, pp. 121–5).

Abraham as he sat in the tent door[u] or to Gideon at
the oak in Ophrat?[v] John the Baptist lived in the
wilderness.[w] But our Saviour was even characterized
by His mixing in the ways of men and feeling with
them. Let us use thankfully the instruction given us
and in remembering the Mother strive to enter more
deeply into the mind of her Son.

And here let me remark on a circumstance just
alluded to—the silence of Scripture concerning the
Virgin Mary as far as the details of her history. It is
expressive. She is mentioned at Christ's incarnation, at
His birth, in His childhood and education, during His
ministry, at His death and afterwards His ascension just
before the day of Pentecost as being present with the
Apostles in prayer.[x] Thus she is continually brought
before our minds. Yet nothing is told us about her.
Hence we gather first that we are to reverence her
memory for His sake. Or, in other words, that she is to
be a subject of our meditation in order to our realizing
and fully developing in our hearts the image of her
Son. And secondly we may observe how entirely we
are guarded against any possible harm to our own
Christian uprightness in thinking of her. Did we pay to
St Paul that honour which we seem called upon to
render to the Virgin,[11] we should be in danger of
following a human standard and debasing our view of
high Christian excellence, because so much is told of

---

[11] The preacher's caution is understandable. He was aware that he dealt
with a delicate subject for Anglicans. Hence he modifies his state-
ments: 'the honour which we *seem* called upon to render to the
Virgin', and again: 'what *seems* a scriptural tone of thought'.
Nevertheless, his personal love and admiration for the Blessed Virgin
Mary, the Mother of Jesus, is quite evident.

him, that, faithful as he was in his obedience, still the history given of him cannot but have upon it those infirmities which all sons of Adam inherit. But in regarding Mary, we look to one whose actions we know not of and cannot, if we would, too closely imitate, whose name only recalls to us bright and pleasant thoughts, the emblem of early devotedness to God, guiltless piety, angelic purity, meekness, modesty and patience, shining only in the light of her Son and in the ineffable radiance of that Spirit of power who came upon her and overshadowed her,[y] and hence receiving the prize of that high salutation of Gabriel: 'Hail, thou that art highly favoured (filled with divine gifts), the Lord is with thee, blessed art thou among women.'[z]

Very much might be said in honour of the Virgin or in the apostle's words: 'of whom we have many things to say and hard to be uttered seeing you now in debt of hearing'.[aa] But, since these times are heartless and unbelieving and your hearts profane, I say no more; lest I should say more than we can bear, lest I mean, I should use words instead of ideas and should outrun the real measure of my own earnestness in my wish to manifest a conformity to Scripture instructions (to what seems a scriptural tone of thought).

I will but sum up what I have said in two brief remarks and so conclude.[12]

[12] These two brief remarks contain the seeds of future developments of Newman's thought on our Lady. Here, in an Anglican setting, he expresses his insights with reserve and discretion. Sacred Scripture consistently calls Mary 'the Mother of Jesus'. Newman, the Anglican, felt he had to refrain from making normal and frequent use of the expression 'Mother of God'. The second remark would seem to have a hint of the possibility of the Immaculate Conception (cf. above, *Introduction* II, pp. 22–4) and the sermon preached a year later, Text II, pp. 120–1).

First, what must we think of her holiness who was
[what Scripture (the Holy Ghost) calls] the Mother of
our Lord [or, as the Church has since expressed it, the
Mother of (Him who is) God]? Remember (we
cannot divide the divine and human nature in Christ
except in idea) as truly as soul and body make but one
and the same person, so God and man was one Christ.
Now, if divine blessings were given us without
consideration of our obedience and faith, then indeed
there is no reason the Virgin should have been better
than other daughters of Adam. But if (as is the way of
Providence) He rewardeth according to our works,
what untold holiness in the Virgin Mary is intimated
to us by the favour of this mysterious blessing from her
God?

Secondly, how shall we duly conceive of her, who
was the only one whom Christ served on earth? His
only natural superior? When we estimate the reverence which her Son showed her, then may we know
how fitly to honour her memory.

Now then let us ascribe to her Son glory for ever
and ever more bless Him for His great condescension
in becoming, as on this day,[13] incarnate to save a
guilty world.

a.	Lk 1:48	b.	Lk 1:42–3	c.	Lk 1:45	d.	Lk 1:28
e.	cf. 2 Cor 5:16	f.	Mk 3:35	g.	2 Cor 5:17	h.	1 Tim 5:8
i.	cf. Jn 19:26–7	j.	cf. Acts 1:11	k.	Jn 13:1	l.	cf. Heb 2:18
m.	cf. Lk 2:35	n.	cf. Mt 26:47–50	o.	cf. Mt 27:26	p.	Mk 3:35
q.	1 Thess 2:20	r.	1 Thess 2:19	s.	cf. 1 Cor 15:3–4	t.	cf. Heb 4:15
u.	cf. Gen 18:1–15	v.	cf. Judg 6:11–12	w.	cf. Mt 3:1	x.	cf. Acts 1:14
y.	cf. Lk 1:35	z.	cf. Lk 1:28	aa.	Heb 5:11		

Lutgart Govaert, *Kardinal Newmans Mariologie und sein persönlicher Werdegang*.
Salzburg und München 1975, pp. 136–9 Preached on 25 March 1831.

[13] Newman delivered this Sermon on 25 March, the Feast of the
Annunciation.

II

THE REVERENCE DUE TO THE VIRGIN MARY[1]

'From henceforth all generations shall call me blessed'
(Lk 1:48).

To-day we celebrate the Annunciation of the Virgin Mary; when the Angel Gabriel was sent to tell her that she was to be the Mother of our Lord, and when the Holy Ghost came upon her, and overshadowed her with the power of the Highest.[a] In that great event was fulfilled her anticipation as expressed in the text: 'All generations have called her blessed.' The Angel began the salutation; he said, 'Hail, thou that art highly favoured; the Lord is with thee; blessed art thou[2] among women'.[b] Again he said, 'Fear not, Mary, for thou hast found favour with God; and, behold, thou shalt conceive in thy womb, and bring forth a Son, and shalt call His name Jesus. He shall be great, and shall be called the Son of the Highest.'[c] Her cousin Elizabeth

---

[1] This sermon develops the thoughts of No. 1 (above). It was preached for the first time on 25 March 1832. It is a very remarkable piece of religious writing and the most outstanding Marian sermon by the Anglican Newman. It is a fine example of a theological meditation, resting firmly on Sacred Scripture. As mentioned in the Introduction, it contains the best summary we have of Newman's Anglican thoughts on our Lady (cf. above, Introduction II, pp. 18–19).

[2] Cf. above: Text I, p. 109, footnote 8.

was the next to greet her with her appropriate title. Though she was filled with the Holy Ghost at the time she spake, yet, far from thinking herself by such a gift equalled to Mary, she was thereby moved to use the lowlier and more reverent language. 'She spake out with a loud voice, and said, *Blessed art thou* among women, and blessed is the fruit of thy womb. And whence is this to me, that the mother of my Lord should come to me?'[d] ... Then she repeated, 'Blessed is she that believed; for there shall be a performance of those things which were told her from the Lord.'[e] Then it was that Mary gave utterance to her feelings in the Hymn[3] which we read in the Evening Service. How many and complicated must they have been! In her was now to be fulfilled that promise which the world had been looking out for during thousands of years. The Seed of the woman, announced to guilty Eve,[f] after long delay, was at length appearing upon earth, and was to be born of her. In her the destinies of the world were to be reversed, and the serpent's head bruised. On her was bestowed the greatest honour ever put upon any individual of our fallen race. God was taking upon Him her flesh, and humbling Himself to be called her offspring;—such is the deep mystery! She of course would feel her own inexpressible unworthiness; and again, her humble lot, her ignorance, her weakness in the eyes of the world. And she had more-over, we may well suppose, that purity and innocence of heart, that bright vision of faith, that confiding trust in her God, which raised all these feelings to an intensity which we, ordinary mortals, cannot understand. *We* cannot understand them; we repeat her hymn day

[3] The hymn is the Magnificat (cf. Lk 1:46–55).

after day,—yet consider for an instant in how different a mode *we* say it from that in which she at first uttered it. *We* even hurry it over, and do not think of the meaning of those words which came from the most highly favoured, awfully gifted of the children of men. 'My soul doth magnify the Lord, and my spirit hath rejoiced in God my Saviour. For He hath regarded the low estate of His handmaiden: for, behold, from henceforth all generations shall call me blessed. For He that is mighty hath done to me great things; and holy is His name. And His mercy is on them that fear Him from generation to generation.'[g]

Now let us consider in what respects the Virgin Mary is Blessed; a title first given her by the Angel, and next by the Church in all ages since to this day.

1. I observe, that in her the curse pronounced on Eve was changed to a blessing. Eve was doomed to bear children in sorrow;[h] but now this very dispensation, in which the token of Divine anger was conveyed, was made the means by which salvation came into the world. Christ might have descended from heaven, as He went back, and as He will come again. He might have taken on Himself a body from the ground, as Adam[i] was given; or been formed, like Eve, in some other divinely-devised way.[j] But, far from this, God sent forth His Son (as St Paul says), 'made of a woman'.[k] For it has been His gracious purpose to turn *all* that is ours from evil to good. Had He so pleased, He might have found, when we sinned, other beings to do Him service, casting us into hell; but He purposed to save and to change *us*. And in like manner all that belongs to us, our reason, our affections, our pursuits, our relations in life, He needs nothing put aside in His disciples, but all sanctified.[4] Therefore, instead of sending His Son from heaven, He sent Him forth as the Son of Mary, to show that all our sorrow and all our corruption can be blessed and changed by Him. The very punishment of the fall, the very taint of birth-sin, admits of a cure by the coming of Christ.

2. But there is another portion of the original punishment of woman, which may be considered as repealed when Christ came.[5] It was said to the woman, 'Thy

[4] Cf. above: Text I, p. 111, footnote 10.

[5] Newman touches here on a topic of extreme relevance at the present time, the dignity and the role of women. The Church, in its official teaching, also looks to Mary in the mystery of the Incarnation as the person in whom every woman finds a model of her true greatness and feminine genius. Pope John Paul II, in one of his Apostolic Letters, makes explicit use of the mystery of the Annunciation and of Mary's role as the second Eve: 'If Mary is described also as the "new Eve", what are the meanings of this analogy? Certainly there are many. Particularly noteworthy is the meaning which sees Mary as the full revelation of all that is included in the biblical word "woman": a revelation commensurate with the mystery of the Redemption. *Mary* means, in a sense, a going beyond the limit spoken of in the Book of Genesis (3:6) and a return to that "beginning" in which one finds the "Woman" as she was intended to be in *creation*, and therefore in the eternal mind of God: in the bosom of the Most Holy Trinity. Mary *is* "the new beginning" of the *dignity and vocation of women*, of each and every woman. A particular key for understanding this can be found in the words which the Evangelist puts on Mary's lips after the Annunciation, during her visit to Elizabeth: "He who is mighty has done great things for me" (Lk 1:49). These words certainly refer to the conception of her Son, who is the "Son of the Most High" (Lk 1:32), the "holy one" of God; but they can also signify *the discovery of her own feminine humanity. He "has done great things for me"*: this is *the discovery of all the richness and personal resources of femininity*, all the eternal originality of the "woman", just as God wanted her to be, a person for her own sake, who discovers herself "by means of a sincere gift of self".' (Apostolic Letter, On the Dignity and Vocation of Women on the Occasion of the Marian Year, *Mulieris Dignitatem*, Vatican City, Libreria Editrice Vaticana, 1988, No. 11).

husband shall rule over thee';[l] a sentence which has been strikingly fulfilled. Man has strength to conquer the thorns and thistles which the earth is cursed with, but the same strength has ever proved the fulfilment of the punishment awarded to the woman. Look abroad through the heathen world, and see how the weaker half of mankind has everywhere been tyrannized over and debased by the strong arm of force. Consider all those Eastern nations, which have never at any time reverenced it, but have heartlessly made it the slave of every bad and cruel purpose. Thus the serpent has triumphed, —making the man still degrade himself by her who originally tempted him, and her, who then tempted, now suffer from him who was seduced. Nay, even under the light of revelation, the punishment on the woman was not removed at once. Still (in the words of the curse), her husband ruled over her. The very practice of polygamy and divorce, which was suffered under the patriarchal and Jewish dispensation proves it.

But when Christ came as the seed of the woman, He vindicated the rights and honour of His mother. Not that the distinction of ranks is destroyed under the Gospel; the woman is still made inferior to man, as he to Christ;[m] but the slavery is done away with. St Peter bids the husband 'give honour unto the wife, *because* the weaker, in that both are heirs of the grace of life'.[n] And St Paul, while enjoining subjection upon her, speaks of the especial blessedness vouchsafed her in being the appointed entrance of the Saviour into the world. 'Adam was first formed, then Eve; and Adam was not deceived, but the woman being deceived was in the transgression.' But 'notwithstanding, she shall be saved through the Child-bearing;'[o] that is, through the birth of Christ from Mary, which was a blessing, as upon all mankind, so peculiarly upon the woman. Accordingly, from that time, Marriage has not only been restored to its original dignity, but even gifted with a spiritual privilege, as the outward symbol of the heavenly union subsisting betwixt Christ and His Church.[p]

Thus has the Blessed Virgin, in bearing our Lord, taken off or lightened the peculiar disgrace which the woman inherited for seducing Adam, sanctifying the one part of it, repealing the other.

3. But further, she is doubtless to be accounted blessed and favoured in herself, as well as in the benefits she has done us. Who can estimate the holiness and perfection of her, who was chosen to be the Mother of Christ? If to him that hath, more is given,[q] and holiness and Divine favour go together (and this we are expressly told), what must have been the transcendent purity of her, whom the Creator Spirit condescended to overshadow with His miraculous presence?[6] What must have been her gifts, who was chosen to be the only near earthly relative of the Son of God, the only one whom He was bound by nature to revere and look up to; the one appointed to train and educate Him, to instruct Him day by day, as He grew in wisdom and in

[6] This paragraph gave rise to much speculation among Anglicans. They took it to mean that the preacher secretly adhered to the Roman Catholic belief in the Immaculate Conception of the Blessed Virgin Mary. To his accusers when this sermon was published three years later (1835), Newman gave an evasive response (cf. above, Introduction, II, p. 24). In the *Apologia* (in 1864), he recalls how he '*made much of*' our Lady's '*Immaculate Purity*' in this Anglican sermon (cf. *Apologia*, p. 165). It would seem that he personally saw the constraining fittingness and evidence for this doctrine but did not profess it explicitly in his Anglican period, wishing to remain loyal to the teaching of his own Church.

stature?[r] This contemplation runs to a higher subject, did we dare follow it; for what, think you, was the sanctified state of that human nature, of which God formed His sinless Son; knowing as we do, 'that which is born of the flesh is flesh',[s] and that 'none can bring a clean thing out of an unclean'?[t]

Now, after dwelling on thoughts such as these, when we turn back again to the Gospels, I think every one must feel some surprise, that we are not told more about the Blessed Virgin than we find there. After the circumstances of Christ's birth and infancy, we hear little of her. Little is said in praise of her. She is mentioned as attending Christ to the cross, and there committed by Him to St John's keeping;[u] and she is mentioned as continuing with the Apostles in prayer after His ascension;[v] and then we hear no more of her. But here again in this silence we find instruction, as much as in the mention of her.

1. It suggests to us that Scripture was written, not to exalt this or that particular Saint, but to give glory to Almighty God. There have been thousands of holy souls in the times of which the Bible history treats, whom we know nothing of, because their lives did not fall upon the line of God's public dealings with man. In Scripture we read not of all the good men who ever were, only of a few, viz. those in whom God's name was especially honoured. Doubtless there have been many widows in Israel, serving God in fastings and prayers, like Anna; but she only is mentioned in Scripture, as being in a situation to glorify the Lord Jesus. She spoke of the Infant Saviour 'to all them that looked for redemption in Jerusalem'.[w] Nay, for what we know, faith like Abraham's, and zeal like David's, have burned in the breasts of thousands whose names have no memorial; because, I say, Scripture is written to show us the course of God's great and marvellous providence, and we hear of those Saints only who were the instruments of His purposes, as either introducing or preaching His Son. Christ's favoured Apostle was St John, His personal friend;[x] yet how little do we know of St John compared with St Paul; —and why? because St Paul was the more illustrious propagator and dispenser of His Truth. As St Paul himself said, that he 'knew no man after the flesh',[y] so His Saviour, with somewhat a similar meaning, has hid from us the knowledge of His more sacred and familiar feelings, His feelings towards His Mother and His friend. These were not to be exposed, as unfit for the world to know,—as dangerous, because not admitting of being known, without a risk lest the honour which those Saints received through grace should eclipse in our minds the honour of Him who honoured them.[7] Had the blessed Mary been more fully disclosed to us

[7] On this point concerning the relative silence of Sacred Scripture on the details of our Lady's life, Newman can speak with unrestrained fervour to his Anglican congregation. The sparse information on her life given by the inspired authors seems to bolster the Anglican claim that excessive veneration of our Lady eclipses the honour due to Christ and the Holy Trinity, and puts a barrier or created image between the soul and its Creator. This, as Newman himself would soon learn, is not true. The Catholic Church, basing itself on the Fathers of the Church, teaches that 'Mary's function as mother of men in no way obscures or diminishes this unique mediation of Christ, but rather shows its power ... It does not hinder in any way the immediate union of the faithful with Christ but on the contrary fosters it' (Vatican II, Dogmatic Constitution on the Church, *Lumen Gentium*, 60). Her subordinate salvific intercession 'is so understood that it neither takes away anything from nor adds anything to the dignity and efficacy of Christ the one Mediator' (*Ibid.* 62).

in the heavenly beauty and sweetness of the spirit within her, true, *she* would have been honoured, *her* gifts would have been clearly seen; but, at the same time, the Giver would have been somewhat less contemplated, because no design or work of His would have been disclosed in her history. She would have seemingly been introduced for *her* sake, not for His sake. When a Saint is seen working *towards* an end appointed by God, we *see* him to be a mere instrument, a servant though a favoured one; and though we admire him, yet, after all, we glorify God in him. We pass on *from* him to the work to which he ministers. But, when any one is introduced, full of gifts, yet without visible and immediate subserviency to God's designs, such a one seems revealed for his own sake. We should rest, perchance, in the thought of him, and think of the creature more than the Creator. Thus it is a dangerous thing, it is too high a privilege, for sinners like ourselves, to know the best and innermost thoughts of God's servants. We cannot bear to see such men in their own place, in the retirement of private life, and the calmness of hope and joy. The higher their gifts, the less fitted they are for being seen. Even St John the Apostle was twice tempted to fall down in worship before an Angel who showed him the things to come.[z] And, if he who had seen the Son of God was thus overcome by the creature, how is it possible we could bear to gaze upon the creature's holiness in its fullness, especially as we should be more able to enter into it, and estimate it, than to comprehend the infinite perfections of the Eternal Godhead? Therefore, many truths are, like the 'things which the seven thunders uttered', 'sealed up'[aa] from us. In particular, it is in mercy to us that so little is revealed about the Blessed Virgin, in mercy to our weakness, though of her there are 'many things to say', yet they are 'hard to be uttered, seeing we are dull of hearing.'[bb]

2. But, further, the more we consider who St Mary was, the more dangerous will such knowledge of her appear to be. Other saints are but influenced or inspired by Christ, and made partakers of Him mystically. But, as to St Mary, Christ derived His manhood from her, and so had an especial unity of nature with her; and this wondrous relationship between God and man it is perhaps impossible for us to dwell much upon without some perversion of feeling. For, truly, she is raised above the condition of sinful beings, though by nature a sinner;[8] she is brought near to God, yet is but a creature, and seems to lack her fitting place in our limited understandings, neither too high nor too low. We cannot combine, in our thought of her, all we should ascribe with all we should withhold. Hence, following the example of Scripture, we had better only think of her with and for her Son, never separating her from Him, but using her name as a memorial of His great condescension in stooping from heaven, and not 'abhorring the Virgin's womb'.[9] And

---

[8] 'by nature a sinner'. Some people would read into these words the demonstration that the author in his Anglican days regarded Mary as being tainted with the original fault of human nature and then saved from her sinful condition, like every other human person. However, as we point out elsewhere, other texts by Newman as an Anglican make this interpretation doubtful.

[9] Words from the hymn *Te Deum*, which is recited or sung in most Sunday and festive Offices at the end of the Office of Readings in The Liturgy of the Hours.

this is the rule of our own Church, which has set apart only such Festivals in honour of the Blessed Mary, as may also be Festivals in honour of our Lord; the Purification commemorating His presentation in the Temple, and the Annunciation commemorating His Incarnation.[10] And, with this caution, the thought of her may be made most profitable to our faith; for nothing is so calculated to impress on our minds that Christ is really partaker of our nature, and in all respects man, save sin only, as to associate Him with the thought of her, by whose ministration He became our brother.

To conclude. Observe the lesson which we gain for ourselves from the history of the Blessed Virgin; that the highest graces of the soul may be matured in private, and without those fierce trials to which the many are exposed in order to their sanctification. So hard are our hearts, that affliction, pain, and anxiety are sent to humble us, and dispose us towards a true faith in the heavenly word, when preached to us. Yet it is only our extreme obstinacy of unbelief which renders this chastisement necessary. The aids which God gives under the Gospel Covenant, have power to

[10] In the Roman Catholic liturgy, too, the feasts in honour of our Lady are closely associated with the person and redemptive work of Christ. 'In celebrating this annual cycle of the mysteries of Christ, holy Church honours the Blessed Mary, Mother of God, with a special love. She is inseparably linked with her Son's saving work. In her the Church admires and exalts the most excellent fruit of redemption, and joyfully contemplates, as in a faultless image, that which she herself desires and hopes wholly to be' (Vatican II, Constitution on the Sacred Liturgy, *Sacrosanctum Concilium*, 103). 'The feasts of the saints proclaim the wonderful works of Christ in his servants and offer to the faithful fitting examples for their imitation' (*Ibid.* 111).

renew and purify our hearts, without uncommon providences to discipline us into receiving them. God gives His Holy Spirit to us silently; and the silent duties of every day (it may be humbly hoped) are blest to the sufficient sanctification of thousands, whom the world knows not of.[11] The Blessed Virgin is a memorial of this; and it is consoling as well as instructive to know it. When we quench the grace of Baptism, then it is that we need severe trials to restore us. This is the case of the multitude, whose best estate is that of chastisement, repentance, supplication, and absolution, again and again. But there are those who go on in a calm and unswerving course, learning day by day to love Him who has redeemed them, and overcoming the sin of their nature by His heavenly grace, as the various temptations to evil successively present themselves. And, of these undefiled followers of the Lamb,[cc] the Blessed Mary is the chief. Strong in the

---

[11] The value of little things, the importance of our ordinary round of common duties, the sureness of normal things as distinct from the extraordinary and the sensational, was a truth dear to the heart of Newman. He contemplated that principle exemplified in an unparalleled fashion in the humble life of the Virgin of Nazareth. He realized that the obedience of faith does not often demand extraordinary deeds but it does call for the drudgery of daily chores and humble duties, not merely for one day or one month or one year, but every day of every month of every year of our mortal existence. Its silent immolation can become a real martyrdom. Hence Newman's well known and simple method of attaining perfection – no specially heroic deeds but the perfect performance, in a spirit of faith and love, of the small actions that make up the round of our daily duties. Perfection does not consist 'in any specially heroic deeds'. For Newman, a person 'is perfect who does the duties of the day perfectly' (cf. Oratory Paper No. 25: *Newman the Oratorian*, Dublin 1969, p. 316). For his similarity with St Thérèse of the Child Jesus on this point, cf. Philip Boyce, *Spiritual Exodus of John Henry Newman and Thérèse of Lisieux*, Dublin and Manchester 1979, pp. 42–3.

Lord, and in the power of His might, she 'staggered not at the promise of God through unbelief';[dd] she believed when Zacharias doubted,—with a faith like Abraham's she believed and was blessed for her belief, and had the performance of those things which were told her by the Lord. And when sorrow came upon her afterwards, it was but the blessed participation of her Son's sacred sorrows, not the sorrow of those who suffer for their sins.

If we, through God's unspeakable gift, have in any measure followed Mary's innocence in our youth, so far let us bless Him who enabled us. But so far as we are conscious of having departed from Him, let us bewail our miserable guilt. Let us acknowledge from the heart that no punishment is too severe for us, no chastisement should be unwelcome (though it is a sore thing to learn to welcome pain), if it tend to burn away the corruption which has propagated itself within us. Let us count all things as gain, which God sends to cleanse away the marks of sin and shame which are upon our foreheads. The day will come at length, when our Lord and Saviour will unveil that Sacred Countenance to the whole world, which no sinner ever yet could see and live. Then will the world be forced to look upon Him, whom they pierced[ee] with their unrepented wickedness; 'all faces will gather blackness'.[ff] Then they will discern, what they do not now believe, the utter deformity of sin; while the Saints of the Lord, who seemed on earth to bear but the countenance of common men, will wake up one by one after His likeness, and be fearful to look upon. And then will be fulfilled the promise pledged to the Church on the Mount of Transfiguration. It will be 'good'[gg] to be with those whose tabernacles might have been a snare to us on earth, had we been allowed to build them. We shall see our Lord, and His Blessed Mother, the Apostles and Prophets, and all those righteous men whom we now read of in history, and long to know. Then we shall be taught in those Mysteries which are now above us. In the words of the Apostle, 'Beloved, now are we the sons of God, and it doth not yet appear what we shall be; but we know that, when He shall appear, we shall be like Him, for we shall see Him as He is: and every man that hath this hope in Him, purifieth himself, even as He is pure.'[hh]

a. cf. Lk 1:35   b. Lk 1:28   c. Lk 1:30–2   d. Lk 1:42–3
e. Lk 1:45   f. cf. Gen 3:15   g. Lk 1:46–50   h. cf. Gen 3:16
i. cf. Gen 2:7   j. cf. Gen 2:21   k. Gal 4:4   l. Gen 3:16
m. cf. Eph 5:22–33   n. 1 Pet 3:7   o. 1 Tim 2:13–15   p. cf. Eph 5:29, 32
q. cf. Mt 13:12   r. cf. Lk 2:40, 52 s. Jn 3:6   t. Job 14:4
u. cf. Jn 19:25–7   v. cf. Acts 1:13–14 w. Lk 2:38   x. cf. Jn 13:23
y. 2 Cor 5:16   z. cf. Rev 19:10   aa. cf. Rev 10:4   bb. Heb 5:11
cc. cf. Rev 7:9–17   dd. Rom 4:20   ee. cf. Is 53:5   ff. Joel 2:6
gg. cf. Mt 17:4   hh. 1 Jn 3:2–3

Parochial and Plain Sermons, London, 1908, Vol. II, pp. 127–38 Preached on 25 March 1832.

III

THE GLORIES OF MARY FOR
THE SAKE OF HER SON[1]

We know, my brethren, that in the natural world
nothing is superfluous, nothing incomplete, nothing
independent; but part answers to part, and all details
combine to form one mighty whole. Order and
harmony are among the first perfections which we
discern in this visible creation; and the more we
examine into it, the more widely and minutely they
are found to belong to it. 'All things are double,' says
the Wise Man, 'one against another; and He hath
made nothing defective'.[a] It is the very character and
definition of 'the heavens and the earth',[b] as
contrasted with the void or chaos which preceded

---

[1] This sermon and the following one (cf. below, pp. 149–66) are taken
from the Volume *Discourses Addressed to Mixed Congregations*. These
were discourses or sermons given in the Oratory Church in
Birmingham, which was then situated in Alcester Street. Belonging to
the first of Newman's Catholic sermons, they were delivered in the
spring and summer of 1849, three and a half years after his conversion
to the Roman Catholic Church and two years after his ordination to
the Catholic priesthood. They did not form part of a Eucharistic or
liturgical celebration. The congregation was a 'mixed' one in the sense
that it included a considerable number of Anglicans.

them, that everything is now subjected to fixed laws; and every motion, and influence, and effect can be accounted for, and, were our knowledge sufficient, could be anticipated. Moreover, it is plain, on the other hand, that it is only in proportion to our observation and our research that this truth becomes apparent; for though a number of things even at first sight are seen to proceed according to an established and beautiful order, yet in other instances the law to which they are conformed is with difficulty discovered; and the words 'chance', and 'hazard', and 'fortune', have come into use as expressions of our ignorance. Accordingly, you may fancy rash and irreligious minds who are engaged day after day in the business of the world, suddenly looking out into the heavens or upon the earth, and criticizing the great Architect, arguing that there are creatures in existence which are rude or defective in their constitution, and asking questions which would but evidence their want of scientific education.

The case is the same as regards the supernatural world. The great truths of Revelation are all connected together and form a whole. Every one can see this in a measure even at a glance, but to understand the full consistency and harmony of Catholic teaching requires study and meditation. Hence, as philosophers of this world bury themselves in museums and laboratories, descend into mines, or wander among woods or on the sea-shore, so the inquirer into heavenly truths dwells in the cell and the oratory, pouring forth his heart in prayer, collecting his thoughts in meditation, dwelling on the idea of Jesus, or of Mary, or of grace, or of eternity, and pondering the words of holy men who have gone before him, till before his mental sight arises the hidden wisdom of the perfect, 'which God predestined before the world unto our glory,'[c] and which He 'reveals unto them by His Spirit'.[d] And, as ignorant men may dispute the beauty and harmony of the visible creation, so men, who for six days in the week are absorbed in worldly toil, who live for wealth, or name, or self-indulgence, or profane knowledge, and do but give their leisure moments to the thought of religion, never raising their souls to God, never asking for His enlightening grace, never chastening their hearts and bodies, never steadily contemplating the objects of faith, but judging hastily and peremptorily according to their private views or the humour of the hour; such men, I say, in like manner, may easily, or will for certain, be surprised and shocked at portions of revealed truth, as if strange, or harsh, or extreme, or inconsistent, and will in whole or in part reject it.

I am going to apply this remark to the subject of the prerogatives with which the Church invests the Blessed Mother of God. They are startling and difficult to those whose imagination is not accustomed to them, and whose reason has not reflected on them; but the more carefully and religiously they are dwelt on, the more, I am sure, will they be found essential to the Catholic faith, and integral to the worship of Christ. This simply is the point which I shall insist on—disputable indeed by aliens from the Church, but most clear to her children—that the glories of Mary are for the sake of Jesus; and that we praise and bless her as the first of creatures, that we may duly confess Him as our sole Creator.[2]

When the Eternal Word decreed to come on earth, He did not purpose, He did not work, by halves; but He came to be a man like any of us, to take a human soul and body, and to make them His own. He did not come in a mere apparent or accidental form, as Angels appear to men; nor did He merely overshadow an existing man, as He overshadows His saints, and call Him by the name of God; but He 'was made flesh'.[e] He attached to Himself a manhood, and became as really and truly man as He was God, so that henceforth He was both God and man, or, in other words, He was One Person in two natures, divine and human. This is a mystery so marvellous, so difficult, that faith alone firmly receives it; the natural man may receive it for a while, may think he receives it, but never really receives it; begins, as soon as he has professed it, secretly to rebel against it, evades it, or revolts from it. This he has done from the first; even in the lifetime of the beloved disciple men arose who said that our Lord had no body at all, or a body framed in the heavens, or that He did not suffer, but another suffered in His stead, or that He was but for a time possessed of the human form which was born and which suffered, coming into it at its baptism, and leaving it before its crucifixion, or, again, that He was

---

[2] Because he was preaching to a congregation made up of both Anglicans and Catholics, Newman uses an ecumenical tone. To those outside the Church of Rome, he endeavours to give a clear explanation of points of Catholic doctrine and belief. One of the great difficulties experienced by Anglicans with regard to Marian devotion was their fear that it would take away from the honour due to Christ, and finally become a form of idolatry by giving a degree of honour to a creature that was the exclusive right of the Creator himself.

a mere man.[3] That 'in the beginning was the Word, and the Word was with God, and the Word was God, and the Word was made flesh and dwelt among us',[f] was too hard a thing for the unregenerate reason.

The case is the same at this day; mere Protestants have seldom any real perception of the doctrine of God and man in one Person. They speak in a dreamy, shadowy way of Christ's divinity; but, when their meaning is sifted, you will find them very slow to commit themselves to any statement sufficient to express the Catholic dogma. They will tell you at once, that the subject is not to be inquired into, for that it is impossible to inquire into it at all without being technical and subtile. Then, when they comment on the Gospels, they will speak of Christ, not simply and consistently as God, but as a being made up of God and man, partly one and partly the other, or between both, or as a man inhabited by a special Divine presence.[4] Sometimes they even go on

---

[3] The preacher makes reference here to various explanations of the mystery of Christ, which circulated before the Council of Nicea (325), consisting of different strands of Gnosticism, that considered Jesus to be 'a mere man'. They distinguished between Christ and Jesus: Christ, the Son of God, would have descended on Jesus at his baptism in the Jordan. This union lasted until shortly before the Passion, when Christ abandoned Jesus again. Such an explanation denied the reality of the Incarnation of the Son of God and of his redemptive sufferings.

[4] Newman refers in these paragraphs to some of the ever-recurring heretical theories of old, that offered erroneous explanations of the mystery of Christ, and which consequently had implications for a correct understanding of the Virgin Mary.

The first stemmed from *Arius*, a priest from Alexandria, in the *fourth century*, who gave rise to the heresy known as Arianism. He taught that only the Father in the Trinity was truly the uncreated God. The Word did not exist in heaven from eternity with the Father but was created 'from things that were not' by the power of the Father. Therefore, as

to deny that He was in heaven the Son of God, saying that He became the Son when He was conceived of the Holy Ghost; and they are shocked, and think it a mark both of reverence and good sense to be shocked, when they hear the Man spoken of simply and plainly as God. They cannot bear to have it said, except as a figure or mode of speaking, that God had a human body, or that God suffered; they think that the 'Atonement', and 'Sanctification through the Spirit', as they speak, is the sum and substance of the Gospel, and they are shy of any dogmatic expression which goes beyond them. Such, I believe, is the ordinary character of the Protestant notions among us as to the divinity of Christ, whether among members of the

---

Newman says, Arians 'deny that Christ was in heaven the Son of God'. The first ecumenical Council, at Nicea in 325, gave a solemn declaration of the true divinity of Christ, refuting Arianism (cf. below, Text VIII, p. 191, footnote 2).

Then there was *Nestorianism*, a renowned Christological heresy of the *fifth century*. The originator of this school of thought was Nestorius, Bishop of Constantinople, who by his explanation of the mystery of the Incarnation destroyed the unity in Christ. He claimed that Christ was a perfect man like any of us with his own human personality. The Son of God dwelt in this humanity as in a temple. According to this theory, Christ was regarded as a human person joined to the divine person of God's Son. Therefore, not one (divine) Person in Christ, but two, a human and a divine. As a result, the Blessed Virgin Mary was mother, not of God, but of the human person of Jesus. Accordingly, she was not the *Theotokos*. This theory was condemned by the Council of Ephesus in 431.

Finally, the *Monophysitism*, or in its extreme form, *Eutychianism*, was another Christological heresy of the *fifth century*. It was so much in opposition to Nestorianism, that it erred in the other extreme. In defending the unity of Christ so strenuously, it not only recognized in him one Divine Person, but also (and this was their error) only one nature, namely, the divine. It needed the Council of Chalcedon in 451 to give the final explanation of the two integral and distinct natures (human and divine) in the One (divine) Person of Christ.

Anglican communion, or dissenters[5] from it, excepting a small remnant of them.

Now, if you would witness against these unchristian
opinions, if you would bring out distinctly and beyond
mistake and evasion, the simple idea of the Catholic
Church that God is man, could you do it better than by
laying down in St John's words that 'God *became*
man'?[g] and again could you express this more emphatically and unequivocally than by declaring that He was
born a man, or that He had a *Mother*?[6] The world allows
that God *is* man; the admission costs it little, for God is
everywhere, and (as it may say) is everything; but it
shrinks from confessing that God is the Son of Mary. It
shrinks, for it is at once confronted with a severe fact,
which violates and shatters its own unbelieving view of
things; the revealed doctrine forthwith takes its true
shape, and receives an historical reality; and the
Almighty is introduced into His own world at a certain
time and in a definite way. Dreams are broken and
shadows depart; the Divine truth is no longer a poetical
expression, or a devotional exaggeration, or a mystical
economy, or a mythical representation. 'Sacrifice and
offering', the shadows of the Law, 'Thou wouldest not,
but a body hast Thou fitted to me.[h] That which was
from the beginning, which we have heard, which we
have seen with our eyes, which we have diligently

---

[5] 'Dissenters' were those who separated from the Established Church in
England, refusing to accept certain beliefs or authorized usages of the
Anglican Church. Later they would also be called 'Nonconformists' or
'Free Churchmen'.

[6] In the following pages, we perceive the preacher's deep faith in the
reality of the Incarnation and in all its consequences: there is a notable
similarity with the theological meditation of St John the Evangelist as
portrayed in his Gospel.

looked upon, and our hands have handled', 'That which we have seen and have heard, declare we unto you';[i]—such is the record of the Apostle, in opposition to those 'spirits' which denied that 'Jesus Christ had appeared in the flesh,' and which 'dissolved'[j] Him by denying either His human nature or His divine. And the confession that Mary is *Deipara*,[7] or the Mother of God, is that safeguard wherewith we seal up and secure the doctrine of the Apostle from all evasion, and that test whereby we detect all the pretences of those bad spirits of 'Antichrist which have gone out into the world'.[k] It declares that He is God; it implies that He is man; it suggests to us that He is God still, though He has become man, and that He is true man though He is God.[8] By witnessing to the *process* of the union, it secures the reality of the two *subjects* of the union, of

---

[7] The term 'Mother of God' (*Theotokos* in Greek; *Deipara* in Latin) was one that Newman himself was loath to use as an Anglican. Now, as a Roman Catholic, he feels free and secure in his witness to the faith. All of these eighteen *Discourses to Mixed Congregations* display a zeal that is typical of a new convert. Richard H. Hutton describes the peculiar genius of these sermons as follows: 'They have more in them of the enthusiasm of a convert than any other of Newman's publications, and altogether contain the most eloquent and elaborate specimens of his eloquence as a preacher, and of his sense, if I may so call it, of the religious advantages of his position as a spokesman of the great Church of Rome. They represent more adequately Dr Newman as he was when he first felt himself 'unmuzzled' ..., than any other of his writings; and though they have not to me quite the delicate charm of the reserve, and I might almost say, the shy passion, of his Oxford sermons, they represent the full-blown blossom of his genius, while the former show it only in bud.' (*Cardinal Newman*. London, Methuen and Co., 1891, p. 197).

[8] Newman now uses all his eloquence, in a more ornate and elaborate style than in the Anglican sermons. Charles Stephen Dessain, in his fine biography of Newman, points out that these *Discourses to Mixed Congregations* were 'not above the head of his mixed audience' even though they contained 'many passages of eloquent beauty' (cf. *John Henry Newman*, London, Nelson, 1966, p. 94).

the divinity and of the manhood. If Mary is the Mother of God, Christ must be literally Emmanuel, God with us.[1] And hence it was, that, when time went on, and the bad spirits and false prophets grew stronger and bolder, and found a way into the Catholic body itself, then the Church, guided by God, could find no more effectual and sure way of expelling them than that of using this word *Deipara* against them; and, on the other hand, when they came up again from the realms of darkness, and plotted the utter overthrow of Christian faith in the sixteenth century, then they could find no more certain expedient for their hateful purpose than that of reviling and blaspheming the prerogatives of Mary, for they knew full well that, if they could once get the world to dishonour the Mother, the dishonour of the Son would follow close. The Church and Satan agreed together in this, that Son and Mother went together; and the experience of three centuries has confirmed their testimony, for Catholics who have honoured the Mother, still worship the Son, while Protestants, who now have ceased to confess the Son, began then by scoffing at the Mother.[9]

You see, then, my brethren, in this particular, the harmonious consistency of the revealed system, and the

---

[9] Newman's personal devotion to Mary shines through these pages. He speaks with deep conviction and filial love. Aware of the audience he addresses, he explains Catholic truths about our Lady without offending his listeners, although at times in forthright language. His theological argumentation is based on Scripture and follows the teaching of the Church. Moreover, it is clothed in elegant English prose – something that for centuries had not been frequent in England. It is no wonder that a noted Anglican said about these sermons: 'Romanism has never been so glorified before' (Benjamin Jowett, well-known for his 'liberal' theological ideas). In fact, not a few Anglicans were received into the Catholic Church as a result of these sermons.

bearing of one dotrine upon another; Mary is exalted
for the sake of Jesus. It was fitting that she, as being a
creature, though the first of creatures, should have an
office of ministration. She, as others, came into the
world to do a work, she had a mission to fulfil; her
grace and her glory are not for her own sake, but for
her Maker's; and to her is committed the custody of the
Incarnation; this is her appointed office,—'A Virgin
shall conceive, and bear a Son, and they shall call His
Name Emmanuel'.[m] As she was once on earth, and was
personally the guardian of her Divine Child, as she
carried Him in her womb, folded Him in her embrace,
and suckled Him at her breast, so now, and to the latest
hour of the Church, do her glories and the devotion
paid her proclaim and define the right faith concerning
Him as God and man. Every church which is dedicated
to her, every altar which is raised under her invocation,
every image which represents her, every litany in her
praise, every Hail Mary for her continual memory,
does but remind us that there was One who, though
He was all-blessed from all eternity, yet for the sake of
sinners, 'did not shrink from the Virgin's womb'.[10]
Thus she is the *Turris Davidica*, as the Church calls her,
'the Tower of David'; the high and strong defence of
the King of the true Israel; and hence the Church also
addresses her in the Antiphon, as having 'alone
destroyed all heresies in the whole world'.[11]

---

[10] Cf. above, p. 124, footnote 9 of the previous sermon.

[11] The antiphon was used at the time in the *Breviarum Romanum*, cf. the
Common of the Feasts of the Blessed Virgin Mary, Matins, 3rd
Nocturn, Antiphon 7, and also in the *Missale Romanum*: cf. the
Common of Our Lady, *Tract* of the Mass '*Salve Sancta Parens*'
(between Septuagesima and Easter) and the second Mass for Our Lady
on Saturdays, '*Vultum tuum*'. Newman considered the mystery of
Mary to be a safeguard of Catholic orthodox teaching.

And here, my brethren, a fresh thought opens upon us, which is naturally implied in what has been said. If the *Deipara* is to witness of Emmanuel, she must be necessarily more than the *Deipara*. For consider; a defence must be strong in order to be a defence; a tower must be, like that Tower of David, 'built with bulwarks'; 'a thousand bucklers hang upon it, all the armour of valiant men'.[n] It would not have sufficed, in order to bring out and impress on us the idea that God is man, had His Mother been an ordinary person. A mother without a home in the Church, without dignity, without gifts, would have been, as far as the defence of the Incarnation goes, no mother at all. She would not have remained in the memory, or the imagination of men. If she is to witness and remind the world that God became man, she must be on a high and eminent station for the purpose. She must be made to fill the mind, in order to suggest the lesson. When she once attracts our attention, then, and not till then, she begins to preach Jesus. 'Why should she have such prerogatives,' we ask, 'unless He be God? and what must He be by nature, when she is so high by grace?' This is why she has other prerogatives besides, namely, the gifts of personal purity and intercessory power, distinct from her maternity; she is personally endowed that she may perform her office well; she is exalted in herself that she may minister to Christ.

For this reason, she has been made more glorious in her person than in her office; her purity is a higher gift than her relationship to God. This is what is implied in Christ's answer to the woman in the crowd, who cried out, when He was preaching, 'Blessed is the womb that bare Thee, and the breasts which Thou hast sucked'.º He replied by pointing out to His disciples a higher blessedness; 'Yea, rather, blessed', He said, 'are they who hear the word of God and keep it'.ᴾ You know, my brethren, that Protestants take these words in disparagement of our Lady's greatness, but they really tell the other way. For consider them; He lays down a principle, that it is more blessed to keep His commandments than to be His Mother; but who, even of Protestants, will say that she did *not* keep His commandments? She kept them surely, and our Lord does but say that such obedience was in a higher line of privilege than her being His Mother; she was more blessed in her detachment from creatures, in her devotion to God, in her virginal purity, in her fullness of grace, than in her maternity. This is the constant teaching of the Holy Fathers: 'More blessed was Mary', says St Augustine, 'in receiving Christ's faith, than in conceiving Christ's flesh';[12] and St Chrysostom declares, that she would not have been blessed, though she had borne Him in the body, had she not heard the word of God and kept it. This, of course, is an impossible case; for she was made holy, that she might be made His Mother, and the two blessednesses cannot be divided. She who was chosen to supply flesh and blood to the Eternal Word, was first filled with grace in soul and body; still, she had a double blessedness, of office and of qualification for it, and the latter was the greater. And it is on this account

[12] This seeming disparagement of Mary was a topic that many Church Fathers commented on. Newman gives a profound, yet a clear and concise, explanation in line with a long Patristic tradition. He refers to these two passages on a number of occasions in his preaching. For the citations from St Augustine and St John Chrysostom cf. below, Text V, p. 169, footnotes 5 and 6.

that the Angel calls her blessed; '*Full of grace*,'[q] he says, 'Blessed among women';[r] and St Elizabeth also, when she cries out, 'Blessed thou that hast *believed*'.[s] Nay, she herself bears a like testimony, when the Angel announced to her the high favour which was coming on her. Though all Jewish women in each successive age had been hoping to be Mother of the Christ, so that marriage was honourable among them, childlessness a reproach, she alone had put aside the desire and the thought of so great a dignity. She, who was to bear the Christ, gave no welcome to the great announcement that she was to bear Him; and why did she thus act towards it? because she had been inspired, the first of womankind, to dedicate her virginity to God, and she did not welcome a privilege which seemed to involve a forfeiture of her vow. How shall this be, she asked, seeing I am to live separate from man? Nor, till the Angel told her that the conception would be miraculous and from the Holy Ghost, did she put aside her 'trouble' of mind, recognize him securely as God's messenger, and bow her head in awe and thankfulness to God's condescension.

Mary then is a specimen, and more than a specimen, in the purity of her soul and body, of what man was before his fall, and what he would have been, had he risen to his full perfection. It had been hard, it had been a victory for the Evil One, had the whole race passed away, nor any one instance in it occurred to show what the Creator had intended it to be in its original state. Adam, you know, was created in the image and after the likeness of God; his frail and imperfect nature, stamped with a Divine seal, was supported and exalted by an indwelling of Divine grace. Impetuous passion did not exist in him, except as a latent element and a possible evil; ignorance was dissipated by the clear light of the Spirit; and reason, sovereign over every motion of his soul, was simply subjected to the will of God. Nay, even his body was preserved from every wayward appetite and affection, and was promised immortality instead of dissolution. Thus he was in a supernatural state; and, had he not sinned, year after year would he have advanced in merit and grace, and in God's favour, till he passed from paradise to heaven. But he fell; and his descendants were born in his likeness; and the world grew worse instead of better, and judgment after judgment cut off generations of sinners in vain, and improvement was hopeless; 'because man was flesh',[t] and, 'the thoughts of his heart were bent upon evil at all times'.[u]

However, a remedy had been determined in heaven; a Redeemer was at hand; God was about to do a great work, and He purposed to do it suitably; 'where sin abounded, grace was to abound more'.[v] Kings of the earth, when they have sons born to them, forthwith scatter some large bounty, or raise some high memorial; they honour the day, or the place, or the heralds of the auspicious event, with some corresponding mark of favour; nor did the coming of Emmanuel innovate on the world's established custom. It was a season of grace and prodigy, and these were to be exhibited in a special manner in the person of His Mother. The course of ages was to be reversed; the tradition of evil was to be broken; a gate of light was to be opened amid the darkness, for the coming of the Just;—a Virgin conceived and bore Him. It was fitting, for His honour and glory, that she, who was the instrument of His bodily presence, should first be a miracle of His grace; it was fitting that she should triumph, where Eve had failed, and should 'bruise the serpent's head'[w] by the spotlessness of her sanctity. In some respects, indeed, the curse was not reversed; Mary came into a fallen world, and resigned herself to its laws; she, as also the Son she bore, was exposed to pain of soul and body, she was subjected to death; but she was not put under the power of sin. As grace was infused into Adam from the first moment of his creation, so that he never had experience of his natural poverty, till sin reduced him to it; so was grace given from the first in still ampler measure to Mary, and she never incurred, in fact, Adam's deprivation. She began where others end, whether in knowledge or in love. She was from the first clothed in sanctity, destined for perseverance, luminous and glorious in God's sight, and incessantly employed in meritorious acts, which continued till her last breath. Her was emphatically 'the path of the just, which, as the shining light, goeth forward and increaseth even to the perfect day';[x] and sinlessness in thought, word, and deed, in small things as well as great, in venial matters as well as grievous, is surely but the natural and obvious sequel of such a beginning. If Adam might have kept himself from sin in his first state, much more shall we expect immaculate perfection in Mary.[13]

Such is her prerogative of sinless perfection, and it is,

[13] Newman makes much of our Lady's purity and holiness. He regarded it as a prerequisite for her divine maternity. Nevertheless, he stresses that our Lady was not simply a passive instrument in God's hands. She actively co-operated with every grace and every divine request. This exalts her to inconceivable heights of sanctity. The previous November Newman had remarked in a letter to an Anglican lady that, in the seemingly disparaging words of Christ in the Gospel 'who

as her maternity, for the sake of Emmanuel; hence she answered the Angel's salutation, *Gratia plena*, with the humble acknowledgement, *Ecce ancilla Domini*, 'Behold the handmaid of the Lord'.[y] And like to this is her third prerogative, which follows both from her maternity and from her purity, and which I will mention as completing the enumeration of her glories. I mean her intercessory power. For, if 'God heareth not sinners, but if a man be a worshipper of Him, and do His will, him He heareth';[z] if 'the continual prayer of a just man availeth much';[aa] if faithful Abraham was required to pray for Abimelech, 'for he was a prophet';[bb] if patient Job was to 'pray for his friends', for he had 'spoken right things before God';[cc] if meek Moses, by lifting up his hands, turned the battle in favour of Israel against Amalec;[dd][14] why should we wonder at hearing that Mary, the only spotless child of Adam's seed, has a transcendent influence with the God of grace? And if the Gentiles at Jerusalem sought Philip, because he was an Apostle, when they desired access to Jesus, and Philip spoke to Andrew, as still more closely in our Lord's confidence, and then both came to Him,[ee] is it strange that the Mother should have power with the Son, distinct in kind from that of the purest angel and the most triumphant saint? If we have faith to admit the Incarnation itself, we must admit it in its fullness; why then should we start at the gracious appointments which

---

is my mother?' (Mt 12:48), 'Catholics found the doctrine that her being Mother of God is not her only title to honour, but that she was made such *on account* of her personal sanctity, which leads on to the doctrine of the Immaculate Conception' (*The Letters and Diaries*, XII, 334).

[14] Newman uses the former Roman Catholic nomenclature of Old Testament names, for example, Amalec for Amalek, Noe for Noah, Elias for Elijah, Eliseus for Elisha, Ahias for Ahijah, etc.

arise out of it, or are necessary to it, or are included in it? If the Creator comes on earth in the form of a servant and a creature,[ff] why may not His Mother, on the other hand, rise to be the Queen of heaven, and be clothed with the sun, and have the moon under her feet?[gg]

I am not proving these doctrines to you, my brethren; the evidence of them lies in the declaration of the Church. The Church is the oracle of religious truth, and dispenses what the apostles committed to her in every time and place. We must take her word, then, without proof, because she is sent to us from God to teach us how to please Him; and that we do so is the test whether we be really Catholics or no. I am not proving then what you already receive, but I am showing you the beauty and the harmony, in one out of many instances, of the Church's teaching; which are so well adapted, as they are divinely intended, to recommend that teaching to the inquirer and to endear it to her children. One word more, and I have done; I have shown you how full of meaning are the truths themselves which the Church teaches concerning the Most Blessed Virgin, and now consider how full of meaning also has been the Church's dispensation of them.

You will find, that, in this respect, as in Mary's prerogatives themselves, there is the same careful reference to the glory of Him who gave them to her. You know, when first He went out to preach, she kept apart from Him; she interfered not with His work; and, even when He was gone up on high,[hh] yet she, a woman, went not out to preach or teach, she seated not herself in the Apostolic chair, she took no part in the priest's office; she did but humbly seek her

Son in the daily Mass of those, who, though her ministers in heaven, were her superiors in the Church on earth. Nor, when she and they had left this lower scene, and she was a Queen upon her Son's right hand, not even then did she ask of Him to publish her name to the ends of the world, or to hold her up to the world's gaze, but she remained waiting for the time, when her own glory should be necessary for His. He indeed had been from the very first proclaimed by Holy Church, and enthroned in His temple, for He was God; ill had it beseemed the living Oracle of Truth to have withholden from the faithful the very object of their adoration; but it was otherwise with Mary. It became her, as a creature, a mother, and a woman, to stand aside and make way for the Creator, to minister to her Son, and to win her way into the world's homage by sweet and gracious persuasion. So when His name was dishonoured, then it was that she did Him service; when Emmanuel was denied, then the Mother of God (as it were) came forward; when heretics said that God was not incarnate, then was the time for her own honours. And then, when as much as this had been accomplished, she had done with strife; she fought not for herself. No fierce controversy, no persecuted confessors, no heresiarch, no anathema, were necessary for her gradual manifestation; as she had increased day by day in grace and merit at Nazareth, while the world knew not of her, so has she raised herself aloft silently, and has grown into her place in the Church by a tranquil influence and a natural process. She was as some fair tree, stretching forth her fruitful branches and her fragrant leaves, and overshadowing the territory of the saints. And thus the Antiphon speaks of her: 'Let thy dwelling be in Jacob, and thine inheritance in Israel, and *strike thy roots* in My elect'.[ii] Again,

> And so in Sion was I established, and in the holy city I likewise rested, and in Jerusalem was my power. And I *took root* in an honourable people, and in the glorious company of the saints was I *detained*. I was exalted like a cedar in Lebanus, and as a cypress in Mount Sion; I have stretched out my branches as the terebinth, and my branches are of honour and grace.[jj][15]

Thus was she reared without hands, and gained a modest victory, and exerts a gentle sway, which she has not claimed. When dispute arose about her among her children, she hushed it; when objections were urged against her, she waived her clams and waited; till now, in this very day, should God so will, she will win at length her most radiant crown, and, without opposing voice, and amid the jubilation of the whole Church, she will be hailed as immaculate in her conception.[16]

Such art thou, Holy Mother, in the creed and in the

---

[15] These words taken from Wisdom texts in the Old Testament (cf. Sir. 24: 11–13; 15–20 in the Vulgate) have been applied to our Lady by the Church's liturgy. In the Tridentine liturgy of Newman's day: cf. for example, *Officium parvum Beatae Mariae Virginis, Ad Matutinum, In Nocturno*, and in the Roman Missal, Mass for the Common of the Feast of Our Lady.

[16] A fine paragraph describing the slow but steady development of Marian doctrine in the course of salvation history and in the life of the Church. The Immaculate Conception would be solemnly declared as a dogma by Pius IX, in 1854, four years after Newman delivered this sermon. This paragraph has implications also for the place of women in the Church and in the work of redemption.

worship of the Church, the defence of many truths, the grace and smiling light of every devotion. In thee, O Mary, is fulfilled, as we can bear it, an original purpose of the Most High. He once had meant to come on earth in heavenly glory, but we sinned; and then He could not safely visit us, except with a shrouded radiance and a bedimmed Majesty, for He was God. So He came Himself in weakness, not in power; and He sent thee, a creature, in His stead, with a creature's comeliness and lustre suited to our state. And now thy very face and form, dear Mother, speak to us of the Eternal; not like earthly beauty, dangerous to look upon, but like the morning star, which is thy emblem, bright and musical, breathing purity, telling of heaven, and infusing peace. O harbinger of day! O hope of the pilgrim! lead us still as thou hast led; in the dark night, across the bleak wilderness, guide us on to our Lord Jesus, guide us home.

> Maria, mater gratiae,
> Dulcis parens clementiae.
> Tu nos ab hoste protege
> Et mortis hora suscipe.[17]

a. Sir 42:24	b. Gen 2:1	c. 1 Cor 2:7	d. 1 Cor 2:10
e. Jn 1:14	f. Jn 1:1, 14	g. Jn 1:14	h. Heb 10:5
i. 1 Jn 1:1, 3	j. cf. 1 Jn 4:2–3	k. 1 Jn 4:3	l. cf. Is 7:14; Mt 1:23
m. Is 7:14	n. Song 4:4	o. Lk 11:27	p. Lk 11:28
q. Lk 1:28	r. Lk 1:42	s. cf. Lk 1:45	t. Gen 6:3
u. Gen 6:5	v. Rom 5:20	w. Gen 3:15	x. Prov 4:18
y. Lk 1:28, 38	z. Jn 9:31	aa. Jas 5:16	bb. Gen 20:7
cc. Job 42:8	dd. cf. Ex 17:11–13	ee. cf. Jn 12:20–22	ff. cf. Phil 2:7
gg. cf. Rev 12:1	hh. cf. Acts 1:9	ii. cf. Sir 24:8	jj. cf. Sir 24:10–13, 16

Discourses Addressed to Mixed Congregations. London, 1909, pp. 342–59. This sermon was in the first volume of Newman's Catholic sermons, preached and published in 1849.

[17] Mary, Mother of grace, gentle parent of clemency; from the enemy defend us, and welcome us at the hour of death.

IV

ON THE FITNESS OF THE GLORIES
OF MARY

You may recollect, my brethren, our Lord's words
when on the day of His resurrection He had joined the
two disciples on their way to Emmaus, and found them
sad and perplexed in consequence of His death. He
said, '*Ought not* Christ to suffer these things, and so
enter into His glory?'[a] He appealed to the fitness and
congruity which existed between this otherwise
surprising event and the other truths which had been
revealed concerning the Divine purpose of saving the
world. And so, too, St Paul, in speaking of the same
wonderful appointment of God; 'It *became* Him,' he
says, 'for whom are all things, and through whom are
all things, who had brought many sons unto glory, to
consummate the Author of their salvation by suffering'.[b] Elsewhere, speaking of prophesying, or the
exposition of what is latent in Divine truth, he bids his
brethren exercise the gift 'according to the *analogy*[1] or

---

[1] The *analogia fidei*, the *analogy* or rule of faith, is one of the methods used
by theologians to determine whether a doctrine is truly part of divine
revelation. It means that the doctrine in question fits in harmoniously
and is seen to be consistent with other known truths of Revelation.

rule of faith';[c] that is, so that the doctrine preached may correspond and fit into what is already received. Thus, you see, it is a great evidence of truth, in the case of revealed teaching, that it is so consistent, that it so hangs together, that one thing springs out of another, that each part requires and is required by the rest.

This great principle, which is exemplified so variously in the structure and history of Catholic doctrine, which will receive more and more illustrations the more carefully and minutely we examine the subject, is brought before us especially at this season, when we are celebrating the Assumption of our Blessed Lady, the Mother of God, into heaven. We receive it on the belief of ages; but, viewed in the light of reason, it is the *fitness*[2] of this termination of her earthly course which so persuasively recommends it to our minds: we feel it 'ought' to be; that it 'becomes' her Lord and Son thus to provide for one who was so singular and special, both in herself and her relations to Him. We find that it is simply in harmony with the substance and main outlines of the doctrine of the Incarnation, and that without it Catholic teaching would have a character of incompleteness, and would disappoint our pious expectations.

[2] Another theological method of argumentation, from which divine revelation is investigated and new intuitions are judged, is the so-called argument from 'convenience', viz. its suitableness or fitness. It is used above all in judging the truth of propositions that contain mysteries of the divine life which go far beyond all human comprehension, or for truths that are but very implicitly revealed in sacred Scripture. A very obvious example of its use is in the demonstration of the doctrine of our Lady's bodily Assumption into heaven. It is easy for the eye of faith to see how *fitting* this truth is. Naturally, such theological argumentation needs in a particular manner and in all cases the final authoritative acceptance and approval of the Church.

Let us direct our thoughts to this subject to-day, my brethren; and with a view of helping you to do so, I will first state what the Church has taught and defined from the first ages concerning the Blessed Virgin, and then you sill see how naturally the devotion which her children show her, and the praises with which they honour her, follow from it.

Now, as you know, it has been held from the first, and defined from an early age, that Mary is the Mother of God. She is not merely the Mother of our Lord's manhood, or of our Lord's body, but she is to be considered the Mother of the Word Himself, the Word incarnate. God, in the person of the Word, the Second Person of the All-glorious Trinity, humbled Himself to become her Son. *Non horruisti Virginis uterum*, as the Church sings, 'Thou didst not disdain the Virgin's womb'.[3] He took the substance of His human flesh from her, and clothed in it He lay within her; and He bore it about with Him after birth, as a sort of badge and witness that He, though God, was hers. He was nursed and tended by her; He was suckled by her; He lay in her arms. As time went on, He ministered to her, and obeyed her. He lived with her for thirty years, in one house, with an uninterrupted intercourse, and with only the saintly Joseph to share it with Him. She was the witness of His growth, of His joys, of His sorrows, of His prayers; she was blest with His smile, with the touch of His hand, with the whisper of His affection, with the expression of His thoughts and His feelings, for that length of time. Now, my brethren, what ought she to be, what is it

[3] Cf. above, Text II, p. 124, footnote 9.

becoming that she should be, who was so favoured?

Such a question was once asked by a heathen king, when he would place one of his subjects in a dignity becoming the relation in which the latter stood towards him. That subject had saved the king's life,[4] and what was to be done to him in return? The king asked, 'What should be done to the man whom the king desireth to honour?' And he received the following answer, 'The man whom the king wisheth to honour ought to be clad in the king's apparel, and to be mounted on the king's saddle, and to receive the royal diadem on his head; and let the first among the king's princes and presidents hold his horse, and let him walk through the streets of the city, and say, Thus shall he be honoured, whom the king hath a mind to honour.'[d] So stands the case with Mary; she gave birth to the Creator, and what recompense shall be made her? what shall be done to her, who had this relationship to the Most High? what shall be the fit accompaniment of one whom the Almighty has deigned to make, not His servant, not His friend, not His intimate, but His superior, the source of His second being, the nurse of His helpless infancy, the teacher of His opening years? I answer, as the king was answered: Nothing is too high for her to whom God owes His human life; no exuberance of grace, no excess of glory, but is becoming, but is to be expected there, where God has lodged Himself, whence God has issued. Let her 'be clad in the king's apparel', that is, let the fullness of the Godhead so flow into her that

---

[4] The king referred to was the Persian king Ahasuerus; the subject was Mordecai who had denounced two of the king's guards who had plotted to assassinate him (cf. Esther 6:1–12).

she may be a figure of the incommunicable sanctity, and beauty, and glory, of God Himself: that she may be the Mirror of Justice, the Mystical Rose, the Tower of Ivory, the House of Gold, the Morning Star. Let her 'receive the king's diadem upon her head', as the Queen of heaven, the Mother of all living, the Health of the weak, the Refuge of sinners, the Comforter of the afflicted.[5] And 'let the first amongst the king's princes walk before her', let angels and prophets, and apostles, and martyrs, and all saints, kiss the hem of her garment and rejoice under the shadow of her throne. Thus is it that King Solomon[6] has risen up to meet his mother, and bowed himself unto her, and caused a seat to be set for the king's mother, and she sits on his right hand.[e]

We should be prepared then, my brethren, to believe that the Mother of God is full of grace and glory, from the very fitness of such a dispensation, even though we had not been taught it; and this fitness will appear still more clear and certain when we contemplate the subject more steadily. Consider then, that it has been the ordinary rule of God's dealings with us, that personal sanctity should be the attendant upon high spiritual dignity of place or work. The angels, who, as the word imports, are God's messengers, are also perfect in holiness; 'without sanctity, no one shall see God';[f] no defiled thing can enter the courts of heaven; and the higher its inhabitants are advanced in their ministry about the throne, the holier are they, and the more absorbed in their

---

[5] Titles attributed to our Lady in the Litany of Loreto.
[6] Newman now changes his reference from King Ahasuerus to King Solomon, who indicates Christ.

contemplation of that Holiness upon which they wait. The Seraphim, who immediately surround the Divine Glory, cry day and night, 'Holy, Holy, Holy, Lord God of Hosts'.[g] So is it also on earth; the prophets have ordinarily not only gifts but graces; they are not only inspired to know and to teach God's will, but inwardly converted to obey it. For surely those only can preach the truth duly who feel it personally; those only transmit it fully from God to man, who have in the transmission made it their own.[7]

I do not say that there are no exceptions to this rule, but they admit of an easy explanation; I do not say that it never pleases Almighty God to convey any intimation of His will through bad men; of course, for all things can be made to serve Him. By all, even the wicked, He accomplishes His purposes, and by the wicked He is glorified. Our Lord's death was brought about by His enemies, who did His will, while they thought they were gratifying their own. Caiaphas, who contrived and effected it, was made use of to predict it.[h] Balaam prophesied good of God's people in an earlier age, by a Divine compulsion, when he wished to prophesy evil.[i] This is true; but in such cases Divine Mercy is plainly overruling the evil, and mani-

---

[7] An important observation not only for preaching but for life in general. It is not so much what we *say* that influences people, but what we *are*; to *appear* as great is no substitute for *being* great. The influence of Newman's own preaching stemmed in no small degree from his personal conviction and holiness. The profound spirituality both of the man and of his teaching conferred on his sermons their power of persuasion. He appeared in the pulpit as a man living in an unseen world, a man with a vision, and an urgency to share it with others. The evident sincerity of his teaching, supported by the experience of his personal life, gave his already gifted speech an ascendancy over the hearts of a large and varied congregation.

festing His power, without recognizing or sanctioning the instrument. And again, it is true, as He tells us Himself, that in the last day 'Many shall say, Lord, Lord, have we not prophesied in Thy Name, and in Thy Name cast out devils, and done many miracles?' and that He shall answer, 'I never knew you'.[j] This, I say, is undeniable; it is undeniable first, that those who have prophesied in God's Name may *afterwards* fall from God, and lose their souls. Let a man be ever so holy now, he may fall away; and, as present grace is no pledge of perseverance, much less are present gifts; but how does this show that gifts and graces do not commonly go together? Again, it is undeniable that those who have had miraculous gifts may nevertheless have *never* been in God's favour, not even when they exercised them; as I will explain presently. But I am now speaking, not of having gifts, but of being prophets. To be a prophet is something much more personal than to possess gifts. It is a sacred office, it implies a mission, and is the high distinction, not of the enemies of God, but of His friends. Such is the Scripture rule. Who was the first prophet and preacher of justice? Enoch, who walked 'by faith', and 'pleased God',[k] and was taken from a rebellious world. Who was the second? 'Noe', who 'condemned the world and was made heir of the justice which is through faith.'[l] Who was the next great prophet? Moses, the lawgiver of the chosen people, who was the 'meekest of all men who dwell on the earth'.[m] Samuel comes next, who served the Lord from his infancy in the Temple;[n] and then David, who, if he fell into sin, repented, and was 'a man after God's heart'.[o] And in like manner Job, Elias, Isaias, Jeremias, Daniel, and above them all St John Baptist, and then again St Peter, St Paul, St John, and the rest, are all especial instances of heroic virtue, and patterns to their brethren. Judas is the exception, but this was by a particular dispensation to enhance our Lord's humiliation and suffering.

Nature itself witnesses to this connexion between sanctity and truth. It anticipates that the fountain from which pure doctrine comes should itself be pure; that the seat of Divine teaching, and the oracle of faith should be the abode of angels; that the consecrated home, in which the Word of God is elaborated, and whence it issues forth for the salvation of the many, should be holy, as that Word itself is holy. Here you see the difference of the office of a prophet and a mere gift, such as that of miracles. Miracles are the simple and direct work of God; the worker of them is but an instrument or organ. And in consequence he need not be holy, because he has not, strictly speaking, a share in the work. So again the power of administering the Sacraments, which also is supernatural and miraculous, does not imply personal holiness; nor is there anything surprising in God's giving to a bad man this gift, or the gift of miracles, any more than in His giving him any natural talent or gift, strength or agility of frame, eloquence, or medical skill. It is otherwise with the office of preaching and prophesying, and to this I have been referring; for the truth first goes into the minds of the speakers, and is apprehended and fashioned there, and then comes out from them as, in one sense, its source and its parent. The Divine word is begotten in them, and the offspring has their features and tells of them. They are not like 'the dumb animal, speaking with man's voice', on which Balaam rode, a mere instrument of God's word;[p] but they have 'received an unction from the Holy One, and they know all things',[q] and 'where the Spirit of the Lord is, there is liberty';[r] and while they deliver what they have received, they enforce what they feel and know. 'We have *known and believed*', says St John, 'the charity which God hath to us'.[s]

So has it been all through the history of the Church; Moses does not write as David; nor Isaias as Jeremias; nor St John as St Paul. And so of the great doctors of the Church, St Athanasius, St Augustine, St Ambrose, St Leo, St Thomas, each has his own manner, each speaks his own words, though he speaks the while the words of God. They speak from themselves, they speak in their own persons, they speak from the heart, from their own experience, with their own arguments, with their own deductions, with their own modes of expression. Now can you fancy, my brethren, such hearts, such feelings to be unholy? how could it be so, without defiling, and thereby nullifying, the word of God? If one drop of corruption makes the purest water worthless, as the slightest savour of bitterness spoils the most delicate viands, how can it be that the word of truth and holiness can proceed profitably from impure lips and an earthly heart? No; as is the tree, so is the fruit; 'beware of false prophets,' says our Lord; and then He adds, 'from their fruits ye shall know them. Do men gather grapes of thorns, or figs of thistles?'[t] Is it not so, my brethren? which of you would go to ask counsel of another, however learned, however gifted, however aged, if you thought him unholy? nay, though you feel and

are sure, as far as absolution goes, that a bad priest
could give it as really as a holy priest, yet for advice,
for comfort, for instruction, you would not go to one
whom you did not respect. 'Out of the abundance of
the heart, the mouth speaketh;'[u] 'a good man out of
the good treasure of his heart bringeth forth good, and
an evil man out of the evil treasure bringeth forth
evil.'[v]

So then is it in the case of the soul; but, as regards
the Blessed Mary, a further thought suggests itself. She
has no chance place in the Divine Dispensation; the
Word of God did not merely come to her and go from
her; He did not pass through her, as He visits us in
Holy Communion. It was no heavenly body which
the Eternal Son assumed, fashioned by the angels, and
brought down to this lower world:[8] no; He imbibed,
He absorbed into His Divine Person, her blood and
the substance of her flesh; by becoming man of her,
He received her lineaments and features, as the appropriate character in which He was to manifest Himself
to mankind. The child is like the parent, and we may
well suppose that by His likeness to her was manifested by her relationship to Him. Her sanctity comes,
not only of her being His mother, but also of His
being her son. 'If the first fruit be holy,' says St Paul,

---

[8] The reality of Christ's humanity is certified by his birth in a natural
way from the Virgin Mary. This is a truth emphasized in Patristic
teaching. For example, St Athanasius writes: 'Gabriel announced the
good news to Mary with all clarity: he did not say simply: "what is
born in you", in case it might be thought that the body had been
introduced into her from outside; he said: "what is born of you",
so that it would be accepted that what she gave birth to, came from her
in the natural way' (*Letter to Epictetus*, 5, in Migne, *Patrologia Graeca* 26,
1058: henceforth abbreviated: *PG*).

'the mass also is holy; if the mass be holy, so are the branches.'[w] And hence the titles which we are accustomed to give her. He is the Wisdom of God, she therefore is the Seat of Wisdom; His Presence is Heaven, she therefore is the Gate of Heaven; He is infinite Mercy, she then is the Mother of Mercy. She is the Mother of 'fair love and fear, and knowledge and holy hope';[x] is it wonderful then that she has left behind her in the Church below 'an odour like cinnamon and balm, and sweetness like to choice myrrh'?[y]

Such, then, is the truth ever cherished in the deep heart of the Church, and witnessed by the keen apprehension of her children, that no limits but those proper to a creature can be assigned to the sanctity of Mary.[9] Therefore, did Abraham believe that a son should be born to him of his aged wife?[z] then Mary's faith must be held as greater when she accepted Gabriel's message. Did Judith consecrate her widowhood to God to the surprise of her people?[aa] much more did Mary, from her first youth, devote her virginity. Did Samuel, when a child, inhabit the Temple, secluded from the world?[bb] Mary too was by her parents lodged in the same holy precincts, even at the age when children first can choose between good and evil. Was Solomon on his birth called 'dear to the Lord?'[cc] and shall not the destined Mother of God be dear to Him from the moment she was born? But further still; St John Baptist was sanctified by the Spirit before his birth;[dd] shall Mary be only equal to him? is it not fitting that her privilege should surpass his? is it

---

[9] These are theological truths indicating the unsuspected greatness of the Mother of God. Newman tries to dispel any fear of Marian 'idolatry' in the hearts of his Anglican listeners.

wonderful, if grace, which anticipated his birth by
three months, should in her case run up to the very
first moment of her being, outstrip the imputation of
sin, and be beforehand with the usurpation of Satan?
Mary must surpass all the saints; the very fact that
certain privileges are known to have been theirs
persuades us, almost from the necessity of the case,
that she had the same and higher. Her conception was
immaculate, in order that she might surpass all saints
in the date as well as the fullness of her sanctification.[10]

But in a festive season, my dear brethren, I must not
weary you with argument, when we should offer
specially to the Blessed Virgin the homage of our love
and loyalty; yet, let me finish as I have begun; I will
be brief, but bear with me if I view her bright
Assumption, as I have viewed her immaculate purity,
rather as a point of doctrine than as a theme for devotion.

It was surely fitting then, it was becoming, that she
should be taken up into heaven and not lie in the grave
till Christ's second coming, who had passed a life of
sanctity and of miracle such as hers. All the works of
God are in a beautiful harmony; they are carried on to
the end as they begin. This is the difficulty which men
of the world find in believing miracles at all; they think
these break the order and consistency of God's visible
word, not knowing that they do but subserve a higher
order of things, and introduce a supernatural perfection. But at least, my brethren, when one miracle is
wrought, it may be expected to draw others after it for

---

[10] To appreciate the force and precision of his argumentation, we should
   remember that the definitive proclamation of the Immaculate
   Conception had not yet been given by the Church.

the completion of what is begun. Miracles must be wrought for some great end; and if the course of things fell back again into a natural order before its termination, how could we but feel a disappointment? and if we were told that this certainly was to be, how could we but judge the information improbable and difficult to believe? Now this applies to the history of our Lady. I say, it would be a greater miracle if, her life being what it was, her death was like that of other men, than if it were such as to correspond to her life. Who can conceive, my brethren, that God should so repay the debt, which He condescended to owe to His Mother, for the elements of His human body, as to allow the flesh and blood from it was taken to moulder in the grave? Do the sons of men thus deal with their mothers? do they not nourish and sustain them in their feebleness, and keep them in life while they are able? Or who can conceive that that virginal frame, which never sinned, was to undergo the death of a sinner? Why should she share the curse of Adam, who had no share in his fall? 'Dust thou art, and into dust thou shalt return',[ee] was the sentence upon sin; she then, who was not a sinner, fitly never saw corruption. She died, then, as we hold, because even our Lord and Saviour died; she died, as she suffered, because she was in this world, because she was in a state of things in which suffering and death are the rule. She lived under their external sway; and, as she obeyed Caesar by coming for enrolment to Bethlehem,[ff] so did she, when God willed it, yield to the tyranny of death, and was dissolved into soul and body, as well as others. But though she died as well as others, she died not as others die; for, through the merits of her Son, by whom she was what she was, by the grace of Christ which in her had anticipated sin, which had filled her with light, which had purified her flesh from all defilement, she was also saved from disease and malady, and all that weakens and decays the bodily frame. Original sin had not been found in her, by the wear of her senses, and the waste of her frame, and the decrepitude of years, propagating death. She died, but her death was a mere fact, not an effect; and, when it was over, it ceased to be. She died that she might live, she died as a matter of form or (as I may call it) an observance, in order to fulfil, what is called, the debt of nature,—not primarily for herself or because of sin, but to submit herself to her condition, to glorify God, to do what her Son did; not however as her Son and Saviour, with any suffering for any special end; not with a martyr's death, for her martyrdom had been in living; not as an atonement, for man could not make it, and One had made it, and made it for all; but in order to finish her course, and to receive her crown.

And therefore she died in private. It became Him, who died for the world, to die in the world's sight; it became the Great Sacrifice to be lifted up on high, as a light that could not be hid. But she, the lily of Eden, who had always dwelt out of the sight of man, fittingly did she die in the garden's shade, and amid the sweet flowers in which she had lived. Her departure made no noise in the world. The Church went about her common duties, preaching, converting, suffering; there were persecutions, there was fleeing from place to place, there were martyrs, there were triumphs; at length the rumour spread abroad that the Mother of God was no longer upon earth. Pilgrims went to and fro; they sought for her relics, but they found them

not; did she die at Ephesus? or did she die at
Jerusalem? reports varied; but her tomb could not be
pointed out, or if it was found, it was open; and
instead of her pure and fragrant body, there was a
growth of lilies from the earth which she had touched.
So inquirers went home marvelling, and waiting for
further light. And then it was said, how that when her
dissolution was at hand, and her soul was to pass in
triumph before the judgment-seat of her Son, the
apostles were suddenly gathered together in the place,
even in the Holy City, to bear part in the joyful ceremonial; how that they buried her with fitting rites;
how that the third day, when they came to the tomb,
they found it empty, and angelic choirs with their glad
voices were heard singing day and night the glories of
their risen Queen. But, however we feel towards the
details of this history (nor is there anything in it which
will be unwelcome or difficult to piety), so much
cannot be doubted, from the consent of the whole
Catholic world and the revelations made to holy souls,
that, as is befitting, she is, soul and body, with her Son
and God in heaven, and that we are enabled to celebrate, not only her death, but her Assumption.[11]

---

[11] For details on Newman's thoughts about the Assumption, cf. above:
Introduction IV, pp. 72–78. Richard H. Hutton recalls the effect of
these words on his non-Catholic listeners. 'I know no passage in
Newman which so thoroughly bewilders the Protestant imagination,
in its unwillingness to accept vague tradition of the most distant and
uncertain origin, as evidence for historic fact, as that in which he deals
with the death of the mother of Christ' (*Cardinal Newman*, pp.
201–2). Hutton, a staunch Protestant at the time but who was to
become more and more sympathetic to High Anglican concepts as
the years went on, mentions the extreme difficulties Protestants found
in accepting the Catholic Church's claim.

And now, my dear brethren, what is befitting in us, if all that I have been telling you is befitting in Mary?[12] If the Mother of Emmanuel ought to be the first of creatures in sanctity and in beauty; if it became her to be free from all sin from the very first, and from the moment she received her first grace to begin to merit more; and if such as was her beginning, such was her end, her conception immaculate and her death an assumption; if she died, but revived, and is exalted on high; what is befitting in the children of such a Mother, but an imitation, in their measure, of her devotion, her meekness, her simplicity, her modesty, and her sweetness? Her glories are not only for the sake of her Son, they are for our sakes also. Let us copy her faith, who received God's message by the angel without a doubt; her patience, who endured St Joseph's surprise without a word; her obedience, who went up to Bethlehem in the winter and bore our Lord in a stable; her meditative spirit, who pondered in her heart what she saw and heard about Him: her fortitude, whose heart the sword went through; her self-surrender, who gave Him up during His ministry and consented to His death.

Above all, let us imitate her purity, who, rather than relinquish her virginity, was willing to lose Him for a Son.[13] O my dear children, young men and

---

[12] Imitation of Mary's virtues is the heart of true devotion. It has been stated authoritatively by the Second Vatican Council: 'Let the faithful remember moreover that true devotion consists neither in sterile nor transitory affection, nor in a certain vain credulity, but proceeds from true faith, by which we are led to recognize the excellence of the Mother of God, and we are moved to a filial love towards our Mother and to the imitation of her virtues' (Dogmatic Constitution on the Church, *Lumen Gentium*, 67).

[13] Cf. the same thought above, pp. 139–141 and below pp. 168–174.

young women,[14] what need have you of the intercession of the Virgin-mother, of her help, of her pattern,
in this respect! What shall bring you forward in the
narrow way, if you live in the world, but the thought
and patronage of Mary? What shall seal your senses,
what shall tranquillise your heart, when sights and
sounds of danger are around you, but Mary? What
shall give you patience and endurance, when you are
wearied out with the length of the conflict with evil,
with the unceasing necessity of precautions, with the
irksomeness of observing them, with the tediousness
of their repetition, with the strain upon your mind,
with your forlorn and cheerless condition, but a
loving communion with her! She will comfort you in
your discouragements, solace you in your fatigues,
raise you after your falls, reward you for your
successes. She will show you her Son, your God and
your all. When you spirit within you is excited, or
relaxed, or depressed, when it loses its balance, when
it is restless and wayward, when it is sick of what it
has, and hankers after what it has not, when your eye
is solicited with evil and your mortal frame trembles
under the shadow of the tempter, what will bring you
to yourselves, to peace and to health, but the cool
breath of the Immaculate and the fragrance of the
Rose of Sharon? It is the boast of the Catholic
Religion, that it has the gift of making the young
heart chaste; and why is this, but that it gives us Jesus
Christ for our food, and Mary for our nursing
Mother? Fulfil this boast in yourselves; prove to the

---

[14] Newman ends with a paragraph of lyrical beauty and intense devotion.

world that you are following no false teaching, vindi-
cate the glory of your Mother Mary, whom the world
blasphemes, in the very face of the world, by the
simplicity of your own deportment, and the sanctity
of your words and deeds. Go to her for the royal heart
of innocence. She is the beautiful gift of God, which
outshines the fascinations of a bad world, and which
no one ever sought in sincerity and was disappointed.
She is the personal type and representative image of
that spiritual life and renovation in grace, 'without
which no one shall see God'.[gg] 'Her spirit is sweeter
than honey, and her heritage than the honeycomb.
They that eat her shall yet be hungry, and they that
drink her shall still thirst. Whoso hearkeneth to her
shall not be confounded, and they that work by her
shall not sin.'[hh]

a. Lk 24:26	b. Heb 2:10	c. cf. Rom 12:6
d. Est 6:6–7	e. cf. 1 Kings 2:19	f. Heb 12:14
g. Is 6:3	h. cf. Jn 18:14	i. cf. Num 24:1–9
j. Mt 7:22–3	k. cf. Gen 5:22; Heb 11:5	l. Heb 11:7
m. Num 12:3	n. 1 Sam 2:18	o. Acts 13:22
p. cf. 2 Pet 2:16; cf. Num 22:28–30	q. 1 Jn 2:20	r. 2 Cor 3:17
s. 1 Jn 4:16	t. Mt 7:15, 16	u. Mt 12:34
v. Mt 12:35; Lk 6:45	w. Rom 11:16	x. Sir 24:18
y. Sir 24:15	z. cf. Gen 18:1–15	aa. cf. Jdt 8:1–8
bb. cf. 1 Sam 1:24–28; 2:18–19	cc. cf. 2 Sam 12:24	dd. cf. Luk 1:41
ee. Gen 3:19	ff. cf. Lk 2:4	gg. Heb 12:14
hh. Sir 24:20–22		

Discourses Addressed to Mixed Congregations, London, 1909, pp. 360–76.
This sermon was in the first volume of Newman's Catholic sermons, preached and
published in 1849.

V

OUR LADY IN THE GOSPEL[1]

There is a passage in the Gospel of this day which may
have struck many of us as needing some illustration.
While our Lord was preaching, a woman in the crowd
cried out,[2] 'Blessed is the womb that bore Thee, and
the breasts which Thou hast sucked'.[a] Our Lord
assents, but instead of dwelling on the good words of
this woman, He goes on to say something further. He
speaks of a greater blessedness. 'Yea,' He says, 'but
blessed are they who hear the word of God and keep
it.'[b] Now, these words of our Lord require notice, if
it were only for this reason, because there are many

---

[1] This sermon was preached in St Chad's Cathedral, Birmingham, on
the third Sunday of Lent, 26 March 1848. It is among the first group
of sermons Newman preached a few months after his return in
December 1847 from Rome, where he had been ordained a priest in
the Catholic Church (30 May 1847).

[2] As an Anglican, Newman wrote out his sermons with exact references
to Scripture. He read them as was customary in the Anglican Church.
After his conversion, he endeavoured to conform to the Catholic
custom of preaching more freely without reading from a prepared text.
Consequently, for most of his Catholic sermons, he only jotted down
a general outline or schematic notes, and when he did write out his
text he gave no scriptural references, or at most incomplete ones.

persons nowadays who think they are said in depreci-
ation of the glory and blessedness of the Most Holy
Virgin Mary; as if our Lord had said, 'My Mother is
blessed, but My true servants are more blessed than
she is'. I shall say some words then on this passage, and
with a peculiar fitness, because we have just passed the
festival of Lady Day,[3] the great feast on which we
commemorate the Annunciation, that is, the visit of
the Angel Gabriel to her, and the miraculous conception of the Son of God, her Lord and Saviour, in her
womb.

Now, a very few words will be sufficient to show
that our Lord's words are no disparagement to the
dignity and glory of His Mother, as the first of creatures and the Queen of all Saints. For consider, He
says that it is a more blessed thing to keep His
commandments than to be His Mother, and do you
think that the Most Holy Mother of God did not keep
the commandments of God? Of course no one—no
Protestant even—no one will deny she did.[4] Well, if
so, what our Lord says is that the Blessed Virgin was
more blessed in that she kept His commandments than
because she was His Mother. And what Catholic
denies this? On the contrary, we all confess it. All
Catholics confess it. The holy Fathers of the Church
tell us again and again that our Lady was more blessed
in doing God's will than in being His Mother. She
was blessed in two ways. She was blessed in being His

---

[3] Lady Day, i.e. the Feast of the Annunciation, 25 March, which fell the
day before this sermon was preached.

[4] Notice the almost colloquial style. Newman is making a noticeable
effort at adapting to Catholic ways, or as he himself expressed it,
'throwing himself into the system'.

Mother; she was blessed in being filled with the spirit of faith and obedience. And the latter blessedness was the greater. I say the holy Fathers say so expressly. St Augustine says: 'More blessed was Mary in receiving the faith of Christ, than in receiving the flesh of Christ.'[5] In like manner St Elizabeth says to her at the Visitation, '*Beata es quae credidisti*—Blessed art thou who didst believe';[c] and St Chrysostom goes so far as to say that she would not have been blessed, even though she had borne Christ in the body, unless she had heard the word of God and kept it.[6]

Now, I have used the expression 'St Chrysostom goes *so far* as to say', not that it is not a plain truth. I say it is a plain truth that the Blessed Virgin would not have been blessed, though she had been the Mother of God, if she had not done His will; but it is an extreme thing to say, for it is supposing a thing impossible, it is

---

[5] Many spiritual authors have been at pains to demonstrate that our Lord's words to the anonymous woman in the crowd (cf. Lk 11:28) were no disparagement to his Blessed Mother. It is no wonder that Newman, who was so familiar with the writings of the Fathers of the Church, should have recalled the best-known defence from Patristic times, namely, that by St Augustine: with these words (Lk 11:27–8), Jesus 'taught us to consider blessed not those who boast of kinship or consanguinity with upright and holy people, but those who by obedience and imitation follow their conduct. Just like Mary who, if she was blessed for having conceived the body of Christ, was much more so because she believed in Christ' (*De sacra Virginitate*, 3.3). Commenting on the same passage elsewhere, St Augustine affirmed: 'My mother, too, whom you call blessed, is blessed because she keeps the word of God, not because the Word was made flesh in her and lived among us. She is blessed because she keeps the very Word of God through whom she was made and who was made flesh in her. People should not be satisfied with joy in a temporal offspring; they should rejoice rather in being joined spiritually to God' (*In Ioannis Evang.*, 10.3.)

[6] *In Matthei Evang.*, 12.48.

supposing that she could be so highly favoured and yet
not be inhabited and possessed by God's grace,
whereas the Angel, when he came, expressly hailed
her as full of grace. '*Ave, gratia plena*'.[d] The two
blessednesses cannot be divided. (Still it is remarkable
that she herself had an opportunity of contrasting and
dividing them, and that she preferred to keep God's
commandments to being His Mother, if she could not
have both.) She who was chosen to be the Mother of
God was also chosen to be *gratia plena*, full of grace.
This you see is an explanation of those high doctrines
which are received among Catholics concerning the
purity and sinlessness of the Blessed Virgin. St
Augustine will not listen to the notion that she ever
committed sin,[7] and the Holy Council of Trent
declares that by special privilege she through all her
life avoided all, even venial sin.[8] And at this time you
know it is the received belief of Catholics that she was
not conceived in original sin, and that her conception
was immaculate.[9]

[7] Newman refers here to a famous passage on our Lady in the writings
of St Augustine where he discusses the sinlessness of the Blessed Virgin
Mary. Scholars discuss whether the Bishop of Hippo includes in this
text freedom from original sin as well as from all personal sin. In
all probability he also includes it at least indirectly, given the all-
embracing Christological grounds he mentions, namely Mary's
relation to her Son: *propter honorem Domini*: 'Hence we exclude the
Blessed Virgin Mary, in whose regard, for the honour of the Lord, I
do not wish any mention of sin to be made' (*De natura et gratia*, 36.42).

[8] Cf. Council of Trent, Decree on Justification, Canon 23: 'If anyone
affirms that a person, once he has been justified, can avoid all sin,
including venial sin, throughout the whole of life, without a special
privilege from God, as the Church believes concerning the Blessed
Virgin, let him be anathema' (Denzinger-Schönmetzer, No. 1573).

[9] Newman is speaking six years before the solemn proclamation of the
dogma of the Immaculate Conception by Pope Pius IX in 1854.

Whence come these doctrines? They come from the great principle contained in our Lord's words on which I am commenting. He says: 'More blessed is it to do God's will than to be God's Mother.'[e] Do not say that Catholics do not feel this deeply—so deeply do they feel it that they are ever enlarging on her virginity, purity, immaculateness, faith, humility, and obedience. Never say, then, that Catholics forget this passage of Scripture. Whenever they keep the Feast of the Immaculate Conception, the Purity,[10] or the like, recollect it is because they make so much of the blessedness of sanctity. The woman in the crowd cried out, 'Blessed is the womb and the breasts of Mary'. She spoke in faith; she did not mean to exclude her higher blessedness, but her words only went a certain way. Therefore our Lord completed them. And therefore His Church after Him, dwelling on the great and sacred mystery of His Incarnation, has ever felt that she, who so immediately ministered to it, must have been most holy. And therefore for the honour of the Son she has ever extolled the glory of the Mother.[11] As we give Him of our best, ascribe to Him what is best, as on earth we make our churches costly and beautiful; as when He was taken down from the Cross, His pious servants wrapped Him in fine linen, and laid Him in a tomb in which never man was laid;[f]

---

[10] The Feast of the Purity of the Blessed Virgin Mary was then celebrated in some places (including England) on the third Sunday of October.

[11] Newman's thought with regard to Marian belief and devotion is closely connected with the mystery of the Incarnation and with Christological truths. Another sermon he was to preach two years later would underline this fact and bear the title: 'The Glories of Mary for the Sake of her Son' (cf. above, Text III, pp. 129–48).

as His dwelling-place in heaven is pure and stainless—
so much more ought to be—so much more was—that
tabernacle from which He took flesh, in which He
lay, holy and immaculate and divine. As a body was
prepared for Him, so was the place of that body
prepared also. Before the Blessed Mary could be
Mother of God, and in order to her being Mother, she
was set apart, sanctified, filled with grace, and made
meet for the presence of the Eternal.

And the holy Fathers have ever gathered the exact
obedience and the sinlessness of the Blessed Virgin
from the very narrative of the Annunciation, when she
became the Mother of God. For when the Angel
appeared to her and declared to her the will of God,
they say that she displayed especially four graces—
humility, faith, obedience, and purity. Nay, these
graces were as it were, preparatory conditions to her
being made the minister of so high a dispensation. So
that if she had not had faith, and humility, and purity,
and obedience, she would not have merited to be
God's Mother. Thus it is common to say that she
conceived Christ in mind before she conceived Him in
body,[12] meaning that the blessedness of faith and
obedience preceded the blessedness of being a Virgin
Mother. Nay, they even say that God waited for her

[12] These thoughts are expressed by various Church Fathers when
commenting on the scene of the Annunciation. In particular, they
stress the living faith of our Lady whereby she spiritually conceived
the Word of God by believing the message announced to her by the
angel Gabriel. St Augustine writes: 'The Blessed Virgin brought by
faith what she had conceived by faith ... full of faith and conceiving
Christ in her mind before she conceived him in her womb' (*Sermon*
215.4). St Leo the Great, in one of his admirable Christmas homilies,
expresses the same idea: 'A royal Virgin ... conceives a son, the God-
Man, in her mind before doing so in her body' (*Sermon* 21.1).

consent before He came into her and took flesh of her. Just as He did no mighty works in one place because they had not faith,[g] so this great miracle, by which He became the Son of a creature, was suspended till she was tried and found meet for it – till she obeyed.[h]

But there is something more to be added to this. I said just now that the two blessednesses could not be divided, that they went together. 'Blessed is the womb', etc.; 'Yea rather, blessed', etc. It is true, but observe this. The holy Fathers always teach that in the Annunciation, when the Angel appeared to our Lady, she showed that she preferred what our Lord called the greater of the two blessednesses to the other. For when the Angel announced to her that she was destined to have that blessedness which Jewish women had age after age looked out for, to be the Mother of the expected Christ, she did not seize the news, as another would, but she waited. She waited till she could be told it was consistent with her virgin state. She was unwilling to accept this most wonderful honour, unwilling till she could be satisfied on this point. 'How shall this be, since I know not man?'[i] They consider that she had made a vow of virginity, and considered that holy estate a greater thing than to bear the Christ. Such is the teaching of the Church, showing distinctly how closely she observes the doctrine of the words of Scripture on which I am commenting, how intimately she considers that the Blessed Mary felt them, viz. that though blessed was the womb that bore Christ and the breasts which He sucked, yet more blessed was the soul who owned that womb and those breasts, more blessed was the soul full of grace, which because it was so gracious was rewarded with the extraordinary privilege to be made the Mother of God.

But now a further question arises which it may be worth considering. It may be asked, Why did our blessed Lord *seem* to extenuate the honour and privilege of His Mother? When the woman said, 'Blessed is the womb', etc., He answered indeed, '*Yea.*' But He went on, 'Yea rather, blessed'.[j] And on another occasion, if not on this, He said when someone told Him that His Mother and brethren were without, 'Who is My Mother?'[k] etc. And at an earlier time, when He began His miracles and His Mother told Him that the guests in the marriage feast had no wine, He said: 'Woman, what have I to do with thee? Mine hour is not yet come.'[l] These passages seem to be coldly worded towards the Blessed Virgin, even though the sense may be satisfactorily explained. What, then, do they mean? Why did He so speak?

Now I shall give two reasons in explanation:

1. The first, which more immediately rises out of what I have been saying is this: that for many centuries the Jewish women had looked out each of them to be the mother of the expected Christ, and had not associated it apparently with any higher sanctity. Therefore they had been so desirous of marriage; therefore marriage was held in such special honour by them. Now, marriage is an ordinance of God, and Christ has made it a sacrament – yet there is a higher state, and that the Jews did not understand. Their whole idea was to associate religion with pleasures of this world. They did not know, commonly speaking, what it was to give up this world for the next. They did not understand that poverty was better than riches, ill name than good name, fast and abstinence than feasting, and virginity than marriage. And therefore when the woman in the crowd cried out upon the blessedness of the womb that bore Him and the breasts that He had sucked, He taught her and all who heard Him that the soul was greater than the body, and that to be united to Him in spirit was more than to be united to Him in flesh.

2. This is one reason, and the other is more interesting to us. You know that our Saviour for the first thirty years of His earthly life lived under the same roof as His Mother. When He returned from Jerusalem at the age of twelve with her and St Joseph, it is expressly said that He was subject to them.[m] This is a very strong expression, but that subjection, that familiar family life, was not to last to the end. Even on the occasion upon which the Evangelist says that He was subject to them, He had said and done what emphatically conveyed to them that He had other duties. For He had left them and stayed in the Temple among the doctors, and when they expressed surprise, He answered, 'Wist ye not that I ought to be in the things which are My Father's?'[n] This was, I say, an anticipation of the time of His ministry, when He was to leave His home. For thirty years He remained there, but as He was steadily observant of His home duties while they were His duties, so was He zealous about His Father's work, when the time came for His performing it. When the time of His mission came, He left His home and His Mother and, dear as she was to Him, He put her aside.

In the Old Testament the Levites are praised because they knew not father or mother when duty to God came in the way. 'Who said to his father and to his mother, I know you not, and to his brothers, I am ignorant of you.' 'They knew not their children.'[o] If such was the conduct of the sacerdotal tribe under the Law, well did it become the great and one Priest of the New Covenant to give a pattern of that virtue which was found and rewarded in Levi. He, too, Himself has said: 'He who loveth father or mother more than Me is not worthy of Me.'[p] And he tells us that 'every one who hath left home or brothers or sisters or father or mother or wife or children or lands for His name's sake, shall receive a hundredfold and shall possess eternal life.'[q] It became, then, Him who gave the precept to set the example; and as He told His followers to leave all they had for the Kingdom's sake, in *His own Person* to do all that He could, to leave all He had, to leave His home and His Mother, when He had to preach the Gospel.

Therefore it was that from the beginning of His ministry, He gave up His Mother. At the time He did His first miracle, He proclaimed it. He did that miracle at her bidding, but He implied, or rather declared, that He was then beginning to separate from her. He said, 'What is between Me and thee?' And again, 'My hour is not yet come';[r] that is 'the hour cometh when I shall acknowledge thee again, O My Mother. The hour cometh when thou rightly and powerfully wilt intercede with Me. The hour cometh when at thy bidding I will do miracles: it cometh, but it is not yet come. And till it is come, What is between thee and Me? I know thee not. For the time I have forgotten thee.'

From that time we have no record of His seeing His Mother till He saw her under His Cross. He parted with her. Once she tried to see Him. A report went about that He was beside Himself. His friends went out to get possession of Him.[s] The Blessed Virgin apparently did not like to be left behind. She went out, too. A message came to Him that they were seeking Him, could not reach Him for the press. Then He said those serious words, 'Who is My Mother?'[t] etc., meaning, as it would appear, that He had left all for God's service, and that, as for our sake He had been born of the Virgin, so for our sake He gave up His Virgin Mother that He might glorify His heavenly Father and do His work.

Such was His separation from the Blessed Mary, but when on the Cross He said, 'It is finished',[u] this time of separation was at an end. And therefore just before it His blessed Mother had joined Him, and He, seeing her, recognized her again. His hour was come, and He said to her of St John, 'Woman, behold thy son', and to St John, 'Behold thy Mother'.[v]

And now, my brethren, in conclusion I will but say one thing. I do not wish your words to outrun your real feeling. I do not wish you to take up books containing the praises of the Ever Blessed Virgin, and to use them and imitate them rashly without consideration. But be sure of this, that if you cannot enter into the warmth of foreign books of devotion, it is a deficiency in you.[13] To use strong words will not

---

[13] This is one of the very few occasions where Newman recommends the warmth of devotion expressed at the time in books from Latin countries. While Faber had no difficulty with it, Newman advocated greater moderation, in line with the English character.

mend the matter; it is a fault within which can only gradually be overcome, but it is a deficiency, for this reason if for no other. Depend upon it, the way to enter into the sufferings of the Son is to enter into the sufferings of the Mother. Place yourselves at the foot of the Cross, see Mary standing there, looking up and pierced with the sword.[w] Imagine her feelings, make them your own. Let her be your great pattern. Feel what she felt and you will worthily mourn over the death and Passion of your and her Saviour. Have her simple faith and you will believe well. Pray to be filled with the grace given to her. Alas, you must have many feelings she had not, the feeling of personal sin, of personal sorrow, of contrition, and self-hate, but these will in a sinner naturally accompany the faith, the humility, the simplicity which were her great ornaments. Lament with her, believe with her, and at length you will experience her blessedness of which the text speaks. None indeed can have her special prerogative and be the Mother of the Highest, but you will have a share in that blessedness of hers which is greater, the blessedness of doing God's will and keeping His commandments.

a. Lk 11:27	b Lk 11:28	c. Lk 1:45
d. Lk 1:28	e. cf. Lk 11:27–8; 8:20–1	f. cf. Mt 27:59–60
g. cf. Mt 13:58	h. cf. Lk 1:26–38	i. Lk 1:34
j. Lk 11:27–8	k. Mt 12:48; Mk 3:33	l. Jn 2:4
m. cf. Lk 2:51	n. Lk 2:49	o. Dt 33:9
p. Mt 10:37	q. Mt 19:29	r. Jn 2:4
s. cf. Mk 3:20–1	t. Mt 12:46–50	u. Jn 19:30
v. Jn 19:26–7	w. cf. Lk 2:35	

Catholic Sermons of Cardinal Newman, Preached on 26 March 1848. London, Burns & Oates, 1957, pp. 92–104.

VI

THE ROSARY – A WAY OF MEDITATING ON THE MYSTERIES OF OUR FAITH

I am not going to make a long address to you,[1] my dear boys, or say anything that you have not often heard before from your superiors, for I know well in what good hands you are, and I know that their instructions come to you with greater force than any you can have from a stranger. If I speak to you at all, it is because I have lately come from the Holy Father, and am, in some sort, his representative,[2] and so in the years to come you may remember that you saw me today and heard me speak in his name, and remember

---

[1] Newman had no text for this short sermon. What we have here is the report given in a newspaper and written from notes taken at the time of preaching. It was delivered on Sunday, 5 October 1879. The Cardinal was then 78 years of age, and was speaking 'from his heart' to the boys at Oscott College, in the north of Birmingham. As it was the Feast of the Holy Rosary, he preached on the text: 'They found Mary and Joseph, and the Infant lying in a manger' (Lk 2:16).

[2] Five months previously, Newman was in Rome to be elevated to the Cardinalate by Pope Leo XIII. He was honoured by many groups and Institutions on his return to England, and gave numerous replies to congratulatory discourses. Cf. *Addresses to Cardinal Newman with his Replies, 1879–1881*. Edited by W.P. Neville. London, Longmans, Green & Co., 1905.

it to your profit. You know that today we keep the
Feast of the Holy Rosary, and I propose to say to you
what occurs to me on this great subject. You know
how that devotion came about; how, at a time when
heresy was very widespread, and had called in the aid
of sophistry, that can so powerfully aid infidelity
against religion, God inspired St Dominic to institute
and spread this devotion. It seems so simple and easy,
but you know God chooses the small things of the
world to humble the great.[a] Of course it was first of all
for the poor and simple, but not for them only, for
everyone who has practised the devotion knows that
there is in it a soothing sweetness that there is in
nothing else.[3] It is difficult to know God by our own
power, because He is incomprehensible. He is invisible to begin with, and therefore incomprehensible.
We can in some way know him, for even among the
heathens there were some who had learned many
truths about Him; but even they found it hard to

---

[3] Newman himself was very fond of his beads. He said: 'to my own feelings nothing is more delightful' (*The Letters and Diaries*, XII, 217). For
him it was not a matter of a mechanical repetition, but a meditation
and contemplation of the mysteries of our Lord's life in the company
of his Mother. He has not told us expressly how he said the Rosary,
but the following advice which he gave to a recent convert whom he
directed probably reflects Newman's own procedure: 'Try it thus, if
you don't so use it at present, but perhaps you do; – viz. before each
mystery, set before you a picture of it, and fix your mind upon that
picture (e.g. the Annunciation, the Agony, etc.) *while* you say the Pater
and 10 Aves, not thinking of the words, only saying them correctly.
Let the exercise be hardly more than a meditation. Perhaps this will
overcome any sense of tedium' (*The Letters and Diaries*, XII, 263).
Needless to say, the material repetition of Paters and Aves has then
reached its scope and becomes genuine prayer (cf. Philip Boyce,
OCD, 'At Prayer with Newman', in *In Search of Light. Life Development
Prayer*. Three Essays on John Henry Newman. Rome, International
Centre of Newman Friends, 1985, p. 82).

conform their lives to their knowledge of Him. And so in His mercy He has given us a revelation of Himself by coming amongst us, to be one of ourselves, with all the relations and qualities of humanity, to gain us over. He came down from Heaven and dwelt amongst us, and died for us. All these things are in the Creed, which contains the chief things that He has revealed to us about Himself. Now the great power of the Rosary lies in this, that it makes the Creed into a prayer; of course, the Creed is in some sense a prayer and a great act of homage to God; but the Rosary gives us the great truths of His life and death to meditate upon, and brings them nearer to our hearts. And so we contemplate all the great mysteries of His life and His birth in the manger; and so too the mysteries of His suffering and His glorified life.[4] But even Christians, with all their knowledge of God, have usually more awe than love of Him, and the special virtue of the Rosary lies in the special way in which it looks at these mysteries; for with all our thoughts of Him are mingled thoughts of His Mother, and in the relations between Mother and Son we have set before us the Holy Family, the home in which God lived. Now the family is, even humanly considered, a sacred thing; how much more the family bound together by supernatural ties, and, above all, that in which God dwelt with His Blessed Mother. This is what I should most wish you to remember in future years. For you will all of you have to go out into the world, and going out into the world means

---

[4] These pages show how Newman, despite his intellectual power and immense learning, could place himself at the level of schoolboys and explain spiritual realities to them in a simple and attractive manner.

leaving home; and, my dear boys, you don't know what the world is now. You look forward to the time when you will go out into the world, and it seems to you very bright and full of promise. It is not wrong for you to look forward to that time; but most men who know the world find it a world of great trouble, and disappointments, and even misery. If it turns out so to you, seek a home in the Holy Family that you think about in the mysteries of the Rosary. Schoolboys know the difference between school and home. You often hear grown-up people say that the happiest time of their life was that passed at school; but when they were at school you know they had a happier time, which was when they went home; that shows there is a good in home which cannot be found elsewhere. So that even if the world should actually prove to be all that you now fancy it, if it should bring you all that you could wish, yet you ought to have in the Holy Family a home with a holiness and sweetness about it that cannot be found elsewhere. This is, my dear boys, what I most earnestly ask you. I ask you when you go out into the world, as you soon must, to make the Holy Family your home, to which you may turn from all the sorrow and care of the world and find a solace, a compensation, and a refuge. And this I say to you, not as if I should speak to you again, not as if I had of myself any claim upon you, but with the claims of the Holy Father, whose representative I am, and in the hope that in the days to come you will remember that I came amongst you and said it to you. And when I speak of the Holy Family I do not mean Our Lord and Our Lady only, but St Joseph too; for as we cannot separate Our Lord from His Mother, so we cannot separate St Joseph from them both; for who but he was their protector in all the scenes of Our Lord's early life? And with Joseph must be included St Elizabeth and St John, whom we naturally think of as part of the Holy Family; we read of them together and see them in pictures together. May you, my dear boys, throughout your life find a home in the Holy Family; the home of Our Lord and His Blessed Mother, St Joseph, St Elizabeth, and St John.

a. cf. 1 Cor 1:27–8

Sayings of Cardinal Newman, Blackrock, Co. Dublin, 1976
(Facsimile Reprint), pp. 44–6.
First published: London, Burns and Oates, 1890.
Preached, without a text, 5 October 1879.

PART TWO

THEOLOGICAL THEMES

VII

ST MARY, OUR PATTERN IN RECEIVING AND STUDYING THE FAITH[1]

But Mary kept all these things, and pondered them in her heart. (Lk 2:19).

Little is told us in Scripture concerning the Blessed Virgin, but there is one grace of which the Evangelists make her the pattern, in a few simple sentences—of Faith. Zacharias questioned the Angel's message, but 'Mary said, Behold the handmaid of the Lord; be it unto me according to thy word.'[a] Accordingly Elisabeth, speaking with an apparent allusion to the contrast thus exhibited between her own highly-favoured husband, righteous Zacharias, and the still more highly-favoured Mary, said, on receiving her

---

[1] This sermon was preached to students and professors of Oxford University on 2 February 1843, the Feast of the Purification of Our Lady. It was the last of a series of sixteen sermons that dealt with various problems of faith and reason. The few pages we reproduce here are the introductory remarks of what was to be a famous and significant sermon on the subject of the development of doctrine. The sermon contains, in embryonic form, the theory the author would later expand in his *Essay on the Development of Christian Doctrine.*

salutation, 'Blessed art thou among women, and blessed is the fruit of thy womb; Blessed is she that believed for there shall be a performance of those things which were told her from the Lord'.[b]

2. But Mary's faith did not end in a mere acquiescence in Divine providences and revelations: as the text informs us, she 'pondered' them.[c] When the shepherds came, and told of the vision of Angels which they had seen at the time of the Nativity, and how one of them announced that the Infant in her arms was 'the Saviour, which is Christ the Lord',[d] while others did but wonder, 'Mary kept all these things, and pondered them in her heart'.[e] Again, when her Son and Saviour had come to the age of twelve years, and had left her for awhile for His Father's service, and had been found, to her surprise, in the Temple, amid the doctors, both hearing them and asking them questions, and had, on her addressing Him, vouchsafed to justify His conduct,[f] we are told, 'His mother kept all these sayings in her heart'.[g] And accordingly, at the marriage-feast in Cana, her faith anticipated His first miracle, and she said to the servants, 'Whatsoever He saith unto you, do it'.[h]

3. Thus St Mary is our pattern of Faith, both in the reception and in the study of Divine Truth. She does not think it enough to accept, she dwells upon it; not enough to possess, she uses it; not enough to assent, she develops it; not enough to submit the Reason, she reasons upon it; not indeed reasoning first, and believing afterwards, with Zacharias, yet first believing without reasoning, next from love and reverence, reasoning after believing.[2] And thus she symbolizes to us, not only the faith of the unlearned, but of the doctors of the Church also, who have to investigate, and weigh, and define, as well as to profess the Gospel; to draw the line between truth and heresy; to anticipate or remedy the various aberrations of wrong reason; to combat pride and recklessness with their own arms; and thus to triumph over the sophist and the innovator.

a. Lk 1:38	b. Lk 1:42, 45	c. cf. Lk 2:19
d. cf. Lk 2:11, 17	e. Lk 2:19	f. cf. Lk 2:41–9
g. Lk 2:51	h. Jn 2:5	

Fifteen Sermons preached before the University of Oxford between AD 1826 and 1843. London, 1909, pp. 312–14.

[2] Newman presents the Blessed Virgin Mary as a model for all true theologians: she accepts the word of God, ponders it in her heart, deepens or develops her understanding of it. The theological method she uses is what a Christian theologian should follow: 'first believing without reasoning, next from love and reverence, receiving after believing'.

VIII

THE DEVELOPMENT OF MARIAN DOCTRINE IN THE EARLY CENTURIES[1]

There was one other subject on which the Arian controversy had a more intimate, though not an immediate influence. Its tendency to give a new interpretation to the texts which speak of our Lord's subordination, has already been noticed; such as admitted of it were henceforth explained more prominently of His manhood than of His Mediatorship or His Sonship. But there were other texts which did not

---

[1] This extract is taken from one of Newman's most famous books: *An Essay on the Development of Christian Doctrine*. From apostolic times there was a body of doctrine which kept developing in a homogeneous way, changing and growing, yet remaining substantially the same. Newman illustrates various arguments in favour of existing developments, one of them using an historical approach (cf. ch. III). He proceeds in chapter IV to give some specific instances, where he analyses the historical evidence that is available to show how certain doctrines or dogmas, professed today though not at first sight evident in apostolic times, were nevertheless truly prefigured and recognizable in the beliefs of the first age of Christianity, and became more pronounced and precise with the passing of the centuries. He pays special attention to the divinity of Christ in the mystery of our Lord's Incarnation. He concludes with the present section on Mary's dignity and grace, consequent on a correct understanding of the divine Sonship of Christ, whose mother she was.

admit of this interpretation, and which, without ceasing to belong to Him, might seem more directly applicable to a creature than to the Creator. He indeed was really the 'Wisdom in whom the Father eternally delighted', yet it would be but natural, if, under the circumstances of Arian misbelief, theologians looked out for other than the Eternal Son to be the immediate object of such descriptions. And thus the controversy opened a question which it did not settle. It discovered a new sphere, if we may so speak, in the realms of light, to which the Church had not yet assigned its inhabitant. Arianism[2] had admitted that our Lord was both the God of the Evangelical Covenant, and the actual Creator of the Universe; but even this was not enough, because it did not confess Him to be the One, Everlasting, Infinite, Supreme Being, but as one who was made by the Supreme. It was not enough in accordance with that heresy to proclaim Him as having an ineffable origin before all

---

[2] The Arian heresy exalted Christ far above all creatures but did not admit that he was consubstantial with the Father and uncreated. Arians maintained that the one true God is the Father who is 'not generated', not created and incommunicable. According to them, the Word had a beginning because it was generated by God the Father. His 'Substance' is different from and created by the Father who alone is 'not generated', uncreated and incommunicable. Consequently, they denied Christ's true and eternal divinity. Although they exalted him to a very sublime position, it was still a subordinate rank between God the Father and creatures. The Council of Nicea in the year 325 reacted against this theological error, defining the Son to be 'the only begotten Son of God, born of the Father before all ages' and 'not created' as creatures are, but 'of the same substance' or 'consubstantial' with the First Person of the Blessed Trinity. St Athanasius (295–373), present as a deacon at the Council of Nicea and as Bishop of Alexandria three years later (in 328), was the heroic defender of the true faith of the Church against Arianism.

worlds; not enough to place Him high above all creatures as the type of all the works of God's Hands; not
enough to make Him the King of all Saints, the
Intercessor for man with God, the Object of worship,
the Image of the Father; not enough, because it was
not all, and between all and anything short of all, there
was an infinite interval. The highest of creatures is
levelled with the lowest in comparison of the One
Creator Himself. That is, the Nicene Council recognized the eventful principle, that, while we believe
and profess any being to be made of a created nature,
such a being is really no God to us, though honoured
by us with whatever high titles and with whatever
homage. Arius or Asterius[3] did all but confess that
Christ was the Almighty; they said much more than St
Bernard or St Alphonso have since said of the Blessed
Mary; yet they left Him a creature and were found
wanting. Thus there was 'a wonder in heaven':[b] a
throne was seen, far above all other created powers,
mediatorial, intercessory; a title archetypal; a crown
bright as the morning star; a glory issuing from the
Eternal Throne; robes pure as the heavens; and a
sceptre over all; and who was the predestined heir of
that Majesty? Since it was not high enough for the
Highest, who was that Wisdom, and what was her
name, 'the Mother of fair love, and fear, and holy
hope',[c] 'exalted like a palm-tree in Engaddi, and a
rose-plant in Jericho',[d] 'created from the beginning

---

[3] Asterius was a sophist who lived in the beginning of the fourth
century. A convert to Christianity, he became an advocate of the
heresy of the Semi-Arians, who made subtle distinctions by which
they maintained that, although the Son was not of the same substance,
he was 'like in substance' to the Father.

before the world',[e] in God's everlasting counsels, and 'in Jerusalem her power'?[f] The vision is found in the Apocalypse, a Woman clothed with the sun, and the moon under her feet, and upon her head a crown of twelve stars.[g][4] The votaries of Mary do not exceed the true faith, unless the blasphemers of her Son came up to it. The Church of Rome is not idolatrous, unless Arianism is orthodoxy.[5]

I am not stating conclusions which were drawn out in the controversy, but of premisses which were laid, broad and deep. It was then shown, it was then determined, that to exalt a creature was no recognition of its divinity. Nor am I speaking of the Semi-Arians, who, holding our Lord's derivation from the Substance of the Father, yet denying His Consubstantiality, really did lie open to the charge of maintaining two Gods, and present no parallel to the

---

[4] The liturgy of the Church applies in a spiritual sense these Old Testament texts of wisdom literature to our Lady. The Woman of the Apocalypse (ch. 12) is usually understood as applying to the Church, but some biblical scholars and theologians also see it as referring to our Lady. Hans-Urs von Balthasar writes: 'The best way to learn something about Mary and how she is related to our present age is to start with chapter 12 of Revelation. This question is at the core of this last book of the Bible which uses visionary images to provide insight into the drama of the world's history' (*Mary for today*, Slough, St Paul Publications, 1989, p. 7). Cf. A. Feuillet, 'Le Messie et sa Mère d'après le chapitre XII de l'Apocalypse': *Revue Biblique* 66 (1959), pp. 55–86; Domenico Bertetto, *Maria nel domma cattolico*, Torino, 1955, pp. 106–50. Cf. also below, Text XII, p. 241, footnote 12.

[5] A very fine conclusion, almost on a triumphant note, proving how untrue was the censure of Marian 'idolatry' levelled at Roman Catholics for their veneration of the Blessed Virgin Mary. Catholics do not elevate our Lady as highly in the order of creation as Arius exalted Christ. Since the Christ of the Arians was not divine, much less is our Lady.

defenders of the prerogatives of St Mary. But I speak of the Arians who taught that the Son's Substance was created; and concerning them it is true that St Athanasius's condemnation of their theology is a vindication of the Medieval. Yet it is not wonderful, considering how Socinians, Sabellians, Nestorians, and the like,[6] abound in these days, without their even knowing it themselves, if those who never rise higher in their notions of our Lord's Divinity, than to consider Him a man singularly inhabited by a Divine Presence, that is, a Catholic Saint,—if such men should mistake the honour paid by the Church to the human Mother for that very honour which, and which alone, is worthy of her Eternal Son.

I have said that there was in the first ages no public and

---

[6] *Socinians* formed an Antitrinitarian sect that arose in the wake of the Reformation. It owes its name to Fausto Sozzini from Siena (1539–1604). They made much use of human reason, interpreting the Bible and the mysteries of religion in the light of reason. They denied the distinction of three Persons in the Trinity. For them, Christ was not a Divine Person.

    Sabellians, the followers of Sabellius in the third Century. He denied the mystery of the Trinity by refusing to admit any real distinction between the three Divine Persons. These were, according to Sabellius, simply three transient 'modalities' or manifestations of God to man. At times God appears as Father, at other times as Son and again as Holy Spirit. The Sabellians understood the word 'person' in its original sense of 'mask'. Some Protestant authors (e.g. in Newman's day, Archbishop Whately in his study on the *Elements of Logic*) took a similar view.

    Nestorians, followers of Nestorius, in the fifth Century. According to him, there were not only two natures in Christ but also two distinct persons, one divine and the other human. He refused to admit expressions such as: 'The Word suffered' or 'Mary is the Mother of God'. He claimed that only the human person of Christ is our High Priest and Redeemer, and that Mary is merely the Mother of (the man) Christ. Cf. above, Text III, pp. 133–4, footnote 4.

ecclesiastical recognition of the place which St Mary holds in the Economy of grace; this was reserved for the fifth century, as the definition of our Lord's proper Divinity had been the work of the fourth. There was a controversy contemporary with those already mentioned, I mean the Nestorian, which brought out the complement of the development, to which they had been subservient; and which, if I may so speak, supplied the subject of that august proposition of which Arianism had provided the predicate. In order to do honour to Christ, in order to defend the true doctrine of the Incarnation, in order to secure a right faith in the manhood of the Eternal Son, the Council of Ephesus determined the Blessed Virgin to be the Mother of God. Thus all heresies of that day, though opposite to each other, tended in a most wonderful way to her exaltation; and the School of Antioch, the fountain of primitive rationalism, led the Church to determine first the conceivable greatness of a creature, and then the incommunicable dignity of the Blessed Virgin.[7]

But the spontaneous or traditional feeling of Christians had in great measure anticipated the formal ecclesiastical decision. Thus the title *Theotokos*, or

[7] The thinkers and theologians of Antioch were renowned for their critical spirit, their love of reasoning, their common sense and grammatical precision. They were opposed to mystical and allegorical interpretations of Scripture (favoured by the Alexandrian School). Despite the general tendency of the Antiochenes to a rationalistic spirit, they had some acute theologians and competent commentators of Sacred Scripture: e.g. St John Chrysostom (+407), Theodore of Mopsuestia (+429) and Theodoret (+c. 460). They would be keen to lay down the limits of what could be correctly attributed to a creature, and thus kept the Church from ascribing too much honour to our Lady.

Mother of God, was familiar to Christians from primitive times, and had been used, among other writers,
by Origen, Eusebius, St Alexander, St Athanasius, St
Ambrose, St Gregory Nazianzen, St Gregory Nyssen,
and St Nilus. She had been called Ever-Virgin by
others, as by St Epiphanius, St Jerome, and Didymus.
By others, 'the Mother of all living',[h] as being the
antitype of Eve; for, as St Epiphanius observes, 'in
truth', not in shadow, 'from Mary was Life itself
brought into the world, that Mary might bear things
living, and might become Mother of living things'.[8] St
Augustine says that all have sinned 'except the Holy
Virgin Mary, concerning whom, for the honour of
the Lord, I wish no question to be raised at all, when
we are treating of sins'.[9] 'She was alone and wrought
the world's salvation', says St Ambrose, alluding to her
conception of the Redeemer. She is signified by the
Pillar of the cloud which guided the Israelites,[i]
according to the same Father; and she had 'so great
grace, as not only to have virginity herself, but to
impart it to those to whom she came'; 'the Rod out
of the stem of Jesse',[j] says St Jerome, and 'the Eastern
gate through which the High Priest alone goes in and
out, yet is ever shut'; the wise woman, says St Nilus,
who 'hath clad all believers, from the fleece of the
Lamb born of her, with the clothing of incorruption,

---

[8] [*Haer.* 78,18]. *Panarion* 78:18: *PG* 42:727. The reference is to St
   Epiphanius, Bishop of Salamis. He was a native of Palestine, entered
   the monastic life and founded a monastery himself. He defended
   orthodox beliefs and refuted the errors of heretics. His most important
   work was the *Panarion*, commonly called the 'Refutation of all the
   Heresies'.
[9] Cf. St Augustine, *De natura et gratia* 36:42. Cf. above, Text V, p. 170,
   footnote 7.

and delivered them from their spiritual nakedness';
'the Mother of Life, of beauty, of majesty, the
Morning Star', according to Antiochus; 'the mystical
new heavens', 'the heavens carrying the Divinity',
'the fruitful vine by whom we are translated from
death unto life', according to St Ephraim; 'the manna
which is delicate, bright, sweet, and virgin, which, as
though coming from heaven, has poured down on all
the people of the Churches a food pleasanter than
honey', according to St Maximus.

St Proclus calls her 'the unsullied shell which
contains the pearl of price', 'the sacred shrine of
sinlessness', 'the golden altar of holocaust', 'the holy
oil of anointing', 'the costly alabaster box of spike-
nard', 'the ark gilt within and without', 'the heifer
whose ashes, that is, the Lord's Body taken from her,
cleanses those who are defiled by the pollution of sin',
'the fair bride of the Canticles', 'the stay (στήριγμα)
of believers', 'the Church's diadem', 'the expression of
orthodoxy'. These are oratorical expressions; but we
use oratory on great subjects, not on small. Elsewhere
he calls her 'God's only bridge to man'; and elsewhere
he breaks forth, 'Run through all creation in your
thoughts, and see if there be equal to, or greater than,
the Holy Virgin Mother of God'.[10]

Theodotus[11] too, one of the Fathers of Ephesus,

---

[10] Passages like these show Newman's familiarity with and respect for
the Fathers of the Church. It was the study of their writings that led
him to the Catholic Church. He himself would say: 'The Fathers
made me a Catholic' (*Difficulties felt by Anglicans*, Vol. II, p. 24).

[11] Theodotus, Bishop of Ancyra, (+*c.* 445), made much of the perpetual
virginity of Mary in order to confirm the doctrine of there being one
divine Person in Christ. (cf. *Homilia 4 in S. Deiparam*: *PG* 77: 1394).

or whoever it is whose Homilies are given to St
Amphilochius: 'As debtors and God's well-affected
servants, let us make confession to God the Word
and to His Mother, of the gift of words, as far as we
are able ... Hail, Mother, clad in light, of the light
which sets not; hail all-undefiled mother of holiness;
hail most pellucid fountain of the life-giving stream!'
After speaking of the Incarnation, he continues,
'Such paradoxes doth the Divine Virgin Mother ever
bring to us in her holy irradiations, for with her is
the Fount of Life, and breasts of the spiritual and
guileless milk; from which to suck the sweetness, we
have even now earnestly run to her, not as in forget-
fulness of what has gone before, but in desire of
what is to come'.

To St Fulgentius[12] is ascribed the following: 'Mary
became the window of heaven, for God through her
poured the True Light upon the world; the heavenly
ladder, for through her did God descend upon earth
... Come, ye virgins, to a Virgin, come ye who
conceive to one who did conceive, ye who bear to
one who bore, mothers to a Mother, ye who give
suck to one who suckled, young women to the
Young.' Lastly, 'Thou has found grace,' says St Peter
Chrysologus, 'how much? he had said above, Full.

---

[12] St Fulgentius (468–533) was made Bishop of Ruspe in North Africa
about 507. A Church Father, he was well-known for his eloquence
and theological doctrine. He strenuously opposed Arianism and on
that account was banished on two occasions. He thoroughly understood and defended the doctrine of the one Person in Christ and its
implications for the honour due to Mary (cf. *De laudibus Mariae ex
partu Salvatoris*, in Migne, *Patrologia Latina*, 65: 899. Henceforth
abbreviated: *PL*).

And full indeed, which with full shower might pour
upon and into the whole creation.'[13]

Such was the state of sentiment on the subject of
the Blessed Virgin, which the Arian, Nestorian, and
Monophysite heresies found in the Church; and on
which the doctrinal decisions consequent upon them
impressed a form and a consistency which has been
handed on in the East and West to this day.

a. cf. Mt 3:17, 17:5	b. Rev 12:1	c. Sir 24:18
d. Sir 24:14	e. cf. Prov 8:22–3	f. Sir 24:11
g. Rev 12:1	h. Gen 3:20	i. cf. Ex. 13:21
j. Is 11:1		

An Essay on the Development of Christian Doctrine.
London, 1909, pp. 142–8.
Written in the months preceding Newman's reception into the Roman
Catholic Church (October 1845) and first published that same year.

[13] Newman indicates his sources for these citations from the writings of
the Fathers of the Church and ancient ecclesiastical writers in a long
footnote, as follows:

Aug. *de Nat. et Grat.* 42. Ambros. *Ep.* 1, 49, § 2. *In Psalm* 118, v.
3. *de Instit. Virg.* 50. Hier. *in Is.* xi. 1, *contr. Pelag.* ii. 4. Nil. *Ep.* i. p.
267. Antioch. ap. Cyr. *de Rect. Fid.* p. 49. Ephr. *Opp. Syr.* t. 3, p. 607.
Max. *Hom.* 45. Procl. *Orat.* vi. pp. 225–228, p. 60, p. 179, 180, ed.
1630. Theodot. *ap. Amphiloch.* pp. 39, &c. Fulgent. *Serm.* 3, p. 125.
Chrysol. *Serm.* 142. A striking passage from another Sermon of the
last-mentioned author, on the words 'She cast in her mind what
manner of salutation,' &c., may be added: 'Quantus sit Deus satis
ignorat ille, qui hujus Virginis mentem non stupet, animum non
miratur. Pavet coelum, tremunt Angeli, creatura non sustinet, natura
non sufficit; et una puella sic Deum in sui pectoris capit, recipit,
oblectat hospitio, ut pacem terris, coelis gloriam, salutem perditis,
vitam mortuis, terrenis cum coelestibus parentelam, ipsius Dei cum
carne commercium, pro ipsâ domûs exigat pensione, pro ipsius uteri
mercede conquirat,' &c. *Serm.* 140. [St Basil, St Chrysostom, and St
Cyril of Alexandria sometimes speak, it is true, in a different tone; on
the subject vid. 'Letter to Dr Pusey,' Note iii., *Diff. of Angl.* vol. 2.]

Cf. below, Text XI, pp. 230–1, footnote 9.

IX

DISTINCTION BETWEEN FAITH AND DEVOTION[1]

I begin by making a distinction which will go far to remove good part of the difficulty of my undertaking, as it presents itself to ordinary inquirers,—the distinction between faith and devotion.[2] I fully grant that *devotion* towards the blessed Virgin has increased among Catholics with the progress of centuries; I do not allow that the *doctrine* concerning her has undergone a growth, for I believe that it has been in substance one and the same from the beginning.

By 'faith' I mean the Creed and assent to the Creed; by 'devotion' I mean such religious honours as belong to the objects of our faith, and the payment of those honours. Faith and devotion are as distinct in fact, as they are in idea. We cannot, indeed, be devout

---

[1] This extract and the following ones (IX–XIII/A; XIV–XV) are taken from Newman's principal study on the Blessed Virgin Mary, namely, his *Letter to Pusey*. For a description of its content and context, see above, Introduction, III, pp. 38–50.

[2] This distinction between devotion to our Lady and doctrine (faith) concerning her is a most important one in understanding Catholic veneration for the Mother of Jesus. Newman was quite original on this point, in so far as he was the first author to give it such prominence. He emphasised that 'it was the principle with Catholics that, while dogma is one, devotion is multiform – that while faith is fixed, devotion is free' (*The Letters and Diaries*, XXII, 98). This helped Protestants to have a more accurate understanding of Catholic beliefs and practices regarding our Lady.

without faith, but we may believe without feeling devotion. Of this phenomenon every one has experience both in himself and in others; and we bear witness to it as often as we speak of realizing a truth[3] or not realizing it. It may be illustrated, with more or less exactness, by matters which come before us in the world. For instance, a great author, or public man, may be acknowledged as such for a course of years; yet there may be an increase, an ebb and flow, and a fashion, in his popularity. And if he takes a lasting place in the minds of his countrymen, he may gradually grow into it, or suddenly be raised to it. The idea of Shakespeare as a great poet, has existed from a very early date in public opinion; and there were at least individuals then who understood him as well, and honoured him as much, as the English people can honour him now; yet, I think, there is a national devotion to him in this day such as never has been before. This has happened, because, as education spreads in the country, there are more men able to enter into his poetical genius, and, among these, more capacity again for deeply and critically understanding him; and yet, from the first, he has exerted a great insensible influence over the nation, as is seen in the circumstance that his phrases and sentences, more than can be numbered, have become almost proverbs among us. And so again in philosophy, and in the arts and sciences, great truths and principles have sometimes been known and acknowledged for a course of years; but, whether from feebleness of intellectual

---

[3] 'To realize' is a word often used by Newman in a very precise and forceful sense. It means knowing a truth in a way that is not simply theoretical, but that has practical consequences in life and conduct.

power in the recipients, or external circumstances of an accidental kind, they have not been turned to account. Thus the Chinese are said to have known of the properties of the magnet from time immemorial, and to have used it for land expeditions, yet not on the sea. Again, the ancients knew of the principle that water finds its own level, but seem to have made little application of their knowledge. And Aristotle was familiar with the principle of induction; yet it was left for Bacon to develop it into an experimental philosophy. Illustrations such as these, though not altogether apposite, serve to convey that distinction between faith and devotion on which I am insisting. It is like the distinction between objective and subjective truth. The sun in the spring-time will have to shine many days before he is able to melt the frost, open the soil, and bring out the leaves; yet he shines out from the first notwithstanding, though he makes his power felt but gradually. It is one and the same sun, though his influence day by day becomes greater; and so in the Catholic Church it is the one Virgin Mother, one and the same from first to last, and Catholics may have ever acknowledged her; and yet, in spite of that acknowledgement, their devotion to her may be scanty in one time and place, and overflowing in another.

This distinction is forcibly brought home to a convert, as a peculiarity of the Catholic religion, on his first introduction to its worship. The faith is everywhere one and the same, but a large liberty is accorded to private judgment and inclination as regards matters of devotion. Any large church, with its collections and groups of people, will illustrate this. The fabric itself is

dedicated to Almighty God, and that, under the invocation of the Blessed Virgin, or some particular Saint;
or again, of some mystery belonging to the Divine
Name or the Incarnation, or of some mystery associated with the Blessed Virgin. Perhaps there are seven
altars or more in it, and these again have their several
Saints. Then there is the Feast proper to this or that
day; and during the celebration of Mass, of all the
worshippers who crowd around the priest, each has
his own particular devotions, with which he follows
the rite. No one interferes with his neighbour; agree-
ing, as it were, to differ, they pursue independently a
common end, and by paths, distinct but converging,
present themselves before God. Then there are
confraternities attached to the church,—of the Sacred
Heart, or of the Precious Blood; associations of prayer
for a good death, or for the repose of departed souls,
or for the conversion of the heathen; devotions
connected with the brown, blue, or red scapular; not
to speak of the great ordinary ritual observed through
the four seasons, or of the constant Presence of the
Blessed Sacrament, or of its ever-recurring rite of
Benediction, and its extraordinary forty hours'
Exposition. Or, again, look through such manuals of
prayers as the *Raccolta*,[4] and you at once will see both
the number and the variety of devotions, which are
open to individual Catholics to choose from, accord-

---

[4] The *Raccolta* was a collection of prayers, novenas and pious practices to
which the Pope had attached indulgences. The first edition was
published in Rome by Telesforo Galli in 1807. Official editions were
later published by the Sacred Congregation for Indulgences and Holy
Relics. Newman's companion and close friend, Ambrose St John,
translated the first English edition.

ing to their religious taste and prospect of personal
edification.

Now these diversified modes of honouring God did
not come to us in a day, or only from the Apostles;
they are the accumulations of centuries; and, as in the
course of years some of them spring up, so others
decline and die. Some are local, in memory of some
particular Saint, who happens to be the Evangelist, or
Patron, or pride of the nation, or who lies entombed
in the church or in the city where it is found; and
these devotions, necessarily, cannot have an earlier
date than the Saint's day of death or interment there.
The first of these sacred observances, long before such
national memories, were the devotions paid to the
Apostles, then those which were paid to the Martyrs;
yet there were Saints nearer to our Lord than either
Martyrs or Apostles; but, as if these sacred persons
were immersed and lost in the effulgence of His glory,
and because they did not manifest themselves, when
in the body, in external works separate from Him, it
happened that for a long while they were less dwelt
upon. However, in process of time, the Apostles, and
then the Martyrs, exerted less influence than before
over the popular mind, and the local Saints, new
creations of God's power, took their place, or again,
the Saints of some religious order here or there established. Then, as comparatively quiet times succeeded,
the religious meditations of holy men and their secret
intercourse with heaven gradually exerted an influence out of doors, and permeated the Christian
populace, by the instrumentality of preaching and by
the ceremonial of the Church. Hence at length those
luminous stars rose in the ecclesiastical heavens, which

were of more august dignity than any which had preceded them, and were late in rising, for the very reason that they were so specially glorious. Those names, I say, which at first sight might have been expected to enter soon into the devotions of the faithful, with better reason might have been looked for at a later date, and actually were late in their coming. St Joseph furnishes the most striking instance of this remark; here is the clearest of instances of the distinction between doctrine and devotion. Who, from his prerogatives and the testimony on which they come to us, had a greater claim to receive an early recognition among the faithful than he? A Saint of Scripture, the foster-father of our Lord, he was an object of the universal and absolute faith of the Christian world from the first, yet the devotion to him is comparatively of late date.[5] When once it began, men seemed surprised that it had not been thought of before; and now, they hold him next to the Blessed Virgin in their religious affection and veneration.

As regards the Blessed Virgin then, I shall postpone the question of devotion for a while, and inquire first into the doctrine of the undivided Church (to use your controversial phrase), on the subject of her prerogatives.

A Letter Addressed to the Rev. E.B. Pusey, DD on occasion of his Eirenicon:
Certain Difficulties felt by Anglicans in Catholic Teaching,
London, 1910, Vol. II, pp. 26–31.
Written in December 1865 and first published at the beginning of 1866.

[5] In the sixteenth century, St Teresa of Avila was instrumental in propagating devotion to St Joseph. It was not until the seventeenth century that his feastday became a holy day of obligation and his name was inserted into the Litany of the Saints.

X

OUR LADY AS SEEN BY THE
FATHERS OF THE CHURCH:
THE SECOND EVE

What is the great rudimental teaching of Antiquity from its earliest date concerning her [the Blessed Virgin]? By 'rudimental teaching', I mean the prima facie view of her person and office, the broad outline laid down of her, the aspect under which she comes to us, in the writings of the Fathers. She is the Second Eve.[1]

Now let us consider what this implies. Eve had a definite, essential position in the First Covenant. The fate of the human race lay with Adam; he it was who represented us. It was in Adam that we fell; though Eve had fallen, still, if Adam had stood, we should not have lost those supernatural privileges which were bestowed upon him as our first father.[2] Yet though Eve was not the head of the race, still, even as regards

---

[1] [*Vide Essay on Development of Doctrine*, 1845, p. 384 etc.] Cf. pp. 415 ff. in later editions. The first point of doctrine on our Lady proposed by Newman is her position and role in salvation history as the Second Eve. This teaching is firmly grounded in Patristic thought. Newman maintains that it is the point which first strikes us in the writings of the Fathers.

[2] This was the opinion expressed by St Thomas Aquinas cf. *Summa Theologiae*, I–II, q.81, a.5.

the race, she had a place of her own; for Adam, to
whom was divinely committed the naming of all
things, named her 'the Mother of all the living',[a] a
name surely expressive, not of a fact only, but of a
dignity; but further, as she thus had her own general
relation to the human race, so again had she her own
special place, as regards its trial and its fall in Adam. In
those primeval events, Eve had an integral share. 'The
woman, being seduced, was in the transgression.'[b] She
listened to the Evil Angel; she offered the fruit to her
husband, and he ate of it. She co-operated, not as an
irresponsible instrument, but intimately and personally
in the sin: she brought it about. As the history stands,
she was a *sine qua non*, a positive, active, cause of it.
And she had her share in its punishment; in the
sentence pronounced on her, she was recognized as a
real agent in the temptation and its issue, and she
suffered accordingly. In that awful transaction there
were three parties concerned,—the serpent, the
woman, and the man; and at the time of their
sentence, an event was announced for a distant future,
in which the three same parties were to meet again,
the serpent, the woman, and the man; but it was to be
a second Adam and a second Eve, and the new Eve
was to be the mother of the new Adam.[3] 'I will put

[3] The parallelism between the three actors in the fall of the human race
 – the serpent (the fallen angel), the woman (Eve) and the man (Adam)
 – and the three agents in its restoration to divine friendship – Gabriel
 (the good Angel), the woman (Mary, the new Eve) and the man
 (Christ, the new or second Adam) – was often illustrated by the
 Church Fathers. Newman uses it to explain the vital role of the Blessed
 Virgin Mary in the work of salvation. As Eve was active and personally involved in the first test of humanity that resulted in the original
 sin of disobedience and the fall, so was Mary actively, freely and
 wholeheartedly involved, by faith and obedience, in the second 'test'

enmity between thee and the woman, and between thy seed and her seed.'[c] The Seed of the woman is the Word Incarnate, and the Woman, whose seed or son He is, is His mother Mary. This interpretation, and the parallelism it involves, seem to me undeniable; but at all events (and this is my point) the parallelism is the doctrine of the Fathers, from the earliest times; and, this being established, we are able, by the position and office of Eve in our fall, to determine the position and office of Mary in our restoration.[4]

I shall adduce passages from their writings, noting their respective countries and dates; and the dates shall extend from their births or conversions to their deaths, since what they propound is at once the

---

that produced a positive result and brought us a Redeemer who restored us again to God's grace and eternal life. The Second Vatican Council repeats this point of Marian doctrine, so dear to the Church Fathers and to Newman: 'Rightly, therefore, the Fathers see Mary not merely as passively engaged by God, but as freely co-operating in the work of man's salvation through faith and obedience. For, as St Irenaeus says, she "being obedient, became the cause of salvation for herself and for the whole human race." Hence not a few of the early Fathers gladly assert with him in their preaching: "the knot of Eve's disobedience was untied by Mary's obedience: what the virgin Eve bound through her disbelief, Mary loosened by her faith." Comparing Mary with Eve, they call her "Mother of the living", and frequently claim: "death through Eve, life through Mary."' (Dogmatic Constitution on the Church, *Lumen Gentium*, 56)

[4] Newman shows, in his *Essay on the Development of Christian Doctrine*, how this point of Marian doctrine, namely, Mary as the Second Eve, was present in the teaching of the Fathers from the earliest times. This early intimation of tendencies, that are fully brought to light later on, is the fifth of the seven notes given by Newman by which a legitimate development may be discerned from a growth that would be a corruption or betrayal of the truth. In other words, a living truth will show from the start tendencies of future genuine development. (Cf. below, Text XVI, pp. 283–7).

doctrine which they had received from the generation before them, and the doctrine which was accepted and recognized as true by the generation to whom they transmitted it.

First, then, St Justin Martyr (AD 120–65), St Irenaeus (120–200), and Tertullian (160–240). Of these Tertullian represents Africa and Rome; St Justin represents Palestine; and St Irenaeus Asia Minor and Gaul;—or rather he represents St John the Evangelist, for he had been taught by the Martyr St Polycarp, who was the intimate associate of St John, as also of other Apostles.

1. St Justin:[5]

> We know that He, before all creatures, proceeded from the Father by His power and will, ... and by means of the Virgin became man, that by what way the disobedience arising from the serpent had its beginning, by that way also it might have an undoing. For Eve, being a Virgin and undefiled, conceiving the word that was from the serpent, brought forth disobedience and death; but the Virgin Mary, taking faith and joy, when the Angel told her the good tidings, that the Spirit of the Lord should come upon her and the power of the Highest overshadow her, and therefore the Holy One that was born of her was Son of God, answered, 'Be it to me according to thy word'.[d6]

---

[5] [I have attempted to translate literally without caring to write English. The original passages are in Note I, infr.]. Cf. *Difficulties felt by Anglicans*, II, 119–24.

[6] [*Tryph*. 100]: *Dialogue with Trypho*, 100: *PG* 6:709.

2. Tertullian:

> God recovered His image and likeness, which the
> devil had seized, by a rival operation. For into Eve,
> as yet a virgin, had crept the word which was the
> framer of death. Equally into a virgin was to be
> introduced the Word of God which was the
> builder-up of life; that, what by that sex had gone
> into perdition by the same sex might be brought
> back to salvation. Eve had believed the serpent;
> Mary believed Gabriel; the fault which the one
> committed by believing, the other by believing has
> blotted out.[7]

3. St Irenaeus:

> With a fitness, Mary the Virgin is found obedient,
> saying, 'Behold Thy handmaid, O Lord; be it to me
> according to Thy word'.[e] But Eve was disobedient;
> for she obeyed not, while she was yet a virgin. As
> she, having indeed Adam for a husband, but as yet
> being a virgin ... becoming disobedient, became
> the cause of death both to herself and to the whole
> human race, so also Mary, having the predestined
> man, and being yet a Virgin, being obedient,
> became both to herself and to the whole human
> race the cause of salvation ... And on account of
> this the Lord said, that the first should be last
> and the last first.[f] And the Prophet signifies the
> same, saying, 'Instead of fathers you have chil-
> dren'.[g] For, whereas the Lord, when born, was the

---

[7] [*De Carn. Christ.* 17]: *De Carne Christi: PL* 2:782.

first-begotten of the dead, and received into His bosom the primitive fathers, He regenerated them into the life of God, He Himself becoming the beginning of the living, since Adam became the beginning of the dying. Therefore also Luke, commencing the line of generations from the Lord, referred it back to Adam,[h] signifying that He regenerated the old fathers, not they Him, into the Gospel of life. And so the knot of Eve's disobedience received its unloosing through the obedience of Mary; for what Eve, a virgin, bound by incredulity, that Mary, a virgin, unloosed by faith.[8]

And again:

As Eve by the speech of an Angel was seduced, so as to flee God, transgressing His word, so also Mary received the good tidings by means of the Angel's speech, so as to bear God within her, being obedient to His word. And, though the one had disobeyed God, yet the other was drawn to obey God; that of the virgin Eve the Virgin Mary might become the advocate. And, as by a virgin the human race had been bound to death, by a virgin it is saved,[9] the balance being preserved, a virgin's disobedience by a Virgin's obedience.[10]

Now, what is especially noticeable in these three

---

[8] [*Adv. Haer.* iii, 22. 34]: *Adversus Haereses* III, 22.34: *PG* 7:958–60.

[9] [Salvatur; some MSS read Solvatur, '[that] it might be loosed;' and so Augustine contr. Jul.i, n.5. This variety of reading does not affect the general sense of the passage. Moreover, the word 'salvation' occurs in the former of these two passages.]

[10] [*Ibid.* v. 19]: *Adversus Haereses* V, 19, 1: *PG* 7: 1175.

writers, is, that they do not speak of the Blessed Virgin merely as the physical instrument of our Lord's taking flesh, but as an intelligent, responsible cause of it; her faith and obedience being accessories to the Incarnation, and gaining it as her reward. As Eve failed in these virtues, and thereby brought on the fall of the race in Adam, so Mary by means of the same had a part in its restoration. You surely imply that the Blessed Virgin was only a physical instrument of our redemption; 'what has been said of her by the Fathers as the chosen *vessel* of the Incarnation, was applied *personally* to her', (that is, by Catholics,) and again 'the Fathers speak of the Blessed Virgin as the *instrument* of our salvation, *in that* she gave birth to the Redeemer';[11] whereas St Augustine, in well-known passages, speaks of her as more exalted by her sanctity than by her relationship to our Lord.[12] However, not to go beyond the doctrine of the Three Fathers, they unanimously declare that she was *not* a mere instrument in the Incarnation, such as David, or Judah, may be considered; they declare she co-operated in our salvation not merely by the descent of the Holy Ghost upon her body, but by specific holy acts, the effect of the Holy Ghost within her soul; that, as Eve forfeited

---

[11] Newman refers here to pages of Pusey's study *An Eirenicon in a letter to the author of 'The Christian Year'*. (Oxford 1865), cf. pp. 151–6. It is to this work that Newman responds in his *Letter to Pusey*. Four years later (1869) in a *Letter to Newman* Pusey would deny that he regarded Mary merely as a physical instrument of the redemption: cf. *First Letter to the Very Rev. J. H. Newman, DD., in Explanation chiefly in regard to the Reverential Love due to the Ever-blessed Theotokos, and the Doctrine of her Immaculate Conception*, Oxford, 1869, pp. 22 ff.

[12] [Opp. t. 8, p. 2, col. 369, t. 6, col. 342]. This is a thought from St Augustine to which Newman often alludes: cf. above, Text V, p. 169, footnote 5.

privileges by sin, so Mary earned privileges by the fruits of grace; that, as Eve was disobedient and unbelieving, so Mary was obedient and believing; that, as Eve was a cause of ruin to all, Mary was a cause of salvation to all; that as Eve made room for Adam's fall, so Mary made room for our Lord's reparation of it; and thus, whereas the free gift was not as the offence, but much greater,[i] it follows that, as Eve co-operated in effecting a great evil, Mary co-operated in effecting a much greater good.[13]

And, besides the run of the argument, which reminds the reader of St Paul's antithetical sentences in tracing the analogy between Adam's work and our Lord's work,[j] it is well to observe the particular words under which the Blessed Virgin's office is described. Tertullian says that Mary 'blotted out' Eve's fault, and 'brought back the female sex,' or 'the human race, to salvation'; and St Irenaeus says that 'by obedience she was the cause or occasion' (whatever was the original

[13] This active, personal, free and responsible co-operation of Mary in the work of salvation is underlined by the Second Vatican Council (cf. Dogmatic Constitution on the Church, *Lumen Gentium*, 56). The Council speaks of our Lady contributing, consenting, co-operating in the work of winning divine mercy and restoring grace; Newman, drawing on the same source from which the Council did – viz., the Fathers – uses similar expressions indicative of Mary's active role: she earned privileges, she was a cause of salvation, obedient and believing, she made room for Christ's redemptive work, co-operating in effecting a great good. Pope John Paul II, in his Encyclical 'On the Mercy of God' in 1980, speaks of our Lady as 'meriting' divine grace in an exceptional way through her holy life and sufferings (*Dives in misericordia*, No. 9). This teaching enhances the Blessed Virgin Mary in our estimation. It also shows why Newman regarded it as containing 'all that Catholics hold concerning her intrinsic gifts and powers' (*Essays Critical and Historical*, II, p. 15, footnote). It makes us aware of what a Mother we have in the spiritual order.

Greek word) 'of salvation to herself and the whole
human race'; that by her the human race is saved; that
by her Eve's complication is disentangled; and that she
is Eve's Advocate, or friend in need. It is supposed by
critics, Protestant as well as Catholic, that the Greek
word for Advocate in the original was Paraclete; it
should be borne in mind, then, when we are accused
of giving our Lady the titles and offices of her Son,
that St Irenaeus bestows on her the special Name and
Office proper to the Holy Ghost.

So much as to the nature of this triple testimony;
now as to the worth of it. For a moment put aside St
Irenaeus, and put together St Justin in the East with
Tertullian in the West. I think I may assume that the
doctrine of these two Fathers about the Blessed
Virgin, was the received doctrine of their own respective times and places; for writers after all are but
witnesses of facts and beliefs, and as such they are
treated by all parties in controversial discussion.[14]
Moreover, the coincidence of doctrine which they
exhibit, and again, the antithetical completeness of it,
show that they themselves did not originate it. The
next question is, Who did? for from one definite
organ or source, place or person, it must have come.

[14] Newman attributes much importance to the fact that each of these
three early writers (St Irenaeus, St Justin and Tertullian) are independent witnesses to the doctrine they expose. From it, he wishes to infer
the apostolicity of this Marian doctrine. Not all authors would agree
with Newman about the independence of these three authors. This
does not weaken the conclusion, however. Even though they were
not independent, they could have received the doctrine from a
common source and would thereby testify to a belief universally
accepted in the second century and stemming from Apostolic teaching. (cf. Francis J. Friedel, *The Mariology of Cardinal Newman*, pp.
197–203).

Then we must inquire, what length of time would it take for such a doctrine to have extended, and to be received, in the second century over so wide an area; that is, to be received before the year 200 in Palestine, Africa, and Rome. Can we refer the common source of these local traditions to a date much later than that of the Apostles, since St John died within twenty years of St Justin's conversion and sixty of Tertullian's birth? Make what allowance you will for whatever possible exceptions can be taken to this representation; and then, after doing so, add to the concordant testimony of these two Fathers the evidence of St Irenaeus, which is so close upon that of the School of St John himself in Asia Minor. 'A three-fold cord', as the wise man says, 'is not quickly broken'.[k] Only suppose there were so early and so broad a testimony, to the effect that our Lord was a mere man, the son of Joseph; should we be able to insist upon the faith of the Holy Trinity as necessary to salvation? Or supposing three such witnesses could be brought to the fact that a consistory of elders governed the local churches, or that each local congregation was an independent Church, or that the Christian community was without priests, could Anglicans maintain their doctrine that the rule of Episcopal succession is necessary to constitute a Church? And then recollect that the Anglican Church especially appeals to the ante-Nicene centuries, and taunts us with having superseded their testimony.

Having then adduced these Three Fathers of the second century, I have at least got so far as this: viz., that no one, who acknowledges the force of early testimony in determining Christian truth, can wonder, no one can complain, can object, that we Catholics should hold a very high doctrine concerning the Blessed Virgin, unless indeed stronger statements can be brought for a contrary conception of her, either of as early, or at least of a later date. But, as far as I know, no statements can be brought from the ante-Nicene literature, to invalidate the testimony of the Three Fathers concerning her; and little can be brought against it from the fourth century, while in that fourth century the current of testimony in her behalf is as strong as in the second; and, as to the fifth, it is far stronger than in any former time, both in its fullness and its authority. That such is the concordant verdict of 'the undivided Church' will to some extent be seen as I proceed.

4. St Cyril of Jerusalem (315–86) speaks for Palestine:

> Since through Eve, a Virgin, came death, it behoved, that through a Virgin, or rather from a Virgin, should life appear; that, as the Serpent had deceived the one, so to the other Gabriel might bring good things.[15]

5. St Ephrem Syrus (he died 378) is a witness for the Syrians proper and the neighbouring Orientals, in contrast to the Graeco-Syrians. A native of Nisibis on the farther side of the Euphrates, he knew no language but Syriac.

Through Eve, the beautiful and desirable glory of

---

[15] *Catechesis* XII, 15: *PG* 33:741.

men was extinguished; but it has revived through Mary.[16]

Again:

In the beginning, by the sin of our first parents, death passed upon all men; today, through Mary we are translated from death unto life. In the beginning, the serpent filled the ears of Eve, and the poison spread thence over the whole body; today, Mary from her ears received the champion of eternal happiness: what, therefore, was an instrument of death, was an instrument of life also.[17]

I have already referred to St Paul's contrast between Adam and our Lord in his Epistle to the Romans, as also in his first Epistle to the Corinthians.[1] Some writers venture to say that there is no doctrinal truth, but a mere rhetorical display, in those passages. It is quite as easy to say so, as to attempt so to dispose of this received comparison, in the writings of the Fathers, between Eve and Mary.

6. St Epiphanius (320–400) speaks for Egypt, Palestine, and Cyprus:

She it is, who is signified by Eve, enigmatically receiving the appellation of the Mother of the living ... It was a wonder, that after the transgression she had this great epithet. And, according to

---

[16] *Opera omnia in sex tomos distributa*, II, p. 318.
[17] *Ibid.*, III, p. 607.

what is material, from that Eve all the race of men on earth is generated. But thus in truth from Mary the Life itself was born in the world, that Mary might bear living things, and become the Mother of living things. Therefore, enigmatically, Mary is called the Mother of living things ... Also, there is another thing to consider as to these women, and wonderful,—as to Eve and Mary. Eve became a cause of death to man ... and Mary a cause of life ... that life might be instead of death, life excluding death which came from the woman, viz., He who through the woman has become our life.[18]

7. By the time of St Jerome (331–420), the contrast between Eve and Mary had almost passed into a proverb. He says 'Death by Eve, life by Mary.'[19] Nor let it be supposed that he, any more than the preceding Fathers, considered the Blessed Virgin a mere physical instrument of giving birth to our Lord, who is the Life. So far from it, in the Epistle from which I have quoted, he is only adding another virtue to that crown which gained for Mary her divine Maternity. They have spoken of faith, joy, and obedience; St Jerome adds, what they had only suggested, virginity. After the manner of the Fathers in his own day, he is setting forth the Blessed Mary to the high-born Roman Lady, whom he is addressing, as the model of the virginal life; and his argument in its behalf is, that it is higher than the marriage-state, not in itself, viewed in any mere natural respect, but as being the

---

[18] *Panarion* 78:18: *PG* 42:728–30.
[19] *Epistola ad Eustochium* 22:21: *PL* 22:407–8.

free act of self-consecration to God, and from the personal religious purpose which it involves.

'Higher wage', he says, 'is due to that which is not a compulsion, but an offering; for, were virginity commanded, marriage would seem to be put out of the question; and it would be most cruel to force men against nature, and to extort from them an angel's life.'[20]

I do not know whose testimony is more important than St Jerome's, the friend of Pope Damasus at Rome, the pupil of St Gregory Nazianzen at Constantinople, and of Didymus in Alexandria, a native of Dalmatia, yet an inhabitant, at different times of his life, of Gaul, Syria, and Palestine.

8. St Jerome speaks for the whole world, except Africa; and for Africa in the fourth century, if we must limit so world-wide an authority to place, witnesses St Augustine (354–430). He repeats the words as if a proverb, 'By a woman death, by a woman life';[21] elsewhere he enlarges on the idea conveyed in it. In one place he quotes St Irenaeus's words, as cited above.[22] In another, he speaks as follows:

> It is a great sacrament that, whereas through woman death became our portion, so life was born to us by woman; that, in the case of both sexes, male and female, the baffled devil should be tormented, when on the overthrow of both sexes he was rejoicing; whose punishment had been

[20] *Ibid.*, 22:20: *PL* 22:407.
[21] *Sermo* 232:2: *PL* 38:1108.
[22] *Adversus Julianum* I, 2, 5: *PL* 44:644. Cf. pp. 211–2.

small, if both sexes had been liberated in us, without our being liberated through both.[23]

9. St Peter Chrysologus (400–50), Bishop of Ravenna, and one of the chief authorities in the Fourth General Council:

> Blessed art thou among women; for among women, on whose womb Eve, who was cursed, brought punishment, Mary, being blest, rejoices, is honoured, and is looked up to. And woman now is truly made through grace the Mother of the living, who had been by nature the mother of the dying ... Heaven feels awe of God, Angels tremble at Him, the creature sustains Him not, nature sufficeth not; and yet one maiden so takes, receives, entertains Him, as a guest within her breast, that, for the very hire of her home, and as the price of her womb, she asks, she obtains peace for the earth, glory for the heavens, salvation for the lost, life for the dead, a heavenly parentage for the earthly, the union of God Himself with human flesh.[24]

It is difficult to express more explicitly, though in oratorical language, that the Blessed Virgin had a real meritorious co-operation, a share which had a 'hire' and a 'price', in the reversal of the fall.

10. St Fulgentius, Bishop of Ruspe in Africa (468–533). The Homily which contains the following

---

[23] *De Agone Christiano*, c. 24: *PL* 40:303.
[24] *Sermo* 140: *PL* 52:576–7.

passage, is placed by Ceillier among his genuine works:

> In the wife of the first man, the wickedness of the devil depraved her seduced mind; in the mother of the Second Man, the grace of God preserved both her mind inviolate and her flesh. On her mind it conferred the most firm faith; from her flesh it took away lust altogether. Since then man was in a miserable way condemned for sin, therefore without sin was in a marvellous way born the God-man.[25]

Accordingly, in the Sermon which follows (if it is his), he continues thus, illustrating her office of universal Mother, as ascribed to her by St Epiphanius:

> Come ye virgins to a Virgin, come ye who conceive to her who conceived, ye who bear to one who bore, mothers to a mother, ye that suckle to one who suckled, young girls to the young girl. It is for this reason that the Virgin Mary has taken on her in our Lord Jesus Christ all these divisions of nature, that to all women who have recourse to her, she may be a succour, and so restore the whole race of women who come to her, being the new Eve, by keeping virginity, as the new Adam the Lord Jesus Christ, recovers the whole race of men.[26]

[25] *Sermo* 2, 6. *De Dupl. Nativitate*: *PL* 65:728.

[26] *Ibid. Sermo* 36: *PL* 65:899–900. Four of the ten Patristic authors quoted by Newman, namely, St Irenaeus, St Cyril of Jerusalem, St Epiphanius and St Jerome, are also cited or referred to by the Second Vatican Council in support of this doctrine of the parallel between Mary and Eve: cf. Dogmatic Constitution on the Church, *Lumen Gentium*, 56.

Such is the rudimental view, as I have called it, which the Fathers have given us of Mary, as the Second Eve, the Mother of the living: I have cited ten authors. I could cite more, were it necessary; except the two last, they write gravely and without any rhetoric. I allow that the two last write in a different style, since the extracts I have made are from their sermons; but I do not see that the colouring conceals the outline. And after all, men use oratory on great subjects, not on small; nor would they, and other Fathers whom I might quote, have lavished their high language upon the Blessed Virgin, such as they gave to no one else, unless they knew well that no one else had such claims, as she had, on their love and veneration.

a. Gen 3:20	b. 1 Tim 2:14	c. Gen 3:15
d. Lk 1:38	e. Lk 1:38	f. cf. Mk 9:35
g. Ps 45:16	h. cf. Lk 3:23–38	i. cf. Rom 5:15
j. cf. Rom 5:12–21	k. Eccles 4:12	l. cf. Rom 5:12–21; 1 Cor 15:21–2

A Letter Addressed to the Rev. E.B. Pusey, DD on occasion of his Eirenicon:
Certain Difficulties felt by Anglicans in Catholic Teaching,
London, 1910, Vol. II, pp. 31–44.
Written in December 1865 and first
published at the beginning of 1866.

XI

MARY'S IMMACULATE HOLINESS[1]

Now I proceed to dwell for a while upon two inferences, which it is obvious to draw from the
rudimental doctrine itself; the first relates to the sanctity of the Blessed Virgin, the second to her dignity.

Her sanctity. She holds, as the Fathers teach us, that
office in our restoration which Eve held in our fall:
now, in the first place, what were Eve's endowments
to enable her to enter upon her trial? She could not
have stood against the wiles of the devil, though she
was innocent and sinless, without the grant of a large
grace. And this she had: a heavenly gift, which was
over and above the additional to that nature of hers,
which she received from Adam, a gift which had been
given to Adam also before her, at the very time (as it
is commonly held) of his original formation. This is
Anglican doctrine, as well as Catholic; it is the

---

[1] Having described the Patristic teaching of Mary as the Second Eve,
Newman now begins to deduce some important conclusions from it.
The first deals with Mary's Immaculate Conception or, in other words,
her sanctity. In many ways, this point is at the core of Newman's
Mariological teaching (cf. above, Introduction IV, pp. 51–64).

doctrine of Bishop Bull.[2] He has written a dissertation on the point. He speaks of the doctrine which 'many of the Schoolmen affirm, that Adam was created in grace, that is, received a principle of grace and divine life from his very creation, or in the moment of the infusion of his soul; of which', he says, 'for my own part I have little doubt'. Again, he says, 'It is abundantly manifest from the many testimonies alleged, that the ancient doctors of the Church did, with a general consent, acknowledge, that our first parents in the state of integrity, had in them something more than nature, that is, were endowed with the divine principle of the Spirit, in order to a supernatural felicity.'

Now, taking this for granted, because I know that you and those who agree with you maintain it as well as we do, I ask you, have you any intention to deny that Mary was as fully endowed as Eve? is it any violent inference, that she, who was to co-operate in the redemption of the world, at least was not less endowed with power from on high, than she who, given as a helpmate to her husband, did in the event but co-operate with him for its ruin? If Eve was raised above human nature by that indwelling moral gift which we call grace, is it rash to say that Mary had

---

[2] George Bull (1634–1710) was Bishop of St Davids (Wales). He was a renowned theologian and High Anglican. His most celebrated treatise was entitled *Defensio fidei Nicaenae* (1685), in which he maintained – against the idea of development proposed by Dionysius Petavius SJ, in his *Opus de Theologicis Dogmatibus* (1643–50) – that the doctrinal elucidation of the Trinity was already known to and developed by the pre-Nicene Fathers. According to Bull, the elucidations of the post-Nicene writers were to be interpreted in the light of what had been taught in earlier times.

even a greater grace? And this consideration gives
significance to the Angel's salutation of her as 'full of
grace',[a]—an interpretation of the original word which
is undoubtedly the right one, as soon as we resist the
common Protestant assumption that grace is a mere
external approbation or acceptance, answering to the
word 'favour', whereas it is, as the Fathers teach, a real
inward condition or superadded quality of soul.[3] And
if Eve had this supernatural inward gift given her from
the first moment of her personal existence, is it possible to deny that Mary too had this gift from the very
first moment of her personal existence? I do not know
how to resist this inference—well, this is simply and
literally the doctrine of the Immaculate Conception. I
say the doctrine of the Immaculate Conception is in
its substance this, and nothing more or less than this
(putting aside the question of degrees of grace); and it
really does seem to me bound up in the doctrine of
the Fathers, that Mary is the second Eve.

It is indeed to me a most strange phenomenon that
so many learned and devout men stumble at this
doctrine; and I can only account for it by supposing
that in matter of fact they do not know what we mean
by the Immaculate Conception; and your Volume
(may I say it?) bears out my suspicion. It is a great
consolation to have reason for thinking so,—reason for
believing that in some sort the persons in question are

[3] Some modern scholars also support this reading of the Greek words
which is clear from the Vulgate and which has been used in all Church
documents: cf. Michael O'Carroll, CSSp, 'Mary, Mother of God' in
The New Dictionary of Theology. Editors: Joseph A. Komonchak, Mary
Collins, Dermot A. Lane. Dublin, Gill & Macmillan, 1992, p. 637;
Domenico Bertetto, *Maria la Serva del Signore*: trattato di Mariologia.
Napoli, 1988, pp. 286–7.

in the position of those great Saints in former times, who are said to have hesitated about the doctrine, when they would not have hesitated at all, if the word 'Conception' had been clearly explained in that sense in which now it is universally received.[4] I do not see how any one who holds with Bull the Catholic doctrine of the supernatural endowments of our first parents, has fair reason for doubting our doctrine about the Blessed Virgin. It has no reference whatever to her parents, but simply to her own person; it does but affirm that, together with the nature which she inherited from her parents, that is, her own nature, she had a superadded fullness of grace, and that from the first moment of her existence. Suppose Eve had stood the trial, and not lost her first grace; and suppose she had eventually had children, those children from the first moment of their existence would, through divine bounty, have received the same privilege that she had ever had; that is, as she was taken from Adam's side, in a garment, so to say, of grace, so they in turn would have received what may be called an immaculate conception. They would have then been conceived in grace, as in fact they are conceived in sin. What is there difficult in this doctrine? What is there unnatural? Mary may be called, as it were, a daughter of Eve unfallen. You believe with us that St John Baptist had grace given to him three months before his birth, at the time that the Blessed Virgin visited his mother. He accordingly was *not* immaculately conceived, because he was

---

[4] There were various misconceptions about the real meaning of the Immaculate Conception. Among them was the one, which Newman goes on to mention, that understood it to refer to Mary's parents who, it was thought, were kept free from all concupiscence in the conception of their child.

alive before grace came to him; but our Lady's case only differs from his in this respect, that to her the grace of God came, not three months merely before the birth, but from the first moment of her being, as it had been given to Eve.

But it may be said, How does this enable us to say that she was conceived without *original sin*? If Anglicans knew what we mean by original sin, they would not ask the question. Our doctrine of original sin is not the same as the Protestant doctrine.[5] 'Original sin', with us, cannot be called sin, in the mere ordinary sense of the word 'sin'; it is a term denoting Adam's sin as transferred to us, or the state to which Adam's sin reduces his children; but by Protestants it seems to be understood as sin, in much the same sense as actual sin. We, with the Fathers, think of it as something negative, Protestants as something positive. Protestants hold that it is a disease, a radical change of nature, an active poison internally corrupting the soul, infecting its primary elements, and disorganizing it; and they fancy that we ascribe a different nature from ours to the Blessed Virgin, different from that of her parents, and from that of fallen Adam. We hold nothing of the kind; we consider that in Adam she died, as others; that she was included, together with the whole race, in Adam's sentence; that she incurred his debt, as we do; but that, for the sake of Him who was to redeem her and us upon the Cross, to her the debt was remitted by anticipation, on her the sentence was not

---

[5] Newman gives an excellent summary of the difference between the Catholic and the Protestant idea of original sin. In Catholic theology it is regarded as the lack of divine grace and friendship that should have been transmitted with human nature but that are missing; in Protestant theology it is seen as a positive corrupting force, or in Newman's words, 'an active poison internally corrupting the soul'.

carried out, except indeed as regards her natural death, for she died when her time came, as others.[6] All this we teach, but we deny that she had original sin; for by original sin we mean, as I have already said, something negative, viz., this only, the *deprivation* of that supernatural unmerited grace which Adam and Eve had on their first formation,—deprivation and the consequences of deprivation. Mary could not merit, any more than they, the restoration of that grace; but it was restored to her by God's free bounty, from the very first moment of her existence, and thereby, in fact, she never came under the original curse, which consisted in the loss of it. And she had this special privilege, in order to fit her to become the Mother of her and our Redeemer, to fit her mentally, spiritually for it; so that, by the aid of the first grace, she might so grow in grace, that, when the Angel came and her Lord was at hand, she might be 'full of grace', prepared as far as a creature could be prepared, to receive Him into her bosom.

[6] Some traditional Catholics found the words 'in Adam she (Mary) died, as others ... she incurred his debt' difficult to accept. Newman gives a perfectly orthodox explanation of his meaning, which basically signifies that our Lady needed to be redeemed like all the offspring of Adam. However, she was redeemed in a unique fashion. In virtue of the foreseen merits of her Divine Son, the sin that all inherit was not allowed to sully her soul in any way. In support of his statement, Newman quotes in an Appendix some passages from two seventeenth-century scholars: the theologian Suárez and the exegete Cornelius a Lapide (cf. *Difficulties felt by Anglicans*, II, pp. 125–7). Not all questions in the mystery of original sin and of Mary's preservation from it through her Immaculate Conception were clarified by the Papal Definition of 1854. The phrase 'the debt of sin' gave rise to numerous studies and theological investigations (cf. above: Introduction, III, pp. 46–47). In all this discussion, it is helpful to remember that the original fault is a 'sin' only in an analogous sense; it is not a personal fault (except in Adam and Eve), and therefore not a 'sin' in the same univocal sense as personal sins.

I have drawn the doctrine of the Immaculate Conception, as an immediate inference, from the primitive doctrine that Mary is the second Eve. The argument seems to me conclusive: and, if it has not been universally taken as such, this has come to pass, because there has not been a clear understanding among Catholics, what exactly was meant by the 'Immaculate Conception'. To many it seemed to imply that the Blessed Virgin did not die in Adam, that she did not come under the penalty of the fall, that she was not redeemed, that she was conceived in some way inconsistent with the verse in the *Miserere* Psalm.[7] If controversy had in earlier days so cleared the subject as to make it plain to all, that the doctrine meant nothing

[7] In former centuries one of the main difficulties raised against the Immaculate Conception of Mary was the certain doctrine of the universal nature of Christ's work of Redemption. It seemed to many that the two doctrines were incompatible. If Mary was not redeemed, how could Christ's redemptive sacrifice be universal? The theological explanation was finally apparent: Mary needed to be redeemed and in fact was redeemed, but in a unique way – by anticipation. On account of the foreseen merits of her Son in his Passion, original sin did not touch her. She was not made immaculate after sin had tainted her, but kept immaculate from the beginning of her existence. Duns Scotus (1264–1308) was the first theologian of note to offer this explanation, showing how it was a more perfect grace to have been preserved rather to have been set free from original sin. Christ's work of Redemption was effective in her in a more excellent manner. This argument was used by Pius IX in the Bull *Ineffabilis Deus*: Mary was 'redeemed in a more exalted fashion': *sublimiori modo redempta*. The same phrase is used by the Vatican Council in the Dogmatic Constitution on the Church (cf. *Lumen Gentium*, 53; Christopher O'Donnell, O Carm, *At Worship with Mary. A Pastoral and Theological Study*. Wilmington, Delaware, Michael Glazier, 1988, pp. 222–3). The verse of the psalm *Miserere* reads: 'Behold, I was brought forth in iniquity, and in sin did my mother conceive me' (Ps. 50 (51):7). It expresses the deep-rooted impurity or sinfulness in every person – not yet the full revelation of the doctrine of original sin, but as it were foreshadowing it and in accord with orthodox teaching.

else than that in fact in her case the general sentence on mankind was not carried out, and that, by means of the indwelling in her of divine grace from the first moment of her being (and this is all the decree of 1854 has declared), I cannot believe that the doctrine would have ever been opposed; for an instinctive sentiment has led Christians jealously to put the Blessed Mary aside when sin comes into discussion. This is expressed in the well-known words of St Augustine, All have sinned 'except the Holy Virgin Mary, concerning whom, for the honour of the Lord, I wish no question to be raised at all, when we are treating of sins';[8] words which, whatever was St Augustine's actual occasion of using them (to which you refer), certainly, in the spirit which they breathe, are well adapted to convey the notion, that, though her parents had no privilege beyond other parents, she had not personally any part in sin whatever. It is true that several great Fathers of the fourth century do imply or assert that on one or two occasions she did sin venially or showed infirmity.

[8] Cf. above, Text V, p. 170, footnote 7.

This is the only real objection which I know of; and as I do not wish to pass it over lightly, I propose to consider it at the end of this Letter.[9]

a. Lk 1:28

*A Letter Addressed to the Rev. E.B. Pusey DD
on occasion of his Eirenicon:
Certain Difficulties felt by Anglicans in Catholic Teaching,*
London, 1910, Vol. II, pp. 44–50.
Written in December 1865 and first published
at the beginning of 1866.

[9] Newman refers to three Church Fathers whose words he takes from that distinguished seventeenth-century theologian, Petavius (*De Incarnatione* XIV, ch. 1), namely, St Basil, St John Chrysostom and St Cyril of Alexandria. On occasion, they attribute a slight sin or imperfection (of doubt or vainglory) to Mary. Newman treats the question at length in *Note III* at the end of the published edition of his *Letter to Pusey*, and shows that these sayings do not represent the mind of the Fathers in general, nor do they transmit an Apostolic tradition. (cf. *Difficulties felt by Anglicans* II, pp. 128–52). For a discussion on this question, cf. Francis J. Friedel, *The Mariology of Cardinal Newman.* New York 1923, pp. 278–87.

XII

THE UNIQUE DIGNITY OF OUR LADY

Now, secondly, her dignity.[1] Here let us suppose that
our first parents had overcome in their trial; and had
gained for their descendants for ever the full possession,
as if by right, of the privileges which were promised to
their obedience,—grace here and glory hereafter. Is it
possible that those descendants, pious and happy from
age to age in their temporal homes, would have forgotten their benefactors? Would they not have followed
them in thought into the heavens, and gratefully
commemorated them on earth? The history of the
temptation, the craft of the serpent, their steadfastness
in obedience,—the loyal vigilance, the sensitive purity
of Eve,—the great issue, salvation wrought out for all
generations,—would have been never from their
minds, ever welcome to their ears. This would have
taken place from the necessity of our nature. Every
nation has its mythical hymns and epics about its first
fathers and its heroes. The great deeds of Charlemagne,

---

[1] Mary's dignity is the second inference drawn by Newman from our
Lady's position as the Second Eve.

Alfred, Cœur de Lion, Louis IX, Wallace,[2] Joan of Arc, do not die; and though their persons are gone from us, we make much of their names. Milton's Adam, after his fall, understands the force of this law and shrinks from the prospect of its operation.

> Who of all ages to succeed, but, feeling
> The evil on him brought by me, will curse
> My head? Ill fare our ancestor impure,
> For this we may thank Adam.[3]

If this anticipation of the first man has not been fulfilled in the event, it is owing to the exigencies of our penal life, our state of perpetual change, and the ignorance and unbelief incurred by the fall; also because, fallen as we are, still from the hopefulness of our nature, we feel more pride in our national great men, than dejection at our national misfortunes. Much more then in the great kingdom and people of God; the Saints are ever in our sight, and not as mere ineffectual ghosts or dim memories, but as if present bodily in their past selves. It is said of them, 'Their works do follow them';[a] what they were here, such are they in heaven and in the Church. As we call them by their earthly names, so we contemplate them in their earthly characters and histories. Their acts, callings, and relations below, are types and anticipations of their present mission above. Even in the case of our Lord Himself, whose native home is the eternal heavens, it is said of Him in His state of glory,

---

[2] *Alfred* was the Anglo-Saxon King of the ninth century (+900). *Cœur de Lion* was the English King Richard I (+1199). William Wallace (+1305) was a renowned freedom fighter from Scotland.

[3] John Milton, *Paradise Lost*, Book X, lines 736–9.

that He is 'a Priest for ever';[b] and when He comes
again, He will be recognized by those who pierced
Him, as being the very same that He was on earth. The
only question is, whether the Blessed Virgin had a part,
a real part, in the economy of grace, whether, when she
was on earth, she secured by her deeds any claim on
our memories; for, if she did, it is impossible we should
put her away from us, merely because she is gone
hence, and should not look at her still according to the
measure of her earthly history, with gratitude and
expectation. If, as St Irenaeus says, she acted the part of
an Advocate, a friend in need, even in her mortal life, if
as St Jerome and St Ambrose say, she was on earth the
great pattern of Virgins, if she had a meritorious share
in bringing about our redemption, if her maternity was
gained by her faith and obedience, if her Divine Son
was subject to her, and if she stood by the Cross
with a mother's heart and drank in to the full those
sufferings which it was her portion to gaze upon, it is
impossible that we should not associate these charac-
teristics of her life on earth with her present state of
blessedness; and this surely she anticipated, when she
said in her hymn that all 'generations should call her
blessed'.[c]

I am aware that, in thus speaking, I am following a
line of thought which is rather a meditation than an
argument in controversy, and I shall not carry it
further; but still, before turning to other topics, it is to
the point to inquire, whether the popular astonish-
ment, excited by our belief in the blessed Virgin's
present dignity, does not arise from the circumstance
that the bulk of men, engaged in matters of this world,
have never calmly considered her historical position in

the Gospels, so as rightly to realize (if I may use the word a second time) what that position imports. I do not claim for the generality of Catholics any greater powers of reflection upon the objects of their faith, than Protestants commonly have; but, putting the run of Catholics aside, there is a sufficient number of religious men among us who, instead of expending their devotional energies (as so many serious Protestants do) on abstract doctrines, such as justification by faith only, or the sufficiency of Holy Scripture, employ themselves in the contemplation of Scripture facts, and bring out before their minds in a tangible form the doctrines involved in them, and give such a substance and colour to the sacred history, as to influence their brethren; and their brethren, though superficial themselves, are drawn by their Catholic instinct to accept conclusions which they could not indeed themselves have elicited, but which, when elicited, they feel to be true. However, it would be out of place to pursue this course of reasoning here; and instead of doing so, I shall take what perhaps you may think a very bold step,—I shall find the doctrine of our Lady's present exaltation in Scripture.

I mean to find it in the vision of the Woman and Child[4] in the twelfth chapter of the Apocalypse:—

[4] Rather than give a theological argument in favour of the dignity of the Blessed Virgin Mary, Newman turns to Scripture (the vision of the Woman and the Child in the Book of the Apocalypse, ch. 12), which he knows will be more appreciated by Anglicans. In a footnote he refers the reader to a discussion of this same point in his *Development of Christian Doctrine*, (p. 384) or, pp. 415–16 in later editions (cf. below, Text XVI, pp. 283–5), and to Bishop Ullathorne's study *The Immaculate Conception of the Mother of God, an Exposition*. London, 1855, p. 77. Newman said that this study by Ullathorne was 'a work full of instruction and of the first authority' (*Difficulties felt by Anglicans*, II, p. 127).

now here two objections will be made to me at once; first that such an interpretation is but poorly supported by the Fathers, and secondly that in ascribing such a picture of the Madonna (as it may be called) to the Apostolic age, I am committing an anachronism.

As to the former of these objections, I answer as follows:—Christians have never gone to Scripture for proof of their doctrines, till there was actual need, from the pressure of controversy; – if in those times the Blessed Virgin's dignity was unchallenged on all hands, as a matter of doctrine, Scripture, as far as its argumentative matter was concerned, was likely to remain a sealed book to them. Thus, to take an instance in point; the Catholic party in the Anglican Church (say, the Nonjurors[5]), unable by their theory of religion simply to take their stand on Tradition, and distressed for proof of their doctrines, had their eyes sharpened to scrutinize and to understand in many places the letter of Holy Scripture, which to others brought no instruction. And the peculiarity of their interpretations is this,—that these have in themselves great logical cogency, yet are but faintly supported by patristical commentators. Such is the use of the word ποιεῖν or *facere* in our Lord's institution of the Holy

[5] 'Nonjurors' was the name given to over 400 clergy and some laity of the Anglican Church who in 1689 refused to take the oath of allegiance to William and Mary, regarding themselves bound in conscience by the oath they had taken to James II. They were men of high moral and traditional values, with deep respect for Scripture. They were deprived of their income and fell into poverty. The bishops among them consecrated other bishops to succeed them and they believed they had the true Anglican succession. They lasted until the end of the eighteenth century when, owing to changed circumstances, they found it possible again to take the oath to the reigning monarch (George III).

Eucharist, which, by a reference to the Old Testament, is found to be a word of sacrifice. Such again is λειτουργούντων in the passage in the Acts 'As they *ministered* to the Lord and fasted',[d] which again is a sacerdotal term. And such the passage in Rom 15:16, in which several terms are used which have an allusion to the sacrificial Eucharistic rite.[6] Such too is St Paul's repeated message to the *household* of Onesiphorus, with no mention of Onesiphorus himself, but in one place with the addition of a prayer that 'he might find mercy of the Lord'[e] in the day of judgment, which, taking into account its wording and the known usage of the first centuries, we can hardly deny is a prayer for his soul. Other texts there are, which ought to find a place in ancient controversies, and the omission of which by the Fathers affords matter for more surprise; those for instance, which, according to Middleton's rule,[7] are real proofs of our Lord's divinity, and yet are passed over by Catholic disputants; for these bear

---

[6] Rom 15:16 reads: '... the grace given to me by God to be a minister of Christ Jesus to the Gentiles in the priestly service of the gospel of God, so that the offering of the Gentiles may be acceptable, sanctified by the Holy Spirit.' One of the 'sacerdotal terms' to which Newman refers in this passage is: *leitourgos*: minister (in public worship). The corresponding verb is in Acts 13:2: 'while they were worshipping' i.e. performing the sacred ministry. *Leitourgein* may simply mean 'serving' the Lord, but the cultic sense is evident from its use in the Old Testament Septuagint (cf. Ex 28:35, 43; 29–30; Num 18:2). The word *poiein* (to do) is used in the institution of the Eucharist: '*Do* this in remembrance of me' (Lk 22:19; 1 Cor 2:24–5).

[7] Conyers Middleton (1683–1750), an English clergyman and theologian. He denied the credibility of miracles after the time of the Apostles. He acknowledged the testimony of the Fathers in matters concerning the beliefs and practices of their own day, but not in any other factual matters they recount.

upon a then existing controversy of the first moment, and of the most urgent exigency.

As to the second objection which I have supposed, so far from allowing it, I consider that it is built upon a mere imaginary fact, and that the truth of the matter lies in the very contrary direction. The Virgin and Child is *not* a mere modern idea; on the contrary, it is represented again and again, as every visitor to Rome is aware, in the paintings of the Catacombs. Mary is there drawn with the Divine Infant in her lap, she with hands extended in prayer, He with His hand in the attitude of blessing.[8] No representation can more forcibly convey the doctrine of the high dignity of the Mother, and, I will add, of her influence with her Son. Why should the memory of His time of subjection be so dear to Christians, and so carefully preserved? The only question to be determined, is the precise date of these remarkable monuments of the first age of Christianity. That they belong to the centuries of what Anglicans call the 'undivided Church' is certain; but lately investigations have been pursued, which place some of them at an earlier date than any one anticipated as possible. I am not in a position to quote largely from the works of the Cavaliere de Rossi,[9] who has thrown so much light upon the subject; but I have his *Imagini Scelte*, published in 1863, and they are sufficient for my

[8] There are various representations of the Mother and Child in the Roman Catacombs. The one Newman refers to is probably that in the Catacomb of St Priscilla on the Via Salaria.

[9] Giovanni Battista de Rossi (1822–94), the famous Roman archaeologist who devoted 50 years of his life to the excavation and study of the catacombs in Rome. He is regarded as the founder of the science of Christian archaeology. He published very many books and studies, some of which are truly monumental.

purpose. In this work he has given us from the Catacombs various representations of the Virgin and Child; the latest of these belong to the early part of the fourth century, but the earliest he believes to be referable to the very age of the Apostles. He comes to this conclusion from the style and the skill of its composition, and from the history, locality, and existing inscriptions of the subterranean in which it is found. However he does not go so far as to insist upon so early a date; yet the utmost concession he makes is to refer the painting to the era of the first Antonines, that is, to a date within half a century of the death of St John.[10] I consider then, that, as you would use in controversy with Protestants, and fairly, the traditional doctrine of the Church in early times, as an explanation of a particular passage of Scripture, or at least as a suggestion, or as a defence, of the sense which you may wish to put upon it, quite apart from the question whether your interpretation itself is directly traditional, so it is lawful for me, though I have not the positive words of the Fathers on my side, to shelter my own interpretation of the Apostle's vision in the Apocalypse under the fact of the extant pictures of Mother and Child in the Roman Catacombs. Again, there is another principle of Scripture interpretation which we should hold as well as you, viz., when we speak of a doctrine being

---

[10] The first of the 'Antonines' was the Roman Emperor Antoninus Pius who died in the year AD 161. He was succeeded by Marcus Aurelius Antoninus (+180). Modern historians of art would date the Virgin and Child images in the Roman Catacombs not to the second century, but at earliest to the first half of the third century. Cf. however, Vincent Ferrer Blehl SJ, *The White Stone. The Spiritual Theology of John Henry Newman*, Petersham MA, St Bede's Publications, 1994, p. 121.

contained in Scripture, we do not necessarily mean
that it is contained there in direct categorical terms, but
that there is no satisfactory way of accounting for the
language and expressions of the sacred writers,
concerning the subject-matter in question, except to
suppose that they held concerning it the opinion which
we hold,—that they would not have spoken as they
have spoken, *unless* they held it. For myself I have ever
felt the truth of this principle, as regards the Scripture
proof of the Holy Trinity; I should not have found out
that doctrine in the sacred text without previous traditional teaching; but, when once it is suggested from
without, it commends itself as the one true interpretation, from its appositeness,—because no other view of
doctrine, which can be ascribed to the inspired writers,
so happily solves the obscurities and seeming inconsis-
tencies of their teaching. And now to apply what I have
been saying to the passage in the Apocalypse.

If there is an Apostle on whom, *à priori*, our eyes
would be fixed, as likely to teach us about the Blessed
Virgin, it is St John, to whom she was committed by
our Lord on the Cross;[f]—with whom, as tradition
goes, she lived at Ephesus till she was taken away. This
anticipation is confirmed *à posteriori*; for, as I have said
above, one of the earliest and fullest of our informants
concerning her dignity, as being the second Eve, is
Irenaeus, who came to Lyons from Asia Minor, and
had been taught by the immediate disciples of St
John.[11] The Apostle's vision is as follows:

[11] Among the 'immediate disciples' of St John was St Polycarp
(*c.*69–*c.*155, Bishop of Smyrna). Tradition has it that St Irenaeus
(130–*c.*200) as a young man knew and listened to St Polycarp in
Smyrna. St Irenaeus calls St Papias (Bishop of Hierapolis) 'a hearer of
John and companion of Polycarp' (*Adversus Haereses*, V, xxxiii).

> A great sign appeared in heaven: A woman clothed with the Sun, and the Moon under her feet; and on her head a crown of twelve stars. And being with child, she cried travailing in birth, and was in pain to be delivered. And there was seen another sign in heaven; and behold a great red dragon ... And the dragon stood before the woman who was ready to be delivered, that, when she should be delivered, he might devour her son. And she brought forth a man child, who was to rule all nations with an iron rod; and her son was taken up to God and to His throne. And the woman fled into the wilderness.[g]

Now I do not deny of course, that under the image of the Woman, the Church is signified; but what I would maintain is this, that the Holy Apostle would not have spoken of the Church under this particular image, *unless* there had existed a blessed Virgin Mary, who was exalted on high, and the object of veneration to all the faithful.

No one doubts that the 'man-child' spoken of is an allusion to our Lord: why then is not 'the Woman' an allusion to His Mother?[12] This surely is the obvious sense of the words; of course they have a further sense also, which is the scope of the image; doubtless the Child represents the children of the Church, and doubtless the Woman represents the Church; this, I grant, is the real or direct sense, but what is the sense

[12] Some ancient as well as modern authors understand 'the woman' in this text of the Apocalypse to refer not only to the Church but also to our Lady. Cf. above, Text VIII, p. 193, footnote 4. Cf. also Candido Pozo, *Maria el la obra de la Salvación*, Madrid, 1974, p. 245; Dominic J. Unger, OFM Cap, 'Cardinal Newman and Apocalypse XII': *Theological Studies* 11 (1950) pp. 356–7.

of the symbol under which that real sense is conveyed? *who* are the Woman and the Child? I answer, they are not personifications but Persons. This is true of the Child, therefore it is true of the Woman.

But again: not only Mother and Child, but a serpent is introduced into the vision. Such a meeting of man, woman, and serpent has not been found in Scripture, since the beginning of Scripture, and now it is found in its end. Moreover, in the passage in the Apocalypse, as if to supply, before Scripture came to an end, what was wanting in its beginning, we are told, and for the first time, that the serpent in Paradise was the evil spirit. If the dragon of St John is the same as the serpent of Moses,[h] and the man-child is 'the seed of the woman',[i] why is not the woman herself she, whose seed the man-child is? And, if the first woman is not an allegory, why is the second? if the first woman is Eve, why is not the second Mary?

But this is not all. The image of the woman, according to general Scripture usage, is too bold and prominent for a mere personification. Scripture is not fond of allegories. We have indeed frequent figures there, as when the sacred writers speak of the arm or sword of the Lord; and so too when they speak of Jerusalem or Samaria in the feminine; or of the Church as a bride or as a vine; but they are not much given to dressing up abstract ideas or generalizations in personal attributes. This is the classical rather than the Scriptural style. Xenophon places Hercules between Virtue and Vice, represented as women; Aeschylus introduces into his drama Force and Violence; Virgil gives personality to public rumour or Fame, and Plautus to Poverty. So on monuments done in the classical style, we see virtues, vices, rivers, renown, death, and the like, turned into human figures of men and women. Certainly I do not deny there are some instances of this method in Scripture, but I say that such poetical compositions are strikingly unlike its usual method. Thus, we at once feel the difference from Scripture, when we betake ourselves to the Pastor of Hermas, and find the Church a woman; to St Methodius, and find Virtue a woman; and to St Gregory's poem, and find Virginity again a woman. Scripture deals with types[13] rather than personifications. Israel stands for the chosen people, David for Christ, Jerusalem for heaven. Consider the remarkable representations, dramatic I may call them, in Jeremiah, Ezechiel, and Hosea: predictions, threatenings, and promises, are acted out by those Prophets. Ezechiel is commanded to shave his head, and to divide and scatter his hair;[j] and Ahias tears his garment, and gives ten out of twelve parts of it to Jeroboam.[k] So too the structure of the imagery in the Apocalypse is not a mere allegorical creation,[14] but is founded on the Jewish ritual. In like manner our Lord's bodily cures are visible types of the power of His grace upon the soul; and His prophecy of the last day is conveyed under that of the fall of Jerusalem. Even His parables

[13] A 'type' (from Greek *typos* meaning an 'impression' or an 'image' or 'example') is an exposition of the sacred text which presents people or events of the Old Testament as prefigurations or patterns of persons and events in the New Testament. The scriptural base for a typological interpretation rests on St Paul's use of the word in the sense of 'example' or 'image' in Rom 5:12 (Adam a 'type' of Christ) and 1 Cor 10:6 (The Israelites in the desert are a 'type' of Christians in their pilgrimage of faith in this world).

[14] An 'allegory' is a continued and developed metaphor in which the single details signify another reality.

are not simply ideal, but relations of occurrences, which did or might take place, under which was conveyed a spiritual meaning. The description of Wisdom in the Proverbs and other sacred books, has brought out the instinct of commentators in this respect. They felt that Wisdom could not be a mere personification, and they determined that it was our Lord: and the later-written of these books, by their own more definite language, warranted that interpretation. Then, when it was found that the Arians used it in derogation of our Lord's divinity, still, unable to tolerate the notion of a mere allegory, commentators applied the description to the Blessed Virgin. Coming back then to the Apocalyptic vision, I ask, If the Woman ought to be some real person, who can it be whom the Apostle saw, and intends, and delineates, but that same Great Mother to whom the chapters in the Proverbs are accommodated?[1] And let it be observed, moreover, that in this passage, from the allusion made in it to the history of the fall, Mary may be said still to be represented under the character of the Second Eve. I make a further remark: it is sometimes asked, Why do not the sacred writers mention our Lady's greatness? I answer, she was, or may have been alive, when the Apostles and Evangelists wrote; there was just one book of Scripture certainly written after her death, and that book does (so to say) canonize and crown her.

But if all this be so, if it is really the Blessed Virgin whom Scripture represents as clothed with the sun, crowned with the stars of heaven, and with the moon as her footstool, what height of glory may we not attribute to her? and what are we to say of those who, through ignorance, run counter to the voice of Scripture, to the testimony of the Fathers, to the traditions of East and West, and speak and act contemptuously towards her whom her Lord delighteth to honour?

a. Rev 14:13   b. Heb 7:21; Ps 110:4   c. Lk 1:48
d. Acts 13:2   e. 2 Tim 1:18   f. cf. Jn 19:26–7
g. Rev 12:1–3a, 4b–6a h. cf. Num 21:4–9   i. Gen 3:15
j. cf. Ezek 5:1–12   k. cf. 1 Kings 11:28–39   l. cf. Prov 8 and 9

A Letter Addressed to the Rev. E.B. Pusey, DD on occasion of his Eirenicon: Certain Difficulties felt by Anglicans in Catholic Teaching, London, 1910, Vol. II, pp. 50–61. Written in December 1865 and first published at the beginning of 1866.

XIII/A

MARY, THE MOTHER OF GOD (THEOTOKOS)

Now I have said all I mean to say on what I have called the rudimental teaching of Antiquity about the Blessed Virgin; but after all I have not insisted on the highest view of her prerogatives, which the Fathers have taught us. You, my dear Friend, who know so well the ancient controversies and Councils, may have been surprised why I should not have yet spoken of her as the *Theotokos*;—but I wished to show on how broad a basis her dignity rests, independent of that wonderful title; and again I have been loath to enlarge upon the force of a word, which is rather matter for devotional thought than for polemical dispute. However, I might as well not write to you at all, as altogether be silent upon it.[1]

[1] One could well wonder why Newman did not begin with this point which indicates Mary's highest prerogative – her Divine Maternity. He himself hints at the answer in these lines. He was fully aware of the ecumenical readership to which his study was directed and knew all the reluctance of Anglicans in using the term 'Mother of God'. He therefore began with the parallel Eve–Mary which offered no special difficulty, and from which he regarded Mary's sinlessness and Immaculate Conception (a sensitive issue at the time and stumbling block for many non-Catholics) flowed 'as an immediate inference'.

It is then an integral portion of the Faith fixed by Ecumenical Council, a portion of it which you hold as well as I, that the Blessed Virgin is *Theotokos*, *Deipara*, or Mother of God;[2] and this word, when thus used, carries with it no admixture of rhetoric, no taint of extravagant affection,—it has nothing else but a well-weighed, grave, dogmatic sense, which corresponds and is adequate to its sound. It intends to express that God is her Son, as truly as any one of us is the son of his own mother. If this be so, what can be said of any creature whatever, which may not be said of her? what can be said too much, so that it does not compromise the attributes of the Creator? He indeed might have created a being more perfect, more admirable, than she is; He might have endued that being, so created, with a richer grant of grace, of power, of blessedness: but in one respect she surpasses all even possible creations, viz., that she is Mother of her Creator. It is this awful title, which both illustrates and connects together the two prerogatives of Mary, on which I have been lately

[2] The Ecumenical Council which gave the solemn dogmatic pronouncement about Mary as the *Theotokos*, the Mother of God, was the Council of Ephesus in 431. It thus made official the title *Theotokos* already applied to the Mother of Jesus by Origen in the third century. This Council solemnly approved the doctrine of St Cyril of Alexandria, namely, that the holy Fathers 'did not doubt to call the Blessed Virgin the Mother of God, not because the nature of the Word or his divinity had the origin of their existence from the Blessed Virgin, but that, since the holy body, animated by a rational soul, which the Word of God substantially united to himself, was born from her, the Word is said to be born according to the flesh' (Denzinger-Schönmetzer, No. 251). 'If anyone does not confess that Emmanuel is truly God, and that therefore the Blessed Virgin is Mother of God (*Theotokos*) for she bore according to the flesh the Word who is from God, let him be anathema' (*ibid.* 252).

enlarging, her sanctity and her greatness. It is the issue of her sanctity; it is the origin of her greatness. What dignity can be too great to attribute to her who is as closely bound up, as intimately one, with the Eternal Word, as a mother is with a son? What outfit of sanctity, what fullness and redundance of grace, what exuberance of merits must have been hers, when once we admit the supposition, which the Fathers justify, that her Maker really did regard those merits, and take them into account, when He condescended 'not to abhor the Virgin's womb'?[3] Is it surprising then that on the one hand she should be immaculate in her Conception? or on the other that she should be honoured with an Assumption, and exalted as a queen with a crown of twelve stars, with the rulers of day and night to do her service? Men sometimes wonder that we call her Mother of life, of mercy, of salvation; what are all these titles compared to that one name, Mother of God?

I shall say no more about this title here. It is scarcely possible to write of it without diverging into a style of composition unsuited to a Letter; so I will but refer to the history and to instances of its use.

The title of *Theotokos*,[4] as ascribed to the Blessed Mary, begins with ecclesiastical writers of a date hardly later than that at which we read of her as the second Eve. It first occurs in the works of Origen (185–254); but he, witnessing for Egypt and Palestine, witnesses also that it was in use before his time; for, as

---

[3] Words from the *Te Deum*.

[4] [*Vid.* Oxford translation of St Athanasius, pp. 420, 440, 447: *Essay on Doct. Development*, pp. 407–9.] In later Editions of the *Essay* it was on pp. 416–8.

Socrates informs us, he 'interpreted how it was to be used, and discussed the question at length'.[5] Within two centuries of his time (431), in the General Council held against Nestorius, it was made part of the formal dogmatic teaching of the Church. At that time, Theodoret,[6] who from his party connexions might have been supposed disinclined to its solemn recognition, owned that 'the ancient and more than ancient heralds of the orthodox faith taught the use of the term according to the Apostolic tradition'. At the same date John of Antioch,[7] the temporary protector of Nestorius, whose heresy lay in the rejection of the term, said, 'This title no ecclesiastical teacher has put aside. Those who have used it are many and eminent; and those who have not used it, have not attacked those who did.' Alexander[8] again, one of the fiercest partisans of Nestorius, witnesses to the use of the word, though he considers it dangerous; 'That in festive solemnities,' he says, 'or in preaching or teaching, *theotokos* should be unguardedly said by the orthodox without explanation is no blame, because such statements were not dogmatic, nor said with evil meaning.' If we look for those Fathers, in the interval between Origen and the Council, to whom Alexander refers as using the term, we find among

---

[5] Socrates, *Historia ecclesiastica* VII, 32.

[6] Theodoret (+458), Bishop of Cyrrhus, might have been supposed to be disinclined to recognize the solemn pronouncement of the Council of Ephesus, because he was a personal friend and admirer of Nestorius.

[7] John of Antioch (+441) was made Bishop of Antioch in 429. For a few years he befriended Nestorius and opposed St Cyril of Alexandria. However, in 443 he was reconciled to Cyril again.

[8] Alexander of Hierapolis (+435) was a determined adversary of St Cyril at the Council of Ephesus and an ardent supporter of Nestorius.

them no less names than Archelaus of Mesopotamia, Eusebius of Palestine, Alexander of Egypt, in the third century; in the fourth, Athanasius, who uses it many times with emphasis, Cyril of Palestine, Gregory Nyssen and Gregory Nazianzen of Cappadocia, Antiochus of Syria, and Ammonius of Thrace:—not to refer to the Emperor Julian, who, having no local or ecclesiastical domicile, is a witness for the whole of Christendom. Another and earlier Emperor, Constantine, in his speech before the assembled Bishops at Nicaea, uses the still more explicit title of 'the Virgin Mother of God'; which is also used by Ambrose of Milan, and by Vincent and Cassian in the south of France, and then by St Leo.

So much for the term; it would be tedious to produce the passages of authors who, using or not using the term, convey the idea. 'Our God was carried in the womb of Mary,' says Ignatius, who was martyred AD 106. 'The Word of God', says Hippolytus, 'was carried in that Virgin frame.' 'The Maker of all', says Amphilochius, 'is born of a Virgin.' 'She did compass without circumscribing the Sun of justice,—the Everlasting is born,' says Chrysostom. 'God dwelt in the womb,' says Proclus. 'When thou hearest that God speaks from the bush,' asks Theodotus, 'in the bush seest thou not the Virgin?' Cassian says, 'Mary bore her Author.' 'The One God only-begotten', says Hilary, 'is introduced into the womb of a Virgin.' 'The Everlasting', says Ambrose, 'came into the Virgin.' 'The closed gate', says Jerome, 'by which alone the Lord God of Israel enters, is the Virgin Mary.' 'That man from heaven', says Capriolus, 'is God conceived in the womb.' 'He is made in thee', says St Augustine, 'who made thee.'[9]

This being the faith of the Fathers about the Blessed Virgin, we need not wonder that it should in no long time be transmuted into devotion. No wonder if their language should become unmeasured, when so great a term as 'Mother of God' had been formally set down as the safe limit of it. No wonder if it should be stronger and stronger as time went on, since only in a long period could the fullness of its import be exhausted. And in matter of fact, and as might be anticipated, (with the few exceptions which I have noted above, and which I am to treat of below), the current of thought in those early ages did uniformly tend to make much of the Blessed Virgin and to increase her honours, not to circumscribe them. Little jealousy was shown of her in those times; but, when any such niggardness of affection occurred, then one Father or other fell upon the offender, with zeal, not to say with fierceness. Thus St Jerome inveighs against Helvidius; thus St Epiphanius denounces Apollinaris; St Cyril, Nestorius; and St Ambrose, Bonosus; on the other hand, each successive insult offered to her by individual adversaries did but bring out more fully the intimate sacred affection with which Christendom regarded her. 'She was alone, and wrought the world's salvation and conceived the redemption of all,' says Ambrose;[10] 'she had so great grace, as not only to

---

[9] These pages show Newman's familiarity with and respect for the Church Fathers and ancient ecclesiastical writers, who witnessed to a living tradition in the Church from the earliest centuries.

[10] [Essay on Doctr. Dev. *ubi supr.*] Newman refers to the same pages of the *Essay on Development* as in footnote 4 above.

preserve virginity herself, but to confer it on those whom she visited.' 'She is the rod out of the stem of Jesse,' says St Jerome, 'and the Eastern gate through which the High Priest alone goes in and out, which still is ever shut.' 'She is the wise woman,' says Nilus, who 'hath clad believers, from the fleece of the Lamb born of her, with the clothing of incorruption, and delivered them from their spiritual nakedness.' 'She is the mother of life, of beauty, of majesty, the morning star,' according to Antiochus. 'The mystical new heavens', 'the heavens carrying the Divinity', 'the fruitful vine', 'by whom we are translated from death unto life,' according to St Ephrem. 'The manna, which is delicate, bright, sweet, and virgin, which, as though coming from heaven, has poured down on all the people of the Churches a food pleasanter than honey,' according to St Maximus.

Basil of Seleucia says, that 'she shines out above all the martyrs as the sun above the stars, and that she mediates between God and men.' 'Run through all creation in your thought,' says Proclus, 'and see if there be one equal or superior to the Holy Virgin, Mother of God.' 'Hail, Mother, clad in light, of the light which sets not,' says Theodotus, or some one else at Ephesus; 'hail, all undefiled mother of holiness; hail, most pellucid fountain of the life-giving stream.' And St Cyril too at Ephesus, 'Hail, Mary, Mother of God, majestic common-treasure of the whole world, the lamp unquenchable, the crown of virginity, the sceptre of orthodoxy, the indissoluble temple, the dwelling of the Illimitable, Mother and Virgin, through whom He in the holy gospels is called blessed who cometh in the name of the Lord,[a] ... through whom the Holy Trinity is sanctified, ... through whom Angels and Archangels rejoice, devils are put to flight, ... and the fallen creature is received up into the heavens, etc., etc.'[11] Such is but a portion of the panegyrical language which St Cyril used in the third Ecumenical Council.

a. Mt 21:9

A Letter Addressed to the Rev. E.B. Pusey, DD on occasion of his Eirenicon:
Certain Difficulties felt by Anglicans in Catholic Teaching,
London, 1910, Vol. II, pp. 61–7.
Written in December 1865 and first published
at the beginning of 1866.

[11] [Opp. t. 6, p. 355].

XIII/B

MARY THEOTOKOS[1]

Mater Dei. Mother of God. See art. ἀντίδοσις ἰδιωμάτων.[2]

[1] During the summer of 1841 Newman began a translation of *Treatises* by St Athanasius against the Arian heresy. The doctrinal cogency of this great saint and theologian was the occasion of another doubt in Newman's mind about the position of the Anglican Church. In the *Apologia*, he writes: 'I had got but a little way in my work [the translation of St Athanasius], when my trouble returned on me. The ghost had come a second time. In the Arian History I found the very same phenomenon, in a far bolder shape, which I had found in the Monophysite. I had not observed it in 1832. Wonderful that this should come upon me! I had not sought it out; I was reading and writing in my own line of study, far from the controversies of the day, on what is called a 'metaphysical' subject; but I saw clearly, that in the history of Arianism, the pure Arians were the Protestants, the semi-Arians were the Anglicans, and that Rome now was what it was then. The truth lay, not with the *Via Media*, but with what was called 'the extreme party' (*Apologia*, p. 139). In 1881, Newman completed the uniform edition of his complete Anglican writings, with the publication of the two volumes of the *Treatises of St Athanasius*. The first volume contains the translation of the text of St Athanasius; the second volume has annotations or notes in alphabetical order by Newman himself where he gives a learned explanation of theological terms and shows his own grasp of these subjects. Among the notes is the present passage, entitled *Mary Theotokos*. Newman elaborates first of all on the history of this Marian title and then on the doctrinal truth which the title conveys. He quotes extensively from the Fathers of the Church.

[2] The author refers to his *Note* on this Greek term 'antidosis idiomaton'

Athanasius gives the title to the Blessed Virgin, *Orat.* iii, 14, 29, 33; iv. 32; *Incarn. c. Ar.* 8, 22.

As to the history of this title, Theodoret, who from his party would rather be disinclined towards it, says that '*the most ancient* (τῶν παλαι καὶ πρόπαλαι) heralds of the orthodox faith taught the faithful to name and believe the Mother of the Lord *Theotokos*, according to *the Apostolical tradition*'. *Haer.* iv. 12. And John of Antioch,[3] whose championship of Nestorius and quarrel with St Cyril are well known, writes to the former, 'This title no ecclesiastical teacher has put aside; those who have used it are many and eminent, and those who have not used it have not attacked those who used it' (*Concil. Eph.* part i, c. 25). And Alexander,[4] the most obstinate or rather furious of all Nestorius's adherents, who died in banishment in Egypt, fully allows the ancient reception of the word, though only into popular use, from which came what he considers the doctrinal corruption. 'That in festive solemnities, or in preaching and teaching, *Theotokos* should be unguardedly said by the orthodox without

---

(*Select Treatises of St Athanasius in Controversy with the Arians*, Vol. II, pp. 367–9). The term is a technical one in theology and signifies 'the communication of attributes'. St Athanasius uses it frequently and it means that the properties of the human nature of Christ can be predicated of the Word in his divinity, and vice versa. This arises from the fact that in Christ there is only one Person who subsists in two natures, a divine and a human nature. Therefore, it is correct to use expressions such as God became man, the only-begotten Son of the Father suffered, died and rose again; etc.

[3] John of Antioch (+441), (cf. above, Text XIII/A, p. 249, footnote 7), like Theodoret, was a friend and supporter of Nestorius. For Theodoret, cf. above, Text XIII/A, p. 249, footnote 6.

[4] For Alexander of Hierapolis (+435), cf. above, Text XIII/A, p. 249, footnote 8.

explanation, is no blame, because such statements were not dogmatic, nor said with evil meaning. But now after the corruption of the whole world,' etc. (Lup. Ephes. *Epp.* 94). He adds that it, as well as ἀνθρωποτόκος 'was used by the great doctors of the Church.' Socrates (*Hist.* vii. 32) says that Origen, in the first tome of his Commentary on the Romans (see de la Rue *in Rom.* lib. i. 5, the original is lost), treated largely of the word; which implies that it was already in use. 'Interpreting', he says, '*how* θεοτόκος is used, he discussed the question at length.' Constantine implies the same, with an allusion to pagan mythology of an unpleasant kind; he says, 'When He had to draw near to a body of this world, and to tarry on earth, the need so requiring, He contrived a sort of irregular birth of Himself, (νόθην τινὰ γένεσιν); for without marriage was there conception, and childbirth, (εἰλείθμια), from a pure Virgin, and a maid, the Mother of God, (θεοῦ μήτηρ κόρη)'. *Ad. Sanct. Coet.* p. 480. The idea must have been familiar to Christians before Constantine's date to be recognized by him, a mere catechumen, and to be virtually commented on by such a parallelism.

For instances of the word θεοτόκος, besides Origen. ap. Socr. vii. 32, see Euseb, *V. Const.* iii. 43; *in Psalm.* cix. 4, p. 703, Montf. Nov. Coll.; Alexandr. *Ep. ad Alex.* ap. Theodor. *Hist.* i. 3, p. 745; Athan. (supra); Cyril. *Cat.* x. 19; Julian Imper. ap. Cyril. *c. Jul.* viii. p. 262; Amphiloch. *Orat.* 4, p. 41 (if Amphil.) ed. 1644; Nyssen. *Ep. ad Eustath.* p. 1093; Chrysost. apud Suicer *Symb.* t. ii. p. 240; Greg. Naz. *Orat.* 29. 4; *Ep.* 101, p. 85, ed. Ben. Antiochus and Ammon. ap. Cyril. *de Recta Fid.* pp. 49, 50; Pseudo-Dion. *contr.*

Samos. 5, p. 240; Pseudo-Basil. *Hom.* t. 2, p. 600, ed. Ben.

Pearson[5] on the Creed (notes on Art. 3), arguing from Ephrem. ap. *Phot. Cod.* 228, p. 775, says the phrase *Mater Dei* originated with St Leo. On the contrary, besides in Constantine's *Oration* as above, it is found, before St Leo. in Ambros. *de Virg.* ii. 7; Cassian. *Incarn.* ii. 5, vii. 25; Vincent. Lir. *Commonit.* 21. It is obvious that θεοτόκος, though framed as a test against Nestorians, was equally effective against Apollinarians and Eutychians,[6] who denied that our Lord had taken human flesh at all, as is observed by Facundus *Def. Trium Cap.* i. 4. And so St Cyril: 'Let it be carefully observed, that nearly this whole contest about the faith has been created against us for our maintaining that the Holy Virgin is Mother of God; now, if we hold', as was the calumny, 'that the Holy Body of Christ our common Saviour was from heaven, and not born of her, how can she be considered as Mother of God?' (*Epp.* pp. 106–7). Yet these sects, as the Arians, maintained the term.[7] See above: *Heresies.*

As to the doctrine, which the term implies and

---

[5] John Pearson (1613–86), a learned Anglican and theologian, was Bishop of Chester. He had a profound knowledge of the Fathers of the Church. His *Exposition of the Creed* (1659) is considered a classic.

[6] The Apollinarians, following Apollinarius (+ *c.* 390), denied the complete human nature of Christ. They maintained that man was made up of body, soul and spirit, but that in Christ, the divine Word took the place of his human spirit. Eutyches (+454) maintained that in Christ there was not only one Person but also one nature, a divine one. His resolute opposition to Nestorius thus made him fall into the opposite error – Monophysitism.

[7] Newman refers to a *Note* entitled *Heresies* he wrote in this same volume, *Select Treatises of St Athanasius*, Vol. II, pp. 143–9.

guards, the following are specimens of it. See St Cyril's quotations in his *de Recta Fide*, p. 49, etc. 'The fleshless', says Atticus, 'becomes flesh, the impalpable is handled, the perfect grows, the unalterable advances, the rich is brought forth in an inn, the coverer of heaven with clouds is swathed, the king is laid in a manger.' Antiochus speaks of Him, our Saviour, 'with whom yesterday in an immaculate bearing Mary travailed, the Mother of life, of beauty, of majesty, the Morning Star,' etc. 'The Maker of all', says St Amphilochius, 'is born to us today of a Virgin.' 'She did compass', says St Chrysostom, 'without circumscribing the Sun of righteousness. Today the Everlasting is born, and becomes what He was not. He who sitteth on a high and lofty throne is placed in a manger, the impalpable, incomposite, and immaterial is wrapped around by human hands; He who snaps the bands of sin, is environed in swathing bands.' And in like manner St Cyril himself, 'As a woman, though bearing the body only, is said to bring forth one who is made up of body and soul, and that will be no injury to the interests of the soul, as if it found in flesh the origin of its existence, so also in the instance of the Blessed Virgin, though she is Mother of the Holy Flesh, yet she bore God of God the Word, as being in truth one with it' (*Adv. Nest.* i. p. 18). 'God dwelt in the womb, yet was not circumscribed; whom the heaven containeth not, the Virgin's frame did not straiten' (Procl. *Orat.* i. p. 60). 'When thou hearest that God speaks from the bush, and Moses falling on his face worships, believest thou, not considering the fire that is seen, but God that speaks? and yet, when I mention the Virgin womb, dost thou abominate and turn away?. . . In the bush seest thou not the Virgin, in the fire the loving-kindness of Him who came?' (Theodotus of Ancyra[8] *ap. Conc. Eph.*) 'Not only did Mary bear her Elder', says Cassian[9] in answer to an objector, 'but her Author, and giving birth to Him from whom she received it, she became parent of her Parent. Surely it is as easy for God to give nativity to Himself, as to man; to be born of man, as to make men born. For God's power is not circumscribed in His own Person, that He should not do in Himself what He can do in all' (*Incarn.* iv. 2). 'The One God Only-begotten, of an ineffable origin from God, is introduced into the womb of the Holy Virgin, and grows into the form of a human body. He who contrives all . . . is brought forth according to the law of a human birth; He at whose voice Archangels tremble . . . and the world's elements are dissolved, is heard in the wailing of an infant' etc. (Hil. *Trin.* ii. 25). '"My beloved is white and ruddy;"[a] white truly, because the Brightness of the Father, ruddy, because the Birth of a Virgin. In Him shines and glows the colour of each nature;. . . He did not begin from a Virgin, but the Everlasting came into a Virgin' (Ambros. *Virgin.* i. n. 46). 'Him, whom, coming in His simple Godhead, not heaven, not earth, not sea, not any creature had endured, Him the inviolate womb of a Virgin carried' (Chrysost. *ap. Cassian.*

---

[8] Theodotus (+*c.* 445), Bishop of Ancyra, became a strong opponent of Nestorius at the Council of Ephesus. Cf. above, Text VIII, p. 197, Footnote 11.

[9] John Cassian (360–435), a monk who came from the East and settled in France. He is well-known for his two monastic studies, the *Institutes* and the *Conferences*. Newman here refers to his seven-volume theological work *De Incarnatione Domini*.

Incarn. vii. 30). 'Happily do some understand by the "closed gate",[b] by which only "the Lord God of Israel enters", that Prince on whom the gate is closed, to be the Virgin Mary, who both before and after her bearing remained a Virgin.' (Jerom. *in Ezek.* 44. init). 'Let them tell us', says Capreolus of Carthage, 'how is that Man from Heaven, if He be not God conceived in the womb?' (ap. *Sirm. Opp.* t. i. p. 216). 'He is made in thee', says St Austin, 'who made thee ... nay, through whom heaven and earth is made;... the Word of God in thee is made flesh, receiving flesh, not losing Godhead. And the Word is joined, is coupled to the flesh, and of this so high wedding thy womb is the nuptial chamber' etc. (*Serm.* 291, 6). 'Say, O blessed Mary', says St Hippolytus, 'what was It which by thee was conceived in the womb, what carried by thee in that virgin frame? It was the Word of God' etc. (ap. *Theod. Eran.* i. p. 55). 'There is one physician,' says St Ignatius, 'fleshly and spiritual, generate and ingenerate, God come in the flesh, in death true life, both from Mary and from God, first passible, then impassible, Jesus Christ our Lord' (*Ep. ad Eph.* 7).

a. Song 5:10   b. cf. Ezek 44:1–3

Select Treatises of St Athanasius in Controversy with the Arians,
London, 1903, Vol. II, pp. 210–15.
Newman worked on St Athanasius between 1841 and 1844.

XIV

THE POWER OF OUR LADY'S PRAYER

I must not close my review of the Catholic doctrine
concerning the Blessed Virgin, without directly
speaking of her intercessory power, though I have
incidentally made mention of it already.[1] It is the
immediate result of two truths, neither of which you
dispute; first, that 'it is good and useful', as the
Council of Trent says, 'suppliantly to invoke the
Saints and to have recourse to their prayers';[2] and
secondly, that the Blessed Mary is singularly dear to
her Son and singularly exalted in sanctity and glory.
However, at the risk of becoming didactic, I will state
somewhat more fully the grounds on which it rests.

To a candid pagan it must have been one of the
most remarkable points of Christianity, on its first
appearance, that the observance of prayer formed so

---

[1] The power of our Lady's prayer is a feature of Newman's Mariology.
It reflects not only his theological conviction but also the experience
of his own personal devotion to the Blessed Virgin Mary. Cf. above:
Introduction, IV, pp. 78–90.

[2] Council of Trent, Session 25, *Decree on the Invocation, the Veneration and
the Relics of the Saints, and on Sacred Images*. Cf. Denzinger-
Schönmetzer, No. 1821.

vital a part of its organization; and that, though its members were scattered all over the world, and its rulers and subjects had so little opportunity of correlative action, yet they, one and all, found the solace of a spiritual intercourse and a real bond of union, in the practice of mutual intercession. Prayer indeed is the very essence of all religion; but in the heathen religions it was either public or personal; it was a state ordinance, or a selfish expedient for the attainment of certain tangible, temporal goods. Very different from this was its exercise among Christians, who were thereby knit together in one body, different, as they were, in races, ranks, and habits, distant from each other in country, and helpless amid hostile populations.[3] Yet it proved sufficient for its purpose. Christians could not correspond; they could not combine; but they could pray one for another. Even their public prayers partook of this character of intercession; for to pray for the welfare of the whole Church was in fact a prayer for all the classes of men and all the individuals of which it was composed. It was in prayer that the Church was founded. For ten days all the Apostles 'persevered with one mind in prayer and supplication, with the women, and Mary the Mother of Jesus, and with his brethren.'[a] Then again at Pentecost 'they were all with one mind in one place;'[b] and the converts then made are said to have

---

[3] This form of Christian prayer is based on the reality of the Communion of Saints in the Mystical Body of Christ. As the *Catechism of the Catholic Church* expresses it: 'In the age of the Church, Christian intercession participates in Christ's, as an expression of the communion of saints. In intercession, he who prays looks "not only to his own interests, but also to the interests of others", even to the point of praying for those who do him harm.' (No. 2635).

'persevered in prayer.'[c] And when, after a while, St Peter was seized and put in prison with a view to his being put to death, 'prayer was made without ceasing'[d] by the Church of God for him; and, when the Angel released him, he took refuge in a house 'where many were gathered together in prayer'.[e]

We are so accustomed to these passages as hardly to be able to do justice to their singular significance; and they are followed up by various passages of the Apostolic Epistles. St Paul enjoins his brethren to 'pray with all prayer and supplication at all times in the Spirit, with all instance and supplication for all saints',[f] to 'pray in every place',[g] 'to make supplication, prayers, intercessions, giving of thanks, for all men'.[h] And in his own person he 'ceases not to give thanks for them, commemorating them in his prayers,'[i] and 'always in all his prayers making supplication for them all with joy'.[j]

Now, was this spiritual bond to cease with life? or had Christians similar duties to their brethren departed? From the witness of the early ages of the Church, it appears that they had; and you, and those who agree with you, would be the last to deny that they were then in the practice of praying, as for the living, so for those also who had passed into the intermediate state between earth and heaven.[4] Did the

[4] To understand why Newman goes to such length to illustrate from Scripture the fact and the power of intercession, we must recall that invocation of the Saints was condemned by the Anglican Church. Since there was no clear distinction made between invocation and intercession, the practice of prayers to our Lady was not accepted as lawful. It was felt that it could easily obscure the role of Christ as the one Mediator between God and man. Moreover, purgatory, 'the intermediate state between earth and heaven' is not a tenet of the Anglican faith.

sacred communion extend further still, on to the
inhabitants of heaven itself? Here too you agree with
us, for you have adopted in your Volume the words
of the Council of Trent which I have quoted above.
But now we are brought to a higher order of thought.

It would be preposterous to pray for those who are
already in glory; but at least they can pray for us, and
we can ask their prayers, and in the Apocalypse at least
Angels are introduced both sending us their blessing
and offering up our prayers before the Divine
Presence. We read there of an angel who 'came and
stood before the altar, having a golden censer'; and
'there was given to him much incense, that he should
offer of the prayers of all saints upon the golden altar
which is before the Throne of God'.[k] On this occasion,
surely the Angel performed the part of a great
Intercessor or Mediator above for the children of the
Church Militant below. Again, in the beginning of the
same book, the sacred writer goes so far as to speak of
'grace and peace' coming to us, not only from the
Almighty, 'but from the seven Spirits that are before
His throne',[l] thus associating the Eternal with the
ministers of His mercies; and this carries us on to the
remarkable passage of St Justin, one of the earliest
Fathers, who, in his Apology, says, 'To Him [God],
and His Son who came from Him and taught us these
things, and the host of the other good Angels who
follow and resemble Him, and the Prophetic Spirit, we
pay veneration and homage'. Further, in the Epistle to
the Hebrews, St Paul introduces, not only Angels, but
'the spirits of the just' into the sacred communion: 'Ye
have come to Mount Zion, to the heavenly Jerusalem,
to myriads of angels, to God the Judge of all, to the

spirits of the just made perfect, and to Jesus the Mediator of the New Testament'.[m] What can be meant by having 'come to the spirits of the just', unless in some way or other, they do us good, whether by blessing or by aiding us? that is, in a word, to speak correctly, by praying for us, for it is surely by prayer that the creature above is able to bless and aid the creature below.

Intercession thus being a first principle of the Church's life, next it is certain again, that the vital force of that intercession, as an availing power, is, (according to the will of God), sanctity. This seems to be suggested by a passage of St Paul, in which the Supreme Intercessor is said to be 'the Spirit': 'the Spirit Himself maketh intercession for us; He maketh intercession for the saints according to God'.[n] And, indeed, the truth thus implied, is expressly brought out for us in other parts of Scripture, in the form both of doctrine and of example. The words of the man born blind speak the common-sense of nature: 'if any man be a worshipper of God, him He heareth'.[o] And Apostles confirm them: 'the prayer of a just man availeth much',[p] and 'whatever we ask, we receive, because we keep his commandments'.[q] Then, as for examples, we read of the Almighty's revealing to Abraham[r] and Moses[s] beforehand, His purposes of wrath, in order that they by their intercessions might avert its execution. To the friends of Job it was said, 'My servant Job shall pray for you; his face I will accept'.[t] Elias by his prayer shut and opened the heavens.[u] Elsewhere we read of 'Jeremias, Moses, and Samuel;'[v] and of 'Noe, Daniel, and Job', as being great mediators between God and His people.[w] One instance is given us, which testifies the continuance of this high office beyond this life. Lazarus, in the parable, is seen in Abraham's bosom.[x] It is usual to pass over this striking passage with the remark that it is a Jewish mode of speech; whereas, Jewish belief or not, it is recognized and sanctioned by our Lord Himself. What do Catholics teach about the Blessed Virgin more wonderful than this? If Abraham, not yet ascended on high, had charge of Lazarus, what offence is it to affirm the like of her, who was not merely as Abraham, 'the friend',[y] but was the very 'Mother of God'?

It may be added, that, though, if sanctity was wanting, it availed nothing for influence with our Lord, to be one of His company, still, as the Gospel shows, He on various occasions actually did allow those who were near Him, to be the channels of introducing supplicants to Him or of gaining miracles from Him, as in the instance of the miracle of the loaves;[z] and if on one occasion, He seems to repel His Mother, when she told Him that wine was wanting for the guests at the marriage feast, it is obvious to remark on it, that, by saying that she was then separated from Him ('What have I to do with thee?'[aa]) *because* His hour was not yet come, He implied, that when that hour was come, such separation would be at an end. Moreover, in fact, He did at her intercession work the miracle to which her words pointed.

I consider it impossible then, for those who believe the Church to be one vast body in heaven and on earth, in which every holy creature of God has his place, and of which prayer is the life, when once they recognize the sanctity and dignity of the Blessed Virgin, not to perceive immediately, that her office above is one of perpetual intercession for the faithful militant, and that our very relation to her must be that of clients to a patron, and that, in the eternal enmity which exists between the woman and the serpent, while the serpent's strength lies in being the Tempter, the weapon of the Second Eve and Mother of God is prayer.

As then these ideas of her sanctity and dignity gradually penetrated the mind of Christendom, so did that of her intercessory power follow close upon them and with them. From the earliest times that mediation is symbolized in those representations of her with uplifted hands, which, whether in plaster or in glass, are still extant in Rome,—that Church, as St Irenaeus says, with which 'every Church, that is, the faithful from every side, must agree, because of its more powerful principality'; 'into which', as Tertullian adds, 'the Apostles poured out, together with their blood, their whole doctrine'. As far indeed as existing documents are concerned, I know of no instance to my purpose earlier than AD 234, but it is a very remarkable one; and, though it has been often quoted in the controversy, an argument is not weaker for frequent use.

St Gregory Nyssen,[5] then, a native of Cappadocia in the fourth century, relates that his namesake, Bishop of Neocaesarea in Pontus, surnamed Thaumaturgus, in the century preceding, shortly before he was called to the priesthood, received in a

---

[5] The author, in a footnote, refers the reader to his *Essay on the Development of Christian Doctrine*, p. 386 (cf. pp. 417–18 in later editions), where he gives as reference: Nyss. *Opp.* t.ii, p. 977; and for his citation from Bull: *Def.F.N.*, ii, 12. Cf. *PG* 10:909–12, 983–6.

vision a Creed, which is still extant, from the Blessed Mary at the hands of St John. The account runs thus: He was deeply pondering theological doctrine, which the heretics of the day depraved.

> In such thoughts [says his namesake of Nyssa] he was passing the night, when one appeared, as if in human form, aged in appearance, saintly in the fashion of his garments, and very venerable both in grace of countenance and general mien. Amazed at the sight, he started from his bed, and asked who it was, and why he came; but, on the other calming the perturbation of his mind with his gentle voice, and saying he had appeared to him by divine command on account of his doubts, in order that the truth of the orthodox faith might be revealed to him, he took courage at the word, and regarded him with a mixture of joy and fright. Then, on his stretching his hand straight forward and pointing with his fingers at something on one side, he followed with his eyes the extended hand, and saw another appearance opposite the former, in shape of a woman, but more than human ... When his eyes could not bear the apparition, he heard them conversing together on the subject of his doubts; and thereby not only gained a true knowledge of the faith, but learned their names, as they addressed each other by their respective appellations. And thus he is said to have heard the person in woman's shape bid 'John the Evangelist' disclose to the young man the mystery of godliness; and he answered that he was ready to comply in this matter with the wish of 'the Mother of the Lord', and

enunciated a formulary, well-turned and complete, and so vanished. He, on the other hand, immediately committed to writing that divine teaching of his mystagogue, and henceforth preached in the Church according to that form, and bequeathed to posterity, as an inheritance, that heavenly teaching, by means of which his people are instructed down to this day, being preserved from all heretical evil.

He proceeds to rehearse the Creed thus given, 'There is One God, Father of a Living Word,' etc. Bull, after quoting it in his work on the Nicene Faith, alludes to this history of its origin, and adds, 'No one should think it incredible that such a providence should befall a man whose whole life was conspicuous for revelations and miracles, as all ecclesiastical writers who have mentioned him (and who has not?) witness with one voice'.

Here our Lady is represented as rescuing a holy soul from intellectual error. This leads me to a further reflection. You seem, in one place of your Volume, to object to the Antiphon, in which it is said of her, 'All heresies thou hast destroyed alone'.[6] Surely the truth of it is verified in this age, as in former times, and especially by the doctrine concerning her, on which I have been dwelling. She is the great exemplar of prayer in a generation, which emphatically denies the power of prayer *in toto*, which determines that fatal laws govern the universe, that there cannot be any direct communication between earth and heaven, that

---

[6] This Antiphon was used in the Divine Office prior to the revision that took place after the Second Vatican Council. Cf. Common of Feasts of the Blessed Virgin Mary, Matins, Third Nocturn, Antiphon 7.

God cannot visit His own earth, and that man cannot influence His providence.[7]

a.	Acts 1:14	b.	Acts 2:1	c.	Acts 2:42
d.	Acts 12:5	e.	Acts 12:12	f.	Eph 6:18
g.	1 Tim 2:8	h.	1 Tim 2:1	i.	1 Thess 1:2
j.	Phil 1:4	k.	Rev 8:3	l.	Rev 1:4
m.	Heb 12:22–4a	n.	cf. Rom 8:26–7	o.	Jn 9:31
p.	Jas 5:16	q.	1 Jn 3:22	r.	cf. Gen 18:22–33
s.	cf. Ex 32:9–14	t.	cf. Job 42:8	u.	1 Kings 17:1–7; 18:1, 41–5
v.	Jer 15:1	w.	cf. Ezek 14:14, 20	x.	cf. Lk 16:19–25
y.	cf. 2 Chron 20:7; Is 41:8; Jas 2:23	z.	cf. Jn 12:20–26; 6:3–14	aa.	cf. Jn 2:4

A Letter Addressed to the Rev. E.B. Pusey, DD
on occasion of his Eirenicon:
Certain Difficulties felt by Anglicans in Catholic Teaching,
London, 1910, Vol. II, pp. 68–76.
Written by Newman in December 1865
and first published at the beginning of 1866.

---

[7] The graphic description in these final lines of Newman's own age is even more pertinent to our contemporary and secular generation that has drifted farther away from the foundations of our faith and relies enthusiastically on the power of its technological conquests.

XV

GENUINE CATHOLIC BELIEF AND
DEVOTION TO THE BLESSED VIRGIN

I cannot help hoping that your own reading of the
Fathers will on the whole bear me out in the above
account of their teaching concerning the Blessed Virgin.
Anglicans seem to me simply to overlook the strength of
the argument adducible from the works of those ancient
doctors in our favour; and they open the attack upon
our mediaeval and modern writers, careless of leaving a
host of primitive opponents in their rear. I do not
include you among such Anglicans, as you know what
the Fathers assert; but, if so, have you not, my dear
Friend, been unjust to yourself in your recent Volume,
and made far too much of the differences which exist
between Anglicans and us on this particular point? It is
the office of an Irenicon to smoothe difficulties; I shall
be pleased if I succeed in removing some of yours. Let
the public judge between us here. Had you happened in
your volume to introduce your notice of our teaching
about the Blessed Virgin, with a notice of the teaching
of the Fathers concerning her, which you follow, ordinary men would have considered that there was not
much to choose between you and us. Though you

appealed ever so much, in your defence, to the authority of the 'undivided Church', they would have said that
you, who had such high notions of the Blessed Mary,
were one of the last men who had a right to accuse us of
quasi-idolatry. When they found you with the Fathers
calling her Mother of God, Second Eve, and Mother of
all Living, the Mother of Life, the Morning Star, the
Mystical New Heaven, the Sceptre of Orthodoxy, the
All-undefiled Mother of Holiness, and the like, they
would have deemed it a poor compensation for such
language, that you protested against her being called a
Co-redemptress or a Priestess. And, if they were violent
Protestants, they would not have read you with the
relish and gratitude with which, as it is, they have
perhaps accepted your testimony against us. Not that
they would have been altogether fair in their view of
you; on the contrary I think there is a real difference
between what you protest against, and what with the
Fathers you hold; but unread men of the world form a
broad practical judgment of the things which come
before them, and they would have felt in this case that
they had the same right to be shocked at you, as you
have to be shocked at us; and further, which is the point
to which I am coming, they would have said, that,
granting some of our modern writers go beyond the
Fathers in this matter, still the line cannot be logically
drawn between the teaching of the Fathers concerning
the Blessed Virgin and our own. This view of the matter
seems to me true and important; I do not think the line
can be satisfactorily drawn, and to this point I shall now
direct my attention.

It is impossible, I say, in a doctrine like this, to draw
the line cleanly between truth and error, right and

wrong. This is ever the case in concrete matters, which have life. Life in this world is motion, and involves a continual process of change. Living things grow into their perfection, into their decline, into their death. No rule of art will suffice to stop the operation of this natural law, whether in the material world or in the human mind. We can indeed encounter disorders, when they occur, by external antagonism and remedies; but we cannot eradicate the process itself, out of which they arise. Life has the same right to decay, as it has to wax strong. This is specially the case with great ideas.[1] You may stifle them; or you may refuse them elbow-room; or again, you may torment them with your continual meddling; or you may let them have free course and range, and be content, instead of anticipating their excesses, to expose and restrain those excesses after they have occurred. But you have only this alternative; and for myself, I prefer much wherever it is possible, to be first generous and then just; to grant full liberty of thought, and to call it to account when abused.

If what I have been saying be true of energetic ideas generally, much more is it the case in matters of religion. Religion acts on the affections; who is to hinder these, when once roused, from gathering in their strength and running wild?[2] They are not gifted with

---

[1] This idea of growth and development is one that is dear to Newman. In his *Essay on the Development of Christian Doctrine*, he wrote the famous lines: 'In a higher world it is otherwise, but here below to live is to change, and to be perfect is to have changed often' (p. 40).

[2] Newman deals here with an important theme in his Mariology, namely, the difference between doctrine and popular devotion. The former is controlled and constant: the latter can take on different and, at times, extreme expressions from one century or culture to another. Popular religiosity always inclines to excess and corruption. It must be constantly checked by the steady hand of doctrine.

any connatural principle within them, which renders them self-governing, and self-adjusting. They hurry right on to their object, and often in their case it is, the more haste, the worse speed. Their object engrosses them, and they see nothing else. And of all passions love is the most unmanageable; nay more, I would not give much for that love which is never extravagant, which always observes the proprieties, and can move about in perfect good taste, under all emergencies. What mother, what husband or wife, what youth or maiden in love, but says a thousand foolish things, in the way of endearment, which the speaker would be sorry for strangers to hear; yet they are not on that account unwelcome to the parties to whom they are addressed. Sometimes by bad luck they are written down, sometimes they get into the newspapers; and what might be even graceful, when it was fresh from the heart, and interpreted by the voice and the countenance, presents but a melancholy exhibition when served up cold for the public eye. So it is with devotional feelings. Burning thoughts and words are as open to criticism as they are beyond it. What is abstractedly extravagant, may in particular persons be becoming and beautiful, and only fall under blame when it is found in others who imitate them. When it is formalized into meditations or exercises, it is as repulsive as love-letters in a police report. Moreover, even holy minds readily adopt and become familiar with language which they would never have originated themselves, when it proceeds from a writer who has the same objects of devotion as they have; and, if they find a stranger ridicule or reprobate supplication or praise which has come to them so recommended, they feel it as keenly as if a direct insult were offered to those to whom that homage is addressed. In the next place, what has power to stir holy and refined souls is potent also with the multitude; and the religion of the multitude is ever vulgar and abnormal; it ever will be tinctured with fanaticism and superstition, while men are what they are. A people's religion is ever a corrupt religion, in spite of the provisions of Holy Church. If she is to be Catholic, you must admit within her net fish of every kind, guests good and bad, vessels of gold, vessels of earth. You may beat religion out of men, if you will, and then their excesses will take a different direction; but if you make use of religion to improve them, they will make use of religion to corrupt it. And then you will have effected that compromise of which our countrymen report so unfavourably from abroad: a high grand faith and worship which compels their admiration, and puerile absurdities among the people which excite their contempt.

Nor is it any safeguard against these excesses in a religious system, that the religion is based upon reason, and developes into a theology. Theology both uses logic and baffles it; and thus logic acts both for the protection and for the perversion of religion. Theology is occupied with supernatural matters, and is ever running into mysteries, which reason can neither explain nor adjust. Its lines of thought come to an abrupt termination, and to pursue them or to complete them is to plunge down the abyss. But logic blunders on, forcing its way, as it can, through thick darkness and ethereal mediums. The Arians went ahead with logic for their directing principle, and so

lost the truth; on the other hand, St Augustine inti-
mates that, if we attempt to find and tie together the
ends of lines which run into infinity we shall only
succeed in contradicting ourselves, when, in his
Treatise on the Holy Trinity, he is unable to find the
logical reason for not speaking of three Gods as well as
of One, and of one Person in the Godhead as well as
of Three. I do not mean to say that logic cannot be
used to set right its own error, or that in the hands of
an able disputant it may not trim the balance of truth.
This was done at the Councils of Antioch and Nicaea,
on occasion of the heresies of Paulus and Arius.[3] But
such a process is circuitous and elaborate; and is
conducted by means of minute subtleties which will
give it the appearance of a game of skill in matters too
grave and practical to deserve a mere scholastic treatment. Accordingly St Augustine, in the Treatise above
mentioned, does no more than simply lay it down that
the statements in question are heretical, that is to say
there are three Gods is Tritheism, and to say there is
but one Person, Sabellianism. That is, good sense and
a large view of truth are the correctives of his logic.
And thus we have arrived at the final resolution of the
whole matter, for good sense and a large view of truth
are rare gifts; whereas all men are bound to be devout,
and most men busy themselves in arguments and
inferences.

Now let me apply what I have been saying to the
teaching of the Church on the subject of the Blessed

---

[3] The Synod of Antioch rejected the erroneous teaching regarding the
Person of Christ by Paul of Samosata, a heretical bishop of the third
century. The first Council of Nicaea (325) condemned the heretical
doctrine of the Arians.

Virgin. I have to recur to a subject of so sacred a nature, that, writing as I am for publication, I need the apology of my purpose for venturing to pursue it. I say then, when once we have mastered the idea, that Mary bore, suckled, and handled the Eternal in the form of a child, what limit is conceivable to the rush and flood of thoughts which such a doctrine involves? What awe and surprise must attend upon the knowledge, that a creature has been brought so close to the Divine Essence? It was the creation of a new idea and of a new sympathy, of a new faith and worship, when the holy Apostles announced that God had become incarnate; then a supreme love and devotion to Him became possible, which seemed hopeless before that revelation. This was the first consequence of their preaching. But, besides this, a second range of thoughts was opened on mankind, unknown before, and unlike any other, as soon as it was understood that that Incarnate God had a mother. The second idea is perfectly distinct from the former, and does not interfere with it. He is God made low, she is a woman made high. I scarcely like to use a familiar illustration on the subject of the Blessed Virgin's dignity among created beings, but it will serve to explain what I mean, when I ask you to consider the difference of feeling, with which we read the respective histories of Maria Theresa and the Maid of Orleans;[4] or with which the middle and lower classes of a nation regard a first minister of the day who has come of an aristocratic house, and one who has risen from the ranks. May God's mercy keep me from the shadow of a thought, dimming the purity or blunting the keenness of that love of Him,

[4] Maria Theresa was Empress of Austria (1740–80). The Maid of Orleans was St Joan of Arc (1412–31), the daughter of a peasant.

which is our sole happiness and our sole salvation! But surely when He became man, He brought home to us His incommunicable attributes with a distinctiveness, which precludes the possibility of our lowering Him merely by our exalting a creature. He alone has an entrance into our soul, reads our secret thoughts, speaks to our heart, applies to us spiritual pardon and strength. On Him we solely depend. He alone is our inward life; He not only regenerates us, but (to use the words appropriated to a higher mystery) *semper gignit*;[5] He is ever renewing our new birth and our heavenly sonship. In this sense He may be called, as in nature, so in grace, our real Father. Mary is only our mother by divine appointment, given us from the Cross; her presence is above not on earth; her office is external, not within us. Her name is not heard in the administration of the Sacraments. Her work is not one of ministration towards us; her power is indirect. It is her prayers that avail, and her prayers are effectual by the *fiat* of Him who is our all in all. Nor need she hear us by any innate power, or any personal gift; but by His manifestation to her of the prayers which we make to her. When Moses was on the Mount, the Almighty told him of the idolatry of his people at the foot of it, in order that he might intercede for them;[a] and thus it is the Divine Presence which is the intermediating Power by which we reach her and she reaches us.[6]

Woe is me, if even by a breath I sully these ineffa-

---

[5] *semper gignit*: he always (continuously) begets (or generates): words applied to God the Father in Trinitarian theology.

[6] These are fine paragraphs written in beautiful English, brimming with a controlled enthusiasm. It is theology clad in a splendid literary garb. Its ecumenical value is significant. More recently, the Second Vatican Council solemnly stated Mary's position in relation to Christ, the sole

ble truths! but still, without prejudice to them, there is, I say, another range of thought quite distinct from them, incommensurate with them, of which the Blessed Virgin is the centre. If we placed our Lord in that centre, we should only be dragging Him from His throne, and making Him an Arian kind of a God; that is, no God at all. He who charges us with making Mary a divinity, is thereby denying the divinity of Jesus. Such a man does not know what divinity is. Our Lord cannot pray for us, as a creature prays, as Mary prays; He cannot inspire those feelings which a creature inspires. To her belongs, as being a creature, a natural claim on our sympathy and familiarity, in that she is nothing else than our fellow. She is our pride,—in the poet's words, 'Our tainted nature's solitary boast'.[7] We look to her without any fear, any

---

Mediator: 'Mary's function as mother of men in no way obscures or diminishes this unique mediation of Christ, but rather shows its power. But the Blessed Virgin's salutary influence on men originates not in any inner necessity but in the disposition of God. It flows forth from the superabundance of the merits of Christ, rests on his mediation, depends entirely on it and draws all its power from it. It does not hinder in any way the immediate union of the faithful with Christ but on the contrary fosters it' (Dogmatic Constitution on the Church, *Lumen Gentium*, 60). And further on: 'The sacred synod ... strongly urges theologians and preachers of the word of God to be careful to refrain as much from all false exaggeration as from too summary an attitude in considering the special dignity of the Mother of God. Following the study of Sacred Scripture, the Fathers, the doctors and liturgy of the Church, and under the guidance of the Church's magisterium, let them rightly illustrate the duties and privileges of the Blessed Virgin which always refer to Christ, the source of all truth, sanctity and devotion. Let them carefully refrain from whatever might by word or deed lead the separated brethren or any others whatsoever into error about the true doctrine of the Church' (*Ibid.* 67).

[7] 'our tainted nature's solitary boast': these oft-quoted lines are from the poem *The Virgin* by William Wordsworth (1770–1850).

remorse, any consciousness that she is able to read us, judge us, punish us. Our heart yearns towards that pure Virgin, that gentle Mother, and our congratulations follow her, as she rises from Nazareth and Ephesus, through the choirs of angels, to her throne on high, so weak, yet so strong; so delicate, yet so glorious; so modest and yet so mighty. She has sketched for us her own portrait in the Magnificat. 'He hath regarded the low estate of His hand-maid; for, behold, from henceforth all generations shall call me blessed. He hath put down the mighty from their seat; and hath exalted the humble. He hath filled the hungry with good things, and the rich he hath sent empty away.'[b] I recollect the strange emotion which took by surprise men and women, young and old, when, at the Coronation of our present Queen,[8] they gazed on the figure of one so like a child, so small, so tender, so shrinking, who had been exalted to so great an inheritance and so vast a rule, who was such a contrast in her own person to the solemn pageant which centred in her. Could it be otherwise with the spectators, if they had human affection? And did not the All-wise know the human heart when He took to Himself a Mother? did He not anticipate our emotion at the sight of such an exaltation in one so simple and so lowly? If He had not meant her to exert that wonderful influence in His Church, which she has in the event exerted, I will use a bold word, He it is who has perverted us. If she is not to attract our homage, why did He make her solitary in her greatness amid His vast creation? If it be idolatry in us to let our

8 Queen Victoria (1819–1901) succeeded King William IV in 1837 at the very young age of eighteen.

affections respond to our faith, He would not have
made her what she is, or He would not have told us
that He had so made her; but, far from this, He has
sent His Prophet to announce to us, 'A Virgin shall
conceive and bear a Son, and they shall call His name
Emmanuel,'[c] and we have the same warrant for
hailing her as God's Mother, as we have for adoring
Him as God.[9]

Christianity is eminently an objective religion. For
the most part it tells us of persons and facts in simple
words, and leaves that announcement to produce its
effect on such hearts as are prepared to receive it. This
at least is its general character; and Butler recognizes it
as such in his Analogy,[10] when speaking of the Second
and Third Persons of the Holy Trinity: 'The internal
worship', he says, 'to the Son and Holy Ghost is no
farther matter of pure revealed command than as the
relations they stand in to us are matters of pure revelation; for the relations being known, the obligations to
such internal worship are *obligations of reason arising out
of those relations themselves*'.[11] It is in this way that the
revealed doctrine of the Incarnation exerted a stronger
and a broader influence on Christians, as they more and
more apprehended and mastered its meaning and its
bearings. It is contained in the brief and simple declara-

---

[9] The author's devotion to and love of our Lady become quite apparent from passages like this one of such intense fervour.

[10] Joseph Butler (1692–1752), Bishop of Durham and renowned English
theologian. He is known for his famous study on *The Analogy of
Religion, Natural and Revealed, to the Constitution and Course of Nature*,
first published in 1736.

[11] Newman refers the reader to his *Essay on the Development of Christian
Doctrine*, p. 50 (cf. p. 48 in later editions), where he quotes this same
passage from Butler.

tion of St John, 'The Word was made flesh';[d] but it required century after century to spread it out in its fullness, and to imprint it energetically on the worship and practice of the Catholic people as well as on their faith. Athanasius was the first and the great teacher of it. He collected together the inspired notices scattered through David, Isaias, St Paul, and St John, and he engraved indelibly upon the imaginations of the faithful, as had never been before, that man is God, and God is man, that in Mary they meet, and that in this sense Mary is the centre of all things. He added nothing to what was known before, nothing to the popular and zealous faith that her Son was God; he has left behind him in his works no such definite passages about her as those of St Irenaeus or St Epiphanius; but he brought the circumstances of the Incarnation home to men's minds, by the multiform evolutions of his analysis, and thereby secured it to us for ever from perversion. Still, however, there was much to be done; we have no proof that Athanasius himself had any special devotion to the Blessed Virgin; but he laid the foundations on which that devotion was to rest, and thus noiselessly and without strife, as the first Temple was built in the Holy City, she grew up into her inheritance, and was 'established in Sion and her power was in Jerusalem'.[e]

a. cf. Ex 32:7–14   b. Lk 1:48, 52–3   c. cf. Is. 7:14; Mt 1:23
d. Jn 1:14   e. cf. Sir 24:10–11

A Letter Addressed to the Rev. E.B. Pusey, DD
on occasion of his Eirenicon:
Certain Difficulties felt by Anglicans in Catholic Teaching,
London, 1910, Vol. II, pp. 77–88.
Written by Newman in December 1865
and first published at the beginning of 1866.

XVI

LATER DEVELOPMENTS IN MARIAN DOCTRINE ANTICIPATED IN EARLY TIMES BY THE FATHERS[1]

The special prerogatives of St Mary, the *Virgo Virginum*, are intimately involved in the doctrine of the Incarnation itself, with which these remarks began, and have already been dwelt upon above. As is well known, they were not fully recognized in the

[1] This passage is taken from Newman's *Essay on the Development of Christian Doctrine*, where he illustrates the fifth Note of genuine development, namely, that the doctrine in question should 'anticipate its future'. In other words, there should be signs at an early stage of future opinions and practices connected with it which will become clear and be developed only at a later date. In these pages, he applies this criterion to the mission of our Lady, and shows how from the beginning she was seen by the Fathers of the Church as the Second Eve and revered for the power of her prayer. Paul VI, in his Apostolic Exhortation *Marialis Cultus* of 1974, teaches that present-day veneration of our Lady derives from a living and perennial Tradition in the Church: 'We wish to emphasize the fact that the veneration which the universal Church today accords to the Blessed Mother of God is a derivation from and extension and unceasing increase of the devotion that the Church of every age has paid to her, with careful attention to truth and with an ever watchful nobility of expression. From perennial Tradition kept alive by reason of the uninterrupted presence of the Spirit and continual attention to the Word, the Church of our time draws motives, arguments and incentives for the veneration that she pays to the Blessed Virgin' (Apostolic Exhortation, For the Right Ordering and Development of Devotion to the Blessed Virgin, *Marialis Cultus*, (1974), 15).

Catholic ritual till a late date, but they were not a new thing in the Church, or strange to her earlier teachers. St Justin, St Irenaeus, and others, had distinctly laid it down, that she not only had an office, but bore a part, and was a voluntary agent, in the actual process of redemption, as Eve had been instrumental and responsible in Adam's fall.[2] They taught that, as the first woman might have foiled the Tempter and did not, so, if Mary had been disobedient or unbelieving on Gabriel's message, the Divine Economy would have been frustrated. And certainly the parallel between 'the Mother of all living'[a] and the Mother of the Redeemer may be gathered from a comparison of the first chapters of Scripture with the last. It was noticed in a former place, that the only passage where the serpent is directly identified with the evil spirit occurs in the twelfth chapter of the Revelation; now it is observable that the recognition, when made, is found in the course of a vision of a 'woman clothed with the sun and the moon under her feet':[b] thus two women are brought into contrast with each other.[3] Moreover, as it is said in the Apocalypse, 'The dragon was wroth with the woman, and went about to make war with the remnant of her seed',[c] so it is prophesied in Genesis, 'I will put enmity between thee and the woman, and between thy seed and her Seed. He[4] shall

---

[2] Cf. above, Text X, pp. 207–22.

[3] Cf. above, Text XII. pp. 235–45; Text VIII, pp. 192–3.

[4] '*He* shall bruise thy head': as already mentioned, this translation follows the Greek and ascribes the victory to one of the woman's sons. This was interpreted by many Fathers as referring to Christ. The Latin Vulgate has '*she* shall bruise', which gave rise to a Mariological interpretation, which became traditional in the Catholic Church, and was used by Pius IX in *Ineffabilis Deus* in 1854 (defining the dogma of the

bruise thy head, and thou shalt bruise His heel.'[d] Also the enmity was to exist, not only between the Serpent and the Seed of the woman, but between the serpent and the woman herself; and here too there is a correspondence in the Apocalyptic vision. If then there is reason for thinking that this mystery at the close of the Scripture record answers to the mystery in the beginning of it, and that 'the Woman' mentioned in both passages is one and the same, then she can be none other than St Mary, thus introduced prophetically to our notice immediately on the transgression of Eve.

Here, however, we are not so much concerned to interpret Scripture as to examine the Fathers. Thus St Justin says, 'Eve, being a virgin and incorrupt, having conceived the word from the Serpent, bore disobedience and death; but Mary the Virgin, receiving faith and joy, when Gabriel the Angel evangelized her, answered, "Be it unto me according to thy word.".'[5] And Tertullian says that, whereas Eve believed the Serpent, and Mary believed Gabriel, 'the fault of Eve in believing, Mary by believing hath blotted out'. St Irenaeus speaks more explicitly: 'As Eve,' he says ... 'becoming disobedient, became the cause of death to herself and to all mankind, so Mary too, having the predestined Man, and yet a Virgin, being obedient, became cause of salvation both to herself and to all mankind'. This becomes the received doctrine in the post-Nicene Church.

One well-known instance occurs in the history of

Immaculate Conception) and by Pius XII in *Munificentissimus Deus* in 1950 (defining the Assumption).

[5] For the following citations from St Justin, Tertullian and St Irenaeus, cf. above, Text X, pp. 209–16.

the third century of St Mary's interposition, and it is remarkable from the names of the two persons, who were, one the subject, the other the historian of it. St Gregory Nyssen, a native of Cappadocia in the fourth century, relates that his namesake Bishop of Neocaesarea, surnamed Thaumaturgus, in the preceding century, shortly before he was called to the priesthood, received in a vision a Creed, which is still extant, from the Blessed Virgin at the hands of St John. The account runs thus: He was deeply pondering theological doctrine, which the heretics of the day depraved.

> In such thoughts [says his namesake of Nyssa] he was passing the night, when one appeared, as if in human form, aged in appearance, saintly in the fashion of his garments, and very venerable both in grace of countenance and general mien ... Following with his eyes his extended hand, he saw another appearance opposite to the former, in shape of a woman, but more than human ... When his eyes could not bear the apparition, he heard them conversing together on the subject of his doubts; and thereby not only gained a true knowledge of the faith, but learned their names, as they addressed each other by their respective appellations. And thus he is said to have heard the person in woman's shape bid 'John the Evangelist' disclose to the young man the mystery of godliness; and he answered that he was ready to comply in this matter with the wish of 'the Mother of the Lord,' and enunciated a formulary, well-turned and complete, and so vanished.

Gregory proceeds to rehearse the Creed thus given. 'There is One God, Father of a Living Word', etc. Bull, after quoting it in his work upon the Nicene Faith, refers to this history of its origin, and adds, 'No one should think it incredible that such a providence should befall a man whose whole life was conspicuous for revelations and miracles, as all ecclesiastical writers who have mentioned him (and who has not ?) witness with one voice'.[6]

It is remarkable that St Gregory Nazianzen relates an instance, even more pointed, of St Mary's intercession, contemporaneous with this appearance to Thaumaturgus; but it is attended with mistake in the narrative, which weakens its cogency as an evidence of the belief, not indeed of the fourth century, in which St Gregory lived, but of the third. He speaks of a Christian woman having recourse to the protection of St Mary, and obtaining the conversion of a heathen who had attempted to practise on her by magical arts. They were both martyred.

In both these instances the Blessed Virgin appears especially in that character of Patroness or Paraclete, which St Irenaeus and other Fathers describe, and which the Medieval Church exhibits,—a loving Mother with clients.[7]

a. Gen 3:20   b. Rev 12:1   c. Rev 12:17   d. Gen 3:15

An Essay on the Development of Christian Doctrine.
London, 1909, pp. 415–18.
Written by Newman in the months preceding
his reception into the Roman Catholic Church (October 1845).

[6] [Nyss. Opp. t. ii. p. 977]
[7] [Def. F. N. ii 12.]

XVII

DEVOTION TO THE VIRGIN MARY DOES NOT OBSCURE THE DIVINE GLORY OF CHRIST[1]

It has been anxiously asked, whether the honours paid to St Mary, which have grown out of devotion to her Almighty Lord and Son, do not, in fact, tend to weaken that devotion; and whether, from the nature of the case, it is possible so to exalt a creature without withdrawing the heart from the Creator.

In addition to what has been said on this subject in foregoing chapters, I would here observe that the question is one of fact, not of presumption or conjecture. The abstract lawfulness of the honours paid to St Mary, and their distinction in theory from the incommunicable worship paid to God, are points which have already been dwelt upon; but here the question turns upon

---

[1] This passage from the *Essay on the Development of Christian Doctrine* illustrates the sixth test of genuine development, namely, that it conserves any antecedent developments and, in what it adds to them, it illustrates and corroborates the original doctrine. Newman maintained that devotion to our Lady flowed as a natural consequence from devotion to her Son. He now illustrates how this Marian devotion does not weaken devotion to Christ. On the contrary, it strengthens our veneration for Christ. Cf. this same teaching solemnly reiterated by the Second Vatican Council: Dogmatic Constitution on the Church, *Lumen Gentium*, 60 and 67.

their practicability or expedience, which must be determined by the fact whether they are practicable, and whether they have been found to be expedient.

1. Here I observe, first, that, to those who admit the authority of the Fathers of Ephesus, the question is in no slight degree answered by their sanction of the θεοτόκος, or 'Mother of God', as a title of St Mary, and as given in order to protect the doctrine of the Incarnation, and to preserve the faith of Catholics from a specious Humanitarianism.[2] And if we take a survey at least of Europe, we shall find that it is not those religious communions which are characterized by devotion towards the Blessed Virgin that have ceased to adore her Eternal Son, but those very bodies, (when allowed by the law,) which have renounced devotion to her. The regard for His glory, which was professed in that keen jealousy of her exaltation, has not been supported by the event. They who were accused of worshipping a creature in His stead, still worship Him; their accusers, who hoped to worship Him so purely, they, wherever obstacles to the development of their principles have been removed, have ceased to worship Him altogether.[3]

2. Next, it must be observed, that the tone of the

[2] Mary's divine Maternity safeguards the doctrine of the Incarnation – this thought is often repeated in Newman's Mariology: cf. above Introduction IV, pp. 69–70. 'Humanitarianism' here is not to be understood in the modern sense of philanthropic actions on behalf of humanity, but in the theological sense of the belief that Jesus Christ was a man *only*.

[3] This historical illustration of the point Newman is making, concerning devotion to Christ and our Lady, is a consideration he returns to on various occasions: cf. above, Text III, p. 137–8.

devotion paid to the Blessed Mary is altogether distinct from that which is paid to her Eternal Son, and to the Holy Trinity, as we must certainly allow on inspection of the Catholic services. The supreme and true worship paid to the Almighty is severe, profound, awful, as well as tender, confiding, and dutiful. Christ is addressed as true God, while He is true Man; as our Creator and Judge, while He is most loving, gentle, and gracious. On the other hand, towards St Mary the language employed is affectionate and ardent, as towards a mere child of Adam; though subdued, as coming from her sinful kindred. How different, for instance, is the tone of the *Dies Irae* from that of the *Stabat Mater*. In the 'Tristis et afflicta Mater Unigeniti',[4] in the 'Virgo virginum, praeclara Mihi jam non sis amara, Poenas mecum divide', in the 'Fac me vere tecum flere', we have an expression of the feelings with which we regard one who is a creature and a mere human being; but in the 'Rex tremendae majestatis qui salvandos salvas gratis, salva me Fons pietatis', the 'Ne me perdas illa die', the 'Juste judex ultionis, donum fac remissionis', the 'Oro supplex et acclinis, cor contritum quasi cinis', the 'Pie Jesu Domine, dona eis requiem',[5] we

---

[4] Words from the *Stabat Mater*, a *Sequence* (hymn between the Gradual and the Gospel) then used for the Feast of the Seven Sorrows of the Blessed Virgin Mary; '[Oh, how] sad and sore distressed,/Was that Mother [highly blessed]/Of the sole-begotten One'; 'Virgin of all virgins best,/Listen to my fond request:/Let me join my plaint with thine;' 'With devoted heart let me weep with thee'.

[5] Words from the *Dies Irae*, a *Sequence* which was said in Masses for the Dead: 'King of tremendous majesty!/Who savest, whom thou savest, free,'/– Thou fount of pity, save thou me.' 'Condemn me not on that last day.' 'Just avenging judge, grant the gift of pardon.' 'With a contrite heart, prostrate I beseech thee.' 'Gentle Lord Jesus, grant to them eternal rest.'

hear the voice of the creature raised in hope and love, yet in deep awe to his Creator, Infinite Benefactor, and Judge.

Or again, how distinct is the language of the Breviary Services on the Festival of Pentecost, or of the Holy Trinity, from the language of the Services for the Assumption! How indescribably majestic, solemn, and soothing is the 'Veni Creator Spiritus', the 'Altissimi donum Dei, Fons vivus, ignis, charitas',[6] or the 'Vera et una Trinitas, una et summa Deitas, sancta et una Unitas', the 'Spes nostra, salus nostra, honor noster, O beata Trinitas', the 'Charitas Pater, gratia Filius, communicatio Spiritus Sanctus, O beata Trinitas'; 'Libera nos, salva nos, vivifica nos, O beata Trinitas!'[7] How fond, on the contrary, how full of sympathy and affection, how stirring and animating, in the Office for the Assumption, is the 'Virgo prudentissima, quo progrederis, quasi aurora valde rutilans? filia Sion, tota formosa et suavis es, pulcra ut luna, electa ut sol'; the 'Sicut dies verni circumdabant eam flores rosarum, et lilia convallium';[8] the 'Maria Virgo assumpta est ad aethereum thalamum in quo

---

[6] From the hymn *Come O Creator Spirit blest*: 'O highest gift of God most high,/O Fount of Life, O Fire of Love'.

[7] Newman here quotes antiphons from the Feast of the Most Holy Trinity: 'The one and true Trinity, the one and highest God, the one and all-holy Unity': 'You are our hope, our salvation and our glory, O Blessed Trinity': 'The Father is love, the Son is grace, the Holy Spirit is the one who unites, O blessed Trinity': 'Grant us freedom, salvation and life, O blessed Trinity'.

[8] Some of these texts are based on the Wisdom literature of the Old Testament: 'Most wise Virgin, where do you go, like a brightening dawn? daughter of Sion, comely and pleasant, beautiful as the moon, choice as the sun': 'As in spring days, the flowers of roses and the lilies of the valleys surround her' (cf. Song 2:1, 6:4, 9–10).

Rex regum stellato sedet solio'; and the 'Gaudent Angeli, laudantes benedicunt Dominum'.[9] And so again, the Antiphon, the 'Ad te clamamus exules filii Hevae, ad te suspiramus gementes et flentes in hac lacrymarum valle', and 'Eia ergo, advocata nostra, illos tuos misericordes oculos ad nos converte', and 'O clemens, O pia, O dulcis Virgo Maria'.[10] Or the Hymn, 'Ave Maris stella, Dei Mater alma', and 'Virgo singularis, inter omnes mitis, nos culpis solutos, mites fac et castos'.[11]

3. Nor does it avail to object that, in this contrast of devotional exercises, the human will supplant the Divine, from the infirmity of our nature; for, I repeat, the question is one of fact, whether it has done so. And next it must be asked, whether the character of much of the Protestant devotion towards our Lord has been that of adoration at all; and not rather such as we pay to an excellent human being, that is, no higher devotion than that which Catholics pay to St Mary, differing from it, however, in often being familiar, rude, and earthly. Carnal minds will ever create a carnal worship for themselves; and to forbid them the service of the Saints will have no tendency to teach them the worship of God.

[9] 'The Virgin Mary has been assumed to the heavenly dwelling-place where the King of kings sits on a throne of stars.' 'The angels rejoice; they sing for joy and praise the Lord.'

[10] From the *Hail, Holy Queen (Salve Regina)*: 'To thee do we cry, poor banished children of Eve. To thee do we send up our sighs, mourning and weeping in this valley of tears. Turn then, most gracious advocate, thine eyes of mercy towards us ... O clement, O loving, O sweet Virgin Mary.'

[11] 'Hail, star of the sea, kind Mother of God.' 'Unique Virgin, meekest of all, make us, when set free from sin, meek and pure.'

Moreover, it must be observed, what is very important, that great and constant as is the devotion which the Catholic pays to the Blessed Mary, it has a special province, and has far more connexion with the public services and the festive aspect of Christianity, and with certain extraordinary offices which she holds, than with what is strictly personal and primary in religion.[12]

Two instances will serve in illustration of this, and they are but samples of many others.[13]

4. For example, St Ignatius' *Spiritual Exercises*[14] are among the most approved methods of devotion in the modern Catholic Church; they proceed from one of the most celebrated of her Saints, and have the praise of Popes, and of the most eminent masters of the spiritual life. A Bull of Paul III's 'approves, praises, and sanc-

---

[12] Expressions of devotion to our Lady are not to be scorned or suppressed. Rather they are to be brought into harmony with the liturgy and with doctrine. When treating of popular devotions of the Christian people, the Second Vatican Council stated that 'such devotions should be so drawn up that they harmonize with the liturgical seasons, accord with the sacred liturgy, are in some way derived from it, and lead the people to it, since in fact the liturgy by its very nature is far superior to any of them' (The Constitution on the Sacred Liturgy, *Sacrosanctum Concilium*, 13).

[13] [*E.g.* the 'De Imitatione', the 'Introduction à la Vie Dévote', the 'Spiritual Combat', the 'Anima Divota', the 'Paradisus Animae', the 'Regula Cleri', the 'Garden of the Soul', etc. etc. (Also, the Roman Catechism, drawn up expressly for Parish instruction, a book in which, out of nearly 600 pages, scarcely half-a-dozen make mention of the Blessed Virgin, though without any disparagement thereby, or thought of disparagement, of her special prerogatives.)]

[14] Newman chooses a work like the *Spiritual Exercises* by St Ignatius because it is one of the most widely used and approved methods of devotion in the Catholic Church. It was precisely these devotional texts and practices that were being questioned by non-Catholics.

tions all and everything contained in them'; indulgences are granted to the performance of them by the same Pope, by Alexander VII, and by Benedict XIV. St Carlo Borromeo declared that he learned more from them than from all other books together; St Francis de Sales calls them 'a holy method of reformation', and they are the model on which all the extraordinary devotions of religious men or bodies, and the course of missions, are conducted. If there is a document which is the authoritative exponent of the inward communion of the members of the modern Catholic Church with their God and Saviour, it is this work.

The Exercises are directed to the removal of obstacles in the way of the soul's receiving and profiting by the gifts of God. They undertake to effect this in three ways; by removing all objects of this world, and, as it were, bringing the soul 'into the solitude where God may speak to its heart'; next, by setting before it the ultimate end of man, and its own deviations from it, the beauty of holiness, and the pattern of Christ; and, lastly, by giving rules for its correction. They consist of a course of prayers, meditations, self-examinations, and the like, which in its complete extent lasts thirty days; and these are divided into three stages,—the *Via Purgativa*, in which sin is the main subject of consideration; the *Via Illuminativa*, which is devoted to the contemplation of our Lord's passion, involving the process of the determination of our calling; and the *Via Unitiva*, in which we proceed to the contemplation of our Lord's resurrection and ascension.

5. No more need be added in order to introduce the remark for which I have referred to these

Exercises; viz. that in a work so highly sanctioned, so widely received, so intimately bearing upon the most sacred points of personal religion, very slight mention occurs of devotion to the Blessed Virgin, Mother of God. There is one mention of her in the rule given for the first Prelude or preparation, in which the person meditating is directed to consider as before him a church, or other place with Christ in it, St Mary, and whatever else is suitable to the subject of meditation. Another is in the third Exercise, in which one of the three addresses is made to our Lady, Christ's Mother, requesting earnestly 'her intercession with her Son'; to which is to be added the Ave Mary. In the beginning of the Second Week there is a form of offering ourselves to God in the presence of 'His infinite goodness', and with the witness of His 'glorious Virgin Mother Mary, and the whole host of heaven'. At the end of the Meditation upon the Angel Gabriel's mission to St Mary, there is an address to each Divine Person, to 'the Word Incarnate and to His Mother'. In the Meditation upon the Two Standards, there is an address prescribed to St Mary to implore grace from her Son through her, with an Ave Mary after it.

In the beginning of the Third Week one address is prescribed to Christ; or three, if devotion incites, to Mother, Son and Father. In the description given of three different modes of prayer we are told, if we would imitate the Blessed Mary, we must recommend ourselves to her, as having power with her Son, and presently the Ave Mary, *Salve Regina*, and other forms are prescribed, as is usual after all prayers. And this is pretty much the whole of the devotion, if it may so be called, which is recommended towards St Mary in the course of so many apparently as a hundred and fifty Meditations, and those chiefly on the events in our Lord's earthly history as recorded in Scripture. It would seem then that whatever be the influence of the doctrines connected with the Blessed Virgin and the Saints in the Catholic Church, at least they do not impede or obscure the freest exercise and the fullest manifestation of the devotional feelings towards God and Christ.

6. The other instance which I give in illustration is of a different kind, but is suitable to mention. About forty little books have come into my possession which are in circulation among the laity at Rome, and answer to the smaller publications of the Christian Knowledge Society among ourselves. They have been taken almost at hazard from a number of such works, and are of various lengths; some running to as many as two or three hundred pages, others consisting of scarce a dozen. They may be divided into three classes: a third part consists of books on practical subjects; another third is upon the Incarnation and Passion; and of the rest, a portion is upon the Sacraments, especially the Holy Eucharist, with two or three for the use of Missions, but the greater part is about the Blessed Virgin.

As to the class on practical subjects, they are on such as the following: 'La Consolazione degl' Infermi'; 'Pensieri di una donna sul vestire moderno'; 'L'Inferno Aperto'; 'Il Purgatorio Aperto'; St Alphonso Liguori's 'Massime eterne'; other Maxims by St Francis de Sales for every day in the year;

'Pratica per ben confessarsi e communicarsi'; and the like.[15]

The titles of the second class on the Incarnation and Passion are such as 'Gesu dalla Croce al cuore del peccatore'; 'Novena del Ss. Natale di G. C.'; Associazione pel culto perpetuo del divin cuore'; 'Compendio della Passione'.[16]

In the third are 'Il Mese Eucaristico', 'Il divoto di Maria', Feasts of the Blessed Virgin, etc.[17]

7. These books in all three divisions are, as even the titles of some of them show, in great measure made up of Meditations; such are the 'Breve e pie Meditazioni' of P. Crasset; the 'Meditazioni per ciascun giorno del mese sulla Passione'; the 'Meditazioni per l'ora Eucaristica'.[18] Now of these it may be said generally, that in the body of the Meditation St Mary is hardly mentioned at all. For instance, in the Meditations on the Passion, a book used for distribution, through two hundred and seventy-seven pages St Mary is not once named. In the Prayers for Mass which are added, she is introduced, at the Confiteor, thus, 'I pray the Virgin, the Angels, the Apostles, and all the Saints of heaven to intercede', etc; and in the Preparation for Penance, she

---

[15] The Italian titles signify: 'The Consolation of the Sick': 'Thoughts of a Woman on modern dress': 'Hell Wide Open': 'Purgatory Wide Open': St Alphonsus Liguori's 'The Eternal Truths': ... 'Preparation for a good Confession and holy Communion'.

[16] 'Jesus speaks from the Cross to the heart of a sinner': 'Novena for Christmas': 'Association for the perpetual worship of the Divine Heart': 'Compendium of the Passion'.

[17] 'A Eucharistic Month': 'Mary's Devotee'.

[18] Fr Crasset's books are entitled: 'Meditations for every day of the month on the Passion', and 'Meditations for a Holy Hour.'

is once addressed, after our Lord, as the Refuge of
sinners, with the Saints and Guardian Angel; and at the
end of the Exercise there is a similar prayer of four lines
for the intercession of St Mary, Angels and Saints of
heaven. In the Exercise for Communion, in a prayer to
our Lord, 'my only and infinite good, my treasure, my
life, my paradise, my all', the merits of the Saints are
mentioned, 'especially of St Mary'. She is also
mentioned with Angels and Saints at the termination.

In a collection of 'Spiritual Lauds' for Missions, of
thirty-six Hymns, we find as many as eleven addressed
to St Mary, or relating to her, among which are translations of the *Ave Maris Stella*, and the *Stabat Mater*,
and the *Salve Regina*; and one is on 'the sinner's
reliance on Mary'. Five, however, which are upon
Repentance, are entirely engaged upon the subjects of
our Lord and sin, with the exception of an address to
St Mary at the end of two of them. Seven others,
upon sin, the Crucifixion, and the Four Last Things,
do not mention the Blessed Virgin's name.

To the Manual for the Perpetual Adoration of the
Divine Heart of Jesus there is appended one chapter
on the Immaculate Conception.

8. One of the most important of these books is the
French *Pensez-y bien*,[19] which seems a favourite, since
there are two translations of it, one of them being the
fifteenth edition; and it is used for distribution in
Missions. In these reflections there is scarcely a word
said of St Mary. At the end there is a Method of reciting the Crown of the Seven Dolours of the Virgin

[19] '*Pensez-y bien*', ('Give it careful consideration'), was written by the
Jesuit, Barthélemy Baudrand (1701–87).

Mary, which contains seven prayers to her, and the *Stabat Mater*.

One of the longest in the whole collection is a tract consisting principally of Meditations on the Holy Communion; under the title of the 'Eucharistic Month', as already mentioned. In these 'Preparations', 'Aspirations', etc, St Mary is but once mentioned, and that in a prayer addressed to our Lord. 'O my sweetest Brother', it says with an allusion to the Canticles, 'who, being made Man for my salvation, hast sucked the milk from the virginal breast of her, who is my Mother by grace', etc. In a small 'Instruction' given to children on their first Communion, there are the following questions and answers: 'Is our Lady in the Host? No. Are the Angels and the Saints? No. Why not? Because they have no place there.'

9. Now coming to those in the third class, which directly relate to the Blessed Mary, such as 'Esercizio ad Onore dell'addolorato cuore di Maria', 'Novena di Preparazione alla festa dell' Assunzione', 'Li Quindici Misteri del Santo Rosario',[20] the principal is Father Segneri's 'Il divoto di Maria',[21] which requires a distinct notice. It is far from the intention of these remarks to deny the high place which the Holy Virgin holds in the

---

[20] 'Devotions in honour of the Sorrowful Heart of Mary': 'Novena in preparation for the Feast of the Assumption': 'The Fifteen Mysteries of the Holy Rosary'.

[21] Fr Paolo Segneri, an Italian Jesuit of the seventeenth century (1624–94), was a renowned preacher. The book analysed by Newman, *Il devoto di Maria* ('Mary's Devotee'), was published in 1678. Newman's intention in quoting from an author such as Segneri is to show that veneration of Christ is far beyond that given to Mary, even by her most ardent devotees.

devotion of Catholics; I am but bringing evidence of its
not interfering with that incommunicable and awful
relation which exists between the creature and the
Creator; and, if the foregoing instances show, as far as
they go, that that relation is preserved inviolate in such
honours as are paid to St Mary, so will this treatise throw
light upon the *rationale* by which the distinction is
preserved between the worship of God and the honour
of an exalted creature, and that in singular accordance
with the remarks made in the foregoing Section.

10.   This work of Segneri is written against persons who
continue in sins under pretence of their devotion to St
Mary, and in consequence he is led to draw out the idea
which good Catholics have of her. The idea is this, that
she is absolutely the first of created beings. Thus the
treatise says, that 'God might have easily made a more
beautiful firmament, and a greener earth, but it was not
possible to make a higher Mother than the Virgin Mary;
and in her formation there has been conferred on mere
creatures all the glory of which they are capable, remaining mere creatures'. And as containing all created
perfection, she has all those attributes, which, as was
noticed above, the Arians and other heretics applied to
our Lord, and which the Church denied of Him as infinitely below His Supreme Majesty. Thus she is 'the
created Idea in the making of the world'; 'which, as
being a more exact copy of the Incarnate Idea than was
elsewhere to be found, was used as the original of the
rest of the creation'. To her are applied the words, 'Ego
primogenita prodivi ex ore Altissimi',[22] because she was

---

[22] 'I came forth, a first-born, from the mouth of the Most High.'

predestinated in the Eternal Mind coevally with the
Incarnation of her Divine Son. But to Him alone the
title of Wisdom Incarnate is reserved. Again, Christ is
the First-born by nature; the Virgin in a less sublime
order, viz. that of adoption. Again, if omnipotence is
ascribed to her, it is a participated omnipotence (as she
and all Saints have a participated sonship, divinity, glory,
holiness, and worship), and is explained by the words,
'Quod Deus imperio, tu prece, Virgo, potes'.[23]

11. Again, a special office is assigned to the Blessed
Virgin, that is, special as compared with all other
Saints; but it is marked off with the utmost precision
from that assigned to our Lord. Thus she is said to
have been made 'the arbitress of every *effect* coming
from God's mercy'. Because she is the Mother of
God, the salvation of mankind is said to be given to
her prayers '*de congruo*, but *de condigno*[24] it is due only
to the blood of the Redeemer'. Merit is ascribed to
Christ, and prayer to St Mary. The whole may be
expressed in the words, '*Unica* spes mea Jesus, et post
Jesum Virgo Maria. Amen.'[25]

Again, a distinct cultus is assigned to Mary, but the
reason of it is said to be the transcendent dignity of her
Son. 'A particular *cultus* is due to the Virgin beyond
comparison greater than that given to any other Saint,
because her dignity belongs to another order, namely
to one which in some sense belongs to the order of

---

[23] 'What God can do with a command, you are able to do by your
prayer.'

[24] Technical theological terms: Something is due *de congruo* when the
recipient has only a certain suitability to receive it; *de condigno* if it is
strictly deserved.

[25] 'Jesus is my sole hope, and, after Jesus, the Virgin Mary. Amen.'

the Hypostatic Union itself, and is necessarily connected with it'. And 'Her being the Mother of God is the source of all the extraordinary honours due to Mary'.

It is remarkable that the 'Monstra te esse Matrem' is explained as 'Show thyself to be *our* Mother'; an interpretation which I think I have found elsewhere in these Tracts, and also in a book commonly used in religious houses, called the 'Journal of Meditations', and elsewhere.[26]

It must be kept in mind that my object here is not to prove the dogmatic accuracy of what these popular publications teach concerning the prerogatives of the Blessed Virgin, but to show that that teaching is not such as to obscure the divine glory of her Son. We must ask for clearer evidence before we are able to admit so grave a charge; and so much may suffice on the Sixth Test of fidelity in the development of an idea, as applied to the Catholic system.

An Essay on the Development of Christian Doctrine,
London, 1909, pp. 425–36.
Written by Newman in the months preceding his reception
into the Roman Catholic Church (October 1845).

[26] [Vid, *Via Media*, Vol. ii. pp. 121–2]; cf. pp. 128–9 in later editions.

XVIII

A MEMORANDUM
ON THE IMMACULATE CONCEPTION[1]

I

1. It is so difficult for me to enter into the feelings of a person who *understands* the doctrine of the Immaculate Conception, and yet objects to it, that I am diffident about attempting to speak on the subject. I was accused of holding it, in one of the first books I wrote, twenty years ago.[2] On the other hand, this very fact may be an argument against an objector—for why should it not have been difficult to me at that time, if there were a real difficulty in receiving it?

2. Does not the objector consider that *Eve* was created, or born, *without* original sin? Why does not *this* shock him? Would he have been inclined to

---

[1] This *Memorandum* was written by Cardinal Newman for one of his friends in the Oxford Movement, Mr Robert I. Wilberforce, formerly Archdeacon Wilberforce, who was one of the leading theologians among the Tractarians. He became a Catholic in 1854. These pages were meant to be of assistance to him in meeting the objections urged by some Protestant friends against the doctrine of the Immaculate Conception. The *italics* in the text are the Cardinal's.

[2] Cf. above, Text II, pp. 120–1, and p. 120, footnote 6.

worship Eve in that first estate of hers? Why, then, Mary?

3. Does he not believe that St John Baptist had the grace of God—i.e., was regenerated, even before his birth? What do we believe of Mary, but that grace was given her at a still earlier period? *All* we say is, that grace was given her from the first moment of her existence.

4. We do not say that she did not owe her salvation to the death of her Son. Just the contrary, we say that she, of all mere children of Adam, is in the truest sense the fruit and the purchase of His Passion. He has done for her more than for anyone else. To others He gives grace and regeneration at a *point* in their earthly existence; to her, from the very beginning.

5. We do not make her *nature* different from others.[3] Though, as St Austin says, we do not like to name her in the same breath with mention of sin,[4] yet, certainly she *would* have been a frail being, like Eve, *without* the grace of God. A more abundant gift of grace made her what she was from the first. It was not her *nature* which secured her perseverance, but the excess of grace which hindered Nature acting as Nature ever will act. There is no difference in *kind* between her

[3] Newman, first of all, mentions certain misconceptions by Anglicans about the true meaning of the Immaculate Conception. Some thought that it meant Mary did not need to be redeemed by Christ; others that the privilege referred to our Lady's mother, St Anne, and still others, reasoning from a false notion of original sin, concluded that her *nature* was different from ours. (Cf. above: *Introduction* IV, pp. 51–64).

[4] Cf. above, Text V, p. 170, footnote 7.

and us, though an inconceivable difference of *degree*. She and we are both simply saved by the grace of Christ.

Thus, sincerely speaking, I really do not see *what* the difficulty is, and should like it set down distinctly in words. I will add that the above statement is no private statement of my own. I never heard of any Catholic who ever had any other view. I never heard of any other put forth by anyone.

II

Next, Was it a primitive doctrine? No one can add to revelation. That was given once for all; but as time goes on, what was given once for all is understood more and more clearly. The greatest Fathers and Saints in this sense have been in error, that, since the matter of which they spoke had not been sifted, and the Church had not spoken, they did not in their *expressions do justice to their own real meaning*..

E.g. **1,** The Athanasian Creed says that the Son is *immensus* (in the Protestant version, 'incomprehensible'). Bishop Bull, though defending the ante-Nicene Fathers, says that it is a marvel that 'nearly all of them have the appearance of being *ignorant* of the invisibility and immensity of the Son of God'. Do I for a moment think they *were* ignorant? No, but that they spoke *inconsistently*, because they were opposing other errors, and did not observe what they said. When the heretic Arius arose, and they saw the use which was made of their admissions, the Fathers retracted them.

2. The great Fathers of the fourth century seem, most of them, to consider our Lord in His human nature *ignorant*, and to have grown in knowledge,[a] as St Luke *seems* to say. This doctrine was *anathematized* by the Church in the next century, when the Monophysites arose.

3. In like manner, there are Fathers who seem to deny original sin, eternal punishment, etc.

4. Further, the famous symbol 'Consubstantial', as applied to the Son, which is in the Nicene Creed, was *condemned* by a great Council of Antioch, with Saints in it, seventy years before. Why? Because that Council meant something else by the word.

Now, as to the doctrine of the Immaculate Conception, it was *implied* in early times, and never *denied*. In the Middle Ages it *was* denied by St Thomas and by St Bernard,[5] but they took the phrase in a

---

[5] St Bernard's (+1157) difficulty stemmed from the Augustinian belief that original sin was transmitted by means of the concupiscence in the act of generation. Moreover, it was then commonly thought that the 'rational' soul was infused after the vegetative and sensitive soul, hence some time after conception. Consequently, it was difficult for St Bernard to see how our Lady could be sanctified before she existed as a human creature (with a 'rational' soul), but he declared himself most willing to accept a different opinion if it were declared by the Holy See. Cf. *Epistula* (174) *ad Canonicos Lugdunenses: PL* 182, 332–6 and Antonio Maria Calero, *La Vergine Maria nel mistero di Cristo e della Chiesa*. Leumann (Torino) 1995, p. 177. A century later, this difficulty was overcome by St Thomas Aquinas. However, he did not see how our Lady could have the privilege of the Immaculate Conception on account of the doctrine of the universal scope of Christ's redemptive work. It seemed to him that if she had been preserved from original sin, the absolute and universal need of redemption would no longer be valid. (Cf. *In IV Sent.*, d.43, q.1, a.4, s.1 and 3; *Summa Theologiae*, III, q.27, a.2).

different sense from that in which the Church now takes it. They understood it with reference to our Lady's mother, and thought it contradicted the text, 'In sin hath my mother conceived me'—whereas *we* do not speak of the Immaculate Conception except as relating to Mary; and the other doctrine (which St Thomas and St Bernard did oppose) *is* really heretical.

III

As to primitive notion about our Blessed Lady, really, the frequent contrast of Mary with Eve seems very strong indeed. It is found in St Justin, St Irenaeus, and Tertullian, three of the earliest Fathers, and in three distinct continents—Gaul, Africa, and Syria. For instance, 'the knot formed by Eve's disobedience was untied by the obedience of Mary; that what the Virgin Eve tied through unbelief, that the Virgin Mary unties through faith.' Again, 'The Virgin Mary becomes the Advocate (Paraclete) of the Virgin Eve, that *as* mankind has been bound to death *through* a Virgin, *through* a Virgin it may be saved, the balance being preserved, a Virgin's disobedience by a Virgin's obedience' (St Irenaeus, *Haer.* v. 19). Again, 'As Eve, becoming disobedient, became *the cause* of death to herself and *to all mankind, so* Mary, too, bearing the predestined Man, and yet a Virgin, being obedient, became the CAUSE OF SALVATION, both to herself and to all mankind.' Again, 'Eve being a Virgin, and incorrupt, bore disobedience and death, but Mary the Virgin, receiving faith and joy, when Gabriel the Angel evangelized her, answered, "Be it unto me,"' etc. Again, 'What Eve failed in believing, Mary by believing *hath* blotted out.'

1. Now, can we refuse to see that, according to these Fathers, who are earliest of the early, Mary was a *typical woman* like Eve, that both were endued with special gifts of grace, and that Mary succeeded where Eve failed?[6]

2. Moreover, what light they cast upon St Alfonso's doctrine, of which a talk is sometimes made, of the two ladders. You see according to these most early Fathers, Mary *undoes* what Eve had done; mankind is *saved through* a Virgin; the *obedience* of Mary becomes the *cause of salvation to all mankind*. Moreover, the distinct way in which Mary does this is pointed out when she is called by the early Fathers an *Advocate*. The word is used of our Lord and the Holy Ghost— of our Lord, as interceding for us in His own Person; of the Holy Ghost, as interceding in the Saints. This is the *white* way, as our Lord's own special way is the *red* way, viz. of atoning Sacrifice.

3. Further still, what light these passages cast on two texts of Scripture. *Our* reading is, '*She* shall bruise thy head'.[b] Now, this fact alone of our reading, '*She* shall bruise', has some weight, for *why* should not, perhaps, our reading be the right one? But take the comparison of Scripture with Scripture, and see how the whole hangs together as we interpret it.[7] A war between a woman and the serpent is spoken of in Genesis. *Who* is the serpent? Scripture nowhere says till the twelfth chapter of the Apocalypse. There at last, for the first time, the

---

[6] For these considerations on Mary as the Second Eve in patristic writings cf. above, Text X, pp. 206–222.

[7] Cf. above, Text XVI, p. 284, footnote 4, and Text XII, pp. 240–5.

'Serpent' is interpreted to mean the Evil Spirit. Now, *how* is he introduced? Why, by the vision *again* of a Woman, his enemy—and just as, in the first vision in Genesis, the Woman has a 'seed', so here a 'Child'.[c] Can we help saying, then, that the Woman is Mary in the third [chapter] of Genesis? And if so, and our reading is right, the first prophecy ever given contrasts the Second Woman with the First—Mary with Eve, just as St Justin, St Irenaeus, and Tertullian do.

4. Moreover, see the direct bearing of this upon the Immaculate Conception. There was *war* between the woman and the Serpent. This is most emphatically fulfilled if she had nothing to do with sin—for, so far as any one sins, he has an alliance with the Evil One.

IV

Now I wish it observed *why* I thus adduce the Fathers and Scripture. *Not* to *prove* the doctrine, but to rid it of any such monstrous improbability as would make a person *scruple* to accept it *when* the Church declares it. A Protestant is apt to say: 'Oh, I really never, never can accept such a doctrine from the hands of the Church, and I had a thousand thousand times rather determine that the Church spoke falsely, than that so terrible a doctrine was true.' Now, my good man, WHY? Do not go off in such a wonderful agitation, like a horse shying at he does not know what. Consider what I have said. Is it, after all, *certainly* irrational? is it *certainly* against Scripture? is it *certainly* against the primitive Fathers? is it *certainly* idolatrous? I cannot help smiling as I put the questions. Rather, may not *something* be said for it from reason, from piety, from antiquity, from the inspired text? You may see no reason at all to believe the voice of the Church; you may not yet have attained to faith in it—but what on earth this doctrine has to do with *shaking* your faith in her, if you have faith, or in sending you to the right-about if you are beginning to think she *may* be from God, is more than my mind can comprehend. Many, many doctrines are far harder than the Immaculate Conception. The doctrine of Original Sin is indefinitely harder. Mary just has *not* this difficulty. It is *no* difficulty to believe that a soul is united to the flesh *without* original sin; the great mystery is that any, that millions on millions, are born with it. Our teaching about Mary has just one difficulty less than our teaching about the state of mankind generally.

I say it distinctly—there may be many excuses at the last day, good and bad for not being Catholics; *one* I cannot conceive: 'O Lord, the doctrine of the Immaculate Conception was so derogatory to Thy grace, so inconsistent with Thy Passion, so at variance with Thy word in Genesis and the Apocalypse, so unlike the teaching of Thy first Saints and Martyrs, as to give me a *right* to reject it at all risks, and Thy Church for teaching it. It is a doctrine as to which my private judgment is fully justified in opposing the Church's judgment.

And this is my plea for living and dying a Protestant.'[8]

a. cf. Lk 2:52
b. Gen 3:15
c. Rev 12:1–17

Meditations and Devotions of the late Cardinal Newman,
London, 1911, pp. 79–86.
Written by Newman to assist his friend, Robert I. Wilberforce,
who was received into the Catholic Church in 1854.

[8] The full flush of Newman's certainty and fervour appears in the passionate lines of these last paragraphs. He himself did not have a major difficulty as an Anglican in seeing the suitability and even the probability of the Immaculate Conception. Yet it was a real difficulty for many Anglicans, especially in the middle of the last century, not only on account of the doctrine itself, but also because of the implications it had for Papal Infallibility – a Pope, and not an Ecumenical Council, raising a Marian truth to the status of a dogma.

XIX/A

LETTER TO ARTHUR OSBORNE ALLEYNE

The Oratory Birmingham May 30 1860

My dear Mr Alleyne[1]

I quite recollect you, but I never heard what became of you—except that someone told me, I think, that you had been at Oriel. It is a real pleasure to me to know, that you can speak well of any thing I have written, for sometimes I am tempted to think that I waste my time in writing at all. When it is brought home to me that persons I know nothing about, and have no reason to suspect are my readers, have been struck or moved by my books, I gain the encouragement which I need.

[1] Arthur Osborne Alleyne (1833–1909) was received into the Catholic Church at the age of 15. Later he reverted to Anglicanism and was ordained a deacon of the Church of England and, in 1862, a priest. He was often strongly drawn to return to the Catholic Church but he never did. This letter by Newman is a response to one by Alleyne the previous day (29 May) asking for a few words of explanation about the Immaculate Conception – a truth which he and many Anglicans found difficult to understand and accept.

As to St Alfonso's 'Theory of truthfulness',[2] I can quite understand a person finding it difficult—indeed I suppose Englishmen will always be at war with Italians on this head. But it *does* surprise me that you find a difficulty in the Immaculate Conception— and, as you say that 'it presents such obstacles to *Anglicans*', I am led to assure you that I for one felt it no obstacle—on the contrary it seems to me the most natural and necessary of doctrines—and I cannot enter into the minds of those who feel it difficult.

This *fact* in itself ought to have weight with you— because it shows that we (Catholics) 'so readily accept it', to use your own words, not simply on the author- ity of others, or because it is popular, but (over and above its being defined) from its intrinsic verisimili- tude.

In a Sermon published in 1835, ten years before I became a Catholic, I say, 'What, think you, was the sanctity and grace of that human nature of which God formed His sinless Son; knowing, as we do, "that what is born of the flesh is flesh",[a] and that "none can bring a *clean thing out of an unclean*"[b]?'[3] I was accused of holding the doctrine of the Immaculate Conception, for it was clear that I connected 'grace' with the Blessed Virgin's *humanity*—as if grace and nature in her case never had been separated. All I could say in

---

[2] St Alphonsus of Liguori writes in his *Theologia moralis*, lib. IV, Tr. 2, (Mechliniae 1845, Vol. II. pp. 316–7), of the circumstances in which *amphibologia* (equivocation) is licit. Newman treats the question in the *Apologia*, Note G, pp. 348–63.

[3] The sermon was on 'The Reverence due to the Virgin Mary' in *Parochial and Plain Sermons*, Vol.II, p. 132. Cf. above, Text II, pp. 115–128.

answer was, that there was nothing against the doctrine in the Thirty-Nine Articles.[4]

St John Baptist was without original sin three months before his birth—what is then strange or unchristian in the doctrine that our Lady was free from it for nine months that is, from her conception? The grace of God in that case was given to her six months earlier than to the Baptist. Is there any thing monstrous in this?

If I am asked for proof of the doctrine being held in the early Church, I answer that it seems included in the general belief that the Blessed Virgin was without sin—and, while not much is said about her at all, when she *is* spoken of, she is spoken of in this aspect. I need not do more than remind you of the well known passage of St Augustine, in which he says that, when Mary is named, he does not wish to make any mention of sin,[5] as if the two names were antagonistic —but what to me is, and ever has been, most striking, is the series of passages from the earliest Fathers in which Mary is contrasted to Eve, as typical contrasts.[6] St Justin (AD 160) St Irenaeus (AD 170) Tertullian (AD 200) all enlarge on this contrast—and later Fathers hand down the Tradition. The very point indeed in which the contrast is made, is that of *obedience*—but, when St Irenaeus says, 'mankind is surrendered to death by a *Virgin*, and is saved by a *Virgin*', he surely implies that as Eve was without sin,

---

[4] It becomes clear from these paragraphs that Newman never had a serious personal difficulty with the Catholic doctrine of the Immaculate Conception.

[5] For St Augustine cf. above, Text V, p. 170, footnote 7.

[6] For Mary as the Second Eve cf. above, Text X, pp. 206–22.

so was Mary. Why indeed is it difficult to suppose that Mary had at least the privilege of Eve?—and Eve had an immaculate conception and birth.

It is impossible in the course of a letter to bring out all I would say—but I think I am right in saying, that the only great historical difficulty of the doctrine is the opposition, if it may be so called, of St Bernard and St Thomas[7]—yet to my mind it is clearly shown that they did not mean by the doctrine what the Church now means—that is, that, as the Fathers of Antioch condemned the ὁμο-ούσιον, without denying the Nicene dogma, so the two saints in question were opposing what no one now thinks of maintaining, or indeed did then.

I wish you were not so far off—or I should hope for the pleasure of a visit from you. That is the only difficulty of an external character—for we have plenty of room, and could give you a bed, (as I have been doing to a friend since I began this letter) at a minute's notice.

I will say Mass for you tomorrow morning—and will not forget you—and, hoping you will let me hear from you again, and assuring you of my kindest wishes, I am, My dear Mr Alleyne,

Sincerely Yours John H Newman of the Oratory
The Revd A. O. Alleyne

a. Jn 3:6   b. Job 14:4

The Letters and Diaries of John Henry Newman,
London, 1969, Vol. XIX, pp. 346–7.
Written on 30 May 1860.

[7] For St Bernard and St Thomas Aquinas, cf. above, Text XVIII, p. 306, footnote 5.

XIX/B

SECOND LETTER TO ARTHUR
OSBORNE ALLEYNE

The Oratory Birmingham June 15 1860

My dear Mr Alleyne,

I have resolved on answering your Author at once; lest, if I delay, I should chance never to do it.

And I begin with a sentence in your own letter. 'It has always seemed to me *so strange* that the Immaculate Conception, which presents such obstacles to Anglicans is accepted so readily by members of the Church of Rome.' I observe on this as follows:

1. The difficulty which Protestants feel in receiving the doctrine lies in this, that they consider it a substantive self-dependent doctrine more than we do.

There are doctrines so intimately one with other doctrines, that they are rather their parts or aspects, than distinct from them; so that to prove the one is to prove the other. On the contrary there are doctrines so distinct from each other, that each requires its own proper proof, and to prove the one is no step at all towards proving the other.

E.g. the doctrine of our Lord's divinity, and that of the Holy Ghost's, are independent of each other. *This* does not imply *that*; to prove the one is not to prove the other. Again: our Lord's birth from Mary is one doctrine, and her sanctity is another. The one indeed tends to imply the other, but still they are independent, and must each be proved by itself, if their truth is to be ascertained by argument at all.

In these two (latter) cases, to say that the second doctrine is an extension of the first, and that it is sufficient to prove the first in order to the reception of the second, few men would allow.

On the other hand, if I say, 'God is Almighty, and is Allwise'; or 'the Son of God, is eternal, and He is incomprehensible', or 'the Holy Ghost is in the unity of the Father and the Son, and He is God', I put together pairs of propositions, which form parts of one idea respectively, and which are such, that to prove the one is virtually to prove the other. If I may not assume this, we never shall come to an end in the numberless points which will have to be proved, in order to a real reception of any one doctrine of the faith; e.g. we shall be obliged to allow that a man may without blasphemy maintain that the Almighty has not the eloquence, or wit, or reasoning power of man, only because it never entered into the mind of the sacred writers and the early Fathers to deny such an extravagance; nay, he may, without any fault, maintain that the Almighty is revengeful, because it is nowhere stated *as a dogma*, that He is not so.

In this then lies the difference of view, taken by Catholics and Protestants respectively, of the doctrine of the Immaculate Conception; that Catholics do not view it as a substantive and independent doctrine, so much as one of a family of doctrines which are intimately united together,[1] whereas Protestants consider it as separate from every other, and as requiring a proof of its own as fully as if it were the only thing that we knew of the Blessed Virgin. Catholics think it not much more of an addition to what they otherwise hold of her, than it would be to say, 'The Son of God is God, *therefore He is immensus*,'[2] whereas Protestants think it as little connected with what Catholics themselves otherwise hold of the Blessed Virgin, as the Doctrine of our Lord's divinity is with that of the divinity of the Holy Ghost.

2. Next, *why* do Protestants thus differ from Catholics in their mode of viewing the doctrine of the Immaculate Conception? I think it arises from the different view which the two religions take of that doctrine, out of which the Immaculate Conception arises, viz the doctrine of original sin.

Protestants consider original sin to be an *infection* of nature, so that man's nature now is not what it was before the fall. Accordingly, to be conceived without

---

[1] With the phrase 'a family of doctrines which are intimately united together', Newman refers to the interdependence of revealed supernatural truths in the corpus of divine Revelation. By comparing one revealed mystery with another one, it is possible to get a deeper understanding of them. This method of investigating and obtaining a more penetrating knowledge of revealed mysteries (technically called the 'analogy of faith': 'the connection of the mysteries themselves with each other') was officially stated by the First Vatican Council in its Dogmatic Constitution *Dei Filius* (cf. Denzinger-Schönmetzer, No. 3016).

[2] *immensus*: not in the popular sense of huge (immense), but in the theological meaning of boundless or immeasurable. Cf. above, p. 305.

original sin is to have a *nature* different from that of other men. Hence, according to them, it is blasphemy to say that our Lord was born of the nature of fallen Adam; and it *is* blasphemy according to their view of that nature. Hence it was the special heresy of Irving[3] in their eyes, that he so taught, and it was the ground of his expulsion from the Scotch Kirk.

Now I do not deny that Catholics consider that the natural powers of man are enfeebled by the fall; but they do not admit any infection of nature. They consider (or, they are free to consider) that the Blessed Virgin, that our Lord Himself, though both of them were without original sin, still both of them had the nature of fallen Adam. For original sin, according to them, consists in the deprivation of the grace of God, which was a gift external and superadded to Adam's nature. The presence of divine grace is the justifying principle, which makes the soul acceptable to Almighty God; moreover, there are degrees of justification, as there are degrees of grace. Not all the grace conceivable would, in the view of a Protestant, destroy original sin; it ever remains an infection, even though it be not imputed; but to a Catholic, on the contrary, the entrance of grace into the soul, as a presence, *ipso facto* destroys original sin. In the view of a Protestant it is no recommendation of the doctrine of our Lady's Immaculate Conception to urge that St John the Baptist was within six months of such a conception himself; but to a Catholic, who believes

---

[3] Edward Irving (1792–1834) was a minister of the Church of Scotland. In 1830 he was excommunicated for a publication in which he declared Christ's human nature to be sinful. In 1833 he was expelled from the Church of Scotland.

that the entrance of grace at the moment of conception is an *ipso facto* reversal of original sin, it acts as a probable argument in favour of her having been saved from original sin, that the Baptist, who was below her in dignity, was sanctified three months before his birth.

3. This difference of view is the cause of what has seemed so strange to you. As a Protestant would think a disputant captious and unfair, who asked for a distinct proof from Scripture, that 'the godhead and manhood were joined in one Person, *never to be divided,*' so a Catholic cannot comprehend why Protestants make so much difficulty and noise about the doctrine which to them is so natural, so intelligible, as the Immaculate Conception. Any passage of the Fathers, which speaks, vaguely but largely, of the grace given to Mary, tells, in his judgment, for the doctrine; for that privilege is but the *fullness* of grace. On the contrary, to a Protestant it does not go one hair's breadth toward proving it, for not all the grace conceivable can overcome, as he thinks, a fault of nature. In like manner, any passage of the Fathers, as that of St Augustine, which generally separates her off from sin,[4] suggests to the Catholic the doctrine that she was without original sin; whereas on the Protestant it has no such effect whatever, because original sin, in his view, is not a state different from Adam's, but a nature different from Adam's. And further, to the Catholic, (at least before he plunges into past controversy,) it is as little surprising that the

---

[4] For this frequent citation from St Augustine, cf. above, Text V, p. 170, footnote 7.

Church should define this point and declare it to be *de fide*, as that the Athanasian Creed should call the Holy Ghost God, though the Nicene does not: to the Protestant on the other hand, it is 'an unwarranted and audacious addition to the articles of faith' etc. etc.

4. You will ask perhaps, 'Why then was there so much controversy about the doctrine or about its definition?' I have alluded to this in the parenthesis of my last sentence, and will now explain why I do not see any difficulty in the matter. From the beginning of the Church even good and holy men have got involved in controversies of words. Such was, in great measure, that of the homoüsion in early times. The word was thought to involve certain consequences, or to imply certain ideas, which were not Catholic; and, as you know, some 60 years before the Nicene Council, in which it was made *de fide*, it was condemned or at least disavowed, by the great Council of Antioch, assembled against Paul of Samosata.[5] In like manner there have been mistaken ideas attached to the word Conception, and as to the sense in which it was used in the formula, 'the Immaculate Conception.' The question of the Homoüsion was soon settled, for it related to a primary article of faith; yet even the homoüsion was not received universally for something like 50 years after the Council, i.e. till the

---

[5] Cf. above, Text XV, p. 276, footnote 3. 'Homoousios' means 'consubstantial' and was used by the Council of Nicea (AD 325) against the Arians: the Son is truly God because eternally begotten of the Father and of the same substance or 'consubstantial' with Him. This had been denied by the Synod of Antioch in 268 because the term was used in a false sense by Paul of Samosata who took it to mean that the Son was not really a Person of his own, distinct from the Father.

Council of Constantinople; but *that* controversy was *settled*. How could it be otherwise? the question was, Whom are we to worship? whom are we to acknowledge as God? It could not remain in suspense. No one pretends that devotion to the Blessed Virgin is necessary in the sense in which devotion to our Lord is necessary. Devotion to our Lord as God is necessary for salvation; devotion to the Blessed Virgin is not necessary for salvation. It may be dispensed with *in toto* as far as salvation is concerned. In the early Church, if we let history be the measure of fact, many were saved without devotion to her. The *devotion* to her has gradually and slowly extended through the Church; the *doctrine* about her being always the same from the first. But the *gradual* growth of the devotion was a cause why that doctrine, in spite of its having been from the first, should have been but slowly recognized, slowly defined. Then, when the devotion had become fixed and living, next, as regards this particular point, the difficulty of words, of which I have spoken, turned up. Men got committed; they took sides; they controverted; it became a national question, a question of rivalry between Orders, an hereditary watchword. Being, as I have said, no vital point of Christian life, nay not necessary for the existence of devotion to our Blessed Lady and even denied by those, like St Bernard, who cherished that devotion with singular zeal, there was a great difficulty, amid the strife of tongues and the heat of party spirit, to settle it. The Popes could but forbid the controversy; but they could not hinder opinions, and every thing they did went one way, – towards the establishment of the doctrine.

So centuries went on; the doctrine became more and more recognized, but its definition seemed as far off as ever. It required the break-up of the religious establishment, it required the French Revolution, to bring the Church into such a state, that the question could be considered on its own merits. Since *then*, things have visibly tended to its formal reception as a point of the Apostolic Faith. Your author says, 'The present Pope *resolved to raise* the question (!) ... In 1849, at the time of his flight to Gaeta, the thought *first* entered his mind.'[6] A person ought to know something about facts before he ventures to write history. I don't profess to be able to do so myself; but I think he will find, if he inquires, that a progress, which was recognized by all Catholics, towards the definition was made in the Pontificate of Gregory XVI. One advance was the leave, continually asked and granted, for priests to use the office of the Immaculate Conception. Another, which I heard of was the Pope's being present at the Mass of the Immaculate Conception. When I first became a Catholic, the general feeling was, 'It must be, yet how is it to be?' This was three years before Gaeta.

5. Now then to go on to the verbal difficulty involved in the word 'Conception'; to which your Author alludes indeed, but hardly does justice. The Protestant argues, 'If, as Catholics grant, original sin is transmitted

---

[6] This quotation and the following ones are taken from John Mason Neale's book: *Voices from the East. Documents on the Present State and Working of the Oriental Church* (London, 1859), which Arthur Alleyne had sent to Newman for consideration. Newman quotes from pages 118, 149, 121.

by descent from Adam, it *must* be a fault of nature and must be inseparable from nature. And so says the text, "In sin hath my Mother conceived me".[a] Either then Mary was not a child of Adam, or she had original sin.' Here again there is a difference between Catholics and Protestants, viz. as to the mode of *derivation* of original sin, which will be best shown by considering, as I said, the meaning of the word, 'Conception'.

Catholics hold, that in conception, viewed *a parte concipientis*, there is, in matter of fact, that deordination of concupiscence, which the text in question calls *sin*; but this is the *conceptio activa*, of which our doctrine says nothing. The Immaculate Conception of the Blessed Virgin is *her conceptio*, the *conceptio à parte concepti*, or the *conceptio passiva*. The concupiscence of the *activa conceptio* is considered (I believe) by Protestants to be the principle of infection; by us, (though nothing on the *mode* of the transmission of original sin has been determined by the Church) concupiscence is viewed as a mere token or badge of original sin, which goes *with* the descent from parent to child, as a civil disability may go, as blacks, by the fact of their descent and by token of their blackness, are slaves in Virginia. Catholics hold that original sin is mainly an external evil, Protestants an internal. According to us, it is not propagated in the way of cause and effect, but by an act of the will of God, exerted and carried out on each child, as it is conceived. I repeat, this is not *de fide*, but it is what I conceive theologians teach. Being such then in one view, the *activa conceptio* is not inconsistent with a suspension of that will, and a reversal of that act on the part of God, as regards the *passiva conceptio* in a particular case; just as a slave state might determine that from a particular day all the children of slaves should be henceforth free; or again, that a particular child born of a particular mother, should be a free child, though all the rest that had been born or should be born, were slaves.

We believe then, that, in a matter of fact, the Blessed Virgin's conception was of this kind; her mother conceived as other mothers, in concupiscence, but that concupiscence was not a token, in that particular case, of the transmission of spiritual disabilities to herself, the child conceived.

You may ask, 'How could concupiscence attend *on* the *conception*, since the conception takes place some *time* after the moment when the concupiscence is indulged?' That is for the Psalmist to answer, not for me: but, if I must explain it, I should say that we ought to distinguish between the material origin of the child, which is at the time of the concupiscence, and the formal origin which is at the time of its quickening, or the creation and infusion of its soul. Of these, the former is coincident with the *activa conceptio*, the latter with the *passiva*. *Thus* the question of 'time' comes in, which your Author thinks so 'subtle, scholastic, and childish,' though, properly speaking, it has nothing to do with our doctrine, but is necessary for the understanding of the Psalm.

Now I believe it will be found, though I have not examined the point myself, that what has been said by great divines against the Immaculate Conception, has been directed against the *activa*; on which matter the whole Church so entirely concurs in their judgment, that certain pictures of St Joachim and St

Anna are on the Index, which represents an active *conceptio* under the image of a Kiss.[7]

6. Having touched upon the interpretation of a text of Scripture, I am led to notice two others, or rather two sets of texts, which are considered by Protestants to be fatal to our doctrine.

The first consists of those which, whether passages of Scripture or otherwise of authority speak of our Lord as the 'only one' of our race without sin. 'The Church' says your Author, 'in the prayers she addresses to the Saviour at High Vespers in Pentecost, adds "because Thou only and alone art without sin",[b] in like manner, in the prayers for the dead'.

1. I answer first; So too the saints say in the Apocalypse, 'Thou only art holy',[c] but are not the Saints themselves holy, as their very name indicates? Of course the Almighty's essential holiness of nature, and His prerogative of being the Fount of holiness are meant in the passage. In like manner, when it is said in the Vespers in question, that our Lord is without sin, it is meant that He is eminently and transcendently sinless. On the other hand, as to *their own* nature, we read 'He putteth no trust in His saints, yea, the heavens are not clean in His sight'.[d]

2. Let us next suppose 'only without sin' to refer to our Lord's Person as composed of two natures. Now, I suppose your Author would allow that there was a sense in which justification was 'by faith *only*', and a

---

[7] One of the misconceptions about the Immaculate Conception was that it depended on Mary's parents who, it was thought, conceived her in a manner in which they did not experience concupiscence.

sense again in which it was *not* 'by faith *only*'; let him give as freely as he takes. Our Lord, as Mediator in two natures, is called the only sinless, because He is sinless apart from grace; His divine nature sufficing to sanctify His human nature, independently of the operation of the Holy Ghost.

3. Let us suppose 'only without sin' to refer simply to His human nature. Then I would have your author recollect the passage in 1 Kings 12: 20. 'There was none that followed the House of David, but the tribe of Judah *only*.'[e] Protestant commentators observe that *of course* Benjamin is included, and give good reasons why it should be so, showing that it is neither fair to others nor expedient for ourselves to press too rigidly the literal text in controversial encounters.

The other set of texts refers to the universality of the Redemption, which implies the universality of the guilt.[8] 'There is another dogma', says your author, 'which it is impossible to harmonize with the new Roman dogma. "If Christ died for all, then were all dead";[f] and "as in Adam all die, even so shall all be made alive"[g]—where, by the bye, for 'then were all dead', read, 'then all died'.

And indeed Catholics do hold that the Blessed Virgin 'died' in Adam;[9] she came under the sentence with the whole race, by anticipation, in the act of Adam's fall; but, as that anticipation was not *carried out*

---

[8] This was the greatest obstacle – the universality of Redemption. It was also regarded as an obstacle by theologians like St Albert the Great and St Thomas Aquinas. For this question cf. above Text XI, p. 229, footnote 7, and Text XVIII, p. 306, footnote 5.

[9] Cf. above, Text XI, pp. 227–9.

in its *fullness* upon *any* man, not on Adam himself, for he did not die 'in the same day'— nor on any one of the race, for they have been all redeemed; nor on the elect, for they, instead of dying, are eternally saved; as all men had *their own* share of the death, greater or less, but some more than others; so Mary had least of all, yet even she had her share. She suffered the hardships of this fallen world, she inherited Adam's debilitated nature, and she died, but, as the elect have not the worst part of that death, eternal death, so she had not even that death of the soul, which is original sin.

'In Adam all die'; yet no man was yet in existence, when Adam fell. They *died* before they *lived*. As the whole race could die, at God's will, before they existed, so one of that whole race could (at the same will) not only die before she was in being, but be made alive again also.

And this last remark suggests to us, how it is that she is to be considered as *really* redeemed by her Son, *though* in fact she had no sin to be forgiven. Your author asks, 'Is the Virgin Mary, or is she not, in the number of the *all*, for whom Jesus Christ died and rose again? Let the defenders of the new dogma give some reply.'

It is not difficult to give it. Yes: she is indisputably among those whom our Lord suffered for and saved; she not only fell in Adam, but she rose in Christ, before she began to be. If she could fall before she was in being, I suppose your author will not deny that she could rise again. In truth, Catholics consider her as the signal and chiefest instance of the power and fullness of redeeming grace; for her Son merited for her that initial grace which was the prevention of original sin.

7. Little remains to say on particular passages of your author. I select those which I think you would wish me to notice.

p. 117: 'In the prayers of the Western Office of the Conception there is not the remotest allusion to her having been conceived without original sin.' The very fact of the Feast implies it. I think it is St Augustine who says that there is no feast day except for what is holy; and who thus accounts for the feast of the Baptist's Nativity, because he was not born in original sin. If then the Conception of our Lady admits of the Festival, the fact is an argument that that Conception was without sin.

p. 118: 'The new devotion was first heard of in the ninth century.' Suppose I say, 'The new doctrine of our Lord's immensity, contradicted by all the ante-Nicene Fathers, was first heard of in the Creed of St Athanasius?' or 'The *Filioque*, protested against by the Orthodox Church to this day, was first heard of in the seventh century?' Whatever principle is adduced to explain the latter statement will avail for the first.

p. 119: 'Error dares to open her lying mouth.' Wonderful, that a writer, can so speak of the Immaculate Conception, when he himself sees nothing antichristian in what most Protestants would think as bad or worse, the ordinary conclusion of the Greek Collects, '*through* the Mother of God.'!

p. 121: 'By the doctrine of even Western Theologians, the hereditary sin of Adam derives itself to all the human race as to a posterity which has its root in the same Adam, when already in a state of sin.' Doubtless; but, according to the will of God, which He may reverse if He pleases at any moment, and in any individual instance. He might have reversed it in the case of the Baptist, or of St John the Evangelist, or of St Joseph, without the suspension of any law of nature.

p. 123: 'The Pope tells us that all was the work of Mary. Is not this to diminish the merits of our Redeemer?' The sinlessness of Mary, (moreover, divinely bestowed,) as little derogates from the incommunicable office of our Lord, as the sin of Eve from the headship of Adam.

p. 124: Your author seems to allow that Mary 'raised herself to the highest degree of holiness and purity, preserved herself intact from all voluntary sin, and was infinitely (!) more glorious than the Seraphim etc.' Here what I have said above may be made use of: If then she was *so much*, the Catholic does not go into any great excess in adding to the '*infinitely* greater glory', that prerogative of grace from her first moment of being. If it is a great addition in the eyes of a Protestant, as it is, this arises from his thinking immunity from original sin to involve a difference of *nature*, and that, whereas it is but a little thing to be gifted with even an *infinite* grace and glory, it is a very great thing indeed to have human nature in a perfectly sound condition.

p. 125: 'If the Christian world has wreathed all these coronets for the Queen of Angels, it is ONLY because she is the Mother of the Son of God'. That is, as indeed the passage goes on to say, she is *called* 'Pure Mother' and the like, '*because* she did carry in her arms a Son who is God over all'. Well, this is to me as repulsive a doctrine as any that can be proposed. So it seems that nothing whatever is implied as to her *sanctity* in the high terms used of her.[10] Why then does not your author consider that she committed voluntary sin as other children of Adam? If 'Burning Bush', 'Pure Dove' 'Virginal Eve', 'Lily', '*Paradise*', and the like are 'ONLY' given her 'because she is the Mother of the Son of God', on what ground does he impute to her any high sanctity at all? He has already told us that '*gratia plena*' is a wrong translation. He says, 'Can you find in the (orthodox doctrine) the least trace of any assertion of her Immaculate Conception?' Nay, if 'Paradise' has 'no trace whatever' of the paradisiacal state of man, which was freedom from original sin, it has no trace of any assertion of her freedom from actual sin either.

p. 127: 'In all the praises addressed during the whole course of this Liturgy to Mary, is there the least allusion to her purity from original sin?' There are frequent allusions to her freedom from sin, and to her grace, generally and largely; and the question is whether freedom from original sin was not as much meant to be included in the general freedom and that fullness of grace, as freedom from other sin; supposing, that is, that original sin consists in deprivation of grace, not in infection of nature, as I have said.

p. 128: 'If this doctrine has been accepted and defended by the Ecumenical Church, as the Pope asserts, his best evidence would have been, either the

---

[10] Newman emphasizes the fact that Mary was not simply a passive instrument in the hands of God. She actively co-operated with Him, a fact which enormously increases her personal sanctity and dignity. This thought was later expounded by Newman in his *Letter to Pusey* (cf. above, Text X, pp. 206–222).

Creeds, as well as the office Books of the Eastern and Western Churches.' I reply, 'If the doctrines of the Holy Ghost's all-righteousness or all-mercifulness, or eternity had been accepted by the Church, the best evidence would have been the Creeds etc' The same answer does for both objections. The Holy Ghost's eternity is involved in His divinity; the Blessed Virgin's immaculateness in her conception is involved in the general declarations of the Fathers about her sinlessness. If all Catholics have not seen this at once, we must recollect that there were at first mistakes among pious and holy men about the attributes of the Holy Spirit.

p. 146: 'We agree entirely that our duty is to glorify by *every possible means* her whom the Almighty invested with majesty.' Well—praising her as exempt from original sin, is, in our judgment, to say the least, not so contrary to the Fathers, as not to be *possible*.

p. 146: 'Since the *earliest ages of Christianity* the orthodox Church has glorified the Blessed Virgin, naming her more precious than the Cherubim, and infinitely (!) more glorious than the Seraphim, supplicating her as the most powerful Mediatress with the Lord, and the mightiest Advocate of the Christian world'. I cannot help thinking, that, whatever be the differences of opinion between Catholics and Protestants, they will here, for once in a way, be in agreement: viz. in judging, that a writer, who holds all this, yet is shocked and indignant at the doctrine that our Lady was without any taint of sin and ever full of grace, is straining out a gnat and swallowing a camel.

Here then I bring my long letter to an end. The

sum of what I have said is this: I fully grant that there is not that formal documentary evidence for the doctrine in question which there is for some other doctrines, but I maintain also that, from its character, it does not require it.

Yours, My dear Mr Alleyne,[11] Most sincerely
John H. Newman
June 17. 1860

a. Ps 50:7   b. cf. 2 Cor 5:21   c. Acts 15:4
d. Job 15:15   e. 1 Kings 12:20   f. 2 Cor 5:14
g. 1 Cor 15:22

The Letters and Diaries of John Henry Newman.
London, 1969, Vol. XIX, pp. 361–70.
Letter dated 15–17 June 1860.

[11] Arthur Alleyne deeply appreciated these two letters. As a token of gratitude, he sent Newman the following month the present of a book in French on our Lady, *La Vierge Marie d'après L'Evangile*, by Auguste Nicolas. Newman thanked him, but added 'with the Apostle, "I seek not yours but you" – and I hope and pray that your book is but a forerunner and pledge of yourself' (*The Letters and Diaries of John Henry Newman*, XIX, 381). His hopes, however, were not fulfilled. Alleyne remained an Anglican clergyman. This correspondence shows the effort Newman was willing to make in order to help an inquirer to understand the teaching of the Catholic Church and to come to the fullness of truth. He truly was a father of many souls.

XIX/C

LETTER TO WILLIAM WILBERFORCE[1]

The Oratory, Birmingham Decr 9 1860

My dear Wilberforce,

Your letter has just come. I shall burn it as soon as I have directed this—and will be quite silent.

Most unfortunately Tuesday is just *the* day that I am, by appointment, busy. A very dear friend, a Protestant, (not from any doubts or thought of becoming a Catholic) whom I have not seen for 8 years, is coming to me just for that one day, having fixed even his *train* a fortnight ago. I cannot then at all *promise myself* liberty to see you on that day, tho', as he has business in Birmingham, I suppose he will be some hours apart from me—To complete it, another friend comes tomorrow evening from Hereford—as I learn this morning—

On Wednesday I am quite disengaged, unless

---

[1] William Wilberforce (1798–1879) was giving thought to the possibility of becoming a Catholic. Unlike Arthur Alleyne, he was received into the Catholic Church about two years after this correspondence (on 6 January 1863).

Monsell, who is coming from Ireland, should make his appearance. I have always been prophesying, since Tuesday was fixed for my friend's coming, that M. would come on *Tuesday*, as I know how strangely perverse things happen. Whether my friend sleeps here Tuesday night, I do not know.

Monday (tomorrow) evening I am quite disengaged, and, as I have said, Wednesday morning—and some time or other on Tuesday.

I will gladly speak out to you, as you wish me, just as the case is. As to the Immaculate Conception, I am perfectly convinced Protestants don't know what our doctrine is. Dear Robert did not, when he wrote his book on the Incarnation as I pointed out to him.[2] There is nothing physical at all in it. The doctrine is simply this—'As St John Baptist's soul was sanctified by the Holy Ghost three months before his birth, so the Blessed Virgin's soul was sanctified, as many months as it had existed before her birth, i.e. from its very first creation.' Physical questions do not come in at all *in the doctrine*—they come in only when, in controversy, we have to *reconcile* our doctrine with the text, 'In sin has my mother conceived me'[a]— *then* we are accustomed to say, 'The Psalmist speaks of the conception of the body—but our doctrine speaks, *not*

---

[2] Robert was a younger brother of William Wilberforce. He had written a book on *The Doctrine of the Incarnation* (London, 1848). Newman pointed out to him on 3 April 1850 (on receiving a copy of the third edition) that Catholics attribute our Lady's immaculate holiness to a 'choice fruit of *grace*' and not to a change of nature. Original sin was regarded in Protestant theology as an infection of nature. Hence an immaculate conception (without original sin) was regarded as the reception of a new and different nature (cf. *The Letters and Diaries of John Henry Newman*, XIII, 456–7). Robert became a Catholic in 1854.

of the body, but of the time when the soul is created, or begins to exist.'

Our doctrine of original sin is *not* that of Protestants. We do *not* hold *infection* of *nature*—but we place original sin in the *absence* of *super*natural grace. Now we say, that the Blessed Virgin had from the first moment of creation the *presence or gift* of grace—AS ADAM HAD – and we only say that *she* was restored (for the sake of the Atonement which was to come) to *Adam's* state, and never was in any other state.

This is the doctrine which the Pope six years ago declared to have been from the beginning of Christianity.[3] I think there is much (in the way of *existing documents*) to show that it *was*—and I don't see (myself) any thing *against* the *notion* of it. Certainly, for myself, in Sermons I published in 1835 I have said, 'What, think you, was the sanctity and *grace* of that human nature, of which God formed his *sinless* Son; knowing, as we do, that "what is born of the flesh, is flesh"[b]—and that "none can bring a clean thing out of an unclean?"[c][4]

As to the opposition made to the doctrine in former ages, as by St Bernard etc, it is *not* an article of faith with us *in the sense* in which they objected to it, but in the sense which I have declared above.

However, you say that the Immac. Concept. is only an illustration of what you would ask—so perhaps I have insisted on it too much.

---

[3] Six years previously Pope Pius IX had declared the doctrine of the Immaculate Conception as a dogma.

[4] Newman quotes from the first edition. Already in the second edition (1836) he had changed 'the sanctity and *grace* of that human nature' to 'the sanctified state of that human nature'. Cf. above, Text II, p. 120.

Certainly a Catholic *is* required, simply to believe, what our Lord delivered to the Apostles to propound and promulgate—and again to believe that the Church has the gift of determining what those things are. But I really do not see there is any thing hard in these requirements, making allowances for the difficulties which the best critics must encounter in arriving at historical facts, and the consequent uncertainty of any private judgments which they may make about them contrary to the Church's doctrine—

Ever Yours affly John H. Newman

W. Wilberforce Esqr

a. Ps 50:7   b. Jn 3:6   c. Job 14:4

The Letters and Diaries of John Henry Newman.
London, 1969,
Vol. XIX, pp. 437–38.
Written on 9 December 1860.

PART THREE

SPIRITUAL AND POETICAL WRITINGS

XX

JESUS SON OF MARY[1]

When our Lord came upon earth, He might have
created a fresh body for Himself out of nothing—or
He might have formed a body for Himself out of the
earth, as He formed Adam. But He preferred to be
born, as other men are born, of a human mother.
Why did He do so? He did so to put honour on all
those earthly relations and connections which are ours
by nature; and to teach us that, though He has begun
a new creation, He does not wish us to cast off the old
creation, as far as it is not sinful. Hence it is our duty
to love and honour our parents, to be affectionate to
our brothers, sisters, friends, husbands, wives, not only
not less, but even more, than it was man's duty before
our Lord came on earth. As we become better
Christians, more consistent and zealous servants of
Jesus, we shall become only more and more anxious
for the good of all around us—our kindred, our
friends, our acquaintances, our neighbours, our superiors, our inferiors, our masters, our employers. And

---

[1] This is a meditation and prayer written by Newman for Good Friday.

this we shall do from the recollection how our Lord loved His Mother. He loves her still in heaven with a special love. He refuses her nothing. We then on earth must feel a tender solicitude for all our relations, all our friends, all whom we know or have dealings with.[2] And moreover, we must love not only those who love us, but those who hate us or injure us, that we may imitate Him, who not only was loving to His Mother, but even suffered Judas, the traitor, to kiss Him,[a] and prayed for His murderers on the cross.[b]

Let us pray God for our relations, friends, well wishers,
and enemies, living and dead.

O Jesus, son of Mary, whom Mary followed to the Cross when Thy disciples fled, and who didst bear her tenderly in mind in the midst of Thy sufferings, even in Thy last words, who didst commit her to Thy best beloved disciple, saying to her, 'Woman, behold thy son,' and to him, 'Behold thy Mother,'[c] we, after Thy pattern, would pray for all who are near and dear to us, and we beg Thy grace to do so continually. We beg Thee to bring them all into the light of Thy truth, or to keep them in Thy truth if they already know it, and to keep them in a state of grace, and to give them the gift of perseverance. We thus pray for our parents, for our fathers and our mothers, for our children, for every one of them, for our brothers and sisters, for every one of our brothers, for every one of our sisters, for our cousins and all our kindred, for our friends,

---

[2] Newman himself had many friends and always remained loyal to them. The loss of friends on becoming a Catholic was one of the great sacrifices of his life. Cf. above, Text I, pp. 106–9, and p. 108, footnote 6.

and our father's friends, for all our old friends, for our
dear and intimate friends, for our teachers, for our
pupils, for our masters and employers, for our servants
or subordinates, for our associates and work-fellows,
for our neighbours, for our superiors and rulers; for
those who wish us well, for those who wish us ill; for
our enemies; for our rivals; for our injurers and for our
slanderers. And not only for the living, but for the
dead, who have died in the grace of God, that He may
shorten their time of expiation, and admit them into
His presence above.

a. cf. Mt 26: 47–9   b. Lk 23: 34   c. Jn 19: 26–7

Meditations and Devotions of the late Cardinal Newman.
London, 1911, pp. 200–2.
Written by Newman as an Oratorian.

XXI

A SHORT SERVICE FOR
ROSARY SUNDAY

In Jesus Christ is the fullness of the Godhead with all its infinite sanctity. In Mary is reflected the sanctity of Jesus, as by His grace it could be found in a creature.

Mary, as the pattern both of maidenhood and maternity, has exalted woman's state and nature,[1] and made the Christian virgin and the Christian mother understand the sacredness of their duties in the sight of God.

Her very image is as a book in which we may read at a glance the mystery of the Incarnation, and the mercy of the Redemption; and withal her own gracious perfections also, who was made by her Divine Son the very type of humility, gentleness, fortitude, purity, patience, love.

What Christian mother can look upon her image and not be moved to pray for gentleness, watchfulness, and obedience like Mary's? What Christian

---

[1] Newman regarded the Blessed Virgin Mary as a model for all women. Mary, by the graces and privileges she received, and by her personal holiness, had greatly exalted the state of woman. (Cf. above: Introduction IV, pp. 70–2).

maiden can look upon her without praying for the gifts of simplicity, modesty, purity, recollection, gentleness such as hers?

Who can repeat her very name without finding in it a music which goes to the heart, and brings before him thoughts of God and Jesus Christ, and heaven above, and fills him with the desire of those graces by which heaven is gained?

Hail then, great Mother of God, Queen of Saints, Royal Lady clothed with the sun and crowned with the stars of heaven,[a] whom all generations have called and shall call blessed.[b] We will take our part in praising thee in our own time and place with all the redeemed of our Lord, and will exalt thee in the full assembly of the saints and glorify thee in the Heavenly Jerusalem.

a. cf. Rev 12:1   b. cf. Lk 1:48

Meditations and Devotions of the late Cardinal Newman.
London, 1911, pp. 261–2.
Written by Newman as an Oratorian.

XXII

AVE MARIS STELLA

Hail, Star of the Sea

Truly art thou a star, O Mary! Our Lord indeed Himself, Jesus Christ, He is the truest and chiefest Star, the bright and morning Star,[a] as St John calls Him; that Star which was foretold from the beginning as destined to rise out of Israel,[b] and which was displayed in figure by the star which appeared to the wise men in the East.[c] But if the wise and learned and they who teach men in justice shall shine as stars for ever and ever;[1] if the angels of the Churches are called stars in the Hand of Christ;[d] if He honoured the apostles even in the days of their flesh by a title, calling them lights of the world;[e] if even those angels who fell from heaven are called by the beloved disciple stars;[f] if lastly all the saints in bliss are called stars, in that they are like stars differing from stars in glory;[g] therefore most assuredly, without any derogation from the honour of our Lord, is Mary His mother called the Star of the Sea, and the more so because even on her

[1] These words of the prophet Daniel (12:3) are applied to Doctors of the Church in the Liturgy of the Hours (cf. Common of Doctors of the Church, Morning Prayer, Benedictus antiphon.)

head she wears a crown of twelve stars.[h] Jesus is the Light of the world, illuminating every man who cometh into it,[i] opening our eyes with the gift of faith, making souls luminous by His Almighty grace; and Mary is the Star, shining with the light of Jesus, fair as the moon, and special as the sun, the star of the heavens, which it is good to look upon, the star of the sea, which is welcome to the tempest-tossed, at whose smile the evil spirit flies, the passions are hushed, and peace is poured upon the soul.

Hail then, Star of the Sea, we joy in the recollection of thee. Pray for us ever at the throne of Grace; plead our cause, pray with us, present our prayers to thy Son and Lord—now and in the honour of death, Mary be thou our help.

a. cf. Rev 22:16   b. cf. Num 24:17   c. cf. Mt 2:2, 9–10
d. cf. Rev 1:20   e. cf. Mt 5:14   f. cf. Rev 9:1
g. cf. 1 Cor 15:41   h. cf. Rev 12:1   i. cf. Jn 1:9; 8:12

Meditations and Devotions of the late Cardinal Newman.
London, 1911, pp. 265–6.
Written by Newman as an Oratorian.

XXIII

CANDLEMAS[1]

(A Song.)

The Angel-lights of Christmas morn,
    Which shot across the sky,
Away they pass at Candlemas,
    They sparkle and they die.

Comfort of earth is brief at best,
    Although it be divine;
Like funeral lights for Christmas gone
    Old Simeon's tapers shine.[2]

And then for eight long weeks and more,
    We wait in twilight grey,
Till the high candle sheds a beam
    On Holy Saturday.

---

[1] This poem and the following one ('The Pilgrim Queen') were written by Newman in 1849, at the Oratory which was then in Alcester Street (Birmingham).

[2] Christmastide in the liturgical calendar of Newman's day lasted until 2 February, the Feast of the Purification (or, as it is now called, the Presentation of our Lord in the Temple).

We wait along the penance-tide
    Of solemn fast and prayer;
While song is hush'd, and lights grow dim
    In the sin-laden air.

And while the sword in Mary's soul[a]
    Is driven home, we hide
In our own hearts, and count the wounds
    Of passion and of pride.

And still, though Candlemas be spent
    And Alleluias o'er,
Mary is music in our need,
    And Jesus light in store.

a. cf. Lk 2:35

Verses on Various Occasions. London, 1910, pp. 279–80.
Written in 1849.

XXIV

THE PILGRIM QUEEN

(A Song.)

There sat a Lady
   all on the ground,
Rays of the morning
   circled her round,
Save thee, and hail to thee,
   Gracious and Fair,
In the chill twilight
   what wouldst thou there?

'Here I sit desolate,'
   sweetly said she,
'Though I'm a queen,
   and my name is Marie:
Robbers have rifled
   my garden and store,
Foes they have stolen
   my heir from my bower.

'They said they could keep Him
    far better than I,
In a palace all His,
    planted deep and raised high.
'Twas a palace of ice,
    hard and cold as were they,
And when summer came,
    it all melted away.[1]

'Next would they barter Him,
    Him the Supreme,
For the spice of the desert,
    and gold of the stream;
And me they bid wander
    in weeds and alone,
In this green merry land
    which once was my own.'[2]

I look'd on that Lady,
    and out from her eyes
Came the deep glowing blue
    of Italy's skies;
And she raised up her head
    and she smiled, as a Queen
On the day of her crowning,
    so bland and serene.

---

[1] Newman refers in these lines to the contention that special veneration given to our Lady would eclipse or endanger the honour due to Christ, her Son. But as history showed, it was precisely those who abandoned devotion to the Mother of Jesus who also lost faith in the divinity of her Son. Cf. above, Text XVII, p. 289.

[2] England was called 'The Dowry of Mary'.

'A moment,' she said,
    'and the dead shall revive;
The giants are failing,
    the Saints are alive;
I am coming to rescue
    my home and my reign,
And Peter and Philip[3]
    are close in my train.'

Verses on Various Occasions. London, 1910, pp. 281–3.
Written in 1849.

[3] Newman refers to St Peter and St Philip Neri.

XXV

THE MONTH OF MARY[1]

(A Song.)

Green are the leaves, and sweet the flowers,
    And rich the hues of May;
We see them in the gardens round,
    And market-paniers gay:
And e'en among our streets, and lanes,
    And alleys, we descry,
By fitful gleams, the fair sunshine,
    The blue transparent sky.

Chorus

O Mother maid, be thou our aid,
    Now in the opening year;
Lest sights of earth to sin give birth,
    And bring the tempter near.

Green is the grass, but wait awhile,
    'Twill grow, and then will wither;
The flowrets, brightly as they smile,
    Shall perish altogether:

[1] Written in 1850, at the Oratory in Alcester Street, Birmingham.

The merry sun, you sure would say,
　　It ne'er could set in gloom;
But earth's best joys have all an end,
　　And sin, a heavy doom.

Chorus

But Mother maid, thou dost not fade;
　　With stars above thy brow,
And the pale moon beneath thy feet,[a]
　　For ever throned art thou.

The green green grass, the glittering grove,
　　The heaven's majestic dome,
They image forth a tenderer bower,
　　A more refulgent home;
They tell us of that Paradise
　　Of everlasting rest,
And that high Tree, all flowers and fruit,
　　The sweetest, yet the best.

Chorus

O Mary, pure and beautiful,
　　Thou art the Queen of May;
Our garlands wear about thy hair,
　　And they will ne'er decay.

a.　cf. Rev 12:1

Verses on Various Occasions. London, 1910, pp. 284–6.
Written in 1850.

XXVI

THE QUEEN OF SEASONS.[1]

(A Song for an inclement May.)

All is divine
  which the Highest has made,
Through the days that He wrought,[a]
  till the day when he stay'd;[b]
Above and below,
  within and around,
From the centre of space,
  to its uttermost bound.

In beauty surpassing
  the Universe smiled,
On the morn of its birth,
  like an innocent child.
Or like the rich bloom
  of some delicate flower;
And the Father rejoiced
  in the work of His power.

---

[1] Written in 1850 at the Oratory.

Yet worlds brighter still,
   and a brighter than those,
And a brighter again,
   He had made, had He chose;
And you never could name
   that conceivable best,
To exhaust the resources
   the Maker possess'd.

But I know of one work
   of His Infinite Hand,
Which special and singular
   ever must stand;
So perfect, so pure,
   and of gifts such a store,
That even Omnipotence
   ne'er shall do more.

The freshness of May,
   and the sweetness of June,
And the fire of July
   in its passionate noon,
Munificent August,
   September serene,
Are together no match
   for my glorious Queen.

O Mary, all months
  and all days are thine own,
In thee lasts their joyousness,
  when they are gone;
And we give to thee May,
  not because it is best,
But because it comes first,
  and is pledge of the rest.

a. cf. Gen 1:1–29   b. cf. Gen 2:2

Verses on Various Occasions. London, 1910, pp. 287–9
Written in 1850.

XXVII

MEDITATIONS ON THE LITANY
OF LORETO FOR THE
MONTH OF MAY[1]

Introductory

May 1: May the Month of Promise

Why is May chosen as the month in which we exercise a special devotion to the Blessed Virgin?

The first reason is because it is the time when the earth bursts forth into its fresh foliage and its green grass after the stern frost and snow of winter, and the

---

[1] These meditations are for each day of the month of May. Newman takes the invocations of the Litany of Loreto as his inspiration. They would probably have formed part of a 'Year-Book of Devotion' which he had hoped to write, but which he never managed to prepare. In these pages we have a manifestation of his own genuine devotion to our Lady – tender, faith-inspired, scriptural and resting on a sure doctrinal foundation. His veneration is not a purely speculative grasp of Mary's greatness: it descends to practical daily life. We can see that he loves her and has unwavering trust in her intercession. These pages offer an example of how cold dogmatic truths can be turned into words of fervent devotion. The meditations are in three sections: May 1–16, on the Immaculate Conception and the Annunciation, treat of the joyful mysteries of our Lady's life. Her dolours are dealt with from May 17–23. Under the general title of the Assumption, we have the glorious mysteries from May 24–31.

raw atmosphere and the wild wind and rain of the early spring. It is because the blossoms are upon the trees and the flowers are in the gardens. It is because the days have got long, and the sun rises early and sets late. For such gladness and joyousness of external Nature is a fit attendant on our devotion to her who is the Mystical Rose and the House of Gold.

A man may say, 'True; but in this climate we have sometimes a bleak, inclement May'. This cannot be denied; but still, so much is true that at least it is the month of *promise* and of *hope*. Even though the weather happen to be bad, it is the month that *begins* and heralds in the summer. We know, for all that may be unpleasant in it, that fine weather is coming, sooner or later. 'Brightness and beautifulness shall', in the Prophet's words, 'appear at the end, and shall not lie: if it make delay, wait for it, for it shall surely come, and shall not be slack.'ᵃ

May then is the month, if not of fulfilment, at least of *promise*; and is not this the very aspect in which we most suitably regard the Blessed Virgin, Holy Mary, to whom this month is dedicated?

The Prophet says, 'There shall come forth a rod out of the root of Jesse, and a flower shall rise out of his root.'ᵇ Who is the flower but our Blessed Lord? Who is the rod, or beautiful stalk or stem or plant out of which the flower grows, but Mary, Mother of our Lord, Mary, Mother of God?

It was prophesied that God should come upon earth. When the time was now full, how was it announced? It was announced by the Angel coming to Mary. 'Hail, full of grace,' said Gabriel, 'the Lord is with thee; blessed art thou among women.'ᶜ She then

was the sure *promise* of the coming Saviour, and therefore May is by a special title her month.

May 2: May the Month of Joy

Why is May called the month of Mary, and especially
dedicated to her? Among other reasons there is this,
that of the Church's year, the ecclesiastical year, it is
at once the most sacred and the most festive and
joyous portion. Who would wish February, March, or
April, to be the month of Mary, considering that it is
the time of Lent and penance? Who again would
choose December, the Advent season—a time of
hope, indeed, because Christmas is coming, but a time
of fasting too? Christmas itself does not last for a
month; and January has indeed the joyful Epiphany,
with its Sundays in succession; but these in most years
are cut short by the urgent coming of Septuagesima.[2]

May on the contrary belongs to the Easter season,
which lasts fifty days, and in that season the whole of
May commonly falls, and the first half always. The
great Feast of the Ascension of our Lord into heaven
is always in May, except once or twice in forty years.
Pentecost, called also Whit-Sunday, the Feast of the
Holy Ghost, is commonly in May, and the Feasts of
the Holy Trinity and Corpus Christi are in May not
unfrequently. May, therefore, is the time in which
there are such frequent Alleluias, because Christ has

[2] In the liturgical cycle prior to its reordering in the wake of the Second
Vatican Council, the Sundays following the Feast of the Epiphany
were enumerated as Sundays 'after the Epiphany'. Depending on the
date of Easter, there could be up to six such Sundays. The three
Sundays immediately preceding Lent were called Septuagesima,
Sexagesima and Quinquagesima respectively.

risen from the grave, Christ has ascended on high, and God the Holy Ghost has come down to take His place.[d]

Here then we have a reason why May is dedicated to the Blessed Mary. She is the first of creatures, the most acceptable child of God, the dearest and nearest to Him. It is fitting then that this month should be hers, in which we especially glory and rejoice in His great Providence to us, in our redemption and sanctification in God the Father, God the Son, and God the Holy Ghost.

But Mary is not only the acceptable handmaid of the Lord. She is also Mother of His Son, and the Queen of all Saints, and in this month the Church has placed the feasts of some of the greatest of them, as if to bear her company. First, however, there is the Feast of the Holy Cross, on the third of May, when we venerate that Precious Blood in which the Cross was bedewed at the time of our Lord's Passion. The Archangel St Michael, and three Apostles, have feast-days in this month: St John, the beloved disciple, St Philip, and St James. Seven Popes, two of them especially famous, St Gregory VII and St Pius V; also two of the greatest Doctors, St Athanasius and St Gregory Nazianzen; two holy Virgins especially favoured by God, St Catherine of Siena (as her feast is kept in England), and St Mary Magdalen of Pazzi; and one holy woman most memorable in the annals of the Church, St Monica, the Mother of St Augustine.[3]

---

[3] Newman speaks of the Church Calendar in use in his day. The seven Popes whose feasts were celebrated or commemorated in May were: Alexander (3rd); Pius V (5th; in England on the 11th); St Peter Celestine (20th); Gregory VII (25th); Eleutherius (26th); John I (27th);

And above all, and nearest to us in this Church, our own holy Patron and Father, St Philip,[4] occupies, with his Novena and Octave, fifteen out of the whole thirty-one days of the month. These are some of the choicest fruits of God's manifold grace, and they form the court of their glorious Queen.

I
On The Immaculate Conception

May 3: Mary is the 'Virgo Purissima', *the Most Pure Virgin*

By the Immaculate Conception of the Blessed Virgin is meant the great revealed truth that she was conceived in the womb of her mother, St Anne, without original sin.[5]

Since the fall of Adam all mankind, his descendants, are conceived and born in sin. 'Behold', says the inspired writer in the Psalm *Miserere*—'Behold, I was conceived in iniquity, and in sin did my mother conceive me.'[e] That sin which belongs to every one of us, and is ours from the first moment of our existence, is the sin of unbelief and disobedience, by which Adam lost Paradise. We, as the children of Adam, are

---

and Felix (30th). The Feast of the Apparition of St Michael, Archangel, was on 8 May; and St John before the Latin Gate on 6 May. In England, St Catherine of Siena was celebrated on 5 May.

[4] St Philip Neri was the Founder of the Oratory. His Feast falls on 26 May.

[5] In this meditation Newman puts into simple words the doctrine of the Immaculate Conception which elsewhere, as we saw, he illustrated in technical language and with theological precision.

heirs to the consequences of his sin, and have forfeited in him that spiritual robe of grace and holiness which he had given him by his Creator at the time that he was made. In this state of forfeiture and disinheritance we are all of us conceived and born; and the ordinary way by which we are taken out of it is the Sacrament of Baptism.

But Mary *never* was in this state; she was by the eternal decree of God exempted from it. From eternity, God, the Father, Son, and Holy Ghost, decreed to create the race of man, and, foreseeing the fall of Adam, decreed to redeem the whole race by the Son's taking flesh and suffering on the Cross. In that same incomprehensible, eternal instant, in which the Son of God was born of the Father, was also the decree passed of man's redemption through Him. He who was born from Eternity was born by an eternal decree to save us in Time, and to redeem the whole race; and Mary's redemption was determined in that special manner which we call the Immaculate Conception. It was decreed, not that she should be *cleansed* from sin, but that she should, from the first moment of her being, be *preserved* from sin; so that the Evil One never had any part in her. Therefore she was a child of Adam and Eve as if they had never fallen; she did not share with them their sin; she inherited the gifts and graces (and more than those) which Adam and Eve possessed in Paradise. This is her prerogative, and the foundation of all those salutary truths which are revealed to us concerning her. Let us say then with all holy souls, *Virgin most pure, conceived without original sin, Mary, pray for us.*

May 4: Mary is the 'Virgo Praedicanda', *the Virgin who is to be proclaimed*

Mary is the *Virgo Praedicanda*, that is, the Virgin who is to be proclaimed, to be heralded, literally, to be *preached*.

We are accustomed to preach abroad that which is wonderful, strange, rare, novel, important. Thus, when our Lord was coming, St John the Baptist *preached* Him; then, the Apostles went into the wide world, and *preached* Christ. What is the highest, the rarest, the choicest prerogative of Mary? It is that she was without sin. When a woman in the crowd cried out to our Lord, 'Blessed is the womb that bare Thee!' He answered, 'More blessed are they who hear the word of God and keep it'.[f] Those words were fulfilled in Mary. She was filled with grace *in order* to be the Mother of God.[6] But it was a higher gift than her maternity to be thus sanctified and thus pure. Our Lord indeed would not have become her son *unless* He had first sanctified her; but still, the greater blessedness was to have that perfect sanctification. *This* then is why she is the *Virgo Praedicanda*; she is deserving to be preached abroad because she never committed any sin, even the least; because sin had no part in her; because through the fullness of God's grace, she never thought a thought, or spoke a word, or did an action, which was displeasing, which was not most pleasing, to Almighty God; because, in her was displayed the greatest triumph over the enemy of souls. Wherefore, when all seemed lost, in order to

---

[6] This was the teaching of Pope Pius IX in the Bull *Ineffabilis Deus* of 1854 (cf. Denzinger-Schönmetzer, No. 2800–1).

show what He could do for us all by dying for us; in order to show what human nature, His work, was capable of becoming; to show how utterly He could bring to naught the utmost efforts, the most concentrated malice of the foe, and reverse all the consequences of the Fall, our Lord began, even before His coming, to do His most wonderful act of redemption, in the person of her who was to be His Mother. By the merit of that Blood which was to be shed, He interposed to hinder her incurring the sin of Adam, before He had made on the Cross atonement for it. And therefore it is that we *preach* her who is the subject of this wonderful grace.

But she was the *Virgo Praedicanda* for another reason. When, why, what things do we preach? We preach what is not known, that it may *become* known. And hence the Apostles are said in Scripture to 'preach Christ'.[g] To whom? To those who knew Him not—to the heathen world. Not to those who knew Him, but to those who did not know Him. Preaching is a gradual work: first one lesson, then another. Thus were the heathen brought into the Church *gradually*. And in like manner, the preaching of Mary to the children of the Church, and the devotion paid to her by them, has *grown*, grown gradually, with successive ages. Not so much preached about her in *early* times as in *later*. First she was preached as the Virgin of Virgins—then as the Mother of God—then as glorious in her Assumption—then as the Advocate of sinners—then as Immaculate in her Conception. And this last has been the special preaching of the present century; and thus that which was earliest in her own history is the latest in the Church's recognition of her.

May 5: Mary is the 'Mater Admirabilis', *the Wonderful Mother*

When Mary, the *Virgo Praedicanda*, the Virgin who is to be proclaimed aloud, is called by the title of *Admirabilis*, it is thereby suggested to us what the *effect* is of the preaching of her as Immaculate in her Conception. The Holy Church proclaims, preaches her, as conceived without original sin; and those who hear, the children of Holy Church, wonder, marvel, are astonished and overcome by the preaching. It is so great a prerogative.

Even created excellence is fearful to think of when it is so high as Mary's. As to the great *Creator*, when Moses desired to see His glory, He Himself says about Himself, 'Thou canst not see My face, for man shall not see Me and live';[h] and St Paul says, 'Our God is a consuming fire'.[i] And when St John, holy as he was, saw only the *Human Nature* of our Lord, as He is in Heaven, 'he fell at His feet as dead'.[j] And so as regards the appearance of angels. The holy Daniel, when St Gabriel appeared to him 'fainted away, and lay in a consternation, with his face close to the ground'.[k] When this great archangel came to Zacharias, the father of St John the Baptist, he too 'was troubled, and fear fell upon him'.[l] But it was otherwise with Mary when the same St Gabriel came to her. She was overcome indeed, and troubled at his *words*, because, humble as she was in her own opinion of herself, he addressed her as 'Full of grace', and 'Blessed among women';[m] but she was able to bear the sight of him.

Hence we learn two things: first, how great a holiness was Mary's, seeing she could endure the presence of an angel, whose brightness smote the holy prophet Daniel even to fainting and almost to death; and secondly, since she is so much holier than that angel, and we so much less holy than Daniel, what great reason we have to call her the *Virgo Admirabilis*, the Wonderful, the Awful Virgin,[7] when we think of her ineffable purity!

There are those who are so thoughtless, so blind, so grovelling as to think that Mary is not as much shocked at wilful sin as her Divine Son is, and that we can make her our friend and advocate, though we go to her without contrition at heart, without even the wish for true repentance and resolution to amend. As if Mary could hate sin less, and love sinners more, than our Lord does! No: she feels a sympathy for those only who wish to *leave* their sins; else, how should she be without sin herself? No: if even to the best of us she is, in the words of Scripture, 'fair as the moon, bright as the sun, and *terrible as an army set in array*',[n] what is she to the impenitent sinner?

May 6: Mary is the 'Domus Aurea', *the House of Gold*

Why is she called a *House*? And why is she called *Golden*? Gold is the most beautiful, the most valuable, of all metals. Silver, copper, and steel may in their way be made good to the eye, but nothing is so rich, so splendid, as gold. We have few opportunities of seeing it in any quantity; but anyone who has seen a large number of bright gold coins knows how magnificent is the look of gold. Hence it is that in Scripture the

---

[7] The word 'awful' as used by Newman in this context means 'worthy of profound respect and reverential fear'.

Holy City is, by a figure of speech, called Golden.
'The City', says St John, 'was pure gold, as it were
transparent glass.'° He means of course to give us a
notion of the wondrous beautifulness of heaven, by
comparing it with what is the most beautiful of all the
substances which we see on earth.

Therefore it is that Mary too is called *golden*;
because her graces, her virtues, her innocence, her
purity, are of that transcendent brilliancy and dazzling
perfection, so costly, so exquisite, that the angels
cannot, so to say, keep their eyes off her any more
than *we* could help gazing upon any great work of
gold.

But observe further, she is a *golden house*, or, I will
rather say, a *golden palace*. Let us imagine we saw a
whole palace or large church all made of gold, from
the foundations to the roof; such, in regard to the
number, the variety, the extent of her spiritual excellences, is Mary.

But why called a *house* or palace? And *whose* palace?
She is the house and the palace of the Great King, of
God Himself. Our Lord, the Co-equal Son of God,
once dwelt in her. He was her Guest; nay, more than
a guest, for a guest comes into a house as well as leaves
it. But our Lord was actually *born in* this holy house.
He took His flesh and His blood from this house, from
the flesh, from the veins of Mary. Rightly then was
she made to be of pure gold, because she was to give
of that gold to form the body of the Son of God. She
was *golden* in her conception, *golden* in her birth. She
went through the fire of her suffering like gold in the
furnace, and when she ascended on high, she was, in
the words of our hymn,

Above all the Angels in glory untold,
Standing next to the King in a vesture of gold.[8]

May 7: Mary is the 'Mater Amabilis', *the Lovable or
Dear Mother*

Why is she '*Amabilis*' thus specially? It is because she
was without sin. Sin is something odious in its very
nature, and grace is something bright, beautiful,
attractive.

However, it may be said that sinlessness was not
enough to make others love her, or to make her dear
to others, and that for two reasons: first, because we
cannot like anyone that is not like ourselves, and *we*
are sinners; and next, because her being holy would
not make her pleasant and winning, because holy
persons whom we fall in with, are not always agree-
able, and we cannot like them, however we may
revere them and look up to them.

Now as to the first of these two questions, we may
grant that bad men do not, cannot like good men; but
our Blessed Virgin Mary is called *Amabilis*, or lovable,
as being such to the *children of the Church*, not to those
outside of it, who know nothing about her; and no
child of Holy Church but has some remains of God's
grace in his soul which makes him sufficiently like
her, however greatly wanting he may be, to allow of
his being able to love her. So we may let this question
pass.

---

[8] This hymn, beginning with the words 'Hail, Mother, most pure!' was
written by Edward Caswall. It was Hymn No 23 in the hymn-book then
in use at the Birmingham Oratory: *Hymns for the use of the Birmingham
Oratory* (London, Basil Montagu Pickering Piccadilly, 1888).

But as to the second question, viz., How are we sure that our Lady, when she was on earth, attracted people round her, and made them love her merely because she was holy?—considering that holy people sometimes have not that gift of drawing others to them.

To explain this point we must recollect that there is a vast difference between the state of a soul such as that of the Blessed Virgin, which has *never* sinned, and a soul, however holy, which has *once* had upon it Adam's sin; for, even after baptism and repentance, it suffers necessarily from the spiritual wounds which are the consequence of that sin. Holy men, indeed, never commit *mortal* sin; nay, sometimes have never committed even one mortal sin in the whole course of their lives. But Mary's holiness went beyond this. She never committed even a *venial* sin, and this special privilege is not known to belong to anyone but Mary.

Now, whatever want of amiableness, sweetness, attractiveness, really exists in holy men arises from the *remains* of sin in them, or again from the want of a holiness powerful enough to overcome the defects of nature, whether of soul or body; but, as to Mary, her holiness was such, that if we saw her, and heard her, we should not be able to tell to those who asked us anything about her except simply that she was angelic and heavenly.

Of course her face was most beautiful; but we should not be able to recollect whether it was beautiful or not; we should not recollect any of her features, because it was her beautiful sinless soul, which looked through her eyes, and spoke through her mouth, and was heard in her voice, and compassed her all about;

when she was still, or when she walked, whether she smiled, or was sad, her sinless soul, this it was which would draw all those to her who had any grace in them, any remains of grace, any love of holy things. There was a divine music in all she said and did—in her mien, her air, her deportment, that charmed every true heart that came near her. Her innocence, her humility and modesty, her simplicity, sincerity, and truthfulness, her unselfishness, her unaffected interest in everyone who came to her, her purity—it was these qualities which made her so lovable; and were we to see her now, neither our first thought nor our second thought would be, what she could do for us with her Son (though she can do so much), but our first thought would be, 'Oh, how beautiful!' and our second thought would be, 'Oh, what ugly hateful creatures are we!'

May 7: Mary is the 'Rosa Mystica,'[9] *the Mystical Rose*

How did Mary become the *Rosa Mystica*, the choice, delicate, perfect flower of God's spiritual creation? It was by being born, nurtured and sheltered in the mystical garden or Paradise[10] of God. Scripture makes use of the figure of a garden, when it would speak of heaven and its blessed inhabitants. A garden is a spot of ground set apart for trees and plants, all good, all various, for things that are sweet to the taste or

[9] This meditation 'Rosa mystica' was written and used in 1874, but the following year it was superseded, and 'Sancta Maria' was written and added instead. It would seem that 'Sancta Maria' was written in 1875 for May 9. Then 'Rosa Mystica' was placed as a duplicate for May 7.

[10] Paradise, originally a Persian word, meant a royal garden or park. It was used by the Greek translators to render the Hebrew 'Garden of Eden'.

fragrant in scent, or beautiful to look upon, or useful for nourishment; and accordingly in its spiritual sense it means the home of blessed spirits and holy souls dwelling there together, souls with both the flowers and the fruits upon them, which by the careful husbandry of God they have come to bear, flowers and fruits of grace, flowers more beautiful and more fragrant than those of any garden, fruits more delicious and exquisite than can be matured by earthly husbandman.

All that God has made speaks of its Maker; the mountains speak of His eternity; the sun of His immensity, and the winds of His Almightiness. In like manner flowers and fruits speak of His sanctity, His love, and His providence; and such as are flowers and fruits, such must be the place where they are found. That is to say, since they are found in a garden, therefore a garden has also excellences which speak of God, because it is their home. For instance, it would be out of place if we found beautiful flowers on the mountain-crag, or rich fruit in the sandy desert. As then by flowers and fruits are meant, in a mystical sense, the gifts and graces of the Holy Ghost, so by a garden is meant mystically a place of spiritual repose, stillness, peace, refreshment, and delight.

Thus our first parents were placed in 'a garden of pleasure' shaded by trees, 'fair to behold and pleasant to eat of',[p] with the Tree of Life in the midst, and a river to water the ground. Thus our Lord, speaking from the cross to the penitent robber, calls the blessed place, the heaven to which He was taking him, 'paradise',[q] or a garden of pleasure. Therefore St John, in the Apocalypse, speaks of heaven, the palace of God, as a garden or paradise, in which was the Tree of Life giving forth its fruits every month.[r]

Such was the garden in which the Mystical Rose, the Immaculate Mary, was sheltered and nursed to be the Mother of the All Holy God, from her birth to her espousals to St Joseph,[11] a term of thirteen years. For three years of it she was in the arms of her holy mother, St Anne, and then for ten years she lived in the temple of God. In those blessed gardens, as they may be called, she lived by herself, continually visited by the dew of God's grace, and growing up a more and more heavenly flower, till at the end of that period she was meet for the inhabitation in her of the Most Holy. This was the outcome of the Immaculate Conception. Excepting her, the fairest rose in the paradise of God has had upon it blight, and has had the risk of canker-worm and locust. All but Mary; she from the first was perfect in her sweetness and her beautifulness, and at length when the angel Gabriel had to come to her, he found her 'full of grace',[s] which had, from her good use of it, accumulated in her from the first moment of her being.

---

[11] Newman echoes in these words a tradition that arose from the apocryphal 'Protoevangelium' of St James (vii–viii) where it is stated that Saints Joachim and Anne presented their child, Mary, in the Temple when she was three years old. The Gospel tells us that she was 'a virgin espoused to a man named Joseph' (Mt 1:18). The time of betrothal lasted about a year. According to Jewish custom, girls were marriageable from about the age of twelve and a half years. The Feast of the Espousals of Our Lady was celebrated in some places and by certain Religious Families on 23 January.

May 8: Mary is the 'Virgo Veneranda', the all-Worshipful Virgin

We use the word '*Venerable*' generally of what is *old*. That is because only what is old has commonly those qualities which excite reverence or veneration.

It is a great history, a great character, a maturity of virtue, goodness, experience, that excite our reverence, and these commonly cannot belong to the young.

But this is not true when we are considering Saints. A short life with them is a long one. Thus Holy Scripture says, 'Venerable age is not that of long time, nor counted by the number of years, but it is the *understanding* of a man that is grey hairs, and a spotless life is old age. The just man, if he be cut short by death, shall be at rest; being made perfect in a short time, he fulfilled a long time.'ᵗ

Nay, there is a heathen writer, who knew nothing of Saints, who lays it down that even to children, to all children, a great reverence should be paid, and that on the ground of their being as yet innocent.[12] And this is a feeling very widely felt and expressed in all countries; so much so that the sight of those who have not sinned (that is, who are not yet old enough to have fallen into mortal sin) has, on the very score of that innocent, smiling youthfulness, often disturbed and turned the plunderer or the assassin in the midst of his guilty doings, filled him with a sudden fear, and brought him,

---

[12] The unlikely heathen author to whom Newman refers is Decimus Iunius Iuvenalis (+ *c.* AD 128) who in his fourteenth *Satura* says that 'the greatest respect is owed to a child, if you are preparing anything shameful, nor should you scorn the years of a child, but the very young (unspeaking) son should be an obstacle to prevent you who are about to sin: *maxima debetur puero reverentia, si quid turpe paras, nec tu pueri contempseris annos, sed peccaturo obstet tibi filius infans.*'

if not to repentance, at least to change of purpose.

And, to pass from the thought of the lowest to the Highest, what shall we say of the Eternal God (if we may safely speak of Him at all) but that He, *because* He is eternal, is ever *young*, without a beginning, and therefore without change, and, in the fullness and perfection of His incomprehensible attributes, now just what He was a million years ago? He is truly called in Scripture the 'Ancient of Days',[u] and is therefore infinitely venerable; yet He needs not old age to make him venerable; He has really nothing of those human attendants on venerableness which the sacred writers are obliged figuratively to ascribe to Him, in order to make us feel that profound abasement and reverential awe which we ought to entertain at the thought of Him.

And so of the great Mother of God, as far as a creature can be like the Creator; her ineffable purity and utter freedom from any shadow of sin, her Immaculate Conception, her ever-virginity—these her prerogatives (in spite of her extreme youth at the time when Gabriel came to her) are such as to lead us to exclaim in the prophetic words of Scripture both with awe and with exultation, 'Thou art the glory of Jerusalem and the joy of Israel; thou art the honour of our people; therefore hath the hand of the Lord strengthened thee, and therefore art thou blessed forever.'[v]

May 9: Mary is 'Sancta Maria,' *the Holy Mary*

God alone can claim the attribute of holiness. Hence we say in the Hymn, '*Tu solus sanctus*',[w] 'Thou only art holy.'[13] By holiness we mean the absence of what-

---

[13] 'Tu Solus Sanctus' in the hymn 'Gloria in excelsis Deo'. Cf. Rev 15:4.

ever sullies, dims, and degrades a rational nature; all that is most opposite and contrary to sin and guilt.

We say that God alone is *holy*, though in truth *all* His high attributes are possessed by Him in that fullness, that it may be truly said that He alone has them. Thus, as to goodness, our Lord said to the young man, 'None is good but God alone'.[x] He too alone is Power, He alone is Wisdom, He alone is Providence, Love, Mercy, Justice, Truth. This is true; but holiness is singled out as His special prerogative, because it marks more than His other attributes, not only His superiority over all His creatures, but emphatically His separation from them. Hence we read in the Book of Job, 'Can man be justified compared with God, or he that is born of a woman appear clean? Behold, even the moon doth not shine, and the stars are not pure,[y] in His sight'. 'Behold, among His saints none is unchangeable, and the Heavens are not pure in His sight.'[z]

This we must receive and understand in the first place; but secondly we know too, that, in His mercy, He has communicated in various measures His great attributes to His rational creatures, and, first of all, as being most necessary, holiness. Thus Adam, from the time of his creation, was gifted, over and above his nature as man, with the grace of God, to unite him to God, and to make him holy.[aa] Grace is therefore called holy grace; and, as being holy, it is the connecting principle between God and man. Adam in Paradise might have had knowledge, and skill, and many virtues; but these gifts did not unite him to his Creator. It was holiness that united him, for it is said by St Paul, 'Without holiness no man shall see God'.[bb]

And so again, when man fell and lost this holy grace, he had various gifts still adhering to him; he might be, in a certain measure, true, merciful, loving, and just; but these virtues did not unite him to God. What he needed was holiness; and therefore the first act of God's goodness to us in the Gospel is to take us out of our *un*holy state by means of the sacrament of Baptism, and by the grace then given us to re-open the communications, so long closed, between the soul and heaven.

We see then the force of our Lady's title, when we call her '*Holy* Mary'. When God would prepare a human mother for His Son, this was why He began by giving her an immaculate conception. He began, not by giving her the gift of love, or truthfulness, or gentleness, or devotion, though according to the occasion she had them all. But He began His great work before she was born; before she could think, speak, or act, by making her *holy*, and thereby, while on earth, a citizen of heaven. '*Tota* pulchra es, Maria!' Nothing of the deformity of sin was ever hers. Thus she differs from all saints. There have been great missionaries, confessors, bishops, doctors, pastors. They have done great works, and have taken with them numberless converts or penitents to heaven. They have suffered much, and have a superabundance of merits to show. But Mary in this way resembles her Divine Son, viz., that, as He, being God, is separate by holiness from all creatures, so she is separate from all Saints and Angels, as being '*full of grace*'.[cc]

II
On The Annunciation

May 10: Mary is the 'Regina Angelorum', *the Queen of Angels*

This great title may be fitly connected with the Maternity of Mary, that is, with the coming upon her of the Holy Ghost at Nazareth after the Angel Gabriel's annunciation to her, and with the consequent birth of our Lord at Bethlehem. She, as the Mother of our Lord, comes nearer to Him than any angel; nearer even than the Seraphim who surround Him, and cry continually, 'Holy, Holy, Holy'.[dd]

The two Archangels who have a special office in the Gospel are St Michael and St Gabriel—and they both of them are associated in the history of the Incarnation with Mary: St Gabriel, when the Holy Ghost came down upon her; and St Michael, when the Divine Child was born.

St Gabriel hailed her as 'Full of grace', and as 'Blessed among women',[ee] and announced to her that the Holy Ghost would come down upon her, and that she would bear a Son who would be the Son of the Highest.

Of St Michael's ministry to her, on the birth of that Divine Son, we learn in the Apocalypse, written by the Apostle St John. We know our Lord came to set up the Kingdom of Heaven among men; and hardly was He born when He was assaulted by the powers of the world who wished to destroy Him. Herod sought to take His life, but he was defeated by St Joseph's carrying His Mother and Him off into Egypt.[ff] But St

John in the Apocalypse tells us that Michael and his angels were the real guardians of Mother and Child, then and on other occasions.

First, St John saw in vision 'a great sign in heaven' (meaning by 'heaven' the Church, or Kingdom of God), 'a woman clothed with the sun, and with the moon under her feet, and on her head a crown of twelve stars';[14] and when she was about to be delivered of her Child there appeared 'a great red dragon', that is, the evil spirit, ready 'to devour her son' when He should be born. The Son was preserved by His own Divine power, but next the evil spirit persecuted her; St Michael, however, and his angels came to the rescue and prevailed against him.

'There was a great battle,' says the sacred writer; 'Michael and his Angels fought with the dragon, and the dragon fought and his angels; and that great dragon was cast out, the old serpent, who is called the devil.'[gg] Now, as then, the Blessed Mother of God has hosts of angels who do her service; and she is their Queen.

May 11: Mary is the 'Speculum Justitiae', *the Mirror of Justice*

Here first we must consider what is meant by *justice*, for the word as used by the Church has not that sense which it bears in ordinary English. By 'justice' is not meant the virtue of fairness, equity, uprightness in our dealings; but it is a word denoting all virtues at once,

[14] The vision of the woman in the Apocalypse is usually taken to signify the Church, but it is also understood to refer to our Lady. Cf. above, Text XII, p. 241, footnote 12.

a perfect, virtuous state of soul—righteousness, or moral perfection; so that it answers very nearly to what is meant by *sanctity*. Therefore when our Lady is called the 'Mirror of Justice', it is meant to say that she is the Mirror of sanctity, holiness, supernatural goodness.

Next, what is meant by calling her a *mirror?* A mirror is a surface which reflects, as still water, polished steel, or a looking-glass. What did Mary reflect? She reflected our Lord—but *He* is infinite *Sanctity*. She then, as far as a creature could, reflected His Divine sanctity, and therefore she is the *Mirror* of Sanctity, or, as the Litany says, of *Justice*.

Do we ask how she came to reflect His Sanctity?— it was by living with Him. We see every day how like people get to each other who live with those they love. When they live with those whom they don't love, as, for instance, the members of a family who quarrel with each other, then the longer they live together the more unlike each other they become; but when they love each other, as husband and wife, parents and children, brothers with brothers or sisters, friends with friends, then in course of time they get surprisingly like each other. All of us perceive this; we are witnesses to it with our own eyes and ears—in the expression of their features, in their voice, in their walk, in their language, even in their handwriting, they become like each other; and so with regard to their minds, as in their opinions, their tastes, their pursuits. And again doubtless in the state of their souls, which we do not see, whether for good or for bad.

Now, consider that Mary loved her Divine Son with an unutterable love; and consider too she had

Him all to herself for thirty years. Do we not see that, as she was full of grace *before* she conceived Him in her womb, she must have had a vast incomprehensible sanctity when she had lived close to God for thirty years?—a sanctity of an angelical order, reflecting back the attributes of God with a fullness and exactness of which no saint upon earth, or hermit, or holy virgin, can even remind us. Truly then she is the *Speculum Justitiae*, the *Mirror* of Divine *Perfection*.

May 12: Mary is the 'Sedes Sapientiae', *the Seat of Wisdom*

Mary has this title in her Litany, because the Son of God, who is also called in Scripture the Word and Wisdom of God, once dwelt in her, and then, after His birth of her, was carried in her arms and seated in her lap in His first years. Thus, being, as it were, the human throne of Him who reigns in heaven, she is called the *Seat of Wisdom*. In the poet's words:[15]

> His throne, thy bosom blest,
> O Mother undefiled,
> That Throne, if aught beneath the skies,
> Beseems the sinless Child.

But the possession of her Son lasted beyond His infancy—He was under her rule,[hh] as St Luke tells us, and lived with her in her house, till He went forth to preach—that is, for at least a whole thirty years. And

---

[15] The poet is John Keble and the poem 'The Purification' is from *The Christian Year: Thoughts in Verse for the Sundays and Holidays throughout the Year*, Oxford–London 1827, p. 283.

this brings us to a reflection about her, cognate to that which was suggested to us yesterday by the title of 'Mirror of Justice'. For if such close and continued intimacy with her Son created in her a sanctity inconceivably great, must not also the knowledge which she gained during those many years from His conversation of present, past, and future, have been so large, and so profound, and so diversified, and so thorough, that, though she was a poor woman without human advantages, she must in her knowledge of creation, of the universe, and of history, have excelled the greatest of philosophers, and in her theological knowledge the greatest of theologians, and in her prophetic discernment the most favoured of prophets?

What was the grand theme of conversation between her and her Son but the nature, the attributes, the providence, and the works of Almighty God? Would not our Lord be ever glorifying the Father who sent Him? Would He not unfold to her the solemn eternal decrees, and the purposes and will of God? Would He not from time to time enlighten her in all those points of doctrine which have been first discussed and then settled in the Church from the time of the Apostles till now, and all that shall be till the end,—nay, these, and far more than these? All that is obscure, all that is fragmentary in revelation, would, so far as the knowledge is possible to man, be brought out to her in clearness and simplicity by Him who is the Light of the World.

And so of the events which are to come. God spoke to the Prophets: we have His communications to them in Scripture. But He spoke to them in figure and parable. There was one, viz., Moses, to whom He vouchsafed to speak face to face. 'If there be among you a prophet of the Lord,' God says, 'I will appear to him in a vision, and I will speak to him in a dream. But it is not so with my servant Moses. ... For I will speak to him mouth to mouth, and plainly, and not by riddles and figures doth he see the Lord.'[ii] This was the great privilege of the inspired Lawgiver of the Jews; but how much was it below that of Mary! Moses had the privilege only now and then, from time to time; but Mary for thirty continuous years saw and heard Him, being all through that time face to face with Him, and being able to ask Him any question which she wished explained, and knowing that the answers she received were from the Eternal God, who neither deceives nor can be deceived.

May 13: Mary is the 'Janua Coeli', *the Gate of Heaven*

Mary is called the *Gate* of Heaven, because it was through her that our Lord passed from heaven to earth. The Prophet Ezechiel, prophesying of Mary, says, 'the gate shall be closed, it shall not be opened, and no man shall pass through it, since the Lord God of Israel has entered through it—and it shall be closed for the Prince, the Prince Himself shall sit in it.'[ij][16]

Now this is fulfilled, not only in our Lord having taken flesh from her, and being her Son, but, more-over, in that she had a place in the economy of

---

[16] The closed gate (cf. Ez 44:2–3) was the Eastern gate of the Temple of Jerusalem. Yahweh had entered by it, so that even the king or prince had to enter the court by another gate in order to reach this closed gate where he could take a ritual meal. Some of the Fathers of the Church, by means of an accommodated sense, took this gate, through which God alone had passed, to be a figure of Mary's perpetual virginity.

Redemption; it is fulfilled in her spirit and will, as well
as in her body. Eve had a part in the fall of man,
though it was Adam who was our representative, and
whose sin made us sinners. It was Eve who began, and
who tempted Adam. Scripture says: 'The woman saw
that the tree was good to eat, and fair to the eyes, and
delightful to behold; and she took of the fruit thereof,
and did eat, and gave to her husband, and he did
eat.'kk It was fitting then in God's mercy that, as the
woman began the *destruction* of the world, so woman
should also begin its *recovery*, and that, as Eve opened
the way for the fatal deed of the first Adam, so Mary
should open the way for the great achievement of the
second Adam,ll even our Lord Jesus Christ, who came
to save the world by dying on the cross for it. Hence
Mary is called by the holy Fathers a second and a
better Eve,[17] as having taken that first step in the salvation of mankind which Eve took in its ruin.

How, and when, did Mary take part, and the initial
part, in the world's restoration? It was when the Angel
Gabriel came to her to announce to her the great
dignity which was to be her portion. St Paul bids us
'present our bodies to God as a reasonable service'.mm
We must not only pray with our lips, and fast, and do
outward penance, and be chaste in our bodies; but we
must be obedient, and pure in our minds. And so, as
regards the Blessed Virgin, it was God's will that she
should undertake *willingly* and with *full understanding*
to be the Mother of our Lord, and not to be a mere
passive instrument whose maternity would have no
merit and no reward. The higher our gifts, the heavier

[17] Cf. above, Text X, pp. 206–22.

our duties. It was no light lot to be so intimately near to the Redeemer of men, as she experienced afterwards when she suffered with him. Therefore, weighing well the Angel's words before giving her answer to them—first she asked whether so great an office would be a forfeiture of that Virginity which she had vowed. When the Angel told her no, then, with the full consent of a full heart, full of God's love to her and her own lowliness, she said, 'Behold the handmaid of the Lord; be it done unto me according to thy word'.[nn] It was by this consent that she became the *Gate of Heaven*.

May 14: Mary is the 'Mater Creatoris', *the Mother of the Creator*

This is a title which, of all others, we should have thought it impossible for any creature to possess. At first sight we might be tempted to say that it throws into confusion our primary ideas of the Creator and the creature, the Eternal and the temporal, the Self-subsisting and the dependent; and yet on further consideration we shall see that we cannot refuse the title to Mary without denying the Divine Incarnation —that is, the great and fundamental truth of revelation, that God became man.

And this was seen from the first age of the Church. Christians were accustomed from the first to call the Blessed Virgin 'The Mother of God', because they saw that it was impossible to deny her that title without denying St John's words, 'The Word' (that is, God the Son) 'was made flesh'.[oo]

And in no long time it was found necessary to

proclaim this truth by the voice of an Ecumenical Council of the Church. For, in consequence of the dislike which men have of a mystery, the error sprang up that our Lord was not really God, but a man, differing from us in this merely—that God dwelt in Him, as God dwells in all good men, only in a higher measure; as the Holy Spirit dwelt in Angels and Prophets, as in a sort of Temple; or again, as our Lord now dwells in the Tabernacle in church. And then the bishops and faithful people found there was no other way of hindering this false, bad view being taught but by declaring distinctly, and making it a point of faith, that Mary was the Mother, not of man only, but of God. And since that time the title of Mary, as *Mother of God*, has become what is called a dogma, or article of faith, in the Church.[18]

But this leads us to a larger view of the subject. Is this title as given to Mary more wonderful than the doctrine that God, without ceasing to be God, should become man? Is it more mysterious that Mary should be Mother of God, than that *God* should be *man?* Yet the latter, as I have said, is the elementary truth of revelation, witnessed by Prophets, Evangelists, and Apostles all through Scripture. And what can be more consoling and joyful than the wonderful promises which follow from this truth, that Mary is the Mother of God?—the great wonder, namely, that we become the brethren of our God; that, if we live well, and die in the grace of God, we shall all of us hereafter be taken up by our Incarnate God to that place where angels dwell; that our bodies shall be raised from the

---

[18] Cf. above, Text III, pp. 131–7; and Text XIII/A, pp. 446–53.

dust, and be taken to Heaven; that we shall be really united to God; that we shall be partakers of the Divine nature; that each of us, soul and body, shall be plunged into the abyss of glory which surrounds the Almighty; that we shall see Him, and share His blessedness, according to the text, 'Whosoever shall do the will of My Father that is in Heaven, the same is My brother, and sister, and mother'.pp

May 15: Mary is the 'Mater Christi', the Mother of Christ

Each of the titles of Mary has its own special meaning and drift, and may be made the subject of a distinct meditation. She is invoked by us as the *Mother of Christ*. What is the force of thus addressing her? It is to bring before us that she it is who from the first was prophesied of, and associated with the hopes and prayers of all holy men, of all true worshippers of God, of all who 'looked for the redemption of Israel'qq in every age before that redemption came.

Our Lord was called the Christ, or the Messias, by the Jewish prophets and the Jewish people. The two words Christ and Messias mean the same. They mean in English the 'Anointed'. In the old time there were three great ministries or offices by means of which God spoke to His chosen people, the Israelites, or, as they were afterward called, the Jews, viz., that of Priest, that of King, and that of Prophet. Those who were chosen by God for one or other of these offices were solemnly anointed with oil—oil signifying the grace of God, which was given to them for the due performance of their high duties. But our Lord was all three, a Priest, a Prophet, and a King—a Priest, because He offered Himself as a sacrifice for our sins; a Prophet, because He revealed to us the Holy Law of God; and a King, because He rules over us. Thus He is the one true Christ.

It was in expectation of this great Messias that the chosen people, the Jews, or Israelites, or Hebrews (for these are different names for the same people), looked out from age to age. He was to come to set all things right. And next to this great question which occupied their minds, namely, *When* was He to come, was the question, *Who* was to be His Mother? It had been told them from the first, not that He should come from heaven, but that He should be born of a Woman. At the time of the fall of Adam, God had said that the *seed* of the *Woman* should bruise the Serpent's head.[rr] Who, then, was to be that Woman thus significantly pointed out to the fallen race of Adam? At the end of many centuries, it was further revealed to the Jews that the great Messias, or Christ, the seed of the Woman, should be born of their race, and of one particular tribe of the twelve tribes into which that race was divided.[ss] From that time every woman of that tribe hoped to have the great privilege of herself being the Mother of the Messias, or Christ; for it stood to reason, since He was so great, the Mother must be great, and good, and blessed too. Hence it was, among other reasons, that they thought so highly of the marriage state, because, not knowing the mystery of the miraculous conception of the Christ when He was actually to come, they thought that the marriage rite was the ordinance necessary for His coming.

Hence it was, if Mary had been as other women, she would have longed for marriage, as opening on her the prospect of bearing the great King. But she was too humble and too pure for such thoughts. She had been inspired to choose that better way of serving God which had not been made known to the Jews— the state of Virginity. She preferred to be His Spouse to being His Mother. Accordingly, when the Angel Gabriel announced to her her high destiny, she shrank from it till she was assured that it would not oblige her to revoke her purpose of a virgin life devoted to her God.

Thus was it that she became the Mother of the Christ, not in that way which pious women for so many ages had expected Him, but, declining the grace of such maternity, she gained it by means of a higher grace. And this is the full meaning of St Elizabeth's words, when the Blessed Virgin came to visit her, which we use in the Hail Mary: 'Blessed art thou among women, and blessed is the fruit of thy womb'.[tt] And therefore it is that in the Devotion called the 'Crown of Twelve Stars'[19] we give praise to God the Holy Ghost, through whom she was *both* Virgin *and* Mother.

May 16: Mary is the 'Mater Salvatoris', *the Mother of the Saviour*

Here again, as in our reflections of yesterday, we must

[19] The devotion called the 'Crown of Twelve Stars' was based on the identification of our Lady with the Woman in the vision of the Apocalypse (ch. 12). As we saw, Newman vigorously defended this interpretation (cf. above, Text XII, pp. 235–45). This image of our Lady with a crown of twelve stars was frequently used in Oratorian iconography.

understand what is meant by calling our Lord a
Saviour, in order to understand why it is used to form
one of the titles given to Mary in her Litany.

The special name by which our Lord was known
before His coming was, as we found yesterday, that of
Messias, or Christ. Thus He was known to the Jews.
But when He actually showed Himself on earth, He
was known by three new titles, the Son of God, the
Son of Man, and the Saviour; the first expressive of His
Divine Nature, the second of His Human, the third of
His Personal Office. Thus the Angel who appeared to
Mary called Him the Son of God;[uu] the angel who
appeared to Joseph called Him *Jesus*, which means in
English, *Saviour*;[vv] and so the Angels, too, called Him a
Saviour when they appeared to the shepherds.[ww] But
He Himself specially calls Himself the Son of Man.[xx]

Not Angels only call Him Saviour, but those two
greatest of the Apostles, St Peter and St Paul, in their
first preachings. St Peter says He is 'a Prince and a
Saviour',[yy] and St Paul says, 'a Saviour, Jesus'.[zz] And
both Angels and Apostles tell us why He is so called—
because He has rescued us from the power of the evil
spirit, and from the guilt and misery of our sins. Thus
the Angel says to Joseph, 'Thou shalt call His name
Jesus, *for* He shall save His people from their *sins*';[ab]
and St Peter, 'God has exalted Him to be Prince and
Saviour, to give repentance to Israel, and remission of
sins'.[ac] And He says Himself, 'The Son of Man is come
to seek and to *save that which is lost*.'[ad]

Now let us consider how this affects our thoughts
of Mary. To rescue slaves from the power of the
Enemy implies a conflict. Our Lord, because He was
a Saviour, was a warrior. He could not deliver the

captives without a fight, nor without personal suffering. Now, who are they who especially hate wars? A
heathen poet answers. 'Wars', he says, 'are hated by
Mothers.'[20] Mothers are just those who especially suffer
in a war. They may glory in the honour gained by
their children; but still such glorying does not wipe
out one particle of the long pain, the anxiety, the
suspense, the desolation, and the anguish which the
mother of a soldier feels. So it was with Mary. For
thirty years she was blessed with the continual presence of her Son—nay, she had Him in subjection.[ae]
But the time came when that war called for Him for
which He had come upon earth. Certainly He came,
not simply to be the Son of Mary, but to be the
Saviour of Man, and therefore at length He parted
from her. She knew *then* what it was to be the mother
of a soldier. He left her side; she saw Him no longer;
she tried in vain to get near Him. He had for years
lived in her embrace, and after that, at least in her
dwelling—but now, in His own words, 'The Son of
Man had not where to lay His head'.[af] And then,
when years had run out, she heard of His arrest, His
mock trial, and His passion. At last she got near Him
– when and where?—on the way to Calvary: and
when He had been lifted upon the Cross. And at
length she held Him again in her arms: yes—when He
was dead. True, He rose from the dead; but still she
did not thereby gain Him, for He ascended on high,
and she did not at once follow Him. No, she remained
on earth many years—in the care, indeed, of His

---

[20] The heathen poet was Quintus Horatius Flaccus who in one of his
odes speaks of wars being hated by mothers: '*bellaque matribus detestata*'
(*Carmina*, lib. I, i, pp. 24–5).

dearest Apostle, St John. But what was even the holiest of men compared with her own Son, and Him the Son of God? O Holy Mary, Mother of our Saviour, in this meditation we have now suddenly passed from the Joyful Mysteries to the Sorrowful, from Gabriel's Annunciation to thee, to the Seven Dolours. That, then, will be the next series of Meditations which we make about thee.

III
Our Lady's Dolours

May 17: Mary is the 'Regina Martyrum', *the Queen of Martyrs*[21]

Why is she so called?—she who never had any blow, or wound, or other injury to her consecrated person. How can she be exalted over those whose bodies suffered the most ruthless violences and the keenest torments for our Lord's sake? She is, indeed, Queen of all Saints, of those who 'walk with Christ in white, for they are worthy;'[ag] but how of those 'who were slain for the Word of God, and for the testimony which they held?'[ah]

To answer this question, it must be recollected that the pains of the soul may be as fierce as those of the body. Bad men who are now in hell, and the elect of God who are in purgatory, are suffering only in their souls, for their bodies are still in the dust; yet how

[21] In a footnote, Newman writes: from this day to the end of the month, being the Novena, and Octave of St Philip (Neri), the Meditations are shorter than the foregoing.

severe is that suffering! And perhaps most people who have lived long can bear witness in their own persons to a sharpness of distress which was like a sword cutting them, to a weight and force of sorrow which seemed to throw them down, though bodily pain there was none.

What an overwhelming horror it must have been for the Blessed Mary to witness the Passion and the Crucifixion of her Son! Her anguish was, as Holy Simeon had announced to her, at the time of that Son's Presentation in the Temple, a sword piercing her soul.[ai] If our Lord Himself could not bear the prospect of what was before Him, and was covered in the thought of it with a bloody sweat,[aj] His soul thus acting upon His body, does not this show how great mental pain can be? and would it have been wonderful though Mary's head and heart had given way as she stood under His Cross?

Thus is she most truly the Queen of *Martyrs*.

May 18: Mary is the 'Vas Insigne Devotionis', *the Most Devout Virgin*

To be *devout* is to be devoted. We know what is meant by a devoted wife or daughter. It is one whose thoughts centre in the person so deeply loved, so tenderly cherished. She follows him about with her eyes; she is ever seeking some means of serving him; and, if her services are very small in their character, that only shows how intimate they are, and how incessant. And especially if the object of her love be weak, or in pain, or near to die, still more intensely does she live in his life, and know nothing but him.

This intense devotion towards our Lord, forgetting

self in love for Him, is instanced in St Paul, who says, 'I know nothing but Jesus Christ and Him crucified'.[ak] And again, 'I live, [yet] now not I, but Christ liveth in me; and [the life] that I now live in the flesh, I live in the faith of the Son of God, who loved me, and delivered Himself for me.'[al]

But great as was St Paul's devotion to our Lord, much greater was that of the Blessed Virgin; because she was His Mother, and because she had Him and all His sufferings actually before her eyes, and because she had the long intimacy of thirty years with Him, and because she was from her special sanctity so ineffably near to Him in spirit. When, then, He was mocked, bruised, scourged, and nailed to the Cross, she felt as keenly as if every indignity and torture inflicted on Him was struck at herself. She could have cried out in agony at every pang of His.

This is called her *com*passion, or her suffering with her Son, and it arose from this that she was the 'Vas insigne *devotionis*'.

May 19: Mary is the 'Vas Honorabile', *the Vessel of Honour*

St Paul calls elect souls vessels of honour: of honour, because they are elect or chosen; and vessels, because, through the love of God, they are filled with God's heavenly and holy grace. How much more then is Mary a vessel of honour by reason of her having within her, not only the grace of God, but the very Son of God, formed as regards His flesh and blood out of her!

But this title '*honorabile*,' as applied to Mary, admits of a further and special meaning. She was a martyr without the rude *dis*honour which accompanied the sufferings of martyrs. The martyrs were seized, haled about, thrust into prison with the vilest criminals, and assailed with the most blasphemous words and foulest speeches which Satan could inspire. Nay, such was the unutterable trial also of the holy women, young ladies, the spouses of Christ, whom the heathen seized, tortured, and put to death. Above all, our Lord Himself, whose sanctity was greater than any created excellence or vessel of grace—even He, as we know well, was buffeted, stripped, scourged, mocked, dragged about, and then stretched, nailed, lifted up on a high cross, to the gaze of a brutal multitude.

But He, who bore the sinner's shame for sinners, spared His Mother, who was sinless, this supreme indignity. Not in the body, but in the soul, she suffered. True, in His Agony she was agonized; in His Passion she suffered a fellow-passion; she was crucified with Him; the spear that pierced His breast pierced through her spirit. Yet there were no visible signs of this intimate martyrdom; she stood up, still, collected, motionless, solitary, under the Cross of her Son,[am] surrounded by Angels, and shrouded in her virginal sanctity from the notice of all who were taking part in His Crucifixion.

May 20: Mary is the 'Vas Spirituale', *the Spiritual Vessel*

To be *spiritual* is to live in the world of spirits—as St Paul says, 'Our conversation is in Heaven'.[an] To be *spiritually*-minded is to see by faith all those good and holy beings who actually surround us, though we see them not with our bodily eyes; to see them by faith as vividly as we see the things of earth—the green country, the blue sky, and the brilliant sunshine. Hence it is that, when saintly souls are favoured with heavenly visions, these visions are but the extraordinary continuations and the crown, by a divine intuition, of objects which, by the ordinary operation of grace, are ever before their minds.

These visions consoled and strengthened the Blessed Virgin in all her sorrows. The Angels who were around her understood her, and she understood them, with a directness which is not to be expected in their intercourse with us who have inherited from Adam the taint of sin. Doubtless; but still let us never forget that as she in her sorrows was comforted by Angels, so it is our privilege in the many trials of life to be comforted, in our degree, by the same heavenly messengers of the Most High; nay, by Almighty God Himself, the third Person of the Holy Trinity, who has taken on Himself the office of being our Paraclete, or Present Help.

Let all those who are in trouble take this comfort to themselves, if they are trying to lead a spiritual life. If they call on God, He will answer them. Though they have no earthly friend, they have Him, who, as He felt for His Mother when He was on the Cross, now that He is in His glory feels for the lowest and feeblest of His people.

May 21: Mary is the 'Consolatrix Afflictorum', *the Consoler of the Afflicted*

St Paul says that his Lord comforted him in all his

tribulation, that he also might be able to comfort them who are in distress, by the encouragement which he received from God.[ao] This is the secret of true consolation: those are able to comfort others who in their own case, have been much tried, and have felt the need of consolation, and have received it. So of our Lord Himself it is said: 'In that He Himself hath suffered and been tempted, He is able to succour those also that are tempted.'[ap]

And this too is why the Blessed Virgin is the comforter of the afflicted. We all know how special a mother's consolation is, and we are allowed to call Mary our Mother from the time that our Lord from the Cross established the relation of mother and son between her and St John. And she especially can console us because she suffered more than mothers in general. Women, at least delicate women, are commonly shielded from rude experience of the highways of the world; but she, after our Lord's Ascension, was sent out into foreign lands almost as the Apostles were, a sheep among wolves. In spite of all St John's care of her, which was as great as was St Joseph's in her younger days, she, more than all the saints of God, was a stranger and a pilgrim upon earth, in proportion to her greater love of Him who *had* been on earth, and had gone away. As, when our Lord was an Infant, she had to flee across the desert to the heathen Egypt,[aq] so, when He had ascended on high, she had to go on shipboard to the heathen Ephesus, where she lived and died.[22]

O ye who are in the midst of rude neighbours or

---

[22] There is an old tradition that our Lady resided for some time with St John at Ephesus where she died. The other equally strong tradition is that she spent her final years in Jerusalem.

scoffing companions, or of wicked acquaintance, or of spiteful enemies, and are helpless, invoke the aid of Mary by the memory of her own sufferings among the heathen Greeks and the heathen Egyptians.

May 22: Mary is the 'Virgo Prudentissima', *the Most Prudent Virgin*

It may not appear at first sight how the virtue of prudence is connected with the trials and sorrows of our Lady's life; yet there is a point of view from which we are reminded of her prudence by those trials. It must be recollected that she is not only the great instance of the contemplative life, but also of the practical; and the practical life is at once a life of penance and of prudence, if it is to be well discharged. Now Mary was as full of external work and hard service as any Sister of Charity at this day. Of course her duties varied according to the seasons of her life, as a young maiden, as a wife, as a mother, and as a widow; but still her life was full of duties day by day and hour by hour. As a stranger in Egypt, she had duties towards the poor heathen among whom she was thrown. As a dweller in Nazareth, she had her duties towards her kinsfolk and neighbours. She had her duties, though unrecorded, during those years in which our Lord was preaching and proclaiming His Kingdom. After He had left this earth, she had her duties towards the Apostles, and especially towards the Evangelists. She had duties towards the Martyrs, and to the Confessors in prison; to the sick, to the ignorant, and to the poor. Afterwards, she had to seek with St John another and a heathen country, where her happy death took place.

But before that death, how much must she have suffered in her life amid an idolatrous population! Doubtless the Angels screened her eyes from the worst crimes there committed. Still, she was full of duties there—and in consequence she was full of merit. All her acts were perfect, all were the best that could be done. Now, always to be awake, guarded, fervent, so as to be able to act not only without sin, but in the best possible way, in the varying circumstances of each day, denotes a life of untiring mindfulness. But of such a life, Prudence is the presiding virtue. It is, then, through the pains and sorrows of her earthly pilgrimage that we are able to invoke her as the *Virgo prudentissima*.

May 23: Mary is the 'Turris Eburnea', *the Ivory Tower*

A Tower is a fabric which rises higher and more conspicuous than other objects in its neighbourhood. Thus, when we say a man 'towers' over his fellows, we mean to signify that they look small in comparison of him.

This quality of greatness is instanced in the Blessed Virgin. Though she suffered more keen and intimate anguish at our Lord's Passion and Crucifixion than any of the Apostles by reason of her being His Mother, yet consider how much more noble she was amid her deep distress than they were. When our Lord underwent His agony, they slept for sorrow. They could not wrestle with their deep disappointment and despondency; they could not master it; it confused, numbed, and overcame their senses.[ar] And soon after, when St Peter was asked by bystanders whether he was not one of our Lord's disciples, he denied it.[as]

Nor was he alone in this cowardice. The Apostles, one and all, forsook our Lord and fled,[at] though St John returned. Nay, still further, they even lost faith in Him, and thought all the great expectations which He had raised in them had ended in a failure. How different this even from the brave conduct of St Mary Magdalen! and still more from that of the Virgin Mother! It is expressly noted of her that she *stood* by the Cross.[au] She did not grovel in the dust, but *stood upright* to receive the blows, the stabs, which the long Passion of her Son inflicted upon her every moment.

In this magnanimity and generosity in suffering she is, as compared with the Apostles, fitly imaged as a *Tower*. But towers, it may be said, are huge, rough, heavy, obtrusive, graceless structures, for the purposes of war, not of peace; with nothing of the beautifulness, refinement, and finish which are conspicuous in Mary. It is true: therefore she is called the Tower of *Ivory*, to suggest to us, by the brightness, purity, and exquisiteness of that material, how transcendent is the loveliness and the gentleness of the Mother of God.

IV
On the Assumption

May 24: Mary is the 'Sancta Dei Genitrix', *the Holy Mother of God*

As soon as we apprehend by faith the great fundamental truth that Mary is the Mother of God, other wonderful truths follow in its train; and one of these is that she was exempt from the ordinary lot of mortals, which is not only to die, but to become earth to earth, ashes to ashes, dust to dust. Die she must, and die she did, as her Divine Son died, for He was man; but various reasons have approved themselves to holy writers, why, although her body was for a while separated from her soul and consigned to the tomb, yet it did not remain there, but was speedily united to her soul again, and raised by our Lord to a new and eternal life of heavenly glory.

And the most obvious reason for so concluding is this—that *other* servants of God have been raised from the grave by the power of God, and it is not to be supposed that our Lord would have granted any such privilege to anyone else without also granting it to His own Mother.

We are told by St Matthew, that after our Lord's death upon the Cross 'the graves were opened, and many bodies of the saints that had slept'—that is, slept the sleep of death, 'arose, and coming out of the tombs after His Resurrection, came into the Holy City, and appeared to many'.[av] St Matthew says, '*many* bodies of the Saints'—that is, the holy Prophets, Priests, and Kings of former times—rose again in anticipation of the last day.

Can we suppose that Abraham, or David, or Isaias, or Ezechias, should have been thus favoured, and not God's own Mother? Had she not a claim on the love of her Son to have what any others had? Was she not nearer to Him than the greatest of the Saints before her? And is it conceivable that the law of the grave should admit of relaxation in their case, and not in hers? Therefore we confidently say that our Lord, having preserved her from sin and the consequences of sin by His Passion, lost no time in pouring out the full merits of that Passion upon her body as well as her soul.

May 25: Mary is the 'Mater Intemerata', *the Sinless Mother*

Another consideration which has led devout minds to believe in the Assumption of our Lady into heaven after her death, without waiting for the general resurrection at the last day, is furnished by the doctrine of her Immaculate Conception.

By her Immaculate Conception is meant, that not only did she never commit any sin whatever, even venial, in thought, word, or deed, but further than this, that the guilt of Adam, or what is called original sin, never was her guilt, as it is the guilt attaching to all other descendants of Adam.

By her Assumption is meant that not only her soul, but her body also, was taken up to heaven upon her death, so that there was no long period of her sleeping in the grave, as is the case with others, even great Saints, who wait for the last day for the resurrection of their bodies.

One reason for believing in our Lady's Assumption is that her Divine Son loved her too much to let her body remain in the grave.[23] A second reason—that now before us – is this, that she was not only dear to the Lord as a mother is dear to a son, but also that she was so transcendently holy, so full, so overflowing with grace. Adam and Eve were created upright and

---

[23] Cf. above *Introduction* IV, pp. 75–6.

sinless, and had a large measure of God's grace bestowed upon them; and, in consequence, their bodies would never have crumbled into dust, had they not sinned; upon which it was said to them, 'Dust thou art, and unto dust thou shalt return'.[aw] If Eve, the beautiful daughter of God, never would have become dust and ashes unless she had sinned, shall we not say that Mary, having never sinned, retained the gift which Eve by sinning lost? What had Mary done to forfeit the privilege given to our first parents in the beginning? Was her comeliness to be turned into corruption, and her fine gold to become dim, without reason assigned? Impossible. Therefore we believe that, though she died for a short hour, as did our Lord Himself,[24] yet, like Him, and by His Almighty power, she was raised again from the grave.

May 26: Mary is the 'Rosa Mystica', *the Mystical Rose*[25]

Mary is the most beautiful flower that ever was seen in the spiritual world. It is by the power of God's grace that from this barren and desolate earth there have ever sprung up at all flowers of holiness and glory. And Mary is the Queen of them. She is the Queen of spiritual flowers; and therefore she is called the *Rose*, for the rose is fitly called of all flowers the most beautiful.

[24] In the definition of the Assumption, the fact of Mary's death was not discussed (cf. Apostolic Constitution: *Munificentissimus Deus* in Denzinger-Schönmetzer, No. 3902). It is the common opinion that she did die. Cf. above, *Introduction*, IV, pp. 72–4.

[25] This meditation is not a repetition of the one for 7 May. The latter was among the Joyful Mysteries; the present one among the Glorious Mysteries. Moreover, after the first year, the one on the 'Mystical Rose' for 7 May was no longer used.

But moreover, she is the *Mystical*, or *hidden* Rose; for mystical means hidden. How is she now 'hidden' from us more than are other saints? What means this singular appellation, which we apply to her specially? The answer to this question introduces us to a third reason for believing in the reunion of her sacred body to her soul, and its assumption into heaven soon after her death, instead of its lingering in the grave until the General Resurrection at the last day.

It is this: if her body was not taken into heaven, where is it? how comes it that it is hidden from us? why do we not hear of her tomb as being here or there? why are not pilgrimages made to it? why are not relics producible of her, as of the saints in general? Is it not even a natural instinct which makes us reverent towards the places where our dead are buried? We bury our great men honourably. St Peter speaks of the sepulchre of David as known in his day, though he had died many hundred years before.[ax] When our Lord's body was taken down from the Cross, He was placed in an honourable tomb.[ay] Such too had been the honour already paid to St John Baptist, his tomb being spoken of by St Mark as generally known.[az] Christians from the earliest times went from other countries to Jerusalem to see the holy places. And, when the time of persecution was over, they paid still more attention to the bodies of the Saints, as of St Stephen, St Mark, St Barnabas, St Peter, St Paul, and other Apostles and Martyrs. These were transported to great cities, and portions of them sent to this place or that. Thus, from the first to this day it has been a great feature and characteristic of the Church to be most tender and reverent towards the bodies of the Saints.

Now, if there was anyone who more than all would be preciously taken care of, it would be our Lady. Why then do we hear nothing of the Blessed Virgin's body and its separate relics? Why is she thus the *hidden* Rose? Is it conceivable that they who had been so reverent and careful of the bodies of the Saints and Martyrs should neglect her—her who was the Queen of Martyrs and the Queen of Saints, who was the very Mother of our Lord? It is impossible. Why then is she thus the *hidden* Rose? Plainly because that sacred body is in heaven, not on earth.

May 27: Mary is the 'Turris Davidica', *the Tower of David*

A Tower in its simplest idea is a fabric for defence against enemies. David, King of Israel, built for this purpose a notable tower; and as he is a figure or type of our Lord, so is his tower a figure denoting our Lord's Virgin Mother.

She is called the *Tower* of David because she had so signally fulfilled the office of defending her Divine Son from the assaults of his foes. It is customary with those who are not Catholics to fancy that the honours we pay to her interfere with the supreme worship which we pay to Him; that in Catholic teaching she eclipses Him. But this is the very reverse of the truth.

For if Mary's glory is so very great, how cannot His be greater still who is the Lord and God of Mary? He is infinitely above His Mother; and all that grace which filled her is but the overflowings and superfluities of His incomprehensible Sanctity. And history teaches us the same lesson. Look at the Protestant countries which threw off all devotion to her three centuries ago, under the notion that to put her from their thoughts would be exalting the praises of her Son. Has that consequence really followed from their profane conduct towards her? Just the reverse—the countries, Germany, Switzerland, England, which so acted, have in great measure ceased to worship Him, and have given up their belief in His divinity,[26] while the Catholic Church, wherever she is to be found, adores Christ as true God and true Man, as firmly as ever she did; and strange indeed would it be, if it ever happened otherwise. Thus Mary is the 'Tower of David'.

May 28: Mary is the 'Virgo Potens', *the Powerful Virgin*

This great universe, which we see by day and by night, or what is called the natural world, is ruled by fixed laws, which the Creator has imposed upon it, and by those wonderful laws is made secure against any substantial injury or loss. One portion of it may conflict with another, and there may be changes in it internally; but, viewed as a whole, it is adapted to stand for ever. Hence the Psalmist says, 'He has established the world, which shall not be moved'.[az]*

Such is the world of nature; but there is another and still more wonderful world. There is a power which avails to alter and subdue this visible world, and to

---

[26] This is not the first time Newman expresses this thought. Cf. for example above, Text 111, p. 137.

suspend and counteract its laws; that is, the world of Angels and Saints, of Holy Church and her children; and the weapon by which they master its laws is the power of prayer.

By prayer all this may be done, which naturally is impossible. Noe prayed, and God said that there never again should be a flood to drown the race of man.[ba] Moses prayed, and ten grievous plagues fell upon the land of Egypt.[cb] Josue prayed, and the sun stood still.[dc] Samuel prayed, and thunder and rain came in wheat-harvest.[ed] Elias prayed, and brought down fire from heaven.[fe] Eliseus prayed, and the dead came to life. Ezechias prayed and the vast army of the Assyrians was smitten and perished.[gf]

This is why the Blessed Virgin is called *Powerful*—nay, sometimes, *All*-powerful, because she has, more than anyone else, more than all Angels and Saints, this great, prevailing gift of prayer. No one has access to the Almighty as His Mother has; none has merit such as hers. Her Son will deny her nothing that she asks; and herein lies her power. While she defends the Church, neither height nor depth, neither men nor evil spirits, neither great monarchs, nor craft of man, nor popular violence, can avail to harm us; for human life is short, but Mary reigns above, a Queen for ever.

May 29: Mary is the 'Auxilium Christianorum', *the Help of Christians*

Our glorious Queen, since her Assumption on high, has been the minister of numberless services to the elect people of God upon earth, and to His Holy Church. This title of 'Help of Christians' relates to those services of which the Divine Office, while recording and referring to the occasion on which it was given her, recounts five, connecting them more or less with the Rosary.

The first was on the first institution of the Devotion of the Rosary by St Dominic, when, with the aid of the Blessed Virgin, he succeeded in arresting and overthrowing the formidable heresy of the Albigenses in the South of France.

The second was the great victory gained by the Christian fleet over the powerful Turkish Sultan, in answer to the intercession of Pope St Pius V and the prayers of the Associations of the Rosary all over the Christian world; in lasting memory of which wonderful mercy Pope Pius introduced her title '*Auxilium Christianorum*' into her Litany; and Pope Gregory XIII, who followed him, dedicated the first Sunday in October, the day of the victory, to Our Lady of the Rosary.

The third was, in the words of the Divine Office, 'the glorious victory won at Vienna, under the guardianship of the Blessed Virgin, over the most savage Sultan of the Turks, who was trampling on the necks of the Christians; in perpetual memory of which benefit Pope Innocent XI dedicated the Sunday in the Octave of her Nativity as the feast of her *august Name*.'[27]

The fourth instance of her aid was the victory over the innumerable force of the same Turks in Hungary on the Feast of St Mary ad Nives, in answer to the solemn supplication of the Confraternities of the Rosary; on occasion of which Popes Clement XI and

---

[27] Later on, this Feast was celebrated on 12 September.

Benedict XIII gave fresh honour and privilege to the Devotion of the Rosary.[28]

And the fifth was her restoration of the Pope's temporal power, at the beginning of this century, after Napoleon the First, Emperor of the French, had taken it from the Holy See; on which occasion Pope Pius VII set apart May 24, the day of this mercy, as the Feast of the *Help of Christians*,[29] for a perpetual thanksgiving.

May 30: Mary is the 'Virgo Fidelis', *the Most Faithful Virgin*

This is one of the titles of the Blessed Virgin, which is especially hers from the time of her Assumption and glorious Coronation at the right hand of her Divine Son. How it belongs to her will be plain by considering some of those other instances in which faithfulness is spoken of in Holy Scripture.

The word *faithfulness* means loyalty to a superior, or exactness in fulfilling an engagement. In the latter sense it is applied even to Almighty God Himself, who, in His great love for us, has vouchsafed to limit His own power in action by His word of promise and His covenant with His creatures. He has given His word that, if we will take Him for our portion and put ourselves into His hands, He will guide us through all trails and temptations, and bring us safe to heaven.

---

[28] The Feast of Our Lady of the Rosary was instituted in gratitude for the victory of the Christian army at Lepanto in 1571. The Feast was later celebrated on 7 October, as it is to the present day.

[29] The Feast of Our Lady, Help of Christians, is no longer celebrated in the universal calendar of the Church.

And to encourage and inspirit us, He reminds us, in various passages of Scripture that He is the *faithful* God, the *faithful* Creator.

And so, His true saints and servants have the special title of 'Faithful', as being true to Him as He is to them; as being simply obedient to his will, zealous for His honour, observant of the sacred interests which He has committed to their keeping. Thus Abraham[ih] is called the Faithful; Moses[ji] is declared to be faithful in all his house; David, on this account, is called the 'man after God's own heart';[kj] St Paul returns thanks that 'God accounted him faithful';[lk] and, at the last day, God will say to all those who have well employed their talents, 'Well done, good and faithful servant'.[ml]

Mary, in like manner, is pre-eminently faithful to her Lord and Son. Let no one for an instant suppose that she is not supremely zealous for His honour, or, as those who are not Catholics fancy, that to exalt her is to be unfaithful to Him. Her true servants are still more truly His. Well as she rewards her friends, she would deem him no friend, but a traitor, who preferred her to Him. As He is zealous for her honour, so is she for His. He is the Fount of grace, and all her gifts are from His goodness. O Mary, teach us ever to worship thy Son as the One Creator, and to be devout to thee as the most highly favoured of creatures.

May 31: Mary is the 'Stella Matutina', *the Morning Star – after the dark night, but always Heralding the Sun*

What is the nearest approach in the way of symbols, in this world of sight and sense, to represent to us the glories of that higher world which is beyond our bodily perceptions? What are the truest tokens and promises here, poor though they may be, of what one day we hope to see hereafter, as being beautiful and rare? Whatever they may be, surely the Blessed Mother of God may claim them as her own. And so it is; two of them are ascribed to her as her titles, in her Litany—the stars above, and flowers below. She is at once the *Rosa Mystica* and the *Stella Matutina*.

And of these two, both of them well suited to her, the Morning Star becomes her best, and that for three reasons.

First, the rose belongs to this earth, but the star is placed in high heaven. Mary now has no part in this nether world. No change, no violence from fire, water, earth, or air, affects the stars above; and they show themselves, ever bright and marvellous, in all regions of this globe, and to all the tribes of men.

And next, the rose has but a short life; its decay is as sure as it was graceful and fragrant in its noon. But Mary, like the stars, abides for ever, as lustrous now as she was on the day of her Assumption; as pure and perfect, when her Son comes in judgment, as she is now.

Lastly, it is Mary's prerogative to be the *Morning* Star, which heralds in the sun. She does not shine for herself, or from herself, but she is the reflection of her and our Redeemer, and she glorifies *Him*. When she appears in the darkness, we know that He is close at hand. He is Alpha and Omega, the First and the Last, the Beginning and the End. Behold He comes quickly, and His reward is with Him, to render to everyone according to his works.[nm] 'Surely I come quickly. Amen. Come, Lord Jesus.'[on]

a. Hab 2:3
b. Is 11:1
c. Lk 1:28
d. cf. Jn 14:25–6
e. Ps 50:5
f. Lk 11:27–8
g. 1 Cor 1:23; cf. Acts 8:5
h. Ex 33:20
i. Heb 12:29
j. Rev 1:17
k. cf. Dan 8:17–18
l. Lk 1:12
m. cf. Lk 1:28–9, 42
n. Song 6:10
o. cf. Rev 21:18, 21
p. cf. Gen 1:8–9
q. cf. Lk 23:43
r. cf. Rev 22:2
s. Lk 1:28
t. cf. Wis 4:7–13
u. Dan 7:9
v. Jdt 15:9–10
w. Rev 15:4
x. Mk 10:18
y. Job 25:4–5
z. Job 15:15
aa. cf. Gen 1:26
bb. Heb 12:14
cc. Lk 1:28
dd. Is 6:3
ee. Lk 1:28, 42
ff. cf. Mt 2:1–18
gg. cf. Rev 12:1–9
hh. cf. Lk 2:51
ii. Num 12:6–8
jj. Ezek 44:2–3
kk. Gen 3:6
ll. 1 Cor 15:45
mm. Rom 12:1
nn. cf. Lk 1:34–8
oo. Jn 1:14
pp. Mt 12:50
qq. cf. Lk 2:26, 38
rr. cf. Gen 3:15
ss. cf. Mic 5:1; Mt 2:6
tt. Lk 1:42
uu. cf. Lk 1:32
vv. cf. Lk 1:21
ww. cf. Lk 2:11
xx. Mt 8:20
yy. Acts 5:31
zz. Acts 13:23
ab. Mt 1:21
ac. Acts 5:31
ad. Lk 19:10
ae. cf. Lk 2:51
af. Mt 8:20
ag. Rev 3:4
ah. Rev 20:4
ai. cf. Lk 2:25–35
aj. Lk 22:44
ak. 1 Cor 2:2
al. Gal 2:20
am. cf. Jn 19:25
an. Phil 3:20
ao. cf. 2 Cor 1:3–4
ap. Heb 2:18
aq. cf. Mt 2:13–15
ar. cf. Mt 26; 40–5
as. cf. Mt 26:69–74
at. cf. Mt 26:56; Mk 14:50
au. cf. Jn 19:25–26
av. Mt 27:52–3
aw. Gen 3:19
ax. cf. Acts 2:29
ay. cf. Mt 27:59–60
az. cf. Mk 6:29
az★. Ps 92:1
ba. cf. Gen 8:20–2
cb. cf. Ex 7:14–12:30
dc. cf. Josh 10:9–14
ed. cf. 1 Sam 12:16–18
fe. cf. 2 Kings 1:1–14
gf. cf. 2 Kings 4:18–37
hg. cf. 2 Kings 19:15–36
ih. Gal 3:9
ji. cf. Num 12:7; Heb 3:2, 5.
kj. cf. 1 Sam 13:14; Acts 13:22
lk. cf. 1 Tim 1:12
ml. Mt 25:21
nm. cf. Rev 22:12–13
on. cf. Rev 22:20

Meditations and Devotions of the late Cardinal Newman,
London, 1911, pp. 1–77.
Written during his Oratorian life.

BIBLIOGRAPHY

I WORKS OF JOHN HENRY NEWMAN

1. From 1886 onwards the 36 volumes of *The Works of Cardinal Newman* (in the uniform edition) were published in London by Longmans, Green, & Co. There were numerous reprints of single volumes. The date in brackets indicates the date of the edition we use in references:

a) WORKS ORIGINALLY WRITTEN DURING NEWMAN'S ANGLICAN YEARS

—*Two Essays on Biblical and Ecclesiastical Miracles*. (1911).
—*Parochial and Plain Sermons*. 8 Vols. (1908–1911).
—*Fifteen Sermons preached before the University of Oxford*. (1909).
—*The Via Media of the Anglican Church. Illustrated in Lectures, Letters and Tracts written between 1830 and 1841*. 2 Vols. (Vol. I: 1911; Vol. II: 1914). [This

edition also contains Newman's *Retractation of anti-Catholic Statements*. October 1845. Cf. Vol. II, pp. 425–33].

—*Sermons bearing on Subjects of the Day*. (1909).

—*The Arians of the Fourth Century*. (1908).

—*Lectures on the Doctrine of Justification*. (1908).

—*Select Treatises of St Athanasius in Controversy with the Arians. Freely translated by John Henry Newman*. 2 Vols. (1903).

—*An Essay on The Development of Christian Doctrine*. (1914).

b) WORKS WRITTEN BY NEWMAN AS A CATHOLIC

—*Loss and Gain. The Story of a Convert*. (1911).

—*Discourses addressed to Mixed Congregations*. (1913).

—*Sermons preached on Various Occasions*. (1913).

—*Certain Difficulties felt by Anglicans in Catholic Teaching*. 2 Vols. (Vol. I: 1908; Vol. II: 1910).

—*Lectures on the Present Position of Catholics in England. Addressed to the Brothers of the Oratory in the Summer of 1851*. (1913).

—*The Idea of a University defined and illustrated*. (1912).

—*Callista. A Tale of the Third Century*. (1910).

—*Apologia pro Vita Sua, being a History of his Religious Opinions*. (1913).

—*An Essay in aid of a Grammar of Assent*. (1913).

c) WORKS WITH MATERIAL WRITTEN DURING ANGLI-
CAN AND CATHOLIC PERIODS

—*Verses on Various Occasions*. (1910).
—*Historical Sketches*. (Vol. I: 1908; Vol. II: 1912; Vol. III: 1913).
—*Essays Critical and Historical*. 2 Vols. (1914).
—*Tracts Theological and Ecclesiastical*. (1913).
—*Discussions and Arguments on Various Subjects*. (1911).

2. Other works by Newman first published after his death and not contained in the uniform edition.

—*Letters and Correspondence of John Henry Newman during his life in the English Church with a brief Autobiography*. Edited, at Cardinal Newman's request, by Anne Mozley. 2 Vols. [First published in 1891]. London, Longmans, Green & Co., 1911.
—*Meditations and Devotions of the late Cardinal Newman*. [First published in 1893]. London Longmans, Green & Co., 1911.
—*Stray Essays on Controversial Points Variously Illustrated*. Birmingham, M. Billing, Son, & Co., 1890. (Printed for private circulation).
—*Sayings of Cardinal Newman*. London, Burns & Oates, 1890. (Facsimile reprint: Dublin, Carraig Books, 1976).
—*My Campaign in Ireland*. Aberdeen, A. King & Co., 1896. (Printed for private circulation).
—*Addresses to Cardinal Newman with his Replies, 1879–1881*. Edited by the Rev. W. P. Neville. London, Longmans, Green & Co., 1905.

—*Sermon Notes of John Henry Cardinal Newman. 1849–1878.* Edited by Fathers of the Birmingham Oratory. [First published in 1913]. London, Longmans, Green & Co., 1914.

—*Correspondence of John Henry Newman with John Keble and Others, 1839–1845.* Edited at the Birmingham Oratory. London, Longmans, Green & Co., 1917.

—*Cardinal Newman and William Froude, F. R. S., a Correspondence.* Edited by Gordon Huntington Harper. Baltimore, The Johns Hopkins Press, 1933.

—*The Newman–Perrone Paper on Development.* Edited by Rev. T. Lynch in *Gregorianum* 16 (1935) pp. 402–44.

—*Cardinal Newman's Theses de Fide and his proposed Introduction to the French Translation of the University Sermons.* Edited by Henry Tristram in Gregorianum 18 (1937) pp. 219–60.

—*John Henry Newman: Autobiographical Writings.* Edited with an Introduction by Henry Tristram of the Oratory. London and New York, Sheed & Ward, 1956.

—*Catholic Sermons of Cardinal Newman. Published, for the first time, from the Cardinal's autograph manuscripts.* Edited at the Birmingham Oratory. London, Burns & Oates, 1957.

—*The Letters and Diaries of John Henry Newman.* Edited at the Birmingham Oratory. Vols. XI–XXII (London, Nelson, 1961–72); Vols. XXIII–XXXI; I–VIII (Oxford, Clarendon Press, 1973–99). Still in progress.

—*On Consulting the Faithful in Matters of Doctrine.* Edited by John Coulson. London, Collins, 1986.

—*Proof of Theism* in *The Argument from Conscience to the Existence of God according to J. H. Newman.* By Adrian J. Boekraad and Henry Tristram. Louvain, Nauwelaerts,

1961, pp. 103–25. Cf. *Further Unpublished Documents regarding the same Subject Matter. Ibid.* pp. 167–99.

—*On the Inspiration of Scripture.* Edited with an Introduction by J. Derek Holmes and Robert Murray SJ, London, Chapman, 1967.

—'Newman's Oratory Papers', in *Newman the Oratorian. His Unpublished Oratory Papers.* Edited with an Introductory Study on the Continuity between his Anglican and his Catholic Ministry by Placid Murray OSB, Dublin, Gill & Macmillan, 1969, pp. 131–467.

—*John Henry Newman. The Philosophical Notebook.* Vol I: *General Introduction to the Study of Newman's Philosophy.* Edited at the Birmingham Oratory by Edward Sillem. Vol II: *The Text.* Edited at the Birmingham Oratory by Edward Sillem and revised by A. J. Boekraad. Louvain, Nauwelaerts, 1969–70.

—*John Henry Newman and the Abbé Jager. A Controversy on Scripture and Tradition (1834–1836).* Edited from the original manuscripts and the French version by Louis Allen. London, Oxford University Press, 1975.

—*The Theological Papers of John Henry Newman on Faith and Certainty.* Partly prepared for publication by Hugo M. de Achaval SJ. Selected and edited by J. Derek Holmes, with a note of introduction by Charles Stephen Dessain. Oxford, Clarendon Press, 1976.

—*The Theological Papers of John Henry Newman: On Biblical Inspiration and on Infallibility.* Selected, edited and introduced by J. Derek Holmes. Oxford, Clarendon Press, 1979.

—*Sermons 1824–1843.* Vol I. Sermons on the Liturgy and Sacraments and on Christ the Mediator. Edited from previously unpublished manuscripts by Placid Murray OSB. Oxford, Clarendon Press, 1991.

—*Sermons 1824–1843*. Vol II. Sermons on Biblical History, Sin and Justification, the Christian Way of Life and Biblical Theology. Edited from previously unpublished manuscripts by Vincent Ferrer Blehl SJ. Oxford, Clarendon Press, 1993.

II SELECT BIBLIOGRAPHY

Alonso, J.M.   'La mariología del Card. Newman y la evolución de su pensamiento': *Ephemerides Mariologicae* 27 (1977) pp. 81–4.

Bertetto, Domenico   *Maria la serva del Signore.* Trattato di mariologia. Napoli, Dehoniane, 1988.

Blehl, Vincent Ferrer, SJ   *The White Stone. The Spiritual Theology of John Henry Newman.* Petersham, Mass., St Bede's Publications, 1994.

Bouyer, Louis   *Newman. His Life and Spirituality.* With a Preface by the Reverend Monsignor H. Francis Davis. London, Burns & Oates, 1958.

Boyce, Philip, OCD   'John Henry Newman: the birth and pursuit of an ideal of Holiness': *Ephemerides Carmeliticae* 30 (1979) pp. 292–318.

Boyce, Philip, OCD   *Spiritual Exodus of John Henry Newman and Thérèse of Lisieux.* Dublin and Manchester, Carmelite Centre of Spirituality/ Koinonia Press, 1979.

Boyce, Philip, OCD   'At Prayer with Newman', in *In Search of Light. Life – Development – Prayer. Three Essays on John Henry Newman.* Rome, International Centre of Newman Friends, 1985, pp. 63–85.

Boyce, Philip, OCD   'Illness and Conversion in Newman's Life', in *Luce nella Solitudine.* Viaggio e crisi di Newman in Sicilia 1833. A cura di Rosario La Delfa e Alessandro Magno. Palermo, Ila Palma, 1989, pp. 51–72.

Calero, Antonio Maria *La Vergine Maria nel mistero di Cristo e della Chiesa*. Saggio di mariologia. Leumann (Torino), Elle Di Ci, 1995.

Chiminelli, Piero *J. H. Newman. L'Annunciatore della 'Seconda Primavera' della Cattolicità in Inghilterra: 1801–1890*. Modena, Paoline, 1964.

Chiminelli, Piero 'Maria nella vita e nel pensiero di J. H. Newman': *Studium* 35 (1939) pp. 285–98.

Church, R. W. *Occasional Papers, selected from the Guardian, The Times, and the Saturday Review 1846–1890*. 2 Vols. London, Macmillan, 1897.

Coulson, John 'John Henry Newman: his genius for Friendship': *The Clergy Review* 62 (1977) pp. 18–21.

Coupet, Jacques, OP 'Le rôle de Marie dans le cheminement de Newman': *Nouveaux Cahiers Mariaux* 17 (1990) pp. 6–12.

Davis, Francis H. 'Doctrina Mariana Cardinalis Newman' in *Alma Socia Christi Vol. XI,* (1953), pp. 233–43. *Acta Congressus Mariologici-mariani Romae anno sancto MCML celebrati*. Romae, Academia Mariana; Officium Libri Catholici.

Davis, Francis H. 'La Mariologie de Newman', in *Maria. Études sur la Sainte Vierge*. Sous la direction d'Hubert du Manoir S J, Paris, 1954, Tome III, pp. [533]–552.

Davis, Francis H. 'Newman and Our Lady': *The Clergy Review* 34 (1949) pp. 369–79.

Dessain, Charles Stephen, CO 'Cardinal Newman and Our Lady': *Our Lady's Digest* 27 (1973) pp. 168–84; 28 (1973) pp. 206–12.

Dessain, Charles Stephen, CO *Cardinal Newman's Teaching about the Blessed Virgin Mary*. London, The Ecumenical Society of the Blessed Virgin Mary, 1971, (19 pp.).

Dessain, Charles Stephen, CO *John Henry Newman*. London, Nelson, 1966.

Dessain, Charles Stephen, CO 'Newman's First Conversion. "A great change of thought" August 1st till December 21st, 1816', in *Newman Studien*. Herausgegeben von Heinrich Fries und Werner Becker. Nürnberg, Bd. 3, (1957), pp. 37–53.

Du Manoir, H., SJ 'Marie, nouvelle Ève, dans l'oeuvre de Newman': *Études Mariales* 14 (1956) pp. [67]–90.

Ffinch, Michael *Newman. Towards the Second Spring*. San Francisco, Ignatius Press, 1991.

Ford, J. T. 'Newman on sensus fidelium and mariology': *Marian Studies* 28 (1977), pp. 120–145.

Friedel, Francis J., SM *The Mariology of Cardinal Newman*. New York, etc., Benzinger Brothers, 1928.

Froude, James Anthony *Short Studies on Great Subjects*. 5 Volumes. London, Longmans, Green & Co., 1907.

Geissler, Hermann 'The Development of Newman's Mariology', in *Newman on Mary. Two Studies in Development*. London, The Ecumenical Society of the Blessed Virgin Mary, (1996/Sept.) pp. 17–24.

Gilley, Sheridan *Newman and his Age*. London, Darton, Longman & Todd, 1990.

Gorce, Denys *Newman et les Pères. (Sources de sa conversion et de sa vie intérieure)*. A l'occasion du Centenaire du Mouvement d'Oxford (1833–1933). Bruges, Charles Beyaert, [1947]. (2nd Ed.).

Gornall, Thomas   'Newman (John Henry), Cardinal, 1801–1890', in *Dictionnaire de Spiritualité Ascétique et Mystique, Doctrine et Histoire*. M. Viller et Collab. Fascicules LXXII–LXXIII. Paris, Beauchesne, 1981, Col. 163–81.

Govaert, Lutgart   'An Ideal of Holiness: Newman's Devotion to Our Lady', in *Newman-Studien*, Bd. 12. Sigmaringendorf, Glock und Lutz, 1988, pp. 198–206.

Govaert, Lutgart   'From Henceforth all Generations Shall Call Me Blessed, (Lk 1:48). J. H. Newman on Our Lady': *Marianum* 53 (1991) pp. 17–41.

Govaert, Lutgart   *Kardinal Newmans Mariologie und sein persönlicher Werdegang*. Salzburg, Anton Pustet, 1975.

Govaert, Lutgart   'Newman's Mariology: Its Development', in *De Cultu Mariano Saeculis XIX–XX*. Actus Congressus Mariologici-Mariani Internationalis . . . anno 1987 celebrati. Roma, Pont. Acad. Mariana Internationalis, 1991, pp. 545–55.

Govaert, Lutgart   'Our Lady in the Thought and Devotion of the Anglican Newman': in *Ampleforth Review* 84 (1979) 20–30.

Graef, Hilda   *God and Myself*. The Spirituality of John Henry Newman. London, Peter Davies, 1967.

Griffin, John R.   'Newman and the Mother of God', in *Faith and Reason* XV, No. 4, (Winter 1989): *Essays in Honor of the Centenary of John Henry Cardinal Newman (1801–1890)*. Front Royal, Virginia, Christendom Press, pp. 91–109.

Griffin, John R.   *A Historical Commentary on the Major Catholic Works of Cardinal Newman*. New York etc., Peter Lang, 1993.

Hardon, J. 'Cardinal Newman, Apologist of Our Lady', in *Review for Religious* 14 (1952) pp. 113–24.

Honoré, Jean *The Spiritual Journey of Newman*. New York, Alba House, 1992.

John Henry Newman. Theologian and Cardinal (Symposium 9–12 October 1979). Roma, Urbaniana University Press; Brescia, Paideia Editrice, 1981.

Hutton, Richard H. *Cardinal Newman*. London, Methuen & Co., 1891. (AMS Press 1976: reprint of 1891 edn).

Ivory, Thomas R. 'When you pray … The Way of Newman', in *The Way* 17 (1977) pp. 145–55.

Kennedy, Finola *John Henry Newman and Frank Duff*. Dublin, Praedicanda Publications, 1990.

Ker, Ian *John Henry Newman. A Biography*. Oxford, Clarendon Press, 1988.

Ker, Ian *The Achievement of John Henry Newman*. London, Collins, 1991.

Komonchak, Joseph A./Collins, Mary/Dermot A. Lane (Eds) *The New Dictionary of Theology*. Dublin, Gill & Macmillan, 1992.

Liddon, Henry Parry *Life of Edward Bouverie Pusey*. In 4 Volumes. London, Longmans, Green & Co., 1893–97.

McGrath, Fergal, SJ *Newman's University. Idea and Reality*. Dublin, Browne & Nolan, 1951.

McHugh, John 'The Second Eve: Newman and Irenaeus', in *The Way. Supplement* 45 (June 1982) pp. 3–21.

McRedmond, Louis *Thrown Among Strangers. John Henry Newman in Ireland*. Dublin, Veritas, 1990.

Morales, José 'La Mariología de John H. Newman',

in *Scripta de María* 3 (1980) pp. 493–524.

Morales, José *Religión Hombre Historia. Estudios Newmanianos.* Pamplona, Ediciones Universidad de Navarra, 1989.

Morrone, Fortunato *Cristo il Figlio di Dio fatto uomo. L'incarnazione del Verbo nel pensiero cristologico di J. H. Newman.* Milano, Jaca Book, 1990.

Mulvey, Beth *St. Mary in the Valley. A History of Maryvale House.* Birmingham, Maryvale Books, 1994.

Murray, Placid, OSB 'Tower of David. A Sketch of Newman's Mariology', in *The Furrow* 27 (1976) pp. 26–34.

O'Carroll, Michael, CSSp. 'Our Lady in Newman and Vatican II', in T*he Downside Review* 89 (1971) pp. 38–63.

O'Donnell, Christopher, O. Carm *At Worship with Mary. A Pastoral and Theological Study.* Wilmington, Delaware, Michael Glazier, 1988.

Olive, Martin M., OP 'Un petit traité de Mariologie selon les Pères des premiers siècles: La "Lettre à Pusey" de Newman (1865)', in *De Primordiis Cultus Mariani.* Acta Congressus Mariologici-Mariani in Lusitania anno 1967 celebrati. Vol: III. *De Fundamento Cultus B. V. Mariae in operibus Sanctorum Patrum et Scriptorum Ecclesiasticorum (post saec. II).* Romae, Pontifica Academia Mariana Internationalis, 1970, pp. 303–32.

Perrott, M.J.L. *Newman's Mariology.* Southampton, Saint Austin Press, 1997.

Pozo, Candido *María en la obra de la salvación.* Madrid 1974.

Pusey, E.B. *An Eirenicon. In a Letter to the Author of*

'The Christian Year'. London, Oxford, John Henry and James Parker; Rivingtons, 1865.

Schneider, Paul Peter, OSB 'Das Marienbild des anglikanischen Newman', in *Newman-Studien*, Bd. 2. Nürnberg, Glock und Lutz, 1954, pp. 103–9.

Stern, Jean, M S 'La Vierge Marie dans le chemin de foi parcouru par John Henry Newman' in *Marianum 53* (1991) pp. 42–68.

Stern, Jean, MS 'Le culte de la Vierge et des saints, et la conversion de Newman au catholicisme', in *La Vie Spirituelle* 117 (1967) II, pp. 156–68.

Stern, Jean, MS 'Le Saint-Esprit et Marie chez Newman et Faber': *Études Mariales*, 26 (1969) pp. 37–56.

Strange, Roderick '*The Development of Newman's Marian Thought and Devotion*', in *International Ecumenical Conference*. London, The Ecumenical Society of the Blessed Virgin Mary, 1980, pp. 61–73.

Strange, Roderick *Newman and the Gospel of Christ*. Oxford University Press, 1981.

Strolz, M.K. (Ed.) *John Henry Newman. Commemorative Essays on the occasion of the Centenary of his Cardinalate 1879 – May – 1979*. Rome 1979.

Strolz, Maria Katharina/Binder, Margarete, (Eds) *John Henry Newman – Lover of Truth*. The Papers of the Academic Symposium and Celebration of the first Centenary of the Death of John Henry Newman. Rome, 26th–28th April 1990. Rome, Urbaniana University Press, 1991.

Trevor, Meriol *Newman. The Pillar of the Cloud*. London, Macmillan & Co Ltd, 1962.

Trevor, Meriol *Newman. Light in Winter.* London, Macmillan & Co Ltd, 1962.

Tristram, Henry, CO *Newman and his Friends.* London, John Lane The Bodley Head Ltd., 1933.

Tristram, Henry, CO 'Dr Russell and Newman's Conversion', in *The Irish Ecclesiastical Record* 66 (1945) pp. 189–200.

Ullathorne, William B. *The Immaculate Conception of the Mother of God.* London, 1855.

Unger, Dominic J. 'Cardinal Newman and Apocalypse XII': *Theological Studies* 11 (1950) pp. 356–67.

Velocci, Giovanni, CSSR 'La Madonna nella vita di Newman', in *Mater Ecclesiae* 16 (1980) pp. 85–98.

Velocci, Giovanni, CSSR 'Maria nella vita e nel pensiero di Newman', in *Sacra Doctrina* 18 (1973), pp. 301–8.

Velocci, Giovanni, CSSR 'Sant' Alfonso visto da Newman'. in *Rivista di vita spirituale 40* (1986) pp. 167–80.

Velocci, Giovanni, CSSR 'La Mariologia del Newman', in *Divinitas* 11 (1967) pp. 1021–46.

Ward, Wilfrid *The Life of John Henry Cardinal Newman. Based on his private Journals and Correspondence.* 2 Vols. London, Longmans, Green & Co., 1912.

Willam, Franz Michel *John Henry Kardinal Newman und die Lehre von der Unbefleckten Empfängnis*, in *De Immaculata Conceptione*. Romae, Academia Mariana Internationalis, 1957, pp. 120–46.

INDEX OF SUBJECTS

INDEX OF NAMES